Lecture Notes in Economics and Mathematical Systems

Managing Editors: M. Beckmann and W. Krelle

359

Eelke de Jong

Exchange Rate Determination and Optimal Economic Policy Under Various Exchange Rate Regimes

Springer-Verlag
Berlin Heidelberg New York London Paris
Tokyo Hong Kong Barcelona Budapest

Author

Dr. Eelke de Jong
Department of Macroeconomics
University of Amsterdam
Jodenbreestraat 23
NL-1011 NH Amsterdam, The Netherlands

ISBN 3-540-54021-0 Springer-Verlag Berlin Heidelberg New York
ISBN 0-387-54021-0 Springer-Verlag New York Berlin Heidelberg

Printing and binding: Druckhaus Beltz, Hemsbach/Bergstr.
2142/3140-543210 – Printed on acid-free paper

CONTENTS

ACKNOWLEDGEMENTS

The research reported in this book was carried out while I was a research fellow at the Faculty of Economics of the University of Groningen and an Assistant Professor at the Faculty of Economics of the University of Amsterdam. At both faculties my promotor Professor H. Jager was my supervisor. I thank him very much for the stimulating way he guided me through this thesis. Each chapter has benefitted from his critical comments. In fact, for more than a decade we two have co-operated on many projects. Hopefully this co-operation will continue in the future.

At the University of Groningen Professor H. de Haan was my co-supervisor and I am grateful to him for his comments and suggestions. I also express my gratitude to the other members of my thesis committee, Professors W. Driehuis, M.M.G. Fase, P. de Grauwe and J.F. Kiviet, and to professor G. Tullio and dr. E. Sterken for comments on the entire manuscript. Professor W.H. Buiter made comments on a preliminary version of Chapter 3. In addition thanks are due to my colleagues at the Universities of Groningen and Amsterdam notably those participating in the research programme "Exchange-rate policy and monetary policy in international dependence" for their discussions, suggestions and comments.

The estimation of the model presented in the Chapters 4, 5 and 6 was labour-intensive. Much of this work has been done by Martin O. Nijkamp, whose efforts have been greatly appreciated. I am grateful too to De Nederlandsche Bank for putting the data-base of the MORKMON model at my disposal. Jeannette J. Capel, Vincent van Polanen Petel and Roland Zwiers carried out various types of activities, such as data collection, estimation and drafting of figures. Hans Amman wrote the optimal control algorithm used for calculating the experiments reported in Chapter 7, and guided me through the use of this programme. Robert Helmink and Netty Nuyten typed parts of the manuscript, Marco van Leeuwen drew some figures, and Mrs. P. Ellman corrected my use of the English language. I am grateful to all these persons and to any others whom I may have forgotten to mention for their contribution in preparing this book.

During my stay at the University of Groningen, the Netherlands Organization for the Advancement of Pure Research (ZWO) provided financial support for the research.

Finally, I want to thank my wife Ike and our two daughters Tineke and Alise for their support in accepting a husband and father who keeps on working when others pay attention to their family. But at last "papa's moeilijke boek" has been accomplished.

Castricum, February 1991

1 INTRODUCTION

1.1 Some characteristics of the floating exchange rate system

The flexible exchange rate system has functioned far less satisfactorily than many anticipated in 1973, when the major industrialized countries decided to let their currencies float. The dominant currencies' exchange rates have fluctuated more than expected.[1] These fluctuations concern both short-term movements - intraday fluctuations and movements during a week or a month - and long-term changes that last for more than a year. Daily percentage changes of one percent are not unusual for the recent float (see MacDonald, 1988, p.8). However, the release of new information can give rise to much larger changes. For example in August 1987 "the dollar moved down 6 percent in two days based on the July trade figures" (Glynn, 1988, p. 36). For the period 1973-1985 MacDonald (1988, p.10) presents minimum and maximum monthly percentage exchange rate changes. These figures clearly illustrate the magnitude of the volatility and also show that the volatility has not diminished as the experience with floating has increased.[2]

In addition to this volatility, exchange rates are also characterized by misalignment: "persistent departure of the exchange rate from its long-run equilibrium" (Williamson, 1983, p.13). Although the measure of misalignment depends upon the exact definition of the exchange rate's long-run equilibrium, there is a widespread feeling that during the greater part of the 1970s the dollar was undervalued, whereas it was overvalued during the first half of the 1980s. Dornbusch and Frankel (1987), for example, consider the purchasing power parity (PPP) as an appropriate measure of the long-term equilibrium. They approximate PPP by means of the real exchange rate of the dollar, using relative consumer price indices for deflating the nominal rate. From the resulting time series, they conclude that the dollar was undervalued from 1977 to 1981 and overvalued from 1982 to 1986 against the currencies of the other members of the Group of Ten. Various studies also reveal that the exchange rates' speed of adjustment toward PPP is very low. Other measures of the long-run exchange

---

[1] Dornbusch and Frankel (1987) present ten characteristics that economists expected floating exchange rates to have in theory. MacDonald (1988, pp. 1-4) presents six claims made by the proponents of flexible exchange rates.

[2] Other studies - such as e.g. Dornbusch and Frankel (1987), Goldstein (1984) and Williamson (1983) - which analyse the period of floating exchange rates reaffirm the characteristics of this period presented in the text.

rate equilibrium, for example Williamson's Fundamental Equilibrium Exchange Rate, reaffirm the above conclusions with regard to the dollar's misalignment.

Another characteristic of the flexible exchange rates' regime is that the trade volume in foreign exchange markets has increased enormously. "From an already hefty $75 billion a day in the late 1970s, forex trading volume mushroomed steadily to $425 billion a day by the third quarter of 1987, according to estimates by Morgan Stanley and Co." (Glynn, 1988, p.35). By September 1989 the worldwide turnover was estimated at more than $500 billion a day (The Economist, September 16, 1989, p. 109). Moreover, inquiries of the foreign exchange markets in the United States and in London reveal that trading by banks and brokers with non-bank customers accounts for only a small part of total volume. Estimates range from 9 to less than 15 per cent (Dornbusch and Frankel, 1987, p.22). The exchange market's total volume is huge compared to the volume of international trade in goods and services and in long-term capital. At an annual rate the foreign exchange transactions' volume lies somewhere between $65 trillion and $100 trillion, whereas trade in goods and services amount to $4 trillion.[3] Both these figures and those of the first paragraph suggest that the connection between the exchange rate (market) and real phenomena is very loose.

In order to explain the exchange rate movements many theoretical and empirical studies have been published. Unfortunately, in general the results of the empirical investigations are disappointing. As a rule the random walk model appears to explain the exchange rate movements better than the exchange rate relations derived from economic theory. The first aim of this study is therefore to investigate the possible explanations for this in order to improve the results.

1.2 Consequences and policy reactions

The effects of exchange rate volatility appear to be quite different from those of misalignments. In general it is taken for granted that in the industrial world economic agents can hedge the exchange rate exposure resulting from the short-term variability by transactions on the forward exchange markets. Accordingly, many empirical studies conclude that short-term exchange rate fluctuations do not harm trade among industrialized countries. Exchange rate volatility can have a detrimental effect on trade among developing countries, because these

---

[3] These figures are obtained from Glynn (1988), p.36. Glynn's article gives an impression of the bankers' attitude toward the foreign exchange market. World exports and world imports each amounted to about $ 2 trillion in 1986 and to more than $ 2.5 trillion in 1988 (IMF, International Financial Statistics).

countries lack well-developed exchange markets.

Misalignments, on the other hand, are considered to be more unfavourable for economic activity, because they give rise to long-lasting changes in competitiveness between countries. Williamson (1983) distinguishes six possible costs of successive periods of an undervalued and overvalued exchange rate. Firstly, in the course of time consumption varies more than it would if the exchange rate were to remain in the neighbourhood of its long-term equilibrium level. Secondly, even if one assumes that full employment is maintained, then there are costs associated with shifting labour and capital between the tradeable and non-tradeable sector. In general, however, an overvaluation will give rise to unemployment in the traded goods sector. The two main reasons are that agents are not sure whether the exchange rate's overvaluation is temporary or permanent and that the reployment of resources between sectors is costly. So it makes sense to start retraining only if there is an expectation that the shift in demand is long-lasting. Fourthly, repeated misalignments create a great uncertainty about the equilibrium level of competitiveness and thus discourage investments, even if the exchange rate was not on average overvalued or undervalued. Fifthly, it is often observed that depreciations lead to strong inflationary pressures but appreciations do not induce equivalent deflationary pressures, so an inflationary bias emerges. Because of this ratchet effect the chances are that misalignments will generate inflation. Finally, it has been argued that overvaluations tend to generate protectionist pressures which are not fully offset by pressure in favour of trade liberalization in times of an undervalued currency.

Although the measurement of the costs is far from easy, various studies indicate that they can be rather high. For instance, Branson and Love (1988) estimate that the overvaluation of the dollar during the period 1980-1985 reduced employment in the American manufacturing sector by almost one million jobs. In some industries the loss in employment was over 10 percent. Branson and Love expect that a dollar depreciation will not easily reverse the employment loss. The reason is that during the period of a high dollar non-U.S. competitors in industries with increasing returns - due to learning, "sunk" costs, or other factors - might have established themselves in the world market. Bergsten and Williamson (1983) find empirical evidence that periods of tension in the U.S.-Japanese trade relations all originate in periods of an overvalued dollar.

In order to avoid the costs of misalignments, the mid-1980s have witnessed a number of proposals which call for reference rates and target zones in order to stabilize the major industrial countries' exchange rates. Williamson (1983) for example pleads for target zones for exchange rates derived from Fundamental Equilibrium Exchange Rates. Countries should adopt suitable exchange rate-oriented monetary policies and make intervention commitments. The target zone proposals have been put into practice in an attempt to gradually unwind the dollar overvaluation. These efforts started in September 1985, when at the Plaza meeting, the finance ministers and central bank governors of the Group of 5 decided to cooperate more closely in order to generate an "orderly appreciation of the main non-dollar currencies against the dollar" (IMF Survey, October 7, 1985, p. 297). On several occasions the major industrialised countries have reaffirmed their concern for exchange rates that are consistent with the underlying fundamentals. In the Louvre Accord of February 1987 they unambiguously opted for a reference rate system when they "agreed to cooperate closely in order to foster stability of exchange rates around their current levels" (IMF Survey, March 9 1987, p.75). These reference rates and target zones of the major currencies are broad and implicit.

For smaller and more open industrial countries more binding regimes are advocated and practised. Most countries of Western Europe, for instance, have participated in various adjustable peg arrangements with a rather small band width. During the 1970s this was the so-called 'snake' arrangement, which proved to be of limited success. Many members resigned in the course of time. Its successor, the European Monetary System (EMS) which was founded in March 1979, appeared to be much more successful. All original members still participate in the exchange rate arrangement. In June 1989 the number of participants has even been enlarged, when Spain announced that the peseta would join the EMS.

Inspired by this success of the EMS and by the Commission's proposals for one internal market after 1992, many are of the opinion that in the future the EMS should be changed into an European Monetary Union (EMU). This view is put into words in the Delors commission's proposals for an EMU. In this report three stages are distinguished. At the end of the third stage Western Europe should be one financial area. The exchange rates between the EMS-currencies should be fixed and capital controls should not be in force.

Some are sceptical with regard to the possibility and/or desirability of a fixed peg for the EMS-currencies. They argue that the success of the EMS can partly be ascribed to some members' use of capital controls. In this way these particular monetary authorities, most notably those of Italy and France, have limited their inhabitants' possibilities for investing in foreign assets in order to defend their currency's exchange rate. During the first stage of the Delors commission's proposals, however, all barriers to the free movement of capital have to be removed. Consequently, in the future the quasi-fixed intra-EMS exchange rates cannot be defended by means of limiting capital flows. Persistent differences in economic performance, especially in rates of inflation, will still require a realignment of the exchange rates. If capital controls are completely removed while inflation differentials persist, the chances are that at times investors expect a devaluation of a 'soft' currency, they will speculate on this and may force the particular central bank to devalue the currency. Thus the monetary authorities would be incapable of deciding the timing of EMS realignments, and the system would be exposed to repeated speculative attacks and devaluations. In order to avoid these undesirable events, one could opt for a more flexible exchange rate system than a fixed peg. A natural candidate is the crawling peg. Thus, it is a small wonder that in a recent article Dornbusch (1988) appears to be an adherent of a crawling peg scheme for the EMS currencies.

Under a crawling peg system the authorities are obliged to defend a certain peg value by maintaining the market rate within a certain band. The peg value can be changed, but only gradually and in small steps. In the literature, however, attention is focused almost exclusively on rules based on the purchasing power parity. Amman and Jager (1987) and Jager and Amman (1986), therefore, study the inherent economic properties of various guidelines. They also determine the optimal peg for a small industrial country. A disadvantage of their analysis is that it is based upon a small Keynesian econometric model. It lacks a supply side so that the influence of net investments on capital stock and a labour market are missing. In addition the financial sector of the model is rather rudimentary. The second objective of the present study is to investigate whether the results obtained in Jager and Amman's analyses still hold if use is made of a model that incorporates these sectors. In this manner some light is shed on the robustness of the peg-rules, which could be used as guidelines in an EMS with free movement of capital.

1.3 Outline of the book

Chapter 2 summarizes the theoretical and empirical studies of exchange rate determination. In accordance with the fact - as mentioned in Section 1.1 - that the exchange market's total volume is many times greater than the volume of international trade in goods and services, modern exchange rate theories stress the importance of financial variables for determining the exchange rate in the short-run. Within this asset approach three different models can be distinguished, *viz.* the portfolio balance, the monetary and the currency substitution model. In the portfolio balance approach the foreign and domestic bonds are considered to be imperfect substitutes, whereas in the monetary approach these two types of bonds are perfectly substitutable. Both approaches exclude non-interest-bearing foreign money from private agents' wealth. The currency substitution approach focuses on the possibility that foreign money is a substitute for domestic money; it is therefore to be considered a part of domestic agents' wealth.

Next, the structure of the majority of empirical studies on exchange rate determination is described. In these studies the exchange rate relation to be estimated is obtained by partly solving the structural model for the exchange rate. The resulting relation is neither a reduced form nor a structural form equation and is often referred to as a quasi- or semi-reduced form. It is argued that its mixed character can give rise to several econometric problems. Thus the semi-reduced form of the exchange rate relation might probably explain a part of the bad performance of exchange rate models mentioned before. Other possible explanations are the assumed speed of adjustment of financial markets, the instability of structural relations and the proxy of exchange rate expectations.

Both theoretical and empirical studies on exchange rate determination highlight the importance of expectations. Various expectation schemes have been proposed during the last few decades. However, none of them has been generally accepted by the practitioners of the economic profession, so that criteria for selecting the most appropriate hypothesis are highly wanting. Therefore, in Chapter 3 three features of hypotheses on expectation formation are developed. These features refer to the availability of the data used, the learning process, and the possibility to determine the parameters of both the model and of the function generating the expectations. Thereafter, these characteristics serve as criteria in assessing existing expectation hypotheses and estimation procedures of models with expectational variables. Our analysis reveals that only weak forms of the rational expectation hypothesis and some proxy variable methods with time-varying parameters meet all three criteria. Examples of such methods are the multi-state Kalman filter and rolling regressions.

In accordance with the conclusions of Chapters 2 and 3, subsequently a structural model of exchange rate determination is developed in which the exchange rate expectations are approximated by rolling regressions. It is a quarterly model of the Dutch economy and is estimated for the period 1970:I-1980:IV. The financial sector of this model is presented in Chapter 4. The equations of the demand for financial assets are specified according to the multi-asset partial adjustment model. A critical review of various variants of this model is presented in the Appendix to Chapter 4. Some preliminary topics - the estimation procedure used, the approximation of exchange rate expectations and the treatment of seasonal influences - are discussed in Section 4.3. Next, the financial sector's accounting and analytical framework is discussed. Five sectors are distinguished, *viz.* the government, the central bank, the banking sector, the non-bank private sector and the foreign sector. No behavioural equations of the first two sectors are estimated. The next three sections contain the estimated relations representing the financial behaviour of the private sector, the banking sector and the foreign sector. Finally in Section 4.8 the relations approximating the government's interest payments and the interest payments on domestic (foreign) holdings of foreign (domestic) assets are presented.

Chapter 5 is devoted to the estimates of the non-financial sector's behavioural equations. These relations are grouped into the following three broad categories: the labour market, the goods market (which also contains international trade relations), and wages and prices. With regard to the labour market it has been assumed that the supply of labour is exogenous, whereas the demand has been derived from a vintage-type production structure. The parameters of this production structure are used for deriving a time series of the utilization rate which is an explanatory variable in many relations. Various demand functions for goods have been estimated, *viz.* the consumption function, the investment function and the foreign trade relations. A behavioural equation of the supply of goods has been estimated. Then the investments in stocks can be obtained by subtracting the demand from the supply of goods. The prices transfer the quantity system into nominal terms.

In Chapter 6 the parts of the model described in the preceding two chapters are brought together and the interaction between the variables is considered. These interactions also come to the fore in the results of the model's simulation during the period 1970:I-1980:IV.

In accordance with our criticism of the use of quasi-reduced form models of exchange rates, the spot rate is derived from the balance of payments identity. The interest rates on short-term and long-term domestic assets are also derived from market equilibrium conditions. This practice of explaining the price of (return on) a financial asset from its market equilibrium is known as the implicit method. It contrasts with the explicit explanation, which consists of the estimation of a relation of the relevant interest rate (exchange rate).

An important characteristic of this method is that the interest rate (exchange rate) is the ultimate result of substituting the relevant estimated relations of the demand for financial assets in the market equilibrium. A drawback is that the researcher cannot directly improve the explanatory power of the interest rate relation. If the resulting estimated values describe the historical data badly, then the researcher should re-examine the underlying demand relations. As far as we know, in the literature no attention has been paid to the conditions under which the implicit method gives reasonable results. This task is accomplished in Section 6.2, which shows in which manner the statistical characteristics of the relevant demand functions determine the explanatory power of the implicit method. It appears that the application of the implicit method gives reasonable results for the exchange rate and the interest rate on short-term assets. For the long-term interest rate the results are somewhat disappointing. From these results we conclude that deriving the exchange rate from the structural form is a good alternative to the usual practice of estimating a semi-reduced form relation of the exchange rate.

Chapter 7 deals with the second objective of this study, namely the determination of a small industrial country's optimal exchange rate parity rule. For this purpose various exchange rate rules are added to the econometric model. In some studies the preferable rule is selected by comparing the simulation results of the resulting models. A drawback of that procedure is that the exchange rate policy is studied in isolation from the other macro-economic policies. The optimal control technique offers an opportunity to take account of the interaction between the various instruments and is therefore used for deriving the optimal policy. The preferred rule is selected as the one for which the sum of the quadratic differences between targets and realizations is the smallest.

The conclusions of this study are presented in Chapter 8.

2 EXCHANGE RATE DETERMINATION: THEORY AND EMPIRICAL TESTS

2.1 Introduction

During the last two decades, many exchange rates have shown large fluctuations. These fluctuations relate to both intraday changes and movements during longer periods: months and years. Concurrently, as has been illustrated in Section 1.1, the link slackened between the exchange rate and the exchange market on one hand and real phenomena such as international trade in goods and services and relative prices on the other. The figures presented in Section 1.1 show that the bulk of the transaction on the foreign exchange market is driven by financial motives.

In order to explain exchange rate changes a large number of theoretical and empirical studies have been published. In accordance with the growing importance of foreign exchange transactions motivated by financial flows, these papers stress that in the short-term the exchange rate is determined by financial markets. Hence, they argue that exchange rate determination is similar to the determination of asset market prices. These theories are, therefore, called asset market approaches of exchange rate determination. The emphasis on financial stocks does not imply that in the asset market approach no importance at all is attached to the trade balance, which played such a dominant role in the traditional explanations of the exchange rate. On the contrary, the approach assumes that the current account balance plays a significant role in the medium-term when the system moves from one short-run equilibrium to another.

Basically three versions of the asset market approach can be distinguished, *viz.* the portfolio balance, the monetary and the currency substitution model. The differences between these versions relate to the number of assets that are assumed to be part of private portfolios and to the assumed degree of substitutability between domestic and foreign assets. In the portfolio balance approach foreign and domestic bonds are considered to be imperfect substitutes, whereas in the monetary approach these two types of bonds are perfectly substitutable. Both approaches exclude non-interest-bearing foreign money from private agents' wealth. The currency substitution approach, on the other hand, focuses on the possibility that foreign money is a substitute for domestic money; foreign money is therefore considered to be part of the domestic agents' wealth. The structure of the short-term equilibrium of these models is discussed in the next section. Section 2.3 describes the current account's role in the adjustment process of many portfolio approaches. The possible influence of exchange rate expectations upon the characteristics of exchange rate models is considered in Section 2.4.

In many empirical studies the asset market approaches are not tested by means of estimating the structural form of the model but by means of estimating a semi- or quasi- reduced form equation. In Section 2.5 we describe the problems associated with this usual way of testing. Section 2.6 deals with other shortcomings of theoretical and empirical studies on exchange rate determination. The concluding remarks are presented in Section 2.7.

2.2 Asset market approaches to exchange rate determination: the short-term

2.2.1 *The portfolio balance approach*

In the portfolio balance approach, the private agents' portfolio consists of domestic money, M, domestic bonds, B, and foreign bonds, F. Both domestic and foreign bonds are assumed to have a fixed price in order to avoid the complications of interest rate changes on bond prices. This can be realized by assuming that these bonds are floating rate notes (Visser, 1989, p. 26) or that the time to maturity is very short (De Jong, 1983, p. 227). Financial capital is assumed to be perfectly mobile, so that actual holdings of the assets always equal their desired holdings.[1] The supply of the various types of assets is given. The demand depends upon the domestic interest rate, r, the expected yield on foreign bonds, $r^* + \overset{\circ}{e}^e$, national income, Y, and financial wealth, W. The expected yield on foreign bonds consists of the foreign interest rate, r^*, and the expected percentage change of the exchange rate, $\overset{\circ}{e}^e$.

Two types of the portfolio balance model can be distinguished, *viz.* the preferred-habitat and the small-country approach. In the preferred-habitat model agents are assumed to be averse to incurring exchange rate risk. The residents of the home country and of the rest of the world hold both domestic- and foreign-currency assets, but if the (expected) yields are equal then they prefer to hold assets denominated in their home currency. Preferred-habitat portfolio balance models can be found in Boughton (1984) and Dooley and Isard (1982). The small-country approach assumes that only domestic residents hold assets denominated in domestic currency. Examples of the small country approach can be found in Branson (1977) and Branson *et al.* (1977).

[1] This definition of perfect capital mobility corresponds with the one presented in Dornbusch and Krugman (1976), p. 554. Some authors understand by perfect capital mobility both continuous equilibrium and perfect substitutability between domestic and foreign bonds (see e.g. De Haan *et al.*, 1979, p. 331 and MacDonald, 1988, pp. 33 and 34).

When the small-country assumptions are applied, the short-term model can be written as

$$M = m(r, r^* + \overset{\circ}{e}{}^e, Y)\cdot W \tag{2.1}$$

$$B = b(r, r^* + \overset{\circ}{e}{}^e, Y)\cdot W \tag{2.2}$$

$$e\cdot F = f(r, r^* + \overset{\circ}{e}{}^e, Y)\cdot W \tag{2.3}$$

$$W = M + B + e\cdot F \tag{2.4}$$

In equation (2.3) the stock of foreign bonds, F, has been multiplied by the exchange rate in order to derive its domestic currency value. Since the stocks of domestic money, M, of domestic bonds, B, and of foreign bonds, F, equal the supply of the various assets, relations (2.1)-(2.3) indicate that the domestic private agents' portfolio is continuously in equilibrium. As a consequence of the small-country assumption, the market for domestic money and that for domestic bonds are also continuously in equilibrium. Equation (2.4) is the definition of private wealth and shows that the three behavioural relations (2.1)-(2.3) are mutually dependent. Hence, the short-run equilibrium is sufficiently described by two of the three first equations in which W is replaced by definition (2.4). These two relations simultaneously determine the exchange rate and the domestic interest rate.

In order to determine the expected percentage change of the exchange rate, the model should be augmented with an equation of expectations formation. One possibility is to assume that the expectations are neutral, i.e. the expected change is zero. Under this assumption Branson (1977) shows that the short-run equilibrium is stable if the domestic bond market (demand for foreign bonds) is more (less) sensitive to changes in the domestic interest rate than to changes in the exchange rate and if the domestic holdings of foreign assets, F, are positive. If $F<0$, the model's instability results from the small-country assumption and from the assumption that the expectations are neutral. Section 2.4 discusses the relevance of the assumed expectations formula. The present section deals with the consequence of the small-country assumption and the changes of the results when this assumption is replaced by the preferred-habitat hypothesis.

Consider the case that the net holdings of foreign assets are positive, $F>0$, and that initially the system is in equilibrium. Assume that the only disturbance from this equilibrium is that the exchange rate is higher than its equilibrium value. Consequently, the proportion of F in the inhabitants' portfolio is greater than its equilibrium value whereas the desired proportion is unaffected. The domestic agents try to sell part of their foreign assets in order to restore the original situation. Therefore, the domestic currency will appreciate. Concluding a depreciation will lead to an appreciation and thus the short-run equilibrium is stable.

Let us now turn to the case where the domestic country has a net debt in foreign currency, $F<0$. A depreciation of the domestic currency from its equilibrium value increases the proportion of the foreign debt in the domestic portfolio, whereas the desired proportion remains at its original level. The inhabitants want to reduce their foreign debt. In order to redeem part of their foreign debt, they need foreign money. This extra demand for foreign assets reinforces the original depreciation of the domestic currency and thus the equilibrium is unstable.

In the preferred-habitat model the short-run equilibrium need not be unstable if $F<0$, because in this model foreigners accept domestic interest bearing assets. Now they accept the domestic assets which inhabitants offer them in exchange for the inhabitants' foreign currency debt. Thus there is a supply of foreign currency, the domestic currency appreciates, and the exchange rate returns to its initial value. Another consequence of the preferred-habitat model is that the equilibrium of the market for domestic interest bearing assets, B, is also determined by the foreigners' demand for these assets (see, e.g. Dooley and Isard, 1982).

2.2.2 *The monetary approach*

The monetary approach differs from the portfolio balance approach in that domestic and foreign bonds are assumed to be perfect substitutes and thus can be aggregated in one asset, BF. Another consequence of the perfect substitutability of domestic and foreign bonds is that the expected yield on both types of assets is the same so that investors are risk neutral with regard to exchange risks, and the uncovered interest parity holds

$$r = r^{*} + \mathring{e}^{e} \tag{2.5}$$

The domestic interest rate is derived from this parity.

The equations corresponding with the portfolio balance relations (2.1)-(2.4) are

$$M = m(r, Y) \cdot W \tag{2.6}$$

$$BF = bf(r, Y) \cdot W \tag{2.7}$$

$$W \;=\; M + B + e{\cdot}F \tag{2.8}$$

where $BF = B + e{\cdot}F$ and because of (2.6) only one interest rate is included in the asset demand functions. Because of the wealth constraint (2.8), one of the two demand functions can be deleted. Usually relation (2.7) is deleted so that the money demand functions remains.

In the majority of studies belonging to the monetary approach, the money demand function differs from (2.7) in that the demand relates to real balances and wealth is excluded. A possible justification for excluding W is that in many cases its time series is highly correlated with that of Y. Then equation (2.7) changes into

$$M/P \;=\; m_r(r,\, Y) \tag{2.9}$$

where P is the domestic price level and $m_r(.)$ is the demand for real money balances. The exchange rate fluctuates in order to equilibrate real demand and supply of money. The exact formula for the exchange rate depends upon the assumed interaction between the exchange rate and the domestic price level.

The most simple monetary model is the flexible price monetary model. In this model the purchasing power parity (PPP) holds at all points in time, that is

$$e \;=\; P/P^* \tag{2.10}$$

Let us assume that the foreigners' money demand has the same shape as (2.9), i.e.

$$M^* / P^* = m_r^*(r^*,\, Y^*) \tag{2.11}$$

Solving (2.9) and (2.10) for P and P^* and substituting the resulting relations in (2.10) gives the exchange rate equation

$$e \;=\; m_r^*(r^*,\, Y^*){\cdot}M \;\;/\;\; m_r(r,Y){\cdot}M^* \tag{2.12}$$

This flexible price monetary model shows some remarkable results that contradict the results of other models. Firstly, an increase in national income gives rise to an appreciating exchange rate, because the real demand for money increases. Given a constant money supply, the price level falls and as a consequence of PPP the exchange rate falls too. This result contrasts with that of the traditional view according to which an increase in Y will lead to an extra demand for imports and thus to a depreciating exchange rate. Secondly, an increase in the domestic interest rate results in a depreciating currency, because the demand for domestic currency declines and, thus, the domestic price rises. This effect is opposite to that of an increasing domestic interest rate in the portfolio balance model. In the portfolio balance approach such a movement increases the attractiveness of domestic bonds so that the demand for assets denominated in domestic currency increases. Consequently, the exchange rate appreciates.

It should be mentioned that these outcomes are not characteristic for all monetary models of the exchange rate but result from the specific assumption applied in the flexible price variant.

Another version of the monetary model is the sticky price monetary model first developed in Dornbusch (1976). In this model PPP does not hold in the short-run but is considered to be a long-term phenomenon. The model consists of the uncovered interest parity, the money demand, money market equilibrium, a relation for the inflation rate, and a function generating the expected changes of the exchange rate.

2.2.3 *The currency substitution model*

Hitherto we have assumed that inhabitants do not hold foreign money. The currency substitution model concentrates on the possible consequences of domestic residents holding foreign money. Allowing domestic investors to hold part of their wealth in foreign currency means that the asset demand system of the portfolio balance model is slightly amended and equals

$$M = m(r, r^* + \mathring{e}^e, \mathring{e}^e, Y) \cdot W \tag{2.13}$$

$$B = b(r, r^* + \mathring{e}^e, \mathring{e}^e, Y) \cdot W \tag{2.14}$$

$$e \cdot F = f(r, r^* + \mathring{e}^e, \mathring{e}^e, Y) \cdot W \tag{2.15}$$

$$e \cdot N = n(r, r^* + \mathring{e}^e, \mathring{e}^e, Y) \cdot W \tag{2.16}$$

$$W = M + B + e \cdot F + e \cdot N \tag{2.17}$$

where N is foreign money. Note that the expected percentage change of the exchange rate is included as a single item in the list of the asset demand functions' arguments. This reflects the currency substitution model's distinction between foreign bonds and foreign money.

For many countries data on the inhabitants' holdings of foreign currency are not available. Hence, the domestic holdings of foreign bonds and currency are aggregated into one single foreign asset. In that case, we are eager to know whether we can derive the presence of currency substitution from the coefficients of the resulting portfolio balance model. In order to shed some light on this issue, let us aggregate the demand for foreign money and bonds in total domestic demand for foreign assets

$$A = F+N = a(r, r^*, \mathring{e}^e, Y)\cdot W \tag{2.18}$$

where a(.) represents the demand for foreign money and foreign bonds. The gross substitutability assumption in (2.13)-(2.16) implies that

$$\delta a/\delta r < 0, \qquad \delta a/\delta r^* > 0, \qquad \delta a/\delta \mathring{e}^e > 0 \tag{2.19}$$

Consequently, all rate-of-return effects in the demand functions for domestic money (2.13), domestic bonds (2.16), and total foreign assets (2.18) are qualitatively the same as they are in the standard portfolio balance model that ignores currency substitution. The size of various coefficients may be affected by currency substitution but this has no effect on the applicability of the standard open economy macro models that ignore the currency substitutability.

In the light of this analysis we conclude "that the financial asset specification in a portfolio balance model with currency substitution is indistinguishable from the standard portfolio balance model, which either rules out currency substitution or implicitly lumps together foreign monetary and non-monetary assets. The sole exception lies in the effect of an increase in domestic income (or some other transaction variable) on the total domestic demand for foreign assets, which *may* be positive if currency substitution is strong whereas it is presumed to be negative or zero in the conventional portfolio balance model" (Cuddington, 1983, pp. 114 and 115).

2.3 The asset market model's dynamics: the current account's role

In the short run the exchange rate is determined by requirements of asset market equilibrium, given existing stocks of the various assets. A short-run equilibrium does not mean that all sectors of the economy are in equilibrium. Mainly three intrinsic sources of the model's dynamics toward the long-term equilibrium can be distinguished: asset accumulation through current account surpluses (deficits), expectations of variables' changes in future periods and if the model contains frictions on the goods markets, a price-adjustment process and/or sometimes an output-adjustment process. The exact form of the adjustment process depends on the specification of the various sectors. A good description of exchange rate dynamics in various models can be found in Obstfeld and Stockman (1985). We will not reproduce their results but concentrate on the role of the current account of the balance of payments, which has such a dominant place in traditional theories. The current account can be part of two sources of dynamics, *viz.* asset accumulation and expectations formation.

In the asset market models and especially in the portfolio balance and currency substitution models, the current account plays a crucial role in the accumulation and decumulation of foreign assets and, consequently, in the adjustment from one short-term equilibrium to another.[2] The current account balance consists of the trade balance and the balance of net income on foreign assets. If the current account is in deficit, F is decreasing. As F changes, the exchange rate changes in order to create a new short-run equilibrium. This new value of the exchange rate influences the balances on the trade account and on the net receipts of interest income. An overview of the adjustment mechanism is depicted in Figure 2.1.

Figure 2.1 Accumulation and exchange rate dynamics

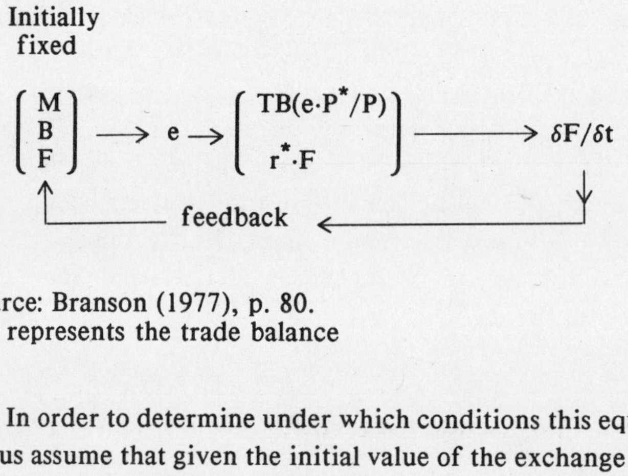

source: Branson (1977), p. 80.
TB represents the trade balance

In order to determine under which conditions this equilibrium will be stable, let us assume that given the initial value of the exchange rate, the balance on the current account is negative. Consequently, the domestic holdings of foreign assets decreases. Neglecting expectations effects, under normal conditions inhabitants do want to increase the proportion of foreign assets in their portfolio and the domestic currency will depreciate. As a result, the real exchange rate, $e{\cdot}P^*/P$,

[2] Obstfeld and Stockman (1985, esp. pp. 954-957) show that when the menu of assets is expanded, the current account, per se, may play no role in exchange rate dynamics.

increases and assuming that the famous Marshall-Lerner elasticity conditions hold, the trade balance improves. This reduces the loss of foreign assets and thus works to stabilize the adjustment process. There is, however, a second and destabilizing channel of adjustment: the balance on the net interest receipts. A decrease of F leads to decreasing net interest receipts and thus to a worsening of the balance on the current account which further propels the decline of F. In order to guarantee that the overall adjustment process will be stable, we assume that the trade balance effect dominates the effect via the balance on net interest receipts.

In some studies the current account determines the long-run real exchange rate's expected change. An example of such an expectations hypothesis is presented in Hooper and Morton (1982). In that study the exchange rate relation is

$$e = \bar{e} - 1/\theta \, [(r - \pi) - (r^* - \pi^*)] \tag{2.20}$$

where π is the inflation rate and a bar above a variable indicates its long-run value. According to this relation, the spot exchange rate moves directly with changes in the underlying equilibrium rate and with changes in the real interest differential.

The equilibrium rate can be divided into its relative price and real components

$$\bar{e} = (p - p^*) + q \tag{2.21}$$

where q is the equilibrium value of the real exchange rate. For deriving the equilibrium real exchange rate, they start with the current account equation

$$CA_t = \Sigma_{i=0}^{t} \gamma_i q_{t-i} + f_1(X^P)_t + f_2(X^t)_t \tag{2.22}$$

According to this relation the current account balance, CA, is a function of current and lagged values of the real exchange rate, q, and transitory, X^t, and permanent, X^P, variables. In the long-run equilibrium, we have

$$\overline{CA} = \gamma\bar{q} + f_1(X^P) \tag{2.23}$$

where $\gamma=\Sigma\gamma_i$ is the long-run response of the current account to the real exchange rate. Assuming that the Marshall-Lerner condition holds, $\gamma>0$. Solving (2.21) for $\bar{q}$ gives

$$\bar{q} = \overline{CA}/\gamma - f_1(X^P)/\gamma \tag{2.24}$$

Hooper and Morton simplify the analysis by assuming that $\overline{CA}$ is constant over time. Under this assumption the change in $\bar{q}$ equals

$$\bar{q}_t - \bar{q}_{t-1} = -[f_1(X^P)_t - f_1(X^P)_{t-1}] / \gamma \tag{2.25}$$

Assuming that the expectations of X^P are static, changes in $f_1(X^P)$ can be derived from non-transitory unexpected changes in the current account

$$f_1(X^P)_t - f_1(X^P)_{t-1} = CA_t - E_{t-1}(CA_t) - CA_t^t \tag{2.26}$$

where $E_{t-1}(CA_t)$ is the expectations in period t-1 of CA in period t, and CA_t^t is the transitory component of the unexpected change in the current account. Hence, the right-hand side of equation (2.26) represents the permanent component of the forecast error with regard to the current account.

Combining (2.25) and (2.26) gives

$$\bar{q}_t - \bar{q}_{t-1} = -[CA_t - E_{t-1}(CA_t) - CA_t^t] / \gamma \tag{2.27}$$

which relates changes in the equilibrium real exchange rate directly to movements in the current account. Integrating (2.27) over time yields

$$\bar{q}_t = q_0 - \Sigma_{i=0}^{t} [CA_{t-i} - E_{t-1-i}(CA_{t-i}) - CA_{t-i}^t] / \gamma \tag{2.28}$$

Thus, the equilibrium real exchange rate is a function of an initial equilibrium rate and the cumulative sum of past permanent unexpected changes in the current account balance. Substituting (2.28) into (2.21) and the result into the exchange rate relation (2.20) shows that the current account balance can influence the spot rate via its influence on the equilibrium real exchange rate.

The discussion presented in this section illustrates that the current account balance can influence the asset market model's dynamics by means of the accumulation or decumulation of foreign assets and its influence on the expected changes in the equilibrium real exchange rate. When specifying the empirical model we will return to these roles of the current account.

2.4 The role of expectations

At the end of the preceding section we discussed a particular form of exchange rate expectations. From the literature it emerges that different expectations assumptions can lead to wide differences in behaviour and that one expectations hypothesis can give rise to different effects in different models. In this subsection we will not deal with all possible expectations hypotheses and all their possible effects in asset market models. We will confine ourselves to some examples that clearly illustrate the consequences of using different expectations schemes.

The first example refers to the stability of the portfolio balance model's short-run equilibrium. Let us assume that the small-country assumption applies and that, initially, the exchange rate expectations are neutral, i.e. the expected change is zero. Hence, a change in the exchange rate only affects the valuation of foreign assets and wealth. As we have shown in Section 2.2.1, if the country is a net debtor then the short-run equilibrium will be unstable.

The introduction of an appropriate expectations scheme can change this unstable system into a stable one. Assume for instance that the agents expect that the exchange rate will return to its initial value. Under such a regressive expectations scheme, a depreciation generates an expected appreciation of the domestic currency. By this, both the demand for domestic assets and the willingness to hold the foreign debt increase. The exchange rate appreciates and thus the short-run equilibrium is stable even if $F<0$.

In general the influence of external shocks, such as changes in economic policy, on the dynamics of a model highly depend upon the particular expectation scheme that has been assumed. In many models the effect of a change in an exogenous variable on the long-term steady state is not influenced by exchange rate expectations, but the immediate effect and the path to the steady state are. For the immediate effect it is important whether the expectations are forward looking or not. Forward looking expectations depend on the expectations of exogenous variables for future periods. The best-known example of this type of expectations is the rational (or perfect foresight) expectation hypothesis. If expectations are forward looking and the endogenous variable concerned can change without costs, as is generally the case for the exchange rate, then an exogenous shock that changes expectations of future exogenous variables often leads to a jump in the endogenous variable.[3] In models with exchange rate expectations that are based on past observations, the exchange rate will not change immediately after an exogenous shock.

Another, related, feature of forward looking expectations is that the announcement of a policy change can give rise to a change in the exchange rate. Generally, the immediate effect of an announcement is similar but less strong

---

[3] These models are unstable, see for instance Ethier (1979), Gray and Turnovsky (1979) and Kouri (1976). The instability problem can be solved by introducing a so-called transversality condition. An economic interpretation of this condition can be found in Kouri (1976).

than the immediate effect of the corresponding policy change. The reason for these reactions of the expectations and the endogenous variables on the announcement of future changes is that the announcement leads to a revision of the expected future values of policy variables. If expectations are not forward looking, then the announcement of a change in the future will have no effect. Since expectations are based on observations only, they will only change at the moment that alterations are put into practice.

The importance of expectations formation for the dynamics toward the new long-run equilibrium can best be illustrated by means of an example. We have chosen the dynamics resulting from an increase in the rate of monetary expansion in the monetary approach model developed in Kouri (1976). In this model it is assumed that the economy only produces traded goods. The world price of these goods is assumed to be constant and equal to 1 so that the domestic price level and the exchange rate are the same variable. The small-country assumption, defined in Section 2.2.1, is applied. In the stationary state of this model the expected rate of inflation equals the actual rate of inflation and hence the rate of change of the money stock, and the stock of real wealth, consisting of money and foreign assets, and its composition are constant. The constancy of real wealth requires that in the long run the current account is zero. Equilibrium on the current account implies that domestic output equals domestic absorption, which consists of private consumption and government expenditure. The composition of real wealth is constant if the stock of wealth is held in desired proportions.

An increase in the monetary expansion is used for financing government expenditure. In the resulting new stationary state the stock of real money has decreased and the stock of foreign assets may have increased or decreased. The stock of real balances decreases because its return, the inverse of the inflation rate, has decreased. Two opposite forces influence the change of the stock of foreign assets. On the one hand it will decrease because the rise of government expenditure generates a deficit on the current account and thus a capital outflow, but on the other hand it will rise due to the substitution effect resulting from the depreciation of the domestic currency. Let us assume that in the long run the stock of foreign assets increases.

Under rational expectations there is an "immediate, discrete devaluation of the exchange rate, after which the exchange rate appreciates relative to its new trend. The sharp depreciation causes the current account to move to a surplus" (Kouri, 1976, p. 209). After the immediate effects the stocks of real money and of foreign assets increase to the new equilibrium.

Under the adaptive expectations hypothesis the change in the expected exchange rate is equal to a fraction of the most recent forecast error. Hence the expected exchange rate does not change immediately after the increase in the rate of monetary expansion. Consequently, the increased government expenditure causes the current account to go into deficit. For a while the stocks of real money and of foreign assets decline by the same amount (their relative price has not yet changed). But after some time the increased inflation rate leads to an expected depreciation of the currency and asset holders substitute domestic money for foreign assets. This capital outflow moves the current account into surplus. The cumulative surpluses exceed the cumulative deficits so that in the long run the stock of foreign assets is greater than in the original equilibrium because of the lower rate of return on domestic assets.

These examples clearly show the crucial role of expectations for exchange rate determination. In this respect, it is disappointing that no expectations scheme is generally accepted as the most appropriate approximation of the agents' expectations. For these two reasons we devote a special chapter (Chapter 3) to this subject.

2.5 Testing asset market approaches by single equation procedures

2.5.1 *The derivation of the exchange rate relation*

In principle three methods for testing exchange rate theories can be distinguished. The first one takes one of the cornerstones of the monetary approach, namely the assumption that the uncovered interest parity (2.5) holds, as a starting point. Using a proxy of the exchange rate's expected percentage change and an assumption of the risk premium's form it tests whether the null hypothesis of no risk premium is valid. This procedure investigates whether the data discriminate between the monetary and the portfolio balance approach. Since it does not analyse the explanatory factors of exchange rate determination, we do not discuss this method.[4] The two other methods explicitly relate the exchange rate to explanatory variables. The structural procedure estimates the structural form of the model, for example relations (2.1)-(2.3), and derives the exchange rate from the resulting equations. This method has hardly ever been used. Studies in which the structural form is applied are Obstfeld (1983) and Smith and Wickens (1986). In almost all studies on the econometric evidence of the asset market approaches use is made of the third method. This procedure tests the particular model by means of a single equation, the exchange rate being the dependent variable. The bad results mentioned in the introduction refer to studies which use this method. In order to detect the possible sources of this

[4] The number of publications containing tests on the existence of a risk premium in the foreign exchange market is enormous. Surveys can be found in Levich (1985) and Hodrick (1987).

disappointing result, the remainder of this chapter is devoted to a description and assessment of this single equation procedure.

The exchange rate relation is obtained either by (partly) solving the structural model for the exchange rate or by deriving the sign of changes in explanatory variables on the exchange rate.

An example of the former variant is the exchange rate relation derived from the flexible price monetary model, such as equation (2.12). In order to illustrate the procedure let us rewrite the equations of the model so that they are suitable for econometric tests. Assume that the money market equilibrium conditions have the form

$$M/P = K \cdot Y^{\alpha} \cdot e^{-\beta r} \tag{2.29}$$

and

$$M^* / P^* = K^* \cdot Y^{*\gamma} \cdot e^{-\delta r^*} \tag{2.30}$$

where K and K^* are constants. Substituting the equations of the price levels that can be derived from these relations into the purchasing power parity expression (2.10) yields the equation corresponding with (2.12)

$$e = \frac{M}{M^*} \cdot \frac{Y^{*\gamma}}{Y^{\alpha}} \cdot \frac{K^*}{K} \cdot e^{\beta r - \delta r^*} \tag{2.31}$$

Taking logarithms of (2.31), we obtain

$$\ln(e) = m - m^* + \gamma y^* - \alpha y + \beta r - \delta r^* \tag{2.32}$$

where, except for the exchange rate, a lower case letter represents the logarithm of a capital letter.

In many studies it is assumed that the coefficients in the money demand functions are identical, so that (2.32) can be rewritten as

$$\ln(e) = m - m^* + \alpha(y^* - y) + \beta(r - r^*) \tag{2.33}$$

Expression (2.33) can be refined further by using the uncovered interest parity for replacing $(r - r^*)$. The derivation of (2.33) is a simple example of the method which obtains the exchange rate relation by analytically solving the structural model. This procedure is very often used for testing the monetary approach.

However, in most cases this method is not suitable for deriving the exchange rate equation of a portfolio balance model, because this model is too complex. Branson *et al.* (1977) obtain an exchange rate equation of a portfolio balance model by determining the short-run multipliers of the explanatory variables on the exchange rate. From this they derive that an exchange rate equation of system (2.1)-(2.4) has the following form

$$e = h(\overset{+}{\Delta M},\ \overset{?}{\Delta B},\ \overset{-}{\Delta F}) \tag{2.34}$$

where the sign of the partial derivative of the exchange rate with respect to a variable is written above the variable concerned. The direction of the immediate effect of a change in the domestic bonds on the exchange rate is undetermined. This variable has therefore been omitted in some empirical studies.

If the model is extended to a world of two countries and the variables with an undetermined sign of their partial derivative in the exchange rate relation are neglected then the following reduced form equation results

$$e = h(\overset{+}{\Delta M},\ \overset{-}{\Delta M^*},\ \overset{-}{\Delta F},\ \overset{+}{\Delta B^*}) \tag{2.35}$$

where B^* is the net foreign holdings of domestic interest bearing assets.

2.5.2 *The nature of the exchange rate equations*

In many articles exchange rate relations like (2.33), (2.34) and (2.35) are labelled the exchange rate model's reduced form equations.[5] Strictly speaking these relations are not reduced form equations because some of the explanatory variables may not be predetermined. For example, the private stock of foreign assets on the right-hand side of (2.34) and (2.35) depends upon the central bank's intervention policy. Moreover, the domestic money stock varies with the unsterilized part of these interventions. The intervention policy in its turn is influenced by the evolution of the exchange rate. Consequently, the exchange rate and its explanatory variables, the stocks of assets on the right-hand side of (2.33), (2.34), and (3.35), are simultaneously determined (see for example Frankel, 1981, pp. 1076-1077, and Hacche and Townend, 1983, p. 139). Moreover, in the relation of the monetary model the domestic interest rate and

---

[5] Note that some authors refer to these single equation models as "structural models". With this term they want to differentiate these models from the pure time series models which explain the exchange rate's current value only from past observations of its own time series. From an econometric point of view the term "structural models" is deceptive, because these equations are not the model's structural form.

the expected depreciation of the domestic currency are most likely to depend on the present value of the spot rate, e. Authors who are aware of this simultaneity therefore refer to these exchange rate relations as *semi- or quasi-reduced form equations*. (see e.g. Meese and Rogoff, 1983a, p. 5, and Gylfason and Helliwell, 1983, p. 823). In order to gain some insight into the advantages and disadvantages of this type of relations, we first discuss the main differences between reduced form and structural form equations.

The reduced form relates each endogenous variable to all predetermined variables and stochastic disturbance terms. It is obtained by solving the original model with respect to the endogenous variables. Since current endogenous variables do not show up as right-hand side variables in the reduced form equations, ordinary least squares (OLS) yields consistent estimates of the parameters. A disadvantage, however, is that very often the structural parameter values cannot be retrieved from the reduced form estimates. Moreover, since the latter are (nonlinear) combinations of several structural form parameters, it is very often unclear which sign and value of the reduced form parameters are implied by a particular theoretical model. Consequently, generally, the reduced form estimates are not helpful for discriminating between different theories. These coefficients only "have a useful interpretation as *comparative static results*, indicating the extent of change in each endogenous variable as any of the predetermined variables change" (Intrilligator, 1978, p. 45).

The structural form of a model consists of the original equations of a particular theory. No subset of equations has been solved for some particular variables. The right-hand sides of the relations contain exogenous, lagged endogenous, as well as current endogenous variables. The presence of the latter necessitates the use of a simultaneous estimation technique for deriving consistent estimates of the parameters; estimated values of these coefficients present a direct test of the underlying theory. It is, therefore, very useful for discriminating between alternative theories (see, e.g. Friedman and Roley, 1980, p. 36 and Obstfeld, 1980, p. 163). Structural estimation is also necessary if one is not only interested in the comparative static results but also in the "channels through which changes in asset supplies influence the exchange rate". (Obstfeld, 1983, p. 163).[6] In addition, the constraints imposed by economic theory on the structural form are far more clear than those imposed on the reduced form, because in the reduced form equations many coefficients are comprised of various parameters of the model's structural form. Another disadvantage of the

[6] See also Keller (1980), p. 89, and Meese and Rogoff (1985). The last two authors write that to "adequately capture the effects of government deficits, it would be necessary to estimate a fully dynamic model of private saving and portfolio behaviour" (Meese and Rogoff, 1985, p. 14).

reduced form is that, generally, each equation contains many explanatory variables. Since it is not unusual for two or more of these variables to be correlated, the estimation of the reduced form parameters is difficult. However, to a great extent it is quite possible to avoid this form of spurious correlation in structural models. In a subsequent section this feature of structural models will be discussed in more detail.

Quasi- or semi-reduced form equations are obtained "at an intermediated step of the model solving process", (Keller, 1984, p. 110). Consequently, the set of explanatory variables of each relation consists of predetermined as well as current endogenous variables. To us it seems that for estimation purposes, the quasi- or semi-reduced form equations combine the disadvantages of both the reduced form and the structural form relations. They share with the reduced form equations the inability to retrieve the structural parameter values from the estimated semi-reduced form coefficients. Ordinary least squares will give rise to inconsistent estimates, so as in the structural form, a simultaneous estimation technique should be used. The resulting parameters cannot be interpreted as the comparative static results of a change of a predetermined variable on an endogenous variable. Nor do the semi-reduced form equations contain sufficient information for deriving the dynamic path of the whole model.[7]

In summing up, the exact nature of the semi- or quasi-reduced form relations, which are a mixture of reduced form and structural form equations, is unclear and incorporates the drawbacks of reduced form and structural form equations, without including the advantages of these particular forms. We therefore conclude that, if possible, the semi- or quasi-reduced form of a model should be avoided. We prefer the structural or reduced form of the model concerned. The ultimate choice between these two types of the model should be guided by the problem at hand.

2.5.3. *Simultaneity*

As has been noted in the previous subsection, the exchange rate, the interest rates, the expected depreciation of the domestic currency and the private stocks of various assets are simultaneously determined. Thus ordinary least squares estimates of the parameters of the structural and of the semi-reduced form will most likely be biased. In order to circumvent biased results arising from

---

[7] Once the parameters of the structural form are obtained, the usefulness of semi-reduced forms lies in "the explanatory contribution and simplifications by means of reducing the system to a more controllable system such as a partial equilibrium" (Keller, 1984, p. 110).

endogenous stocks of assets, some authors have derived a reaction function of the central bank's intervention policy (Branson *et al.*, 1977, and Murphy and Van Duyne ,1980, among others). The resulting system is estimated by a simultaneous estimation technique, mostly an instrumental variables (IV) procedure. Usually an IV-method is also applied to obtain consistent estimates of the parameters of a model in which the simultaneity arises from one of the other factors mentioned above (see, e.g. Hooper, 1983, Hooper and Morton, 1982, and Edison ,1985).

According to some authors the differences between OLS-estimates and IV-estimates appear to be very small. A reason for this might be that the instrumental variables chosen were not exogenous but endogenous. Meese and Rogoff (1983b) extensively studied this possibility. They estimated a Vector Autoregressive (VAR) system consisting of the logarithm of the relative money supplies, the short-term interest differential, the long-term interest differential, the domestic and foreign trade balances and the logarithm of the exchange rate. This system was estimated for the following combinations of countries: U.S. - Germany, U.S. - Japan and U.S. - U.K. during the period March 1973 - June 1981. Each variable is regressed on lagged values of all variables. The dynamic interactions among the variables is best studied with use of the moving average (MA) representation of the system, which is derived by inverting the autoregressive system to express each endogenous variable in the terms of the disturbances. The disturbances are also known as the innovations. This moving average representation is used to study the system's response to "typical shocks", which are positive residuals of one standard deviation unit in each equation.[8] The forecast errors derived from these shocks are used for investigating whether the variables are exogenous. Abstracting from coefficient uncertainty, a variable is considered to be exogenous if for all forecast horizons the variable's own disturbances account for all of its forecast error variance. The share of the variable's own innovation in the explanation of its forecast error variance ranges from 0.52 to 0.94 at the one-month forecast horizon. At the three-month forecast horizon this fraction lies between 0.33 and 0.92. It decreases sharply if the forecast horizon is lengthened to 12 or 36 months. These results indicate that no variable can be considered to be exogenous to the entire system. Hence, it is

[8] It should be noted that these experiments are complicated by the fact that the disturbance terms are in general contemporaneously correlated. So to simulate a typical shock to a given variable it is necessary to recognize that the expectation of other disturbances in the system, conditional on the particular shock of interest, is usually non-zero. The solution to this problem is to specify a variable ordering. This ordering specifies that the first variable is predetermined with respect to the other variables, that the second variable is predetermined with respect to all but the first etc. Since the ordering is not unique, Meese and Rogoff use two ordering schemes. For more details, see Meese and Rogoff (1983b) and Sims (1980).

difficult to find legitimate instrumental variables with which to estimate the parameters of the models consistently. Consistent estimation, thus, requires a careful selection of the regressors and the instrumental variables.[9]

Do these results indicate that the single equation (quasi-reduced) form models' bad performance - mentioned in Section 2.5.1 - can be ascribed to inconsistently estimated coefficients? In order to investigate this possibility Meese and Rogoff (1983b) explore a range of constrained coefficient models. They find that for the models they considered this unimpressive performance cannot be attributed to inconsistent estimates.

An alternative solution would be the estimation of the structural form relations by means of a full information estimation method. As is well-known the application of such a method necessitates the researcher to specify the equation carefully, because a misspecification in one relation biases the estimates of all parameters.

2.5.4. *Multicollinearity and sign reversals*

Generally, the exchange rate and its various foreign and domestic explanatory variables are simultaneously determined. As has been discussed in the previous subsection the collinearity between the exchange rate and the explanatory variables can give rise to biased estimates. In this subsection attention will be paid to the consequences of the collinearity among the explanatory variables and to the possible solutions of the associated problems.

As is well-known, multicollinearity reduces the precision of the estimates (see e.g. Johnston, 1972, p. 160). Sometimes this loss of precision incorrectly gives rise to coefficients which are not significantly different from zero. The true situation may be that the variable has an effect but that the set of observations has not enabled us to pick it up. Another consequence is that the parameter estimates are very sensitive to particular sets of data, and can dramatically change when a few observations are added or deleted.

Multicollinearity is caused by the fact that the set of explanatory variables does not contain enough information to obtain satisfactory estimates of all relevant parameters. The best and obvious solution to this problem is to add some new information to the data set. One piece of additional information may be a priori restrictions on the parameters. In exchange rate models a popular

---

[9] Kiviet (1985) presents sequences of tests to solve empirically the problem of both finding an adequate specification of the structural form and composing a set of admissible instrumental variables. In Section 4.3.2 we review various procedures for selecting instrumental variables and justify our selection procedure.

restriction is the assumed equivalence of the parameters in the domestic and foreign money demand equation.[10] In Section 2.5.1 this assumption changes exchange rate equation (2.32) in (2.33). In the latter the foreign and domestic variables are replaced by their difference (e.g., y and y* are replaced by y - y*). Haynes and Stone (1981 and 1982) show that this subtraction of foreign from domestic variables can lead to sign reversals.

Assume that the true model is

$$e = \alpha_0 + \alpha m + \alpha^* m^* + \epsilon \tag{2.36}$$

and that the restriction is introduced that $\beta = -\alpha = \alpha^*$, so that (2.36) changes in

$$e = \alpha_0 + \beta(m^* - m) + \epsilon \tag{2.37}$$

In the Appendix to their paper Haynes and Stone (1982) prove that the ordinary least squares (OLS) estimator of β equals

$$\hat{\beta} = \omega_1 \hat{\alpha}^* - \omega_2 \hat{\alpha} \tag{2.38}$$

where $\omega_1 = [\ \mathrm{var}\ (m^*) - \mathrm{cov}\ (m, m^*)\ ] / D$

$\omega_2 = [\ \mathrm{var}\ (m) - \mathrm{cov}\ (m, m^*)\ ] / D$

$D = \mathrm{var}\ (m) + \mathrm{var}\ (m^*) - 2\ \mathrm{cov}\ (m, m^*)$

and $\hat{\alpha}$ and $\hat{\alpha}^*$ are the unconstrained OLS estimators of α and α^* in equation (2.36). The definitions of ω_1 and ω_2 imply

$$\omega_1 + \omega_2 = 1 \tag{2.39}$$

The expectation of (2.38) is

$$E\,(\hat{\beta}) = \omega_1 \alpha^* - \omega_2 \alpha \tag{2.40}$$

If the restriction $\beta = -\alpha = \alpha^*$ is correct then $E(\beta) = -\alpha = \alpha^*$. If not, then $E(\hat{\beta})$ depends upon α, α^* and the weights ω_1 and ω_2.

---

[10] Studies in which the magnitude of the parameters of foreign and domestic variables are assumed to be equal are e.g. Driskill (1981a and 1981b). Driskill and Sheffrin (1981), Frankel (1979b), Hooper and Morton (1982) and Woo (1985).

New problems arise if m and m* are positively correlated, then ω_1 or ω_2 may be negative. If the variances of the money supplies differ, then the probability of a negative ω_1 or ω_2 is a function of the strength of the correlation; the stronger the correlation, ceteris paribus, the greater the probability that ω_1 or ω_2 will be negative.[11] This implies that $E(\hat{\beta})$ is not bounded by $-\alpha$ and α^*. In fact $E(\hat{\beta})$ and α^* may differ in sign.

If more explanatory variables are included in the equation then the bias introduced by the constraint in general biases all other coefficients even if the other coefficients are not themselves a source of bias. The empirical work presented in Haynes and Stone (1981 and 1982) shows that the parameters may be biased considerably if the various domestic and foreign coefficients are wrongly supposed to be of equal size. They therefore suggest that the validity of the constraint should be tested before it is imposed.[12] This discussion clearly shows that assuming domestic and foreign parameters to be equal - so that the two corresponding variables in the exchange rate relation can be replaced by their difference - in many cases does not solve the multicollinearity problem of this quasi-reduced form equation.

Additional information, used to reduce the consequences of multicollinearity, may also be reflected in the form of previous estimates of some of the coefficients or a proxy of an unobservable variable. An example of the latter type of information is presented in Hooper and Morton (1982). Their exchange rate relation contains some variables which represent the expected real exchange rate, *viz.* the equilibrium current account balance (see Section 2.3) and a parameter reflecting the expected speed of adjustment of the actual towards the equilibrium current account balance. They first run a regression of the real exchange rate. From these results they obtain, among other things, an estimate of the equilibrium current account. In the second stage they estimate the nominal exchange rate equation with the values of the equilibrium current account and of the expectations' speed of adjustment constrained to their estimate obtained in the first stage.

Rasulo and Sykes Wilford (1980) present a procedure in which previous estimates of coefficients are used to reduce the multicollinearity problem. They suggest that the domestic and foreign money demand equations are estimated first. From these estimations the parameters α and α^* in (2.36) can be obtained.

---

[11] If the direct correlation is perfect and the variances are equal then the weights are undefined because the denominator equals zero. Similar problems arise if the two variables are aggregated and their correlation is negative. See Haynes and Stone (1982) for more details.

[12] Besides Haynes and Stone (1981 and 1982), Clements and Frenkel (1981) also test for this constraint.

They then construct a new variable $\hat{m} = \hat{\alpha}^* m^* - \hat{\alpha} m$, which is substituted in (2.36)

$$e = \alpha_0 + \beta (\hat{\alpha}^* m^* - \hat{\alpha} m) + \epsilon \qquad (2.41)$$

Estimates of α_0 and β are obtained by estimating (2.41). This procedure does not constrain the coefficients α and α^* to be equal. However, it introduces a new parameter, β, which does not appear in the theoretical model. We, therefore, prefer to estimate

$$e - (\hat{\alpha}^* m^* - \hat{\alpha} m) = \alpha_0 + \epsilon \qquad (2.42)$$

which corresponds with the original equation. In fact this is a well-known procedure for handling the multicollinearity problem.[13]

2.6 Other possible shortcomings of the theory and the empirical tests

2.6.1 *Introduction*

In the preceding section we have put forward factors that might explain the disappointing results of the econometric evidence on exchange rate behaviour. All these arguments directly refer to consequences of testing exchange rate models by means of a single exchange rate relation. In this section we draw attention to factors which are not connected with single equation tests only They refer to both assumptions used in the asset market models as well as to problems connected with testing these models. The items to be reviewed are: the asset markets' speed of adjustment, the purchasing power parity, the instability of structural relations and of time series, expectations proxies, the measurement of asset stocks and aspects of exchange rate determination that are not incorporated in empirical asset market models.

2.6.2 *The financial markets' speed of adjustment*

In the short-run model of Section 2.2 stocks of financial assets are assumed to be constant and assets markets are assumed to clear instantaneously. Thus actual stocks of assets are assumed to be always equal to desired stocks.

---

[13] See e.g. Johnston, 1972, p. 165. Other methods for handling the consequence of multicollinearity can be found in textbooks on econometrics (e.g. Johnston, 1972, and Judge *et al*., 1980).

Several authors argue that these assumptions might be too restrictive. Firstly, it implies that the model describes extremely short-run behaviour. The time interval "is short enough to disregard flow market conditions such as the state of the current account" (Bisignano and Hoover, 1982, p. 20). The appropriateness of this assumption, which implies that stocks of financial assets are constant, is questionable in empirical studies which use quarterly data. Secondly, Isard (1983) notes that the assumption of instantaneously clearing financial markets implies that market participants review their full information sets every day; that they re-evaluate their currency position continuously. These implications are at variance with the internal decision processes of banks and corporations. Both banks and non-banks generally instruct their foreign exchange managers to avoid exposing their firms to large risks through open foreign currency positions. Moreover, the "upper level decisions about portfolio stocks are normally reviewed only periodically, reflecting the costs of top management's time, so that the stock-adjustment response to new information may be gradual" (Isard, 1983, p. 18).[14] A third argument to the detriment of the short-run model's assumptions is that the assumption of continuous clearing asset markets is not validated by the results of econometric studies on money demand. These studies find a highly significant partial adjustment mechanism.[15]

Despite these arguments against the assumption of perfect capital mobility, there are only a few studies on exchange rates in which this assumption is not made. Frenkel and Rodriguez (1982) present a variant of Dornbusch's (1976) monetary model in which the speed of adjustment in asset markets is less than infinity. They assume that capital flows are proportional to $r - r^* + \mathring{e}^e$, the difference between the net rates of return on domestic and foreign assets. The international flow of capital can be specified as

$$NCI = \beta(r - r^* + \mathring{e}^e) \tag{2.43}$$

where NCI denotes net capital inflow and β stands for the speed of adjustment in asset markets. When capital is perfectly mobile, $\beta=\infty$, and the mobility of capital ensures that the uncovered interest parity (2.5) holds all the time. Since the speed of adjustment in asset markets is finite, the equilibrium condition for the balance of payments (which is a flow condition) should be introduced

$$CA + NCI - \Delta RES = 0.0 \tag{2.44}$$

---

[14] For more details see Isard (1983), pp. 15-18 and the literature cited therein. See also De Grauwe (1988), p. 12.

[15] See Hacche and Townend (1983) pp. 138, 139 and Woo (1985), pp. 2 and 3 and the literature cited in these publications.

where CA stands for the current account balance and ΔRES for the purchase or sale of foreign exchange by the domestic monetary authorities. In this model capital flows (which result from a stock adjustment process) together with the other items in the balance of payments determine the exchange rate in such a manner that balance of payments equality would be maintained at all times. Genberg (1981) therefore calls this the balance of payments model.

In empirical tests a possible reason for the neglect of the possibility that the asset markets' speed of adjustment is less than infinity might be that a partial-adjustment specification increases the multicollinearity problems of the semi-reduced form equation, because it introduces an additional explanatory variable, namely the asset stock lagged one period (see e.g. Driskill, 1981b, p. 363). One might wonder whether this is an argument against the partial-adjustment scheme or against the use of the semi-reduced form of the model. Woo (1985) estimated a monetary model of the exchange rate in which the money demand equations are of the partial-adjustment type. He claims that this alteration considerably improves the model. It outperforms the random walk model in every case under the mean-absolute error criteria.[16]

From the foregoing arguments we conclude that it is preferable to use a specification of the asset demand functions that includes the possibility of non-instantaneous adjustment. In the empirical part we therefore apply the partial adjustment model. In this model the estimated values of the parameters reflecting the demand's speed of adjustment inform us whether the assumption of immediately adjusting financial markets is valid.

2.6.3 *The purchasing power parity*

The purchasing power parity (2.10) is one of the cornerstones of various asset market models, especially of models belonging to the monetary approach. For example in the flexible price monetary model it is assumed that this parity holds all the time, whereas in the sticky price monetary model it is regarded as a long-term phenomenon (see Section 2.2.2).

A necessary but not sufficient condition for PPP to hold is validity of the Law of One Price (LOP), which says that apart from transportation costs similar goods have the same price in each and every market. Isard (1977) studies the most disaggregated groupings of manufactured goods for which prices are

---

[16] Meese and Rogoff ascribe this good performance of the monetary approach model to the particular sample period and exchange rate used by Woo. See Meese and Rogoff (1985), p. 5, note 6.

available and finds that for the period 1970-1975 the LOP fails to hold. Even in commodity markets, where goods are more homogeneous than in markets of industrial goods, the LOP is not valid in the short run, though it tends to be so in the longer run (see, e.g. Protopapadakis and Stoll, 1986).

Even if the LOP were valid, this would not necessarily imply that PPP holds, because PPP refers to aggregate price indices. Reasons why PPP can fail to be valid when LOP holds are: differences in consumer preferences, different relative productivities between sectors and different relative prices between tradeables and non-tradeables (see, Officer, 1976, pp. 13-26). Since according to several studies LOP is not valid in the short run, it should not come as a surprise that many studies find that PPP fails to hold in the short run for many exchange rates during the 1970s and 1980s.[17] Although the results for the long run are slightly less clear, generally the studies conclude that PPP is unlikely to be valid as a long-run phenomenon. Even Hakkio (1984), who finds relatively favourable results with regard to the validity of PPP, concludes that in all likelihood "there is no tendency for PPP to hold 'in the long run'" (Hakkio, 1984, 276). Neighbouring countries and periods characterized by hyperinflation form possible exceptions to this rule. Frenkel (1981) discovers that if the internal relative prices in neighbouring countries do not shift dramatically, then PPP is likely to be valid for the corresponding currencies. Many studies conclude that PPP holds in the 1920's, a period characterized by hyperinflation.

From this we conclude that, except for neighbouring countries and periods of hyperinflation, PPP is most likely to be invalid. In all other cases the failure of exchange rate models might be ascribed to incorrectly assuming that PPP is valid.

2.6.4 *The instability of structural relations and time series*

Another explanation of the asset market models' bad performance might be that the structural equations changed during the period concerned. This argument has been put forward in Frankel (1981), p. 1079, Hacche and Townend (1983), pp. 139 and 153, and Meese and Rogoff (1983a), p. 18, among others.

The parameter instability argument mostly refers to the money demand functions. After 1973 a downward shift in the U.S. money demand has been

---

[17] A review of studies with regard to the validity of the purchasing power parity can be found in Officer (1976), MacDonald (1988), pp. 214-218 and Visser (1989), pp. 38 and 39. See also the papers in the May 1978 issue of the Journal of International Economics.

observed, whereas there has been an upward shift in German money demand.[18] Consequently, stable money demand relations have proved difficult to estimate: "shifts in velocity, partly in response to institutional changes, appear the norm rather than the exception in recent experiences". (Hacche and Townend, 1983, p. 139). The ultimately preferred exchange rate equation should therefore be tested for structural stability.[19]

Recently, there has been a growing awareness that the conventional tests are based upon the assumption that the relevant variables time series are stationary. If these series are non-stationary then the conventional procedure consists of taking first differences of the data and investigating whether the resulting time series is stationary. Generally, the first differences and/or the percentage changes appear to be stationary. Consequently, the relation has to be estimated for the variables' first differences or percentage changes. Meese and Singleton (1982) show that the logarithms of the spot and forward rate are non-stationary. Baillie and Selover (1987) report similar results for the nominal exchange rate and some of its explanatory variables, *viz.* relative money supply and long-term interest rate differentials. Thus, these studies indicate that non-stationarity of the relevant variables' time series might cause the exchange model's bad performance.[20]

2.6.5 *The expectations proxy*

Expectations play an important role in the asset market views of the exchange rate. Direct observations of expectations, such as survey data, are scarce and/or are of an inappropriate form. In empirical studies one therefore mostly has to introduce some assumptions with regard to the way in which market participants form their expectations. There is, however, no guarantee that the resulting expectations proxy is an adequate measure of the true expectations. In fact studies of survey data reveal that one popular expectations assumption, *viz.* the rational expectations hypothesis, cannot be validated.[21] It seems therefore likely

---

[18] See Frankel (1981), p. 1079.

[19] Lafrance and Racette carried out some tests for structural stability. These tests indicate that they cannot reject stability of their preferred equation. See Lafrance and Racette, 1985, pp. 246, 247.

[20] Baillie and Selover (1987), however, find that even if the time series are appropriately differentiated the estimated coefficients do not support the monetary model or the purchasing power parity.

[21] See e.g. Frankel and Froot (1985) and Dominguez (1986).

that the failure of exchange rate models to predict the future exchange rate can partly be ascribed to the use of inappropriate expectations proxies.[22] In the next chapter we deal extensively with the problem of selecting an adequate expectations proxy. So at present no further attention is paid to this subject.

2.6.6 *The measurement and nature of assets stocks*

In asset market approaches money stocks are one of the determining factors of the exchange rate (see e.g. equations (2.32)-(2.35). According to the portfolio balance model stocks of domestic and foreign interest bearing assets as well as domestic and foreign wealth also affect the exchange rate. Theory does not specify the exact definition of the money stock to be used in empirical studies. Generally, this is not considered a great drawback: various stocks of money are readily available. If desirable, one can test the exchange rate model's sensitivity for different definitions of the money stock.

However, data on the privately held interest bearing assets, subdivided by currency of denomination, as well as of private wealth are scarce and incomplete. These figures have to be approximated. In many studies the following approximation method is used. For a particular period a benchmark value of the stock is estimated. Thereafter, the stocks of subsequent (preceding) periods are estimated by adding (subtracting) the corresponding flows to (from) the benchmark value.[23] It is only under rather restrictive assumptions with regard to the currency denomination of these flows that this procedure yields the stock of domestically held foreign currency assets. If, for example this method is used for approximating the amount of interest bearing assets denominated in US dollars in the portfolio of non-US residents, then the assumption has to be made that the capital outflows published in the non-US country's balance of payments statistics refer to US dollar denominated assets only. It is well known, however, that these flows are denominated in various foreign currencies as well as in the domestic

---

[22] Hacche and Townend are of the opinion that in the case of exchange rates, the inadequate treatment of expectations in empirical estimation has been at least as responsible for the model's failure as the possible instability of the underlying economic structure. See Hacche and Townend (1983), p. 158.

[23] This procedure for approximating wealth and asset variables has been used in e.g. Bisignano and Hoover (1982), Branson *et al.* (1977), Frankel (1982a and 1982b) and Murphy and Van Duyne (1980). The detailed description of the data in Appendix 4 to Frankel (1982b) clearly illustrates the difficulties in deriving the stocks.

currency.[24] Even more restrictive assumptions are needed to claim that the net foreign asset stock can be approximated by cumulating current account balances, diminished by changes in official reserves and adding the result to the benchmark figure (see Branson *et al.*, 1977, among others).

A point of dispute is whether or not to include claims on private agents in the stock of interest bearing assets. Theory is not very clear on this subject. Branson *et al.* (1977) used net foreign asset positions which contain assets issued by both the private and the government sectors. Bisignano and Hoover (1982) explicitly distinguish claims on the foreign private sector from those on the foreign government. Frankel (1984), on the other hand, only considers "outside" assets (government issued liabilities held by the private sector). As he has argued in Frankel (1979a), under certain conditions all exchange risk associated with "inside" assets can be diversified away. The exchange risk of assets issued by the government only disappears if these assets are considered net wealth by the private sector because they imply offsetting liabilities in the form of future taxation. The governments' indebtedness is thus more often relevant for exchange rate determination than "inside" assets which are relevant only under certain conditions.

As far as we know all portfolio assets have been distinguished by currency of denomination. Isard suggested it was useful to distinguish the assets "by the countries on whose macroeconomic policies, productivity performance, creditworthiness, taxes and capital controls their yields depend" (Isard, 1983, p. 14). This introduces the possibility to model "the link between the perceived variance of real returns on equities and perceptions about the effectiveness of macroeconomic policies in particular, or country-specific exogenous variables in general". (ibid, p. 15).

In conclusion the exchange rate models's bad performance might be caused by two factors. First, theory is rather vague with regard to the precise definition of financial stocks. What is the most relevant definition of money and do bonds refer to "outside" assets only? Secondly, according to the exchange rate theory foreign and domestic assets differ by their currency of denomination. However, there are hardly any data on a particular country's holdings by currency of denomination.

---

[24] For example at the end of 1980 nearly 75 percent of Germany's private claims on foreigners were denominated in marks, while nearly 40 percent of its liabilities to foreigners were denominated in currencies other than marks. See Hooper *et al.* (1983), p. 43.

2.6.7 *Omitted aspects of exchange rate determination*

In addition to inappropriate assumptions in the theoretical model or inadequate proxies of relevant variables, the asset market approaches' bad performance might also be due to the neglect of some possibly important aspects of exchange rate determination.

The first factor to be considered is the omission of the stock of domestic interest bearing assets in the exchange rate equation. As is illustrated in equation (2.34), this stock enters the exchange rate equation of the portfolio balance approach. Because of the indeterminacy of the corresponding sign, some authors, e.g. Branson *et al.* (1977) and Murphy and Van Duyne (1980), drop the stock of domestic interest bearing assets held by inhabitants from the exchange rate equation, which is ultimately selected for estimation. This questionable procedure might worsen the empirical result.

The second factor usually omitted emerges because the approximated assets stocks do not include capital gains/losses resulting from movements in asset prices. This omission has already been noted by Branson *et al.* (1977. p. 317), but as far as we know hitherto no study has considered the empirical relevance of these capital gains or losses.

The (perceptive) degree of uncertainty about exchange rates appears in some theoretical models. For example, in Miles and Stewart (1980) exchange rate risk is one of the determining variables of the currency composition of money demand. Marwah and Klein (1983) and Marwah, Klein and Bodken (1985) include the uncertainty of relative yields in the capital flow equations of a model, which simultaneously determines capital flows and exchange rates. In general, however, exchange rate risk is excluded from empirical studies of exchange rate determination.

Many studies of exchange rate determination are confined to bilateral rates. This practice neglects the influences of third countries and thus might give rise to biased results.[25]

Another restrictive assumption applied in nearly all studies is that the portfolio is made up of currencies and interest bearing assets only. No attention is paid to the possibility that other assets, e.g. equities and gold, are included in

---

[25] Two methods, that account for third-country effects can be distinguished. In the first procedure the foreign variables do not refer to one single country but are weighted averages of several countries' variables. This method is used in e.g. Fukao (1983) and Hooper (1983). The exchange rate variable can be a bilateral rate, Fukao, or an effective exchange rate, Hooper. The second method for accounting for third-country effects consists of the estimation of a multilateral exchange rate model. Good examples are the OECD and EPA models. The mechanism of exchange rate determination in these models is briefly described in Amano (1986).

the private sector's portfolios. The gold price especially might be a good additional explaining variable of some exchange rates, because in times of turbulence gold is very often used as an alternative investment.[26]

Recently, Gavin (1989) added the stock market to a monetary model. The stock market is broadly interpreted as all marketable claims on the future profits of firms, and forms the link between future profits and interest rate fluctuations, and current investment and consumption decisions. He shows that the introduction of the stock market can, in some circumstances, give rise to output and asset price dynamics that differ from that of the standard model. For example, if stock market effects dominate, then a monetary expansion can give rise to a real exchange rate appreciation, rather than a depreciation. The reason is the following. The monetary expansion leads to a decline in the short-run real interest rate. Aggregate demand and output increase, and the stock price jumps upward. The demand for real money increases, because the output and the price level increase. Real money supply decreases, however, requiring an equilibrating increase in the nominal interest rate. Assuming a gradually declining rate of inflation this generates a sharp increase of the short-run real interest rate to a level above the foreign interest rate. This increase of the interest rate leads to an exchange rate appreciation, because the current level of the real exchange rate consists of its long-run level minus the integral over the entire future of the difference between the domestic and foreign real interest rate (compare equation (2.20)).

Gavin also shows that, under some circumstances, the announcement of a fiscal expansion may not have the conventional contractionary properties, but may instead be expansionary. The reason for this is that the anticipated expansion, by generating a future period with high profits, leads to an increase in the current stock prices, which in turn gives rise to an expansion in aggregate demand and output.

The last omitted factor we want to mention is the specification of the goods market. Very often this market is neglected or represented by a very simple relation. This simplification also might account for the bad performance of exchange rate models (see, e.g. Meese and Rogoff, 1983b, p. 95).

---

[26] As far as we know only Lorenzo Bini Smaghi and Daniel Gros add the dollar price of gold to the explaining variables of the mark-dollar rate. The study by Bini Smaghi and Gros is referred to in Frankel (1981), pp. 1080, 1081.

2.7 Concluding remarks

In this chapter we have discussed the main characteristics of the modern asset market view of exchange rate determination. According to this approach, in the short run the stocks of the various financial assets are constant and the exchange rate, its expectation and the interest rate move in order to equilibrate demand and supply of financial assets. Along with, among other things, the current account, exchange rate expectations can play an important role in the model's dynamics.

Next we critically assessed the common practice of testing exchange rate models by semi-reduced form equations. From this discussion we concluded that the precise nature of the semi-reduced form relations is unclear. These equations do not contain the detailed information of the structural form and cannot be interpreted as the comparative static effects as is the case of reduced form parameters. To us these semi-reduced form equations appeared to be inadequate for the testing of theories. This opinion is also based on the exposition of the simultaneity and the multicollinearity problems of these relations. These problems appeared to be more severe in the semi-reduced form equations than in structural relations. It appeared that the exchange rate and many of its explanatory variables are simultaneously determined. Under such conditions unbiased parameter estimates can only be obtained when the estimation procedure and the specification are carefully selected. Very often the explanatory variables of the semi-reduced form equations appeared to be highly collinear. This correlation results from the use of both a domestic variable and its foreign counterpart in the same relation. Mostly these variables are highly correlated. The usual practice of constraining the foreign and domestic parameters to be of equal value but of opposite sign can lead to sign reversal. These problems are far less severe if the structural form is estimated instead of a semi-reduced form equation.

In this study we therefore prefer to estimate the structural form of a model for exchange rate determination. When specifying and estimating this model we shall also try to avoid - as far as we can - the shortcomings of exchange rate models mentioned in the previous sections. One of these weaknesses is the possibly inappropriate approximation of exchange rate expectations. Because these expectations play a critical role in various parts of the model, in the next chapter we first critically assess the various methods for approximating expectations.

3 EXPECTATIONS FORMATION: CRITERIA AND AN ASSESSMENT

3.1 Introduction

As has been illustrated in Section 2.4 the characteristics of a particular model largely depend upon the exchange rate expectations. In general expectations play an important role in modern theoretical and empirical studies of economic phenomena. The way in which expectations are formed significantly affects the dynamic properties of economic models and, among other things, the effectiveness of monetary and fiscal policy (see, e.g. Chouraqui, Driscoll and Strauss-Khan, 1988).

During the last decades various expectations hypotheses have been proposed but none of them has been generally accepted by the practitioners of the economic profession. The adaptive expectations hypothesis, for example, has been advocated in Cagan (1956). It is, however, rejected by the adherents of the rational expectations hypothesis, because it does not exclude the possibility of systematic forecasting errors for many periods in succession and because it is entirely backward looking. The rational expectations hypothesis, on the other hand, avoids systematic forecasting errors and contains a forward-looking part but has in turn often been criticized because of the huge amount of information which the economic agents are assumed to possess (See e.g. Friedman, 1979, and Friedman and Roley, 1979). Given this controversy, it is not surprising that a recent study on exchange rate simulations with four econometric multi-country models concludes that "a most wanting aspect of future research would be the determination of expected exchange rates" (Amano,1986, p.148). Of course, generally this also goes for the expectations of other variables. "The neglect or mistreatment of the adjustment of expectations is perhaps the most fundamental criticism of conventional macro models" (Siebrand, 1988, p. 112).

The first stage of a research project on the formation of expectations should be the formulation of the essential elements of expectations formation. When these characteristics are known, they can, in the second stage, be used for assessing the existing hypotheses on expectations formation and the estimation procedures of econometric models with expectational variables. Hopefully at least one of these hypotheses and methods contains all essential features of expectations formation. If not, then the results of the assessment might indicate the hypothesis or hypotheses and method(s) that serve best as the starting point for developing correct procedures.

In this chapter[1] we execute the two stages mentioned in the preceding paragraph. First, in the next section, we develop three features of hypotheses on expectations formation. Thereafter, these characteristics serve as criteria in assessing existing expectations hypotheses (Section 3.3) and in assessing estimation procedures of models with expectational variables (Section 3.4).[2] The conclusions are summarized in Section 3.5. To our knowledge this is the first time that the three criteria developed in Section 3.2 are used for a systematic evaluation of expectations hypotheses and of estimation methods of models with expectational variables. In other studies only one or two criteria are applied for assessing a few methods or hypotheses.

3.2 Criteria of hypotheses on expectations formation

In order to facilitate the discussion in the rest of the chapter, we first sketch the problem and explain the notation. Let us consider the equation

$$y_t = {}_tz^e_{t+1}\,\alpha + X_t\,\beta + u_t \qquad t = 1,...,T \tag{3.1}$$

where y_t is the observation at time t of the dependent variable, which might be part of a simultaneous model, X_t is the 1 x k matrix of observations on both the other current endogenous variables and the predetermined variables included in the equation, and u_t is a disturbance term. The disturbances u_t, t = 1,...,T, are assumed to be independently and identically distributed with zero mean and finite variance. The parameters that have to be estimated are represented by the k x 1 vector β and the scalar α. The term ${}_tz^e_{t+1}$ is the conditional expectation of z_{t+1} formed at time t. This expectation is conditional on the information available at time t, i.e.

$${}_tz^e_{t+1} = E(z_{t+1} \mid I_t) \qquad t = 1,...,T \tag{3.2}$$

where I_t represents the set of information available at the time the expectation is formed and E(.) is the expectation operator. Generally, the expectation is unobserved and remains to be specified. Many authors assume that the

---

[1] This chapter is a slightly shortened version of De Jong (1988). Subjects that are presented in De Jong (1988) but that are not contained in this chapter are: some examples and a discussion of the differences between our definition of the weak form of rational expectations and that of some other writers.

[2] We thus do not consider methods used in simulation experiments such as e.g. Gelauff (1988).

expectations-generating function is linear, i.e.

$$ {}_t z^e_{t+1} = I_t \delta + v_t \tag{3.3} $$

where v_t is a disturbance term and δ is a vector of parameters.

As equation (3.1) illustrates, we assume that the parameters of the model are constant. The expectational variable can be exogenous or endogenous. It is only for convenience that this term is assumed to consist of just one variable and that the lead time is assumed to be one period. The essence of this chapter equally applies to relations with two or more expectational variables and lead times longer than one period. The same holds for expectations of z_t formed at time t-j, (j > 0). Given this model, the researcher's problem is to select or construct a plausible approximation of the unobserved expectation, ${}_t z^e_{t+1}$.

In order to judge whether a particular proxy is useful, we develop three characteristics of expectations formation. The first feature of such a proxy is derived from the frequently mentioned character of expectations that they are based on available data only and therefore should "not be based on any information that becomes available only after date t" (Barro, 1977, p. 106). Assuming that information lags do not exist and that agents know the true value of past and present observations of the variables this implies that the information set I_t contains observations of economic variables up to time t only. Henceforth we will refer to this criterion as the data-availability criterion.[3]

The second feature of expectations formation is that it contains a learning process which generates the expectations. This implies that there should be a feedback from the forecasting performance of the expectations-generating function to the form of this formula. The reason for incorporating such a process in expectations hypotheses is that as a consequence of the introduction of expectations, economic theory no longer assumes that the environment is known to the decision-maker, but "it incorporates in the theory the processes of acquiring knowledge about that environment. In doing so it forces us to include in our model of economic man some of his properties as a learning, estimating, searching, information processing organism" (Simon, 1959, p. 269).[4]

The third and last feature demands of expectations hypotheses and of

---

[3] With Barro, Muth (1961), Lucas (1976), pp. 27 and 37, Shiller (1978), pp. 3, 4 and 6, Begg (1982), p. 18 and Keynes (1936), p. 147 also state that expectations should be based on available information only.

[4] The same reason for the inclusion of a learning-process in the expectation generating function can be found in Cyert and De Groot (1974), p. 522 and Sheffrin (1983), p. 4.

estimation procedures that they should enable us to disentangle the influence of the expectations from the effect of a variable on the expectation itself, i.e. separate estimates of the parameters α in (3.1) and δ in (3.3) should be obtained (see also, Fase and Van Nieuwkerk,1975, p. 304). Henceforth, we will refer to this feature as the identification criterion on expectations formation. Two reasons for imposing this condition on expectations schemes can be mentioned. The first reason is closely related to Lucas' critique on econometric policy evaluation, *viz.* that a change in policy changes the parameter values of the model, because the expectations are affected (see Lucas, 1976). Then the knowledge of α in (3.1) and δ in (3.3) can facilitate the evaluation of different policy rules. Most likely under the different rules the parameter α remains constant, and δ changes in a more or less predictable manner. The second reason for imposing the identification criterion is that it serves us in testing and improving an econometric model. If, for instance, the coefficient of an expectational variable appears to be statistically insignificant or has the wrong sign, we would be eager to know whether expectations have no influence or the expectations proxy is wrong. We thus "must avoid testing the expectations hypothesis and the model containing the expectations variables simultaneously" (Fase and Van Nieuwkerk, 1975, p. 304).

These three criteria on expectations formation are not of equal importance and one or two of them need not apply. It is self-evident that expectations can be derived from available data only, and thus that the data-availability condition should always be imposed. In some studies it suffices to require that the expectations proxy meets this criterion only. If, for example, we are only interested in estimating the influence of expectations, it suffices to impose the data-availability criterion upon the proxy, although then the identification criterion might be useful too. A correct evaluation of different policy rules, however, requires that the identification criterion is met and that a learning process is included in the model[5], because the results of such an analysis highly

[5] See also Begg (1982), p. 11, Shiller (1978), pp. 1 and 3, Muth (1961) and Currie (1985), p. 288. Sims (1982) takes an opposite view. He argues that explicit identification of expectation formation mechanisms is not necessary for policy analysis. In his opinion policy analysis only requires a valid reduced form model. This reduced form "will make relatively precise conditional projections for the effects of policy actions or sequences of actions that are close in form to what has been observed historically" (Sims, 1982, p. 118). The economy's response to policy actions can be derived from the analysis "of a sufficiently long stretch of data" (ibid, p. 120). These quotations illustrate that Sims' argument only applies if a) the alternative policies do not deviate much from the policy historically observed, and b) the time series are long and are influenced by different policy rules so that the effects of these different rules can accurately be estimated. If these conditions are not met Sims admits that "explicit modeling of expectation formation and its dependence on policy could be useful" and that "explicit

depend on the way economic agents revise their expectations.[6]

3.3 An assessment of expectations hypotheses

3.3.1 *Introduction*

This section presents a review and an assessment of various hypotheses of expectations formation. The three features presented in the previous section serve as criteria for the assessment. The expectations postulates are divided into three broad categories. The first group consists of hypotheses according to which the expectations are in a more or less mechanical way derived from the information set. These postulates which we call *non-rational* are treated in Section 3.3.1. They have been criticized by the adherents of the rational expectations hypothesis, because the expectations are not derived from the relevant economic theory. The second and third group are two types of the rational expectations hypothesis, *viz.* the *strong forms* and the *weak forms of rational expectations.* They are presented in Sections 3.3.2 and 3.3.3, respectively.

3.3.2 *Non-rational expectations hypotheses*

Two groups of non-rational expectations hypotheses can be distinguished. The first group consists of hypotheses which assume that the expectations of the

---

modeling of the connection of expectation formation mechanisms to policy in an accurately identified model would allow better use of the data" (ibid., p. 120).

[6] In some studies, Bigman (1984) for example, the expectations are assumed to satisfy one or both of the two consistency properties of expectations defined in Burmeister and Turnovsky (1977). These properties are the "weak consistency" condition which asserts "that the expectation formed at time t for that same instant must equal the actual value prevailing at that time" (ibid, p. 381), and the "strong consistency" condition according to which "the expected instantaneous rate of change at time t must equal the actual instantaneous rate of change at that time" (ibid, p. 381). Underlying the weak consistency criterion is the assumption that information lags do not exist. Then the agents need not form expectations of the current value of the variables, because they observe these values already. Since under these conditions no expectations are formed, we do not consider the weak consistency criterion an appropriate condition for expectation formation. As noted by Burmeister and Turnovsky, the strong consistency criterion is equal to the assumption of perfect myopic foresight. This is itself an expectation hypothesis and not a condition of an expectation hypothesis.

future value of a particular variable are based on the variable's own history only. The hypotheses belonging to the second group do not restrict the information set to the variable's own history, but also utilize the observations of other variables. In contrast to the rational expectations hypotheses, the hypotheses belonging to the second group do not exploit the structure of the relevant theory when deriving the expectation.

The hypotheses belonging to the first group can be derived from the following autoregressive integrated moving average, ARIMA(p,d,q)-model[7]

$$\Phi_p(B)(1-B)^d z_{t+1} = \Theta_q(B)\, a_{t+1} \tag{3.4}$$

where z_{t+1} is a variable, a_{t+1} is an independently distributed error term with expectation zero, and p,d, and q represent the order of the various parts. From now on this term will be interpreted as the forecasting error of the expectations hypothesis at hand. The assumption that the expected value of a_{t+1} is zero then implies that we assume that the economic agents think that their expectations are unbiased. The term $(1-B)^d$, which is known as the integrated part, is the difference operator of order d, B is the backshift operator ($B^n z_t = z_{t-n}$) and the autoregressive operator $\Phi(B)$ and the moving average operator $\Theta(B)$ are polynomials of order p and q respectively, i.e.

$$\Phi_p(B) = 1 - \phi_1 B - \phi_2 B^2 - \dots - \phi_p B^p \tag{3.5-a}$$

$$\Theta_q(B) = 1 - \theta_1 B - \theta_2 B^2 - \dots - \theta_q B^q \tag{3.5-b}$$

Using the autoregressive and integrated parts of the ARIMA model we can derive expectations hypotheses which assume that the expected value is a weighted sum of past observation only. For example, the ARIMA(0,1,0) model yields the static expectations postulate, whereas the ARIMA(1,1,0) model generates the extrapolative or bandwagon (Frankel and Froot, 1985) expectations hypothesis. To illustrate the procedure, let us assume the ARIMA(1,1,0) model:

$$(1 - \phi_1 B)(1 - B) z_{t+1} = a_{t+1} \tag{3.6}$$

which is equal to

$$z_{t+1} - z_t - \phi_1(z_t - z_{t-1}) = a_{t+1} \tag{3.7}$$

---

[7] Fase and Van Nieuwkerk (1975) inspired us to use ARIMA models as the general framework for the non-rational expectations hypotheses.

Taking expectations conditional on the information set available at time t we obtain

$$E(z_{t+1} \mid I_t) = z_t + \phi_1(z_t - z_{t-1}) \tag{3.8}$$

The static, neutral or unitary expectations hypothesis is obtained from this equation by neglecting the autoregressive part, that is by assuming that $\phi_1 = 0$. Autoregressive expectations, however, neglect the integrated part. The most general form of the latter is

$$E(z_{t+1} \mid I_t) = \Sigma_{i=1}^{p} \theta_i \, z_{t-i} \tag{3.9}$$

As is shown in e.g. Fase and Van Nieuwkerk (1975), the moving average part introduces an error correction mechanism into the expectations formation. An example of such a hypothesis is the well-known adaptive expectations postulate which can be derived from an ARIMA(0,1,1) model as follows

$$(1 - B)\, z_{t+1} = (1 - \theta_1 B)\, a_{t+1} \tag{3.10}$$

Taking expectations of this expression conditional on the information set available at time t and noting that a_t is the *realized* forecasting error, i.e. $a_t = z_t - E(z_t \mid I_{t-1})$ we obtain

$$E(z_{t+1} \mid I_t) = z_t + E(a_{t+1} \mid I_t) - \theta_1 a_t$$

$$= z_t - \theta_1 (z_t - E(z_t \mid I_{t-1})) \tag{3.11}$$

By subtracting $E(z_t \mid I_{t-1})$ from both sides, relation (3.11) can be rewritten as

$$E(z_{t+1} \mid I_t) - E(z_t \mid I_{t-1}) = \mu\, (z_t - E(z_t \mid I_{t-1})) \tag{3.12}$$

Adaptive expectations were introduced by Cagan in his study on the monetary dynamics of hyperinflation (See Cagan, 1956, p. 37), where he showed that this hypothesis can be written as a special form of (3.9):[8] the weight of z_{t-i} is equal to $\theta_1 \cdot (1-\theta_1)^i$. This once again illustrates that the hypotheses considered so far

[8] See Cagan (1956), pp. 36-41. He derives the formula for a continuous time model. A derivation of the equivalent formula for the discrete time model is presented in Begg (1982), pp. 23,24.

make use of only the variable's own history.

The regressive expectations hypothesis does not restrict the set of information to the past observations of the variable in question, and so belongs to the second group mentioned in the beginning of this section. It assumes that the agents expect a gradual return of the variable to a particular level, say $\tilde{z}_t$, i.e.

$$
\begin{aligned}
{}_t z^e_{t+1} &= (1 - \theta)\, z_t + \theta \tilde{z}_t \\
&= z_t + \theta\, (\tilde{z}_t - z_t) \qquad 0 < \theta < 1
\end{aligned}
\tag{3.13}
$$

The variable $\tilde{z}_t$ can be a certain initial value or an (expected) long-term equilibrium. In the latter case the expectations depend on the (expected) evolution of the entire system. The regressive expectations mechanism is consistent with dynamic models in which variables gradually converge toward their long-run equilibrium values (see e.g. Dornbusch, 1976).

When assessing these hypotheses and hypotheses that are derived from them,[9] we assume that the value of the relevant parameters is based on information which was already available at time t=1. If in addition it is assumed that $\tilde{z}_t$ is derived from past and present observations only, then all hypotheses pass the data-availability test.

The results with regard to the learning process incorporated in the formulas are less satisfactory. Except for the adaptive expectations hypotheses, no postulate contains any learning. There is not even any feedback from the present forecasting error to the expectation of future events. While this criticism does not apply to the adaptive expectations scheme, several problems still remain.[10] First, some regard as a disadvantage of adaptive expectations, that no economic theory is offered to explain the size of the adjustment parameter θ. Except for simplicity why should θ remain constant? Since in general revisions of expectations are costless, would it not be more realistic to assume that θ increases with the size of the forecasting error? Secondly, partly because of the fixed θ, there remains the possibility of systematic forecasting errors for many periods in succession. Correctly anticipated values of z will be generated only if the economy is in a static equilibrium for a sufficient time. In reality, however, this is an exceptional circumstance. Thirdly, the learning process contains past and present observations of z only. No account is taken of the possibility that z is embodied in a larger simultaneous model. Consequently the adaptive expectations

---

[9] See De Jong (1988), pp.441,442 for expectations hypotheses that are constructed as a combination of the hypotheses presented in the text.

[10] The critique on the learning-process of the adaptive expectations, presented in this paragraph, draws on Begg (1982), pp. 24-26.

scheme does not fit well in a macroeconomic general equilibrium system. The adaptive expectations hypothesis can be defended against these points of criticisms by arguing that more sophisticated learning would not be profitable. In that case, however, one should indicate the circumstances under which this type of expectations dominates alternative formulas.

With regard to the identification criterion we note that the parameters of the expectations-generating functions (3.8), (3.9), (3.12), (3.13), and the parameter α in (3.1) can be estimated, provided that the variables in the right-hand sides of the expectations-generating functions are not elements of X_t in (3.1). In one of the following sections more attention will be paid to the case where this assumption does not hold. If the autoregressive expectations hypothesis is used, however, the assumption that z_{t-i}, i=0,...,n are not contained in X_t appears to be insufficient for identifying all parameters namely: α, and θ_i, i=0,...,p. Substituting (3.9) in (3.1) then yields

$$y_t = \alpha \Sigma_{i=1}^{p} \theta_i z_{t-i} + X_t \beta + u_t \tag{3.14}$$

The parameters of this relation cannot be identified, because the first term of the right-hand side of (3.14) contains p+1 parameters and only p variables. Consequently, an additional constraint should be imposed on α, θ_i, i = 1,...,p. Usually, it is assumed that

$$\Sigma_{i=1}^{p} \theta_i = 1 \tag{3.15}$$

Notice that in the formulas of the static and bandwagon expectations hypotheses, this constraint is imposed on the parameters. In fact this is why α and the parameters of the relevant expectations-generating functions can be estimated.

Sargent (1971) questioned the adequacy of (3.15). He noted that the constraint has often been justified by the following type of argument. Suppose that z increases from a fixed value, which has been its value for more than p+1 periods, to another fixed value, staying there indefinitely. Then it is reasonable to expect that eventually people will catch on and expect z to continue at its new value. "This is taken to imply that the weights ... sum to unity" (Sargent, 1971, p. 722). The weakness of this justification of (3.15) is that during the periods concerned, the variable in question almost never followed the pattern of this mental experiment. "This is an important shortcoming because what form of expectations generator is reasonable depends on the actual behavior of the variable about which the expectations are being formed". (Sargent, 1971, p.

722).[11]

This criticism applies to all expectations schemes presented in this section. With a view toward circumventing it, the adherents of the rational expectations hypothesis derive the expectations proxy from the relevant model. The next two sections are devoted to various forms of this hypothesis.

3.3.3 *Strong forms of the rational expectations hypothesis*

In order to meet the shortcomings of the simple and more or less mechanical expectations-generating functions presented in the previous section, the rational expectations hypothesis states that expectations should be derived from the model in question. Or to put it in the classical phrase of Muth, "... expectations, since they are informed predictions of future events, are essentially the same as the predictions of the relevant economic theory" (Muth, 1961, p.316). Thus, the rational expectations theory equates the subjective probability distribution held by market participants of future economic variables to the true conditional distribution based on all information available at the time the expectations are formed.[12] This definition represents the strong form of the rational expectations hypothesis.[13]

This concept of rational expectations is ambiguous. Most adherents of rational expectations do not explain explicitly enough what they mean by rational expectations. Does it refer to individual expectations, or to a purely macroeconomic phenomenon? Does it incorporate a theory of how expectations are formed, or is it restricted to the outcome of expectations formation processes, leaving the processes themselves unexplained? In order to provide a basis for evaluating the adequacy of the rational expectations hypothesis, Snippe (1986) develops a taxonomy of the rational expectations concept. He distinguishes three

---

[11] Sargent also showed, that when the actual observations of z evolve according to the pth order autoregressive process in (3.14), the imposition of (3.15) would imply an extremely strong serial correlation of z. Most variables never display such a high "drift". This once again illustrates the inadequacy of (3.15). See Sargent (1971) for details.

[12] See also Lucas and Sargent (1981), p. xvi, Sheffrin (1983), p. 8 and Shiller (1978), p. 4.

[13] The distinction between the strong and weak forms of rational expectations has been introduced in Fischer (1980). This taxonomy has been developed further by Snippe (1986).

varieties of the strong form of rational expectations, *viz*. the descriptive version, the micro "as if" variety and the macro "as if" variety. Each variant assumes different answers to the questions mentioned above. The descriptive version is a theory of the *formation* of expectations, i.e. it includes postulates about the set of information available and about the way agents make use of this information. The outcome of this process is the definition of the strong form of rational expectations stated in the previous paragraph. The "as if" varieties only refer to the outcome of the process. They do not incorporate any process which might generate the outcome, but are only hypotheses "about expectations rather than their formation" (Snippe, 1986, p. 430). Since the "as if" forms do not meet the criterion concerning the learning process, the rest of this section is mainly concerned with investigating whether it is reasonable to assume that the descriptive variety of the strong form of rational expectations does contain a learning process. Where appropriate, attention is paid to the differences between this version and the "as if" varieties.

In order to be able to study a possible learning process some insight has to be gained into the assumptions underlying the rational expectations hypothesis and into its consequences for the estimation of a model. Consider the familiar simultaneous model[14] with m equations for m endogenous variables represented by the column vector y_t. The expectations of some of these variables directly affect the behaviour of the model at time t. Assume that there are $m_1<m$ expectational variables which all refer to expectations of one period ahead and are represented by ${}_{t-1}y^e_{1,t}$. For convenience it is supposed that the corresponding endogenous variables are the first m_1 components of the column vector y_t. The model also contains k exogenous variables denoted by the column vector x_t. It can be shown that the reduced form of the model can be written as

$$y_t = \Pi_1 ({}_{t-1}y^e_{1,t}) + \Pi_2 x_t + v_t \qquad (3.16)$$

where v_t is a vector of independently distributed disturbance terms. Since the expectations ${}_{t-1}y^e_{1,t}$ are not directly observed, (3.16) is termed the unobservable reduced form. The rational expectation of $y_{1,t}$ appears to be

$${}_{t-1}y^e_{1,t} = (I-\Pi_{11})^{-1}\,\Pi_{12}({}_{t-1}x^e_t) \qquad (3.17)$$

where Π_{11} and Π_{12} are $(m_1 \times m_1)$ and $(m_1 \times k)$ submatrices of Π_1 and Π_2 respectively.

---

[14] An extensive presentation of the model and a derivation of the results can be found in Wallis (1980) and Begg (1982), pp. 90-98.

According to this relation, the expectations of the endogenous variable, $y_{1,t}$, depend on the conditional expectations of the exogenous variable x_t, which are unobserved. In order to obtain the latter expectations, most authors assume that the exogenous variables are generated by a vector autoregressive moving average model. Because our aim is merely to illustrate the procedure, we postulate a simple process of x_t. Suppose that the exogenous variables are generated by a vector autoregressive process of order p

$$\begin{aligned} x_t &= \phi_1 x_{t-1} + \phi_2 x_{t-2} + .. + \phi_p x_{t-p} + e_t \\ &= \Phi(B)\, x_{t-1} + e_t \end{aligned} \tag{3.18}$$

where e_t is a vector of disturbance terms. The rational expectation of the exogenous variables is

$${}_{t-1}x^e_t = \phi_1 x_{t-1} + \phi_2 x_{t-2} + .. + \phi_p x_{t-p} \tag{3.19}$$

Substituting the right-hand side of (3.19) in (3.17) and the resulting expression of ${}_{t-1}y^e_{1,t}$ in (3.16), we arrive at equations in which all variables are observed.

$$y_t = \Pi_1\, (I-\Pi_{11})^{-1}\, \Pi_{12}\, \Phi(B)\, x_{t-1} + \Pi_2 x_t + v_t \tag{3.20}$$

These equations are known as the observable reduced form. Because the exogenous variables are generated by an autoregressive process, the relations (3.20) are also the final form relations in which each endogenous variable is given as a distributed lag function of the exogenous variables.[15]

Note that for a given exogenous variable the shape of the lag distribution is the same in every equation with the exception of the leading coefficient. This shape is given by the optimal forecasting weights $\Phi(B)$ and imposes cross-equation restrictions on the parameters of the model. When discussing full information estimation methods, we will return to this feature of the rational expectations model.

The derivation of the observable reduced form becomes more complicated if the lead time of the expectations is greater than one period, that is if the model contains expectational variables of the form ${}_{t-j}z^e_t$ or ${}_{t-1}z^e_{t-1+j}$ $(j>1)$. For convenience we assume that the expectations are of the form ${}_{t-1}y^e_{1,t+1}$.

---

[15] If the exogenous variables generating model contains a moving average part, some reformulating is necessary for deriving the final form from the observable reduced form. See Wallis (1980).

Partitioning the equations and matrices in the same manner as in (3.17) gives us the following unobservable reduced form of $y_{1,t}$

$$y_{1,t} = \Pi_{11} ({}_{t-1}y^e_{1,t+1}) + \Pi_{12} x_t + v_{1,t} \tag{3.21}$$

The rational expectation at time t-1 of $y_{1,t+1}$ can be shown to be equal to[16]

$${}_{t-1}y^e_{1,t+1} = \Sigma^{\infty}_{i=0} \Pi^i_{11} \Pi_{12} ({}_{t-1}x^e_{t+i+1}) \tag{3.22}$$

Equation (3.22) illustrates an important feature of dynamic rational expectations models, *viz.* that the rational expectations of endogenous variables are a weighted sum of the conditional expectations of the exogenous variables of all future periods.[17] Relation (3.19) is used for transforming the unobservable equation (3.22) into the observable form

$${}_{t-1}y^e_{1,t+1} = F_1 x_{t-1} + F_2 x_{t-2} + \ldots + F_p x_{t-p} \tag{3.23}$$

where the $(m_1 \times k)$ matrices F_j, j=1,...,p are calculated by means of successively applying the chain rule of forecasting.[18] Substituting (3.23) into equation (3.21) then gives us an observable reduced form.

To assist in an assessment of the rational expectations hypothesis we draw attention to the information set underlying this postulate. Equations (3.17), (3.19) and (3.23) show that the individuals are assumed to know the reduced form coefficients of the model and observe past values of all relevant variables.[19]

---

[16] In deriving (3.22) the following property of rational expectation models has been used

$$E\{ E(y_{t+i+j} \mid I_{t+i}) \mid I_t\} = E(y_{t+i+j} \mid I_t)$$

i.e. at time t the individuals have no information about how they will change their expectation of y_{t+i+j} at some intermediate time t+i. This illustrates that the rational expectation of y_{t+i+j} is their best forecast conditioned on I_t.

[17] See also Mussa (1978), pp. 58, 59.

[18] For more details, see Begg (1982), pp. 96, 97.

[19] Compare the following quotations from Begg (1982). The "... information set has three components: knowledge of the structure of the model; knowledge of government policies in operation; and knowledge of the past values of economic variables". (p. 72) On page 92 Begg writes, "Assume that individuals forming expectations at the end of time t-1 know the parameters of the model

Many authors have argued that this information set is too large to be compatible with profit maximizing behaviour, because the acquisition of this knowledge is too costly (Bigman (1984), Buiter (1980), Darby (1976) and Feige and Pearce (1976), among others). Adherents of the rational expectations hypothesis have suggested that the collection of this information is not very costly because individuals who lack even elementary skills in forecasting, can "draw on outside advisers. A number of groups forecast key macroeconomic variables regularly, and these are available for only the price of a newspaper" (Currie, 1985, p. 289). This way of reasoning, however, does not solve the econometrician's problem of selecting the best way to model expectations in econometric models, because this argument gives rise to the following circular reasoning. When incorporating expectations in the econometric model the econometrician should derive these expectations from the estimated coefficients of the model. However, he does not know the estimated values of these parameters, because he has not yet estimated the model. The economic agents, on the contrary, are supposed to derive their expectations from these estimated coefficients, which are unknown to the producer of these estimates. This is a highly inconsistent and implausible thought experiment.[20] Furthermore, if all agents use the model for expectations formation, the structure of the model would change and the model's forecasts would no longer be valid.[21]

Another way to justify this version of the rational expectations hypothesis is by formulating a learning process and deriving the conditions under which this yields a rational expectations solution.[22] The problem mentioned before, namely that expectations change the structure of the model, is valid here too. It implies that a rationally learning agent takes into account the effect of his learning and

---

and know the history of all variables in the model up to and including time t-1". Benjamin M. Friedman is of the opinion that *future values* of predetermined variables are also included in the information set (see Friedman, 1979, p. 26). However as equation (3.22) illustrates, this rational expectation does not depend on the *future values* of predetermined variables but on the *expectations of the future values* of these variables. These expectations are derived from the observations of the predetermined variables during the periods up to the time the expectations are formed. These observations are already included in the set of information.

[20] Compare Shiller (1978), p. 34.

[21] See Harris and Purvis (1981), p. 844, Bray (1982), p. 319 and Blume and Easley (1982), p. 34.

[22] A brief survey of this literature is presented in Blume, Bray and Easley (1982). The following part of this section is based to a great extent on that study. Chapter 3 of Pesaran (1988) contains a brief review of some learning models.

the influence of the learning of others on the structure of the economy. "The necessary structure for such an analysis requires a degree of sophistication on the part of the individuals that seems highly implausible". (Blume and Easley, 1982, p. 341). Many authors, thus, do not incorporate this feedback mechanism from forecasts to outcomes in the learning process.

An important difference between the various studies on the learning process concerns the assumption with regard the form of the formula used for learning. In one group of studies this form is assumed to be consistent with the form implied by the model, while in the other group it is only by chance that this form is consistent with that derived from the model. Generally it can be shown if the form of the formula is consistent with that of the model, in the long-run the learning process converges to the rational expectations model. This suggests, however, that the rational expectations hypothesis is a long-run phenomenon. The earlier mentioned rational expectations school's criticism of the adaptive expectations hypothesis, namely that the latter is justified by referring to a non-existing long-run situation, seems to apply to the rational expectations hypothesis as well. Moreover this framework is "extraordinarily demanding in terms of the information, understanding, and calculating ability of agents" (Blume, *et al.*, 1982, p. 314). If the form of the formula is not consistent with that implied by the model, then far-reaching assumptions have to be introduced in order to be able to study the learning process and very often the process does not converge to the rational expectations solution. In this case the convergence depends upon the assumed parameter values and priors.

Summing up the preceding discussion we conclude that the learning processes which generate rational expectations are too demanding in terms of the information required and the understanding ability of individuals. Moreover it is only in the long-run that these processes converge to the rational expectations solution so that it is unreasonable to assume that during every period these expectations can be obtained by learning. Hence, the rational expectations hypothesis does not meet our criterion that an expectations hypothesis should incorporate a learning process.[23]

Hitherto we have assumed more or less tacitly that the rational expectations hypothesis includes the way agents come to their expectations. Many adherents of the rational expectations hypothesis, Muth included, have opposed this

---

[23] Note that this hypothesis also does not meet one of Muth's aims. In his introduction Muth criticized other studies because they do not "... include an explanation of the way expectations are formed" (Muth, 1961, p. 316). He thereafter stresses the importance of knowledge of the kind of information used "... and how it is put together to frame an estimate of future conditions" (ibid. p. 316).

interpretation of the postulate. Muth, for example, writes that the hypothesis "*does not* assert that the scratch work of entrepreneurs resembles the system of equations in any way" (Muth, 1961, p. 317). The agents are only assumed to act *as if* they know the model's structure, data and coefficients.[24] As it is explicitly stated that these "as if" varieties of the rational expectations hypothesis do not incorporate any learning mechanism, they do not meet our learning criterion.

The above-mentioned considerations with regard to the learning process are also useful for examining whether the strong form varieties of the rational expectations are based on data which are available at the time the expectations are generated. Both the descriptive and the "as if" version of the rational expectations hypothesis use the same information set. This set of information comprises "knowledge of the structure of the model; knowledge of government policies; and knowledge of the past values of economic variables" (Begg, 1982, p. 72). When estimating a rational expectations model, knowledge of the structure of the model appears to include knowledge of the parameters of the model (Begg, 1982, p. 92). It is highly unlikely that for every period - especially those at the beginning of the sample - the agents can derive the correct parameter values only from the data which are available up to the time the expectations are formed. For estimating the coefficients, the econometrician has to use all periods included in the sample. There is no reason to propose "that everyone else knew them all along" (Shiller, 1978, p. 34). Consequently we conclude that part of the information set is derived from data which become available after the period in which the expectations are formed. The strong form of the rational expectations hypothesis, thus, does not pass the data-availability criterion.[25]

Generally, the rational expectations hypothesis does not enable us to separate the direct effect of a predetermined variable on the endogenous variable from its indirect effect on the latter. This indirect effect results from the variables' role in explaining the expectations of endogenous variables.[26]

To sum up, the various versions of the strong form of rational expectations

---

[24] See Begg (1982), p. 30. Snippe (1986) distinguishes the macro "as if" variety and the micro "as if" variety of the rational expectations hypothesis. Since our criticism applies to both versions we do not discriminate between them.

[25] In order to avoid any misunderstanding we want to stress here that our data-availability criterion does not question the plausibility of the rational expectations' forward looking part, as represented by the sum in the right-hand side of (3.23). We only argue that this forward looking part should be based on available data. Thus the estimates of the data parameter Π_{12} and Π^{i}_{11}, $i = 0,...\infty$ and the expectations ${}_{t-1}x^{e}_{t+i+1}$, $i = 0,...,\infty$ in (3.23) should be derived from available data only. Consequently, jumps in expectations caused by unexpected (announcements of) changes in policy rules remain possible.

[26] For an illustrative example, see De Jong (1988), pp. 449,450.

do not meet any of our three criteria. It is especially the absence of a plausible process which could generate the expectations which is considered to be a great shortcoming. Consequently, in my view the strong form of the rational expectations hypothesis remains "essentially a black box" (Cyert and De Groot, 1974, p. 522).

3.3.4 *Weak forms of the rational expectations hypothesis*

As the discussion in the former section reveals, the strong form of the rational expectations hypothesis is rather disappointing. It does not pass any of the three criteria developed in Section 3.2. In the literature the ambiguity and/or implausibility of the assumptions on the acquisition of information and on the learning process are regarded to be the most serious defects of this expectations hypothesis (see, e.g. Friedman, 1979, Cyert and De Groot, 1974 and Buiter, 1980). In particular, the assumption about the huge amount of information, which the agents are assumed to possess, has often been criticized. Many regard the acquisition of this state of knowledge too costly to be achieved as a result of a more or less deliberate weighing of costs against benefits.

This criticism of the strong form of rational expectations has inspired some authors to propose alternative hypotheses, which are less demanding with respect to the information - availability assumption. The various postulates differ in the way the set of information is reduced. In the present section they are all treated as varieties of the weak form of rational expectations.

The weak form of the rational expectations hypothesis bears the following characteristics. Firstly, it takes account of the fact that expectations depend "on a deliberate and costly acquisition of information" (Snippe, 1986, p. 433). The resulting set of available information is likely to be smaller than in the case of the strong form of rational expectations. Secondly, it assumes that "individuals form expectations optimally on the basis of the information available to them and the cost of using that information" (Fischer, 1980, p. 212). Thus, the weak form of rational expectations assumes that every stage of the expectations-generating process is determined by cost/benefit considerations.

All approaches considered in this section assume that the costs of optimally utilizing the available information are negligible. The economic agents are, therefore, assumed to put the information together in such a way as to extract the best forecast of the variable concerned, z_{t+1} in equation (3.1).

Differences between the various variants of the weak form of rational expectations refer to the assumed size and content of the information set. Mostly it is assumed that the costs associated with the acquisition of the variable's own history are negligible compared to the predictive benefits to be gained from using this information. The information set then consists of a) the entire history of only the variable concerned (Sargent, 1973, for example), or; b) the observations of this variable after a particular date (De Jong, 1986, among others) or c) the last K observations of it (bounded memory).[27] The set of information can of course be extended by the observations of other variables. A necessary condition for utilizing an additional time series is "that the time series serves as a leading indicator in the sense of incrementally improving on the forecasts of the autoregressive models". (Feige and Pearce, 1976, p. 519). This time series will be included in the information set if the benefits resulting from improved predictions outweigh the costs of acquiring and utilizing the time series.

When assessing these weak forms of rational expectations it should first be noted that their main feature is the emphasis on the cost benefit considerations of expectations formation. The actual costs and benefits associated with an expectations formula depend on the particular problem at hand. Nevertheless some general criteria for determining an appropriate information set have been presented. In this respect the weak forms of rational expectations seem to be more realistic than the strong forms of this hypothesis. A full appreciation of these weak forms, however, requires knowledge of the exact formula utilized for deriving the expectations from the set of information. In the above discussion no attention has been given to these formulas; they are the subject of the next section. We therefore postpone our final judgement of these hypotheses until Section 3.5.

3.4 An assessment of estimation methods for models with expectations

3.4.1 *Introduction*

The present section is devoted to a review and an assessment of procedures proposed for estimating models with expectations. All methods considered are limited information estimation methods. In the literature full information methods have also been proposed for estimating models with expectations. As far as we know, these procedures have been derived for the estimation of models with strong forms of rational expectations only. They exploit the cross-equation restrictions mentioned in Section 3.3.2. (see for example Hansen and Sargent,

---

[27] The term expectation with bounded memory is taken from Fourgeaud *et al.* (1984) Their information set does not consist of the history of the variable concerned but of exogenous variables.

1982, and Wallis, 1980). As the use of these methods is restricted to this type of rational expectations models, our conclusions are the same as those stated in Section 3.3.2., namely that none of the criteria mentioned in 3.2 is met.[28]

3.4.2 *Survey data and proxies derived from forward rates and term structures*

It is sometimes asserted that the natural way of incorporating expectations in econometric models is to use direct observations of these expectations. Thereafter, the well-known estimation methods can be used for estimating the parameters of the model.

In the literature several limitations of utilizing survey data have been put forward. First, the survey data may not give an accurate measure of the actual expectation, because "people may not do what they say" (Sheffrin, 1983, p. 22). Second, survey data are rather sparse, being only available for particular variables and relatively short time periods (see Currie, 1985, Dominguez, 1986, and Frankel and Froot, 1985 and 1986, among others). A third disadvantage is that many survey data only elicit qualitative information, whereas quantitative measurements are required for the estimation of the model. The ultimate result then depends on the method used for the conversion of qualitative responses into quantitative measurements (see e.g. Pesaran, 1985, and Mayer and Mors, 1985). Sheffrin (1983) mentioned a fourth limitation of survey data, namely that the "surveys are used to determine average expectations but in many market situations the marginal participant plays the key role" (Sheffrin, 1983, p. 22).[29]

Another more or less direct method for obtaining the unobserved expectations consists of deriving an expectational variable from a theoretical hypothesis. In many studies, for example, the forward exchange rate has been used as a direct measure of the expected future spot rate (e.g. Abraham, 1985, Van Loo, 1983, Obstfeld, 1983, and Cuddington and Gluck, 1983). The forward rate can be regarded as a good measure of the future spot rate if the agents consider the foreign assets as perfect substitutes of domestic assets and if there are no restrictions on international capital movements. Recent research, however, indicates that foreign and domestic assets are most likely to be imperfect substitutes (Fukao, 1983, Jacobs, 1982, De Grauwe, Fratianni and Nabli, 1985,

---

[28] A comparison of the pros and cons of limited versus full information methods is presented in Begg (1982), pp. 113 and 114. Part II of Pesaran (1988) deals with various econometric issues of linear rational expectations models.

[29] See also Koedijk and Ott (1987), p. 9. Dominguez claims that surveys of professional forecasters circumvent many of the problems mentioned in the text. See Dominguez (1986), pp. 26 and 27.

among others). Then the forward rate and the expected future spot rate are separated by a risk premium, which is also unobservable (see for example, Dornbusch, 1983). Under these conditions the approximation of the expectations depends on the approximation of the risk premium. This description clearly illustrates a considerable disadvantage of the use of the forward rate, namely that the validity of the inferences about the expectations is conditioned on the underlying hypothesis.[30]

These methods meet two of the three tests on expectations formation developed in Section 3.2. The data-availability assumption is met. Most likely the interviewed agent bases his expectations on available data. This is also true for the proxies obtained by applying one of the theories mentioned above. Replacing the unobserved expectations in the model by the expectations measured by surveys or derived from the theory enables us to discriminate between the effect of the expectations on the endogenous variable and the effect of variables included in the information set on expectations. Thus the identification test is also met. Problems arise with regard to the criterion concerning the inclusion of a reasonable learning process. As far as we know the survey data contain information of the expectation of a particular variable only. The respondents are not asked to mention some *reasons* why they expect this particular value or movement of the variable concerned. The proxies obtained by a theoretical hypothesis also just refer to a proxy and not to hypothesis for arriving at that expectation. So the methods described in this section only inform us about the agent's expectations and not about the manner in which he forms his expectations. Consequently for many experiments with econometric models these expectations have to be augmented with a hypothesis of the process by which the expectations are formed (See Begg, 1982, p. 10).

3.4.3 *The substitution approach*

In contrast with the procedures of the preceding two sections, the methods to be described in this and following sections pay attention to the information utilized for deriving expectations, i.e. the matrix I_t in equation (3.2). For convenience this relation and equation (3.1) are reproduced

$$y_t = {}_t z^e_{t+1}\alpha + X_t\beta + u_t \qquad t = 1,...,T \qquad (3.1)$$

[30] This criticism also applies to studies in which expectations are obtained by exploiting the term structure of interest rates (e.g. Frankel, 1979 and 1982b, and Murphy and Van Duyne, 1980), or "by comparing the yields on otherwise comparable debt securities with different call provisions" (Friedman, 1980, p. 454).

$$ {}_{t}z^{e}_{t+1} = E(z_{t+1} \mid I_t) \qquad t = 1,...,T \tag{3.2} $$

It is assumed that the expectations-generating function is linear, i.e.

$$ {}_{t}z^{e}_{t+1} = I_t\delta + v_t \qquad t = 1,...,T \tag{3.3} $$

In many studies equation (3.3) is substituted in (3.1) and the resulting relation

$$ y_t = I_t\delta.\alpha + X_t\beta + u'_t \qquad t = 1,...,T \tag{3.24} $$

where

$$ u'_t = u_t + v_t\alpha \tag{3.25} $$

is estimated (see e.g. Jager, 1982, Pauly and Petersen, 1986, and Hooper, 1986).

Equation (3.3) holds for the entire period, t=1,...,T say. If it is assumed that the agents base their estimate of δ on information which was already available during period t=1 then the substitution method passes the data availability test. The procedure does not, however, meet the other two criteria. The first disadvantage is illustrated by equation (3.3). It shows that the relation between the expectation and the set of information is assumed to be fixed, so that does not contain a learning process. The second disadvantage relates to the identification-test. As equation (3.24) clearly indicates, the procedure delivers an estimate of the product $\delta.\alpha$. Unless prior information about α or δ is available, no separate estimates of these parameters can be derived from this product. An additional problem arises if the matrices I and X have a variable in common. Then, the corresponding parameter is $\delta_i.\alpha + \beta_i$, where the index i refers to the i-th variable. The estimation of (3.24) yields an estimate of this compound parameter only and thus once again it is impossible to separate the two different effects of a variable from each other.[31] In this case the different effects are the direct influence of a variable on y, measured by β_i, and the effect on y resulting from its part in approximating the expectation, measured by $\delta_i.\alpha$.

---

[31] The drawback of testing the expectation hypothesis and the model containing the expectation simultaneously is also mentioned in Fase and Van Nieuwkerk (1975), p. 304.

3.4.4 *Proxy variable methods with constant parameters*

In the preceding section the expectations-generating function (3.3) was used only for eliminating the unobserved expectation in relation (3.1). No proxy of this expectation was calculated before equation (3.24) was estimated. Contrasted with that practice, the first step of the methods to be presented in this and the next section, consists of the construction of a proxy variable, $\hat{z}_t$. Thereafter this proxy is substituted in equation (3.1). The resulting equation, which is to be estimated is

$$y_t = \hat{z}_t\alpha + X_t\beta + w_t \tag{3.26}$$

where

$$w_t = u_t + ({}_tz^e_{t+1} - \hat{z}_t)\alpha \tag{3.27}$$

As a consequence of the "errors in variables" nature of this procedure, $\hat{z}_t$ and w_t are correlated. Generally, ordinary least squares will yield inconsistent estimates, whereas an instrumental variable method can solve this inconsistency problem (see Section 4.3.2). Different procedures have been suggested for calculating the proxy $\hat{z}_t$.

Frequently, the proxy $\hat{z}_t$ is derived in the following manner. Suppose, z is generated by the process

$$z_t = I_{t-1}\cdot\delta + v_t \qquad t = 1,\ldots,T \tag{3.28}$$

where v_t is an error term drawn independently of the errors in (3.1) from a normal distribution with zero mean. The estimation of this relation gives us the estimated values of the parameters, $\hat{\delta}$. Then the proxy, $\hat{z}_t$, of the expectation $E(z_{t+1} \mid I_t)$

$$\hat{z}_t = I_t\cdot\hat{\delta} \tag{3.29}$$

is a minimum variance unbiased predictor of z_t under the normality assumption introduced above. It should be noted that in many instances this proxy is not equal to the best forecast in the sense of minimizing a certain loss function. Very often the best forecast will be biased (see Zellner, 1986, for some examples). The conclusions to be presented below with regard to the appropriateness of (3.29) for approximating expectations also apply to these biased formulas.

In many studies the matrix I_{t-1} is assumed to consist of lagged values of z only. The resulting lag structure in (3.28) can be estimated by ordinary least squares, the method suggested in Almon (1965) or the techniques mentioned in Box and Jenkins (1976) for estimating ARIMA-models. The latter models have been used in e.g. Adam and Mélard (1987), Jacobs (1982), Fischer (1981), Viaene and De Vries (1985) and Feige and Pearce (1976).

Another possibility is to assume that, along with past values of z, I_{t-1} contains past values of other variables. These variables are selected because: a) they are suggested by economic theory, b) they significantly - measured by the well-known t-statistic - contribute to the explanation of z (MacDonald, 1983); c) they serve as a leading indicator in the sense of incrementally improving on the forecasts of autoregressive models (Feige and Pearce, 1976). Recently the vector autoregressive model, which is the multiple-variables version of the simple autoregressive model, has been very popular. It has been used by e.g. Branson (1984), and Saracoglu (1984).

Hitherto, only equation (3.28) has been used for selecting the appropriate proxy. There is no feedback from the proxy's performance in explaining y to the selection procedure of $\hat{z}$. Iterative methods, on the other hand, explicitly condition the choice of the proxy on the resulting quality of equation (3.26). Some methods for calculating a rational expectations proxy make use of an iterative technique. The aim of these procedures is to estimate the model in such a way that ultimately the parameter values in the expectations-generating function of the endogenous variables are equal to the relevant parameters of the model. In order to achieve this goal, the model is estimated at each iteration using the expectations proxy derived in the preceding iteration. The resulting new estimates of the model's parameters are used for calculating the expectations proxy, which is used in the next iteration. A simple one equation example can be found in Dooley and Isard (1982). Fair (1984, ch. 11) presents a more generally applicable iterative procedure for estimating models with rational expectations. A disadvantage of the iteration methods is, that the convergence of the algorithm is not guaranteed.[32]

Another proxy variable method for estimating a model with rational expectations has been suggested by McCallum (1976). He argues that rational expectations are equal to the corresponding realized variables plus a forecasting error uncorrelated with the variables which are available and utilized by market

---

[32] Dooley and Isard mention two additional disadvantages which bear upon their application of the iterative procedure. For details see Dooley and Isard (1982), p. 267.

participants in forming expectations,[33] i.e

$$_{t-1}z_t^e = E(z_t \mid I_{t-1}) = z_t + \mu_t \quad (3.30)$$

where $\mu_t = {}_{t-1}z_t^e - z_t$, $t = 1,...,T$, are forecasting errors which are uncorrelated with I_{t-1}, and which are identically distributed with mean zero and constant variance. Substituting (3.30) in

$$y_t = {}_{t-1}z_t^e \alpha + X_t \beta + u_t \quad (3.31)$$

we obtain

$$y_t = z_t \alpha + X_t \beta + e_t \quad (3.32)$$

where

$$e_t = u_t + \mu_t \alpha$$

$$= u_t + ({}_{t-1}z_t^e - z_t) \alpha \quad (3.33)$$

A disadvantage of the McCallum proposal is that it cannot be used when the equation includes on the right-hand side both a current endogenous variable and its own rational expectation one period earlier. This is because once the substitution has been made, the current value of the endogenous variable enters twice and it is impossible to identify separately the relevant elements of α and β.[34] An advantage of this proposal is that, it offers us a rather simple limited information estimation procedure for simultaneous equation models with rational expectations.[35,36] That may be one of the reasons why Cumby *et al.* (1983)

---

[33] As relation (3.30) illustrates, no parameter δ, relating the expectation proxy to an information set, has been estimated for deriving McCallum's proxy, and thus it can be argued that this procedure also belongs to the proxy variable methods with time-varying parameters. We have categorized it in the group of proxy variable methods with constant parameters because it shares with these methods the same (dis)advantages.

[34] For problems associated with the estimation of models in which the McCallum proxy is representing rational expectations, one is referred to Begg (1982), p.110, De Jong (1988), pp. 457 and 458, and Wallis (1980).

[35] A comparison with other limited information methods can be found in Begg (1982), pp. 110 and 111.

extended the applicability of this method to the estimation of rational expectations models with autocorrelated residuals and predetermined but not strictly exogenous instruments.

The last approach, which we want to consider in this section, is only applicable when the particular expectational variable is an explanatory variable in two or more equations of the model. In addition it is required that one relation has a special form which enables us to calculate the parameter δ in the expectations-generating function (3.3).[37] De Jong (1985), for example, presented an equation where theory suggests that the coefficient of the expectations term, the parameter α in (3.1), is equal to 1. Substitution of the expectations-generating function (3.3) in this relation yields

$$y_{2,t} = I_t \delta + X_{2,t} \beta + u_{2,t} \tag{3.34}$$

Provided that no variable of I_t is included in $X_{2,t}$, estimations of the parameters can be obtained. Thereafter the expectations proxy $\hat{z}_t = I_t \hat{\delta}$ is calculated and substituted in (3.1).[38]

As this example clearly illustrates, the present method employs a substitution approach with prior information for deriving a proxy of the expectational variable, and thus can be considered as a combination of the substitution and proxy variable approach.

This procedure has two disadvantages. The first, which has already been mentioned, is that in order to obtain estimates of δ and β in (3.34), the variables in $X_{2,t}$ should not be contained in I_t. The second drawback is that the identification of δ requires that the expectations-generating function and/or the added equation show some special form (e.g. that a particular coefficient is equal to a known value).

---

[36] McCallum claims that his method can also be used for estimating the parameters of models with partly rational expectations, as defined in Section 3.3. In De Jong (1986) we criticize this assertion.

[37] Note that both the present procedure and the multiple indicator approach suggest adding an equation to the original system. A difference between the two methods is that the multiple indicator approach does not introduce restrictions on the form of the added equation or on the expectations generating function. For more details about the multiple indicator approach see Attfield (1980) and the literature cited there.

[38] Kohlhagen (1977) presented a model where the expectations' coefficient in this relation is not equal to 1, but where this equation and the expectation generating function have a special form so that the parameters represented by the vector δ can be calculated from the estimated coefficients of the additional equation.

An assessment of all proxy variable methods reveals that they meet only one of the three criteria of Section 3.2. Provided that the last-described procedure conforms to the restriction mentioned above, all methods meet the identification criterion. The criteria concerning the data-availability and the learning process are not met. The data-availability test is not passed, because the expectations- generating function (3.29) and the process equation (3.1) are estimated for the same period. Consequently the estimated value δ contains information of all observations on z and I. Thus, the expectations proxy of the first period, $\hat{z}_1 = \hat{\delta}\, I_1$, is partly based on data of the periods 2 through T. At time 1 these data are not yet available. It does not become clear how the agents can have access to this information of future periods. This leads us to the learning process. The coefficients of the expectations-generating function do not change as time elapses. Hence during the sample period, t = 1,...,T, the agents do not learn.

3.4.5 *Proxy variable methods with time-varying parameters*

The procedures to be presented in this section seek to circumvent the two disadvantages of the proxy variable methods with constant parameters, namely that the proxy of period t is partly based on information which is not yet available and that the method does not include a learning process. As has already been indicated in the preceding section, these drawbacks arise from the assumption that the parameters in the expectations-generating function are constant. The present procedures assume that these coefficients change as time passes by, i.e.

$$z_t = I_{t-1}\, \delta_t + v_t \qquad t = 1,\dots,T \qquad (3.35)$$

The corresponding unbiased proxy is

$$\hat{z}_t = I_t\, \hat{\delta}_t \qquad t = 1,\dots,T \qquad (3.36)$$

Of course the remarks with regard to the unbiasedness of (3.29) also apply to (3.36). Each period the parameter vector δ is re-estimated. This estimator is based on current and past observations only. The time series of the expectations proxy thus obtained is substituted in the process equation (3.1). The resulting equation can be consistently estimated by an instrumental variables method or sometimes by the ordinary least squares procedure.

The procedures considered in this section can be applied when the information set I_t contains past and present values of z only and if this set also contains the past and present observations of other variables. The first method to be considered is the simple Kalman filter which augments the model with the following equation

$$\delta_t = f_t \, \delta_{t-1} + e_t \qquad t = 1,\dots,T \qquad (3.37)$$

where f_t is a known parameter. An application of the Kalman filter requires an estimate of δ_0 and assumptions with regard to f_t and the processes of v_t and e_t.[39] Then the filter algorithm produces a forecast for each period on the basis of these assumptions together with the actual data included in I_t. A disadvantage of the simple Kalman filter is that "there is no feedback from the data to the algorithm" (Bomhoff and Korteweg, 1983, p. 200). Bomhoff and Korteweg, therefore, use a so-called multi-state Kalman filter. Such a filter is a weighted average of a number of simple Kalman filters. The simple filters differ in the assumptions that have been made with regard to the process of v_t and e_t. The weight of each model's forecast in the multi-state filter "depends in a Bayesian manner both on prior probabilities and on the likelihood of the most recent observations....The prior probabilities are updated in the course of time, in view of the evolution of the posterior probabilities" (ibid. Appendix, pp. 4 and 6).[40]

In Blume and Easley (1982), Bray (1982, proposition 5), Capel and De Jong(1988a and 1988b), Gottfries (1985) and De Jong (1986) a "rolling regressions" procedure is used for approximating expectations. The most general form of this method is presented in De Jong (1986), where the dimension of the parameter vector δ_t, which hitherto was assumed to be constant, is assumed to depend upon the period in question, i.e. δ_t is a $1 \times l_t$ vector and I_t is a $l_t \times n_t$ matrix. The time varying dimension l_t indicates that in each period the agents re-estimate the lag structure of the forecasting equation. The ultimately chosen specification shows the best forecasting performance over the recent past. This represents the feedback from the data to the algorithm. So the relevant disadvantage of the preceding methods does not apply. The time varying dimension n_t of the information set represents the assumption that in general the set of information grows as time passes by. Generally $n_t = n_{t-1} + 1$. Under the assumption of bounded memory this condition becomes $n_t = n_{t-1} = n$. It is, of course, assumed that $l_t < n_t$. The present method formalizes the assumption that at each time the agents' expectations are equal to the best forecast of z_t subject to the available data, I_t, i.e. the agents are assumed to form their expectations in

---

[39] For details concerning the Kalman filter see Athans (1974).

[40] More details of the multi-state Kalman filter can be found in the Appendix to Bomhoff and Korteweg (1983) and in Kool (1989).

a partly rational manner (see, Section 3.3.3). We once again would like to stress that the best forecast can be biased.[41]

When assessing the procedures described above, we assume that the a priori values, which are needed for calculating the proxy $\hat{z}_1$, are based on information that is available at time t=1. This implies that the sample also contains observations relating to the periods before t=1. Under these conditions the present procedures explicitly take into consideration that expectations are based on available data only and the procedures pass the data availability test. As with the proxy variable methods of the preceding section, the present proxy variable procedures meet the identification criterion too. With regard to the test on the learning process, it should first be noted that in all procedures the parameter vector of the forecasting equation is revised to include the effect of recent observations. In the simple Kalman filter and the simple "rolling regressions" procedure this revision is very mechanical. These two procedures do not contain feedback from the data to the specification of the forecasting equation. The agents are thus assumed to gain no additional information on the true structure of the process of the variable concerned, but to update the parameter estimates only. Hence the learning process is rather limited. The learning implied by the multi-state Kalman filter and by the most general form of the "rolling regressions" procedure is more satisfactory because the specification of the forecasting function depends on the recent performance of this equation. Thus these methods also pass the test on the learning process.

3.5 Concluding remarks

In this chapter we presented three criteria for assessing methods of expectations formation, viz. a data availability criterium, a criterium concerns the learning process and an identification criterium. The first two criteria are considered to be of most importance. They state that expectations should be based on available information only and that the formation of expectations includes a learning process.

The three criteria were used for assessing the various expectations hypotheses and methods for estimating models with expectations. This assessment revealed that, of the hypotheses considered, the weak forms of the rational

---

[41] See Zellner (1986). The "rolling regressions" procedures presented in the text assume that the database is updated with the latest observation. Swany and Schinasi (1986) demonstrate that this "rolling" does not necessarily yield predictions that are close to actual data. The minimization of the mean squared prediction errors may even exclude the most recent data.

expectations hypotheses best meet the three criteria. Our final judgement of these hypothesis depends on the particular method used for approximating the expectations. From the assessment of the various estimation methods we concluded that, provided that the prior values are appropriately chosen, the multi-state Kalman filter and the "rolling regressions" approach meet all three criteria. One of these two methods should, thus, be used for approximating weak forms of the rational expectations hypothesis. The exact form of the expectations-generating function and the variables to be included in the information set depend on the particular problem at hand. In this chapter we confined ourselves to the first stage of a research project on expectations formation, *viz.* the determination of the essential elements of expectations formation.

In the next chapter (Section 4.3.5) the results are used for deriving exchange rate expectations.

4 THE FINANCIAL SECTOR OF THE MODEL

4.1 Introduction

In this chapter a structural portfolio model of exchange rate determination is estimated for the Netherlands. The specification of the equations and the estimation procedure used seek to circumvent some of the weak points of many other studies on exchange rate determination mentioned in Chapter 2. This structural model of exchange rate determination forms the monetary sector of a quarterly model of the Dutch economy. The other relations of this model and the simulation results of the entire model are presented in the next chapters.

This chapter is organized as follows. In the next section attention is paid to the specification of the financial relations. Some preliminary subjects - the estimation procedure, the approximation of exchange rate expectations and the treatment of seasonal influences - are discussed in Section 4.3. After these two more or less introductory sections the accounting and analytical framework of the financial part of the model is presented in 4.4. The next three sections contain the estimated relations representing the financial behaviour of the three sectors distinguished, *viz.* the private sector, the banking sector and the foreign sector. These relations determine the interest rates and the sectors' demand for the various assets during a period. In the portfolio balance approach of the exchange rate, the interest payments and receipts play an important role. Therefore, in Section 4.8 the government's interest payments and the interest receipts (payments) on domestic (foreign) holdings of foreign (domestic) assets are approximated.

4.2 The specification of the financial relations

In almost all studies on exchange rate determination actual stocks of assets are assumed to be equal to desired stocks at every moment in time. In Chapter 2 we have argued that this portfolio balance assumption is most likely to be at variance with, among other things, the market participants' behaviour and with the empirical studies of money demand. A more general specification is desirable, which allows for a gradual evolution of actual toward desired stocks of assets or a continuous equality between the two. In this study we therefore model the various sectors' portfolio selection process by the partial adjustments model. The present section describes this specification. A review and a critique on alternative specifications of the multi-asset partial adjustment model is presented in Appendix A to this chapter.

Christofides (1976) has shown that the multi-asset partial adjustment relations are the solution of the following optimization problem. Minimize the quadratic cost function

$$C = \Sigma_{i=1}^{n} a_i(A_{it}^{d} - A_{it})^2 + \Sigma_{i=1}^{n} b_i(A_{it} - A_{i,t-i})^2 \tag{4.1}$$

subject to the constraint

$$W_t = \Sigma_{i=1}^{n} A_{it} = \Sigma_{i=1}^{n} A_{it}^{d} \tag{4.2}$$

Where A_{it}^{d} (A_{it}) is the desired (actual) stock of asset i at the end of period t, W_t is the wealth at the end of period t, n is the number of assets and the coefficients a_i (b_i), i = 1,..., n, measure the cost per unit of being out of equilibrium (of adjusting assets positions). The constraint (4.2) is known as the "wealth conservation condition" (Christofides, 1976, p. 301) or as the "rational desires hypothesis" (Ladenson, 1971, p. 179). The solutions of this minimization problem are derived in Christofides (1976) and represented by the following system of equations

$$\Delta A_{it} = \Sigma_{j=1}^{n} \delta_{ij} (A^{d}_{jt} - A_{j,t-1}) \qquad i = 1,...,n \tag{4.3}$$

The wealth conservation condition (4.2) requires that

$$\Sigma_{i=1}^{n} \delta_{ij} = 1 \qquad j = 1,...,n \tag{4.4}$$

The desired stock requires a behavioural specification. Familiar is the linear homogeneous form

$$A_{jt}^{d} = [\, \Sigma_{k=1}^{n} \beta_{jk} r_{kt} + \Sigma_{h=1}^{m} \gamma_{jh} X_{ht} + \alpha_j \,] \cdot W_t \qquad j = 1,...n \tag{4.5}$$

where r_{kt} is the (expected) rate of return on the k-th asset at time t, X_{ht} are the values in period t of additional variables which influence the portfolio allocation, and β_{jk}, γ_{jh} and α_j are fixed coefficients which satisfy the constraints

$$\Sigma_{j=1}^{n} \beta_{jk} = 0 \quad \text{for all k} \tag{4.6-a}$$

$$\Sigma_{j=1}^{n} \gamma_{jh} = 0 \quad \text{for all h} \tag{4.6-b}$$

$$\Sigma_{i=1}^{n} \alpha_i = 1 \tag{4.6-c}$$

This specification of the desired stocks ensures that any shift in the assets' shares in the desired portfolio is due to movements of either relevant yields, r_{kt}, or other variables, X_{ht}, rather than to overall growth of the total portfolio.[1]

The portfolio adjustment model employed in the next sections consists of equations (4.3), in which A^d_{jt} is replaced by formula (4.5), for j=1,...,n, i.e.

$$\Delta A_{it} = \Sigma^n_{j=1}\,\delta_{ij}\,\alpha_j\,W_t + \Sigma^n_{j=1}\,\delta_{ij}\,\Sigma^n_{k=1}\,\beta_{jk}\,r_{kt}\,W_t$$

$$+ \Sigma^n_{j=1}\,\delta_{ij}\,\Sigma^m_{h=1}\,\gamma_{jh}\,X_{ht}\,W_t - \Sigma^n_{j=1}\,\delta_{ij}\,A_{j,t-1} + v_{it} \qquad i = 1,\dots,n \qquad (4.7)$$

This relation describes the changes in asset holdings resulting from the particular sector's preferences and from a change in wealth. The holdings of asset stocks are, however, also determined by the behaviour of other sectors, e.g. the monetary authorities. This influence is represented by Z which is added to the set of explanatory variables.[2] The resulting equation is divided by W_{t-1} in order to correct for contemporaneous heteroscedasticity of the residuals

$$\frac{\Delta A_{it}}{W_{t-1}} = \Sigma^n_{j=1}\,\delta_{ij}\cdot\alpha_j\,\frac{W_t}{W_{t-1}} + \Sigma^n_{j=1}\,\delta_{ij}\,\Sigma^n_{k=1}\,\beta_{jk}\,r_{kt}\,\frac{W_t}{W_{t-1}}$$

$$+ \Sigma^n_{j=1}\,\delta_{ij}\,\Sigma^m_{h=1}\,\gamma_{jh}\,\frac{X_{ht}\cdot W_t}{W_{t-1}} - \Sigma^n_{j=1}\,\delta_{ij}\,\frac{A_{j,t-1}}{W_{t-1}}$$

$$+ \mu_i\,\frac{Z_t}{W_{t-1}} + \frac{v_{it}}{W_{t-1}} \qquad i = 1,\dots,n \qquad (4.8)$$

Relation (4.8) is the general form of the equations estimated in Sections 4.5 through 4.7.

4.3 Preliminary issues of the empirical part

4.3.1 *Introduction*

Most of the econometric issues that pertain to the modelling in general are dealt

---

[1] For a rationale of this assumption see Friedman (1977), p. 664, and the literature cited in his footnote 4.

[2] A similar approach has been used in Backus *et al.* (1980) and Van Loo (1983).

with in the present section. Successively the following subjects pass in review: aspects of the estimation procedure, *viz.* the handling of cross-equations restrictions and the selection of the instrumental variables, the data used, the definition of the exchange rate variable and the method used for approximating exchange rate expectations. Readers not interested in these details can safely skip this section.

4.3.2 *The estimation procedure: the cross-equation restrictions*

Each sector's balance-sheet identity introduces some additional restrictions to the estimation procedure, Firstly, account has to be taken of the resulting cross-equation restrictions on the coefficients presented in Section 4.2 (relations (4.4), (4.6-a) (4.6-b) and (4.6-c)). Secondly, per sector the disturbance terms v_{it} in equations (4.8) sum to zero and are thus contemporaneously correlated. Consequently, per sector the variance-covariance matrix of the disturbances is singular and thus the simultaneous estimation of the sector's asset demand functions is precluded, while in many cases the OLS estimates are not efficient (see a standard textbook, e.g. Johnston, 1972).

It can be shown, that when the set of explanatory variables is the same for each relation, the OLS estimates automatically satisfy the adding-up constraints (see, e.g. Denton, 1978).[3] These OLS estimates form the basis of the estimation procedure employed in some studies by Backus and his fellow authors (see, Backus *et al.*, 1980, and Backus and Purvis ,1980, for example). They also present prior values based on their own view and Theil-Goldberger mixed estimates which are comprised of the prior and OLS coefficients. An advantage of this method is that the sample information and the author's priors of the parameters' value are clearly presented.[4] Disadvantages are that all ultimately chosen estimates depend on the priors and are not efficient, and that many estimated coefficients appear to have the wrong sign.

In order to circumvent the latter disadvantage, the standard procedure is to delete the wrongly signed coefficients. Then, however, the OLS estimates no longer automatically satisfy the cross-equation restrictions. Moreover, a procedure which in a correct way eliminates the wrongly signed coefficients is rather complicated, because many of the model's structural parameters are not

---

[3] A survey of estimation methods for portfolio models subject to adding-up restrictions can be found in Owen (1986), pp. 59-76.

[4] A more extensive defence of this Bayesian approach can be found in Smith and Brainard (1976).

equal to a particular estimated coefficient. For example, the structural parameter representing the second interest rate's effect on the demand for the first asset, β_{12}, in equation (4.5) forms part of the estimated coefficients of $r_2 \cdot W_t/W_{t-1}$ in all relations (4.8). These estimated coefficients are

$$c_{12} = \Sigma_{j=1}^{n} \delta_{ij} \cdot \beta_{j2} \qquad i=1,...,n \tag{4.9}$$

The estimates of δ_{ij} are equal to the estimated parameters of A_{t-1}/W_{t-1}. By substituting these estimated values into (4.9) we obtain n equations in the n unknown parameters β_{j2}, j = 1,...,n.

In a correct estimation procedure at each stage equations like (4.9) are used for calculating the estimated values of the coefficients in the relation of the desired assets (4.5) in order to verify whether the estimates obtained are plausible. If this verification is not made one can easily arrive at unwanted results. Two examples from recently published empirical studies are presented in De Jong (1990). The first one concerns the estimates provided by Van Loo (1983) of corporate financial behaviour. It can easily be verified that these estimates preclude the determination of some structural coefficients β_{jk}, j = 1,...,n and k = 1,...,n. The second example is taken from Kuipers *et al.* (1990). It appears that in that study some of the own interest rate effects, the coefficients β_{jk} j=k, are negative.

Note that all products of parameters in (4.9) consist of an adjustment parameter, δ_{ij}, multiplied by another coefficient. Hence, the estimation procedure is much less complicated when the adjustment parameters are already known. This notion forms the basis of the two-stage estimation procedure developed in De Nederlandsche Bank (1984). In the first stage all explanatory variables are included in the relation, but only the adjustment coefficients, δ_{ij}, are constrained to be equal to their theoretically correct sign. Conditional on these estimates, in the second stage the remaining parameters are estimated. A drawback of this procedure is that it does not take account of the contemporaneous correlation between the disturbances of each sector's equations. Consequently, the estimated coefficients are asymptotically less efficient than Zellner's seemingly unrelated regression estimates (SURE).[5]

Since SURE is a simultaneous estimation method, the earlier mentioned problem of the singular variance-covariance matrix of disturbances comes to the fore. A solution to this problem consists of deleting one of the equations from the system (see e.g. Theil, 1971). The coefficients of this particular relation result from the adding-up restrictions and the estimated parameters in the other relations. A disadvantage of this procedure is that a variable that significantly

---

[5] See e.g. Johnston (1972), pp. 238-241 for a brief description of SURE.

influences the omitted endogenous variable but insignificantly affects each of the remaining endogenous variables most probably will not appear in the ultimately preferred specification. Hence the choice of the specification may depend upon the relation omitted from the estimation process.

In subsequent sections a slightly amended version of the two-stage procedure[6] has been employed for estimating the parameters. The amendment is that during the first stage wrongly signed and highly insignificant coefficients, which are not a product of an adjustment parameter and another coefficient, are deleted from the relations. The adding-up restrictions are accounted for by cross-equation restrictions. The first stage ends when the adjustment parameters and the coefficients of Z_t still included in (4.8) are rightly signed and significant. The coefficients β_{jk} (and if relevant γ_{jh}) remain to be estimated. During the second stage the adjustment parameters are fixed at the values obtained at the end of the first stage. Equation (4.9) illustrates that given these values the coefficients β_{jk} can be calculated. Those that are wrongly signed are excluded from the first regression of the second stage. If one or more coefficients in this regression appears to have the wrong sign then the relations are re-estimated until the signs of all coefficients correspond with their theoretically expected token.

An advantage of this procedure is that it enables us to delete wrongly signed coefficients from the relations without introducing the misspecification bias associated with the SURE method where one equation has to be deleted. Furthermore, it takes account of all cross-equation restrictions. A drawback is that the consequences of the contemporaneous correlation between the disturbances are neglected.

A disadvantage which the preferred method shares with almost all other procedures is that it is unclear to what extent the ultimately preferred and published coefficients are influenced by the researcher's estimation strategy. In order to elucidate the effect of this influence and in order to obtain some preliminary information on the appropriate structure of the equations, we have first regressed each dependent variable on the set of all plausible explanatory variables. These regressions are reported in Appendices B and C. Since this set is the same for each endogenous variable, the adding-up restrictions are automatically satisfied (see Denton,1978).

---

[6] The LSQ-procedure in the TSP-package is used for simultaneously estimating the equations.

4.3.3 *The estimation procedure: the choice of instrumental variables*

There are two reasons why estimating relations (4.8) by OLS would yield inconsistent estimates. Firstly, recall that the variables r_{kt} (k=1,...,n) in (4.8) are the (expected) rates of return on the assets. These rates and the flows of assets, ΔA_{it} (i=1,..,n), are simultaneously determined. Thus the variables r_{kt} are correlated with the disturbance term v_{it} and the OLS estimates will be biased and inconsistent.

Another reason for this correlation between v_{it} and r_{kt} results from the "errors in variables" problem. According to theory the optimal allocation of assets depends upon the expected yields. In the empirical model these expected yields are approximated by the observed interest rates and a proxy of the expected exchange rate (see Section 4.3.5). In order to illustrate the problem, suppose that the third asset is a foreign asset with expected rate of return $r_{f,t} + \mathring{e}^e_t$. When estimating (4.8) the unobserved percentage change of the expected exchange rate $\mathring{e}^e$ is replaced by the proxy, $\hat{\mathring{e}}^e_t$. Then the regression contains the explanatory variable $r_{f,t} + \hat{\mathring{e}}^e_t$ and the disturbance term

$$v'_{it} = v_{it} + \Sigma^n_{j=1} \delta_{ij} \beta_{j,3} (\mathring{e}^e_t - \hat{\mathring{e}}^e_t) \tag{4.10}$$

Consequently the proxy and the disturbance term (4.10) are correlated with each other.

Instrumental variables methods can be used for solving the problems mentioned.[7] These procedures replace the variables r_k by a set of fitted values $\hat{r}_k$ obtained from a regression of r_k on a set of instrumental variables. These instrumental variables should be highly correlated with r_k and should have as small a covariance as possible with the equation error, v'_i.

Two stage least squares (2SLS) is a well-known instrumental variables method that uses the entire set of predetermined variables as the set of instrumental variables. Small-sample theory, however, indicates that these estimates are biased, though they are asymptotically unbiased. The small sample bias of the 2SLS estimates is illustrated in studies in which the 2SLS estimates appear to be almost identical to the OLS estimates.[8] Thus the set of instruments should be reduced. The way in which the list of instruments has been truncated in the present study is a practical mixture of the causal ordering procedure

---

[7] The essence of the instrumental variables approach can be found in textbooks such as Johnston (1972) and Theil (1971). An extensive study of this method is presented in Bowden and Turkington (1984).

[8] See e.g. Jager (1981).

suggested by Fisher (1965) and the use of canonical correlations proposed by Bowden and Turkington (1984).[9]

Fisher proposes to use the model in order to determine those predetermined variables that influence the particular variable most. This method is very time consuming, because one has to apply this method for each variable which has to be replaced by an instrumental variables estimate. Some additional disadvantages are mentioned in Fisher and Mitchell (1970). In accordance with the reasoning behind Fisher's causal ordering procedure the set of instrumental variables has been restricted to the predetermined variables of the financial sector and the variables in the conditioning set of the expected exchange rate.

The next example illustrates that the variables in the conditioning set of the expected exchange rate proxy are good candidates for serving as instrumental variables. Assume that the conditioning set consists of the variables I_t. Then the expectation $E(e_t \mid I_{t-1})$ is approximated by $\hat{e}_t = I_{t-1}\,\hat{\theta}$, where the vector of coefficients $\hat{\theta}$ is obtained from the regression

$$e_t = I_{t-1}\,\theta + w_t \tag{4.11}$$

where w_t is a disturbance term. By assumption, I_t and w_t are uncorrelated and thus the variables in the conditioning set are orthogonal to the approximation error, $\mathring{e}^e - \hat{\mathring{e}}^e$ and highly correlated with the proxy $\hat{\mathring{e}}^e$. They therefore are included in the set of instrumental variables.

Bowden and Turkington (1974) use canonical correlation in order to reduce the number of instrumental variables. In correspondence with their attention to the correlation between the instrumental variables and the endogenous variables concerned we have selected those predetermined variables of the monetary sector that have a correlation coefficient with one of the (expected) rates of return which exceeds 0.5. All instrumental variables thus obtained are used as instruments of the expected rates of return.[10]

To conclude, our procedure for selecting the instrumental variables can be regarded as a practical mixture of the causal ordering procedure suggested by Fisher (1965) and the use of canonical correlations proposed by Bowden and Turkington (1984).[11] As the former, it restricts the set of instruments to those predetermined variables that most likely cause the replaced variables, whereas

---

[9] Other methods for reducing the number of instrumental variables are listed in Brundy and Jorgenson (1971) and Bowden and Turkington (1984).

[10] The use of a different set of instruments per endogenous variable would have led to inconsistent estimates. See Mitchell and Fisher (1970).

[11] Other methods for reducing the number of instrumental variables are listed in Brundy and Jorgenson (1971) and Bowden and Turkington (1984).

it shares with the latter the attention to the correlation between the instruments and the endogenous variables concerned.

4.3.4 *The data used*

Quarterly data have been used to estimate the model's parameters. It can be argued that the time-period implicitly postulated in the theoretical models of exchange rate determination is shorter than one quarter. Thus monthly or weekly data are recommended for estimating the financial relations. However, the most appropriate time-period of some behavioural equations in the real part of the model, e.g. the investment in plant and equipment, is longer than one quarter. Moreover, data of many real phenomena of the Dutch economy are only available on an annual basis. It is only recently that approximations of the corresponding quarterly figures have been published. We have, therefore, chosen quarterly data because the associated time-period is the shortest for which data on all relevant time series is available.

For several reasons these quarterly figures are not adjusted for seasonal patterns.[12] Firstly, the use of seasonally adjusted time series would violate the data-availability criterion of expectations formation, presented in Chapter 3. For many time series the definite value is published some years after the preliminary value. Hence the seasonally adjusted value of the former incorporates the information of future periods. That is expectations proxies based on seasonally adjusted time series implicitly make use of information which would not have been available at the time the expectations actually were formed.[13]

Secondly, one aim of the monetary policy in the Netherlands is to reduce those fluctuations in financial variables that are caused by seasonal factors. This aim is part of the central bank's responsibility for providing a smoothly functioning financial system.[14] Because in the present study we are interested in the effectiveness and appropriateness of monetary policy we should explicitly take account of the possibility that this policy is influenced by seasons.

Thirdly, the use of seasonally adjusted data can easily give rise to wrong conclusions. For example, the parameter estimates and the error term in the regression equations are likely to be distorted when the variables are adjusted by

---

[12] Driehuis (1972), pp. 9 and 10 lists some reasons in favour of the use of seasonally adjusted data.

[13] The same argument against the use of seasonally adjusted times series can be found in Meese and Rogoff (1983[a]), p. 9.

[14] See Den Dunnen (1985), p.9. Quotations on the seasonal influences of the Dutch monetary policy can be found in Den Dunnen (1985), pp. 58, 61, 76, 80 and in De Wilde (1975).

different methods. If the same method is applied to all series then the relationship between them is not disturbed but the error term is still affected. If, for instance, the original equations' error term is not autocorrelated, then the disturbance term of the regression equations with adjusted time series is a high-order moving average process, and ordinary least squares estimates will not be fully efficient.[15]

Another consequence of the use of adjusted data is that the number of degrees of freedom decreases. In many studies no correction is made for this. Consequently, the application of t-tests overstates the statistical significance of parameter estimates.

Finally, a number of studies in which the unadjusted and seasonally adjusted series have been compared by spectral analysis suggest that some methods of seasonal adjustment remove from the series more than only the seasonal variation.[16]

In the present study seasonal influences are represented by seasonal dummies.

4.3.5 *The effective exchange rate*

In the theoretical models on exchange rate determination presented in previous chapters it has been implicitly assumed that the foreign sector consists of one country. Consequently, the model contains one exchange rate. Actually, however, there are many bilateral exchange rates. In the empirical model these bilateral exchange rates are represented by an effective exchange rate, which is a weighted average of bilateral rates. The value of an effective exchange rate depends on the choice of:[17] a) the base period; b) the mathematical formulation of the average (arithmetic or geometric); c) the number of countries included; and d) the weights attached to each country.

The base period of the effective exchange rate is 1977. The main reason for selecting this period is that 1977 is also the base for the other indices in the model. The geometric average is used as the technique of averaging because three disadvantages that pertain to the use of the arithmetic average do not hold for the use of the geometric average.[18] The drawbacks of the arithmetic average arise

---

[15] See Wallis (1974).

[16] See the studies mentioned in Thomas and Wallis (1971).

[17] Anema and Jepma (1978) and Rhomberg (1976) discuss the various characteristics of effective exchange rate indices.

[18] Brodsky (1982) extensively discusses the differences between the geometric and arithmetic effective exchange rates. The advantages of the geometric effective exchange rate presented in the text are based on his analysis.

from the fundamental ambiguity, that "the" exchange rate can be defined as the price of domestic currency in terms of foreign currency as well as the price of foreign currency in terms of the domestic currency.

The first disadvantage of the arithmetic average is that its value depends on the definition of exchange rate. In order to illustrate the problems, let R_{it} denote the price of the home currency at time t in terms of the currency of the i-th country, and S_{it} the price of the currency of the i-th country at time t in terms of that of the home country. The two exchange rates are linked by $R_{it} = 1/S_{it}$. For a given set of weights w_i, we can define four possible effective exchange rate indices:

Arithmetic	Geometric
$EER1 = 100\ \Sigma_i\ w_i\ R_{it}/R_{i0}$	$EER3 = 100\ \Pi_i\ (R_{it}/R_{i0})^{w_i}$
$EER2 = 100/(\Sigma_i\ w_i\ S_{it}/S_{i0})$	$EER4 = 100/[\Pi_i\ (S_{it}/S_{i0})^{w_i}]$

where Π_i represents the multiplication operant.
Since $1/(R_{it}/R_{i0}) = S_{it}/S_{i0}$, the two geometric effective rates are equal.

The second disadvantage of the arithmetic average is that, appreciating and depreciating currencies are treated differently. The EER1 gives greater weight to currencies that have depreciated to a significant extent vis-à-vis the home currency (indicated by a large index R_{it}/R_{i0}), whereas EER2 gives greater weight to currencies which have appreciated significantly vis-à-vis the home currency (manifested by a large S_{it}/S_{i0}). This asymmetry arises from the fact that the "distance" between 0 and 1 is much smaller than that between 1 and infinity. Thus, in the case of EER1, an index R_{it}/R_{i0} to the amount of 10000 will have a much greater influence on the calculated average than an index R_{it}/R_{i0} of 0.0001, even though the magnitudes of two exchange rate changes are identical. The geometric average, on the other hand, treats appreciating and depreciating currencies in an entirely symmetric manner.

The third reason for preferring the geometric average is that the percentage change of the geometric effective exchange rate is independent of the base period, whereas for the arithmetic indices the result depends on the choice of an initial period.[19]

The number of currencies included and the weight of each currency in the

---

[19] For the geometric average this property follows at once from the fact that $[R_{i2}/R_{i0}]/[R_{i1}/R_{i0}] = R_{i2}/R_{i1}$. The derivation of the relative change in the arithmetic indices can be found in Brodsky (1982), p. 552.

Table 4.1 The Netherlands' most important trading partners

Country	Share in Dutch foreign trade (1975)[a]	Weight in MERM-index[b]
Belgium and Luxembourg	16.7	6.4
France	11.6	14.0
Germany	35.8	20.2
Italy	5.5	12.1
United Kingdom	9.6	3.2
United States	8.2	19.3

a Source: CBS, Maandstatistiek van de buitenlandse handel per land.
b Source: Artus and McGuirk (1981), Table 7. These weights are derived from the trade balance effects of a 10 percent devaluation in the IMF's Multilateral Exchange Rate Model (MERM). A description of this model and of the assumptions underlying the weights presented in the table can be found in Artus and McGuirk (1981). The Figure 6.4 in the row of Belgium and Luxembourg refers to Belgium only.

Table 4.2 The use of foreign currencies as an invoice currency of the Netherlands' foreign trade payments
(% of commodity imports or exports)

	Imports		Exports	
	1973	1976	1973	1976
US dollars	16.2	22.7	10.1	13.0
Pound sterling	10.9	7.6	10.7	4.7
Deutsche marks	24.8	21.6	21.5	21.1
Other currencies	21.9	16.7	12.4	11.0

Source: Van Nieuwkerk (1979), Table 2.

Table 4.3 The distribution of foreign assets and liabilities of Dutch banks by currency
(% of total amount)

	Assets		Liabilities	
	1975	1977	1975	1977
US dollars	50	47	58	51
pound sterling	1	3	6	5
Swiss franc	9	8	6	6
Deutsche mark	19	22	13	15

Source: Den Butter *et al.* (1979), Table 1.

index are determined by the aim of the study. In this respect two aims of the present study are relevant, namely the explanation of exchange rate fluctuations and the evaluation of various exchange rate regimes.

As has been discussed in Chapter 2, according to the modern theories of exchange rate determination the exchange rate is determined by both trade relations and financial capital flows. Tables 4.1 and 4.2 present some figures with regard to the Netherlands' foreign trade in the 1970s. Both the most important trading partners and invoice currencies are listed.

Table 4.3 shows some figures with regard to the currency composition of the Dutch commercial banks' foreign currency assets and liabilities. Data on the currency denomination of capital flows of the non-bank private sector are scarce. Available data suggest in this respect that the US dollar, the Deutsche mark and the Swiss franc are important currencies.[20] From the figures presented above we conclude that for the Netherlands important currencies are the US dollar, the Deutsche mark, the pound sterling, the French franc and the Swiss franc.

The data presented above indicate the currencies that play an important role in the foreign relations of the Netherlands. This information is relevant for calculating the currencies' weights in the effective exchange rate. In order to determine the number of currencies in the index, the second objective of the present study, namely evaluating different exchange rate regimes comes to the fore. In this respect three regimes are distinguished, *viz.* a floating exchange rate regime, a regime of fixed exchange rates, and of an adjustable peg regime. Since the fall of the system of Bretton Woods, the US dollar, the pound sterling and the Swiss franc have been floating against the Dutch guilder, whereas the remaining currencies in the tables have been participants in an exchange rate arrangement during the entire period (the Belgian franc and the Deutsche mark) or during a certain time interval (the French franc and the Italian lire). In order to reduce the number of expectations-generating formulas for the exchange rate, for each exchange rate regime some characteristic exchange rates have been selected as its representative rate. The Deutsche mark represents the fixed peg regime, the French franc the adjustable peg system and the US dollar and pound sterling represent the system of freely floating rates. Although the US dollar is the most important currency of the latter two, the pound sterling is also distinguished because the correlation between its rate and the dollar is not high and because of its role as a reserve currency, although this role is diminishing. The correlation coefficient between the Swiss franc and the Deutsche mark is positive and high. This result certainly reflects the Swiss monetary authorities' objective of stabilizing the franc's value with respect to the Deutsche mark. Because of this peculiar position, we decided to include the Swiss franc in the group of pegged

[20] See Van Nieuwkerk (1981), p. 259.

exchange rates.

To sum up, the Deutsche mark, the US dollar, the pound sterling and the French franc are included in the index. These four exchange rates reflect the various exchange rate regimes that were in force during the 1970s. The US dollar and the pound sterling represent the regime of freely floating exchange rates. The Deutsche mark and the French franc are representatives of a fixed and an adjustable peg system, respectively.

The weights of the currencies in the index are calculated from the weights used in Holtham (1986). When deriving these weights account was taken of: (a) the effects of trade flows, (b) the relative importance of reserve currencies and (c) the fact that a certain currency also represents some other currencies. The trade flow effects are derived from the Multilateral Exchange Rate Model. The reserve currency influence is obtained from data "on different currencies' commercial banks' holdings of foreign currencies and the currency composition of official reserves" (Holtham, 1986, p. 215).[21] The weights eventually obtained are: US dollar 0.318, Deutsche mark 0.51, French franc 0.117, pound sterling 0.055. These weights are also used for calculating the foreign interest rates.

4.3.6 *The proxy of exchange rate expectations*

The proxy of exchange rate expectations is obtained by means of the rolling regressions method presented in Chapter 3. When considering the multi-state Kalman filter and the rolling regressions method, we decided in favour of the latter, because the expectations proxies are derived for each of the four exchange rates separately. As argued above each exchange rate represents a particular exchange rate regime, so that it is not reasonable to apply the assumption underlying the multi-state Kalman filter, that for each exchange rate the economic agents form their expectations as a weighted average of various expectations- generating functions.

The rolling regressions procedure implicitly assumes that the time series of the exchange rate is stationary. A unit-roots test and a coefficient test have been calculated to check for non-stationarity of the level and the relative first difference of the four exchange rates included in the effective exchange rate. The results of these tests are presented in Table 4.4. Fuller (1976) gives a good description of this unit-roots test and presents the critical values of the statistic τ. A brief summary of this procedure is presented in the footnote to Table 4.4. The results presented in Table 4.4 show that the time series of the exchange rates'

---

[21] No data on capital flows are considered because no reliable data on the currency decomposition of these flows are available.

Table 4.4 Stability tests of the exchange rates

Regression: $X = C + X_{-1} + \Delta X_{-1}$

Dependent variable:	guilders per US dollars			guilders per pound sterling			
			Level				
C	X_{-1}	ΔX_{-1}	$\hat{\tau}$	C	X_{-1}	ΔX_{-1}	$\hat{\tau}$
	0.986 (0.005)		-2.58		0.985 (0.005)		-2.99
0.050 (0.07)	0.969 (0.03)		-1.16	0.085 (0.11)	0.972 (0.02)		-1.54
	0.988 (0.006)	0.115 (0.16)	-2.12		0.987 (0.01)	0.156 (0.16)	-2.30
0.058 (0.08)	0.967 (0.03)	0.132 (0.16)	-1.20	0.092 (0.12)	0.973 (0.02)	0.163 (0.16)	-1.46
			Relative differences				
C	X_{-1}	ΔX_{-1}	$\hat{\tau}$	C	X_{-1}	ΔX_{-1}	$\hat{\tau}$
	0.176 (0.16)		-5.27		0.227 (0.15)		-5.00
-0.011 (0.006)	0.069 (0.16)		-5.68	-0.010 (0.006)	0.135 (0.16)		-5.33
	0.076 (0.20)	0.126 (0.16)	-4.56		0.412 (0.20)	-.234 (0.16)	-3.00
-0.014 (0.01)	-0.141 (0.22)	0.232 (0.16)	-5.21	-0.008 (0.007)	0.291 (0.22)	-.172 (0.16)	-3.23

Table 4.4 (continued)

Dependent variable	guilders per French franc			guilders per Deutsche Mark			
			Level				
c	x_{-1}	Δx_{-1}	$\hat{\tau}$	c	x_{-1}	Δx_{-1}	$\hat{\tau}$
	0.993 (0.004)		-1.82		1.00 (0.002)		0.98
0.006 (0.02)	0.981 (0.03)		-0.56	0.12 (0.07)	0.88 (0.06)		-1.79
	0.994 (0.004)	0.179 (0.14)	-1.40		1.00 (0.002)	-.09 (0.13)	1.10
0.009 (0.02)	0.978 (0.03)	0.186 (0.14)	-0.66	0.12 (0.07)	0.89 (0.06)	-.09 (0.13)	-1.79
			Relative differences				
c	x_{-1}	Δx_{-1}	$\hat{\tau}$	c	x_{-1}	Δx_{-1}	$\hat{\tau}$
	0.217 (0.14)		-5.52		-.038 (0.13)		-8.30
-0.006 (0.004)	0.162 (0.15)		-5.71	0.003 (0.002)	-0.073 (0.13)		-8.40
	0.147 (0.17)	0.102 (0.14)	-4.94		-0.143 (0.18)	0.101 (0.19)	-6.31
-0.007 (0.004)	0.042 (0.18)	0.157 (0.14)	-5.24	0.004 (0.002)	-0.237 (0.19)	0.150 (0.13)	-6.51

Standard errors between parentheses. The statistic τ is defined as $\hat{\tau} = (\hat{\alpha} - 1)/\hat{s}$ where $\hat{\alpha}$ is the estimated coefficient for x_{-1} and $\hat{s}$ is its standard deviation. The critical values at the 5% level are -2.25 or -3.22 as the equation is estimated with or without an intercept for 50 observations (see Fuller, 1976, p. 373). The time series is considered to be stationary if $\hat{\tau}$ is smaller than this critical value.

relative first differences is a stationary process, whereas the exchange rates' level is non-stationary. We therefore decided to calculate a proxy of the expected relative change of the exchange rate.

The expected relative change of the Dutch guilder/US dollar and of the Dutch guilder/pound sterling exchange rate are assumed to be a function of the difference between the two expected inflation rates and of the expected value of the difference between the balance of current account of the countries concerned:

$$\overset{o}{e}{}^{e}_{i,t+1} = \alpha_{o,t} \{ \overset{o}{p}{}^{e}_{N,t+1} - \overset{o}{p}{}^{e}_{i,t+1} \} + \alpha_{1,t} \{ e_{i,t+1} CA_{i,t+1} - CA_{N,t+1} \}^{e}$$

$$i = US, UK \qquad (4.12)$$

where

$\overset{o}{e}{}^{e}_{US}(\overset{o}{e}{}^{e}_{UK})$ = the expected relative change of the Dutch guilder/ US dollar (Dutch guilder/pound sterling rate).

$\overset{o}{p}{}^{e}_{N}$ = the expected inflation rate in the Netherlands.

$\overset{o}{p}{}^{e}_{US}(\overset{o}{p}{}^{e}_{UK})$ = the expected rate of inflation in the United States (United Kingdom).

CA_N, CA_{US}, CA_{UK} = the balance of current account of the Netherlands, the United States and the United Kingdom, respectively. All in local currency.

$e_{US}(e_{UK})$ = the Dutch guilder/US dollar (Dutch guilder/pound sterling) exchange rate.

Indices of consumer prices are used for deriving the rates of inflation. Equation (4.12) is very similar to the expectations formula used in Hooper (1983 and 1986), Hooper and Morton (1982) and Pauly and Peterson (1986). The rationale behind this relation is discussed in Section 2.3, where it is shown that under certain assumptions changes in the equilibrium real exchange rate are directly related to movements in the current account. By definition the nominal exchange rate's percentage change is the sum of the real exchange rate's percentage change and the difference between the inflation rates. Consequently, the expected percentage change of the bilateral exchange rate is influenced by the difference between the expected Dutch current account balance corrected for the expected current account balance of the foreign country concerned and the expected domestic and foreign inflation rates.[22] The pressure of a country on the foreign

[22] According to Frankel and Froot (1985), the expected relative inflation is among the determinants of survey data of the expected exchange rate. Thus, although according to the literature mentioned in section 2.6.3, the purchasing power parity does not hold, agents use this parity for deriving their expectations. Since in this section we are modelling the parivate agents' expectation formation,

exchange market is assumed to be reflected in the size of CA. Note that all variables in (4.12) are related to the goods market. This does not mean that in this respect we deny the importance of capital flows, but it reflects our assumption that the expectations moving these flows are anchored in the real sector of the economy. Moreover the coefficients α in (4.12) can be smaller than 1 which would reflect the assumption that the economic agents expect the exchange rate will gradually incorporate the real factors. The resulting expectations proxy is a member of the class of weak forms of rational expectations (see Chapter 3). In accordance with the discussion in Chapter 3, the coefficients in equation (4.12) are estimated by the rolling regressions technique.[23]

When approximating the expected relative first difference of the Dutch guilder/French franc and the Dutch guilder/Deutsche mark rate, the restrictions on exchange rate changes exerted by the EEC exchange rate arrangements is captured by the relative difference of the actual exchange rate from its parity rate.

The resulting formula of the expected relative first difference of the Dutch guilder/French franc is

$$\overset{\circ}{e}{}^{e}_{FR,t+1} = \alpha_{0t}\{\overset{\circ}{p}{}^{e}_{N,t+1} - \overset{\circ}{p}{}^{e}_{FR,t+1}\} + \alpha_{1t}\{e_{FR,t+1}CA_{FR,t+1} - CA_{N,t+1}\}^{e}$$
$$+ \alpha_{2t}\{\tilde{e}_{FR} - e_{FR})/e_{FR} \tag{4.13}$$

where $\tilde{e}_{FR}$ is the parity value of the Dutch guilder/French franc rate and the other variables have a similar meaning as those in (4.12). The parity value is set equal to the market rate during periods in which France was not a member of an exchange rate arrangement. The last term in (4.13) reflects the assumption that if France is a member of an exchange arrangement the agents in the private sector expect the central banks to defend the parity rate. The agents take into account that the authorities can defend the parity rate agreed upon only if this rate roughly fits the rate implied by the fundamental determinants. Thus the expected inflation differential and the expected relative current accounts remain in the formula of the expected relative change of the exchange rate to incorporate the possibility of speculative movements against the parity rate.

The expected relative change of the Dutch guilder/Deutsche mark is solely determined by the exchange rate arrangement

---

the relative prices are used as an explanatory variable.

[23] Note that although Pauly and Peterson use the substitution method, they consider the rolling regression technique as a probably superior alternative. Their most important argument for not applying this procedure is that it introduces "the need for an extra loop in the maxi-LINK solution to update the expectational variable" (Pauly and Peterson, 1986, p. 155).

$$\overset{\circ}{e}{}^{e}_{WG} = (\tilde{e}_{WG} - e_{WG})/e_{WG} \tag{4.14}$$

where $\tilde{e}_{WG}$ is the parity rate of the Dutch guilder/Deutsche mark exchange. Thus it is assumed that the private agents have confidence in the Dutch central bank's aim of a stable exchange rate between the Dutch guilder and the currency of the low-inflation country West-Germany. This is a kind of regressive expectations, where the expected equilibrium rate corresponds with the parity rate.

The expected inflation terms and the expected relative current account $(e_i.CA_i - CA_N)^e$, i = US, UK and FR in equations (4.12) and (4.13) are assumed to be generated by autoregressive processes. The expectations of these variables are obtained by a rolling regression of the assumed autoregressive process. For example, the expected inflation rate in the Netherlands is derived as

$$\overset{\circ}{p}_{Nt} = \Sigma^{q}_{i=1}\, \beta_{it}\, \overset{\circ}{p}_{N,t-i} \tag{4.15}$$

where q represents the degree of the autoregressive process. The equation is re-estimated for every period t where t starts with 1970:I and ends with 1980:IV. The vector $\overset{\circ}{p}_{Nt}$ contains observations of the inflation rate from 1967:III up to and including period 1980:IV, where the quarters 1967:III - 1969:IV serve as the starting period from which the first estimates are obtained. The resulting expected inflation is

$$\overset{\circ}{p}{}^{e}_{N,t+1} = \Sigma^{q}_{i=1}\, \hat{\beta}_{it}\, \overset{\circ}{p}_{N,t-i+1} \tag{4.16}$$

From some preliminary regressions it appeared that an autoregressive process of the second order describes the inflation rates reasonably well; we therefore assume that q=2 in the expected inflation generating functions. The current account differentials show a strong seasonal pattern so that a fourth-order autoregressive process, q=4, seems to be a good choice.

The resulting time series of the expected inflation rates and the expected relative current accounts are substituted in (4.12) and (4.13). Thereafter, the expected exchange rate is obtained by rolling regressions estimates of this equation on data from the same period as that used for estimating the parameters of (4.15).

The expected relative change of the exchange rate used in the model is a weighted average of the four expected relative changes described above. The weights are those determined for the effective exchange rate.

4.4 The accounting and analytical framework of the financial model

The accounting framework underlying our specification of the monetary part of the model is presented in Table 4.5. The different sectors are listed in the headings of the columns 1-5. Throughout the book the following superscripts are used for representing the sectors

cb = central bank
b = banks
p = private sector
g = government
f = foreign sector

Table 4.5 The accounting framework (stocks at the end of 1978)*

Sectors	1	2	3	4	5	6	7
Assets and liabilities	Central Bank	Banks	Private sector	Government	Foreigners	Total	Yield
Money	-18714	-41473	59481	706		0	-
Unborrowed reserves	4225	-4225				0	r_{cb}
International monetary reserves	21983				-21983	0	$r_{sf}+\mathring{e}^e$
Short-term domestic assets		-14082	29275	-16333	1140	0	r_s
Short-term bank loans		62835	-62835			0	r_{sl}
Net foreign assets		1612	68544		-70156	0	$r_f+\mathring{e}^e$
Long-term domestic assets		6565	77491	-138750	54694	0	r_l

* Amounts are in millions of guilders. Source: See the Appendix containing the list of symbols and description of the data of the quarterly model.

Banks are defined as the money-creating institutions exclusive of the central bank and the government. The private sector is heterogeneous, because it includes households, corporations, institutional investors, and mortgage banks. The government consists of the central and the local government.

The rows in Table 4.5 show the different assets and liabilities, namely

M1 = money consisting of currency and demand deposits.
RU = unborrowed reserves of banks
RES = international monetary reserves of the central bank
NDAS = net domestic assets, short-term
LS = short-term bank loans
NFA = net foreign assets of banks and the non-bank private sector
NDAL = net domestic assets, long-term

The precise definitions and sources of these and all other variables of the empirical model are listed in the Appendix to this book. Assets (liabilities) enter with a positive (negative) sign in the table.

The seventh column in Table 4.5 lists the yields on the various assets. They are

r_{cb} = official discount rate
r_s = interest rate on short-term domestic assets
r_l = interest rate on long-term domestic assets
r_{sf} = interest rate on short-term foreign assets
r_f = interest rate on foreign assets
$\mathring{e}^e$ = expected relative change of the exchange rate
r_{ls} = interest rate on short-term bank loans

Money, which consists of currency and demand deposits, is assumed to be non-interest bearing because the interest on demand deposits is low and constant and that on currency is zero. The foreign investments in domestic assets are assumed to be liabilities of the private sector, because no reliable data are available for decomposing these investments in liabilities of the private sector and the government. The foreign short-term and long-term assets are included in one single asset. The number of interest-bearing assets has been restricted to the most relevant ones. From earlier studies of the Dutch financial sector and from a principal components analysis of interest rates, it appears that there are mainly two interest rates,[24] *viz.* a short-term interest rate and a long-term interest rate. All other interest rates can be largely explained by one or both of these two rates. Thus apart from the interest rate on short-term bank loans, only two domestic interest rates are endogenous in the present model, *viz.* the interest rate on short-term assets and the interest rate on long-term assets.

---

[24] The principal components analysis of interest rates is presented in Dongelmans and Fase (1975). The studies of the Dutch financial sector are De Nederlandsche Bank (1984), Van Loo (1983), Van den Berg, Don and Sandee (1983).

Residents of the rest of the world hold assets denominated in Dutch guilders and Dutch inhabitants hold foreign assets. Hence, according to the terminology of Section 2.2.1, the model belongs to the preferred-habitat approach of exchange rate determination.

4.5 The private sector's financial behaviour

The private sector's assets and liabilities are shown in the sector's balance sheet in Table 4.6. The short-term domestic assets consist of the non-interest bearing

Table 4.6 Balance sheet of the private sector
(end 1978, millions of guilders)

Assets				Liabilities
M1		59481	LS	62835
$NDAS^p$		30415	$NDAS^f$	1140
NDALS	72947		$NDAL^f$	54694
$NDALC^p$	4544			
$NDAL^p$		77491		
NFA^p		68544	W^p	117262
		235931		235931

money stock M1 (currency and demand deposits) and short-term net domestic assets, $NDAS^p$ (short-term time and saving deposits with banks). The corresponding item in Table 4.5 is comprised of the private sector's short-term assets $NDAS^p$ minus the short-term claims by foreigners $NDAS^f$ (29275 = 30415 - 1140). The stock of long-term net domestic assets, $NDAL^p$, at the end of 1978 is made up of the cumulative net supply on the capital market, $NDALC^p$, and of the stock of long-term deposits with banks, NDALS, which at the end of 1978 were equal to 4544 and 72947 millions of guilders, respectively. The private sector's foreign assets consist of both long- and short-term claims. The private sector's short-term liabilities comprise short-term bank loans granted to the private sector, LS, and short-term domestic assets held by foreigners, $NDAS^f$. The long-term liabilities consist of the long-term net domestic assets held by foreigners. The private sector's net financial wealth, W^p, is the balancing item of the balance sheet.

Except for the balancing item W^p, behavioural equations are estimated for all entries in Table 4.6. Relations of the foreigners' holdings of domestic assets are presented in Section 4.6. Presently, equations are described for the changes in the private sector's holdings of the remaining four assets and one liability.

As explanatory variables of these changes we have considered
- the stocks of assets lagged one period
- the (expected) yields

- a measure of the utilization of production capacity, q
- the level of nominal national income, Y
- the presence and size of the gross credit ceiling, ncc
- seasonal dummies, S1, S2, S3

The assets are assumed to be gross substitutes. In contrast to some other studies (De Nederlandsche Bank, 1983, and Hasselman *et al.*, 1983, e.g.) the coefficients of the yields are not constrained to be symmetrical.[25] In addition to the expected yield on foreign interest bearing assets, the expected change of the exchange rate has been included in the set of explanatory variables to test for currency substitution (see Chapter 2). The utilization of production capacity captures the influence of the stage of the business cycle on the allocation of financial wealth. We expect that an increase in economic activity will lead to a rise in the private sector's holdings of short-term assets. The value of national income reflects the transaction motive. During the first part of our sample period gross credit ceilings were in force in the form of a maximum permissible growth percentage for short-term bank loans granted to the private sector. This instrument of the central bank is expected to have reduced the private sector's holdings of short-term bank loans.[26] Finally, seasonal dummies are included to capture potential seasonal influences on the allocation of the private sector's financial wealth.

From the unrestricted estimates presented in Appendix B it appears that in equation (4.8) the absolute value of the estimated adjustment parameter δ_{11} is high, whereas the estimates of δ_{1j}, j = 2,...,5 and δ_{i1}, i = 2,...,5 have a wrong sign or are statistically insignificant. Consequently, it has been assumed that the demand for currency and demand deposits reaches its equilibrium value within a quarter: i.e. $\delta_{11} = 1$ and $\delta_{i1} = \delta_{1j} = 0$, i, j = 2,...,5.

The preferred estimates of the first stage are presented in the upper part of Table 4.7. In accordance with the procedure described in Section 4.3.1, at the beginning of the second stage the interest rates' long-term coefficients - the β_{jk} in equation (4.8) - that are off-diagonal and positive are set at zero. This regression revealed that the long-term coefficient of $r_f+\mathring{e}^e$ (r_l) in the equation of $\Delta NDAL^p$ ($-\Delta LS$) also had to be constrained to zero. The ultimate results of the estimation process are presented in the lower part of Table 4.7.

The influence of the gross credit ceiling appeared to be statistically

---

[25] Roley showed that, if the assets demand equations are derived from the frequently used mean-variance model, the symmetry restrictions imply that investors exhibit constant risk aversion with respect to the mean of the argument of the utility function (see Roley, 1983, for details).

[26] More details on the gross credit ceilings can be found in Van Loo (1983), p.181.

Table 4.7 Estimates of the private sector's financial behaviour*

Results of the first stage

	$\frac{M1_{-1}}{FA^P_{-1}}$	$\frac{NDAS^P_{-1}}{FA^P_{-1}}$	$\frac{NDAL^P_{-1}}{FA^P_{-1}}$	$\frac{NFA^P_{-1}}{FA^P_{-1}}$	$\frac{-LS_{-1}}{FA^P_{-1}}$	r_s	r_l	$r_f + \dot{e}^e$	r_{ls}	$\frac{Y_{-1}}{FA^P_{-1}}$	q	ncc	s1
$\Delta M1 / FA^P_{-1}$	-1	0	0	0	0	-.0121 (4.33)	-.0245 (2.84)	-.0011 (0.54)	0.0	0.7072 (5.12)	-.1262 (2.79)	-.0027 (0.75)	0.0037 (0.94)
$\Delta NDAS^P / FA^P_{-1}$	0	-.6887 (7.77)	-.5781 (7.32)	0	-.1721 (4.76)	0.0515 (4.71)	0.0179 (1.50)	-.0060 (2.34)	-.0409 (4.26)	-.4144 (2.50)	0.0389 (0.59)	0.0	0.0015 (0.31)
$\Delta NDAL^P / FA^P_{-1}$	0	0	-.1439 (1.71)	0	-.1119 (5.33)	-.0176 (3.83)	-.0200 (1.11)	0.0035 (1.88)	0.0203 (2.85)	-.1832 (1.64)	-.0764 (1.73)	0.0	-.0052 (1.89)
$\Delta FA^P / FA^P_{-1}$	0	-.2665 (8.71)	-.2780 (8.84)	-.6366 (3.79)	-.4860 (11.39)	-.0051 (2.05)	0.0147 (2.94)	0.0019 (0.93)	0.0041 (1.03)	-.0174 (0.25)	0.1032 (3.96)	0.0	0.0
$-\Delta LS / FA^P_{-1}$	0	-.0448 (1.39)	0.0	-.3634 (3.79)	-.2300 (2.90)	-.0167 (4.11)	0.0119 (1.36)	0.0017 (0.98)	0.0166 (1.48)	-.0922 (0.77)	0.0606 (1.47)	0.0027 (0.92)	0.0
Σ	-1	-1	-1	-1	-1	0	0	0	0	0	0	0	0

Results of the second stage

	$\frac{M1_{-1}}{FA^P_{-1}}$	$\frac{NDAS^P_{-1}}{FA^P_{-1}}$	$\frac{NDAL^P_{-1}}{FA^P_{-1}}$	$\frac{NFA^P_{-1}}{FA^P_{-1}}$	$\frac{-LS_{-1}}{FA^P_{-1}}$	r_s	r_l	$r_f + \dot{e}^e$	r_{ls}	$\frac{Y_{-1}}{FA^P_{-1}}$	q	ncc	s1
$\Delta M1 / FA^P_{-1}$	-1	0	0	0	0	-.0138 (5.86)	-.0219 (2.94)	-.0005 (0.23)	0.0	0.7719 (6.38)	-.1298 (2.89)	0.0	0.0046 (1.39)
$\Delta NDAS^P / FA^P_{-1}$	0	-.6887 (-)	-.5781 (-)	0	-.1721 (-)	0.0486	0.0126	-.0054	-.0356	-.4474 (3.34)	0.0514 (1.04)	0.0	0.0004 (0.11)
$\Delta NDAL^P / FA^P_{-1}$	0	0	-.1439 (-)	0	-.1119 (-)	-0.0085	0.0031	0.0	0.0033	-.0993 (0.91)	-.1406 (3.72)	0.0	-.0050 (2.02)
$\Delta FA^P / FA^P_{-1}$	0	-.2665 (-)	-.2780 (-)	-.6366 (-)	-.4860 (-)	-0.0129	0.0061	0.0032	0.0143	-.0300 (0.45)	0.1286 (5.52)	0.0	0.0
$-\Delta LS / FA^P_{-1}$	0	-.0448 (-)	0	-.3634 (-)	-.2300 (-)	-0.0134	0.0	0.0027	0.0179	-.1951 (2.22)	0.0903 (3.02)	0.0	0.0
Σ	-1	-1	-1	-1	-1	0	0	0	0	0	0	0	0

Table 4.7 (continued)

	s2	s3	FA^p/FA^p_{-1}	R^2 (adj.)	see	DW	r_s	r_l	$r_f + \mathring{e}^e$	r_{ls}	Y/FA^p_{-1}
Results of the first stage											Long-term coefficients**
$\Delta M1 / FA^p_{-1}$	0.0213 (6.39)	0.0064 (2.76)	0.2429 (5.29)	.841	.008	1.03	-.0121 (4.33)	-.0245 (2.85)	-.0012 (0.53)	0.0	0.7072
$\Delta NDAS^p / FA^p_{-1}$	-.0168 (4.45)	0.0	0.4245 (5.43)	.754	.009	1.53	0.3733	0.1022	-.0124	0.0385	-2.4240
$\Delta NDAL^p / FA^p_{-1}$	0.0	0.0	0.2075 (5.38)	.685	.007	1.67	0.2131	-.0609	-.0078	-.2765	4.3060
$\Delta FA^p / FA^p_{-1}$	0.0	-.0064 (5.76)	0.1284 (5.46)	-.203	.004	2.31	0.2268	0.0835	-.0198	-.2990	4.5837
$-\Delta LS / FA^p_{-1}$	-.0045 (2.25)	0.0	-.0034 (.13)	.207	.006	2.07	-.4316	-.1002	0.0412	0.5370	-7.1729
Σ	0	0	1.0				0.0	0.0	0.0	0.0	0.0
Results of the second stage											
$\Delta M1 / FA^p_{-1}$	0.0220 (7.72)	0.0066 (3.06)	0.2164 (7.13)	.840	.008	.98	-.0138 (5.86)	-.0219 (2.94)	-.0005 (0.23)	0.0	0.7719
$\Delta NDAS^p / FA^p_{-1}$	-.0175 (5.70)	0.0	0.4278 (12.78)	.812	.008	1.55	0.0894 (9.56)	0.0	-.0078 (2.46)	0.0	-3.7139
$\Delta NDAL^p / FA^p_{-1}$	0.0	0.0	0.2150 (9.87)	.724	.007	1.64	0.0	0.0219 (3.24)	0.0	-.1140 (5.84)	6.3416
$\Delta FA^p / FA^p_{-1}$	0.0	-.0066 (5.44)	0.1150 (9.26)	.611	.004	1.74	0.0	0.0	0.0082 (4.13)	-.0621 (4.42)	5.6411
$-\Delta LS / FA^p_{-1}$	-.0045 (2.57)	0.0	0.0248 (1.49)	.225	.006	1.88	-.0756 (11.96)	0.0	0.0	0.1761 (6.92)	-9.0407
Σ	0.0	0.0	0.0				0.0	0.0	0.0	0.0	0.0

* The figures between brackets are the absolute values of the t-statistic. The variables: r_s, r_l, $r_f + \mathring{e}^e$ and r_{ls} are multiplied by FA^p/FA^p_{-1}. During the second stage of the estimation procedure the interest rates' coefficients are derived by multiplying the adjustment parameters and the long-term coefficients

** Long-term coefficients are the parameters B_{jk} in equation (4.8). Coefficients that appeared to be wrongly signed are zero. Non-zero coefficients for which no absolute value of the t-statistic are published are obtained by inverting the coefficient matrix of adjustment parameters.

insignificant. The coefficients of national income are in accordance with the transaction motive i.e. it positively influences the demand for money. Note that the coefficient of Y in the demand relation of net foreign assets is insignificant and negative, so that at first sight the currency substitution model presented in Chapter 2 has to be rejected. The corresponding long-term parameter (5.6411) is positive, however, and thus confirms the existence of the currency substitution model. Since no t-statistic of this parameter is derived no definite conclusion with regard to the relevance of the currency substitution model can be made.

4.6 The banks' financial behaviour

The banks' balance sheet containing the assets and liabilities underlying the figures presented in the accounting framework (Table 4.5) is shown below.

Table 4.8 Balance sheet of the banking sector
(end 1978 millions of guilders)

Assets			Liabilities
RU	-4225	D	41507
$NDAS^b$	17567	$NDAS^p$	30415
$NDAL^b$	79512	$NDAS^g$	1234
NFA^b	1612	NDALS	72947
LS	62835	W^b	11198
	157301		157301

It is assumed that the volume of LS, D, $NDAS^p$ and NDALS which forms part of $NDAL^p$ are determined by the private sector, whereas the banks determine the relevant interest rates. The short-term domestic assets held by the government, $NDAS^g$, are assumed to be exogenous. In the present section relations are estimated for the change in the remaining assets

RU =unborrowed reserves of banks

$NDAS^b$ =short-term government debt held by banks

$NDAL^b$ =the banks' net holdings of long-term domestic assets

NFA^b =the banks' net holdings of foreign assets

The explanatory variables of the flows of these items can be divided into five groups. The first four variables are the one-period lagged stocks of the endogenous variables; their coefficients are minus the adjustment parameter δ_{ij}. The second group consists of the assets' yields. The central bank's discount rate has been deleted from the explanatory variables because it is highly correlated with the domestic short-term interest rate. Including both variables would most likely bias the results.[27] As will be shown below, the official discount rate is an explanatory variable of the rate on short-term loans and thus indirectly influences the other domestic rates. The third group comprises two variables, *viz.* the private sector's holdings of short-term time and savings deposits, $NDAS^p$, and that sector's long-term claims on banks, NDALS. These two variables reflect the banks' matching behaviour; an increase (decrease) of their short (long)-term liabilities will be offset by an increase (decrease) of their short (long)-term assets.

The fourth group of explanatory variables consists of instruments of monetary policy. The following five tools have been included in the specification.[28] First there are, dollarswaps, SWAP, which are temporary purchases of dollars by De Nederlandsche Bank N.V. from the banks for a specified period. These arrangements are expected to increase the banks' holdings of short-term domestic assets, especially unborrowed reserves, and to decrease their holdings of foreign assets.

Secondly, the central bank's direct intervention on the foreign exchange market measured by the change of the monetary reserves,[29] ΔRES, influences ΔRU and ΔNFA^b in the same way as the dollarswaps.

Thirdly, special loans granted at market rates, SPL, are introduced in 1975 to meet the banks' demand for cash balances. The special loans are included in the banks' demand for discounts and advances, RL, and thus directly influence the unborrowed reserves, $RU = R - RL$, which consists of the banks' reserves, R, minus the banks' borrowed reserves, RL. A rise in SPL thus decreases ΔRU. It raises the funds available for investments and therefore positively influences $\Delta NDAS^b$ and ΔNFA^b.

Fourthly, there is the change in the holdings of required reserves, ΔRR. Banks do not receive any interest payments on these reserves. An increase in required reserves may necessitate a rise in bank reserves, R, and thus RU, which goes at the expense of the banks' holdings of other assets.

---

[27] The same reasoning can be found in Sterken (1986), p. 25.

[28] An extensive description of the instruments of Dutch monetary policy can be found in Den Dunnen (1985). Van Loo (1983) presents the most detailed econometric study of the influence of monetary policy measures on the banks' behaviour.

[29] It should be noted that the change in the central bank's monetary reserves is a rough measure of the bank's intervention on the foreign exchange market. Therefore, the central bank's holdings of foreign currency reserves have been corrected for some institutional aspects. See the list of symbols for details. This proxy has been used, because the Dutch central bank does not publish a time series of its interventions on the foreign exchange market. See Den Dunnen (1985), pp. 92 and 93 for details.

Finally, from mid-1973 to November 1979 the liquidity-reserve arrangement has been used.[30] According to this arrangement banks were required to hold a minimal amount of short-term assets, mainly treasury bills, corresponding to a certain percentage of their short-term liabilities. The central bank had the power to change this percentage, lq. Of course the interest payments received by the banks were equal to the relevant market rates. The arrangement also contained a different percentage for the minimal amount of the banking sector's long-term domestic assets in relation to their long-term liabilities. In practice the arrangement mostly referred to the short-term liabilities/assets. We, therefore, only considered the liquidity percentage for the short-term liabilities. In the equations the change of the liquidity percentage is related to the private sector's holdings of domestic short-term assets, $\Delta lq \cdot NDAS^p$. An increase lq is expected to increase the banks' holdings of domestic short-term assets, $NDAS^b$. Since the total arrangement also referred to the banks' domestic long-term liabilities, it might be that the coefficient in the $\Delta NDASL^b$ equation is positive too. We expect that this coefficient is smaller than the corresponding one in the relation of the banks' short-term domestic assets.

The last group of explanatory variables comprises the seasonal dummies and the term $FA^b/FA^b(-1)$.

The ultimately preferred estimates of the estimation procedure's first (second) stage are presented in the upper (lower) part of Table 4.9. When comparing these results with the list of explanatory variables described above, it emerges that the dollarswaps and the required reserves had to be excluded from the regressions because they did not show up with a right sign in at least two equations. The coefficient of $\Delta lq \cdot NDAS^p$ is positive in both the relation of the banks' holdings of short-term and long-term domestic assets. As noted above this corresponds with the fact that the liquidity-reserve arrangement referred to both short-term and long-term liabilities. Furthermore, it appears that the instruments of monetary policy do not determine the banks' holdings of long-term domestic assets significantly. This most probably reflects the central bank's ability to control the money market more directly than the capital market.

As in many other studies of the Dutch financial sector, the volume of short-term bank loans granted to the private sector is assumed to be determined by the private sector's financial behaviour (see Section 4.5). The interest rate on these loans, r_{ls}, is set by the banks. Until August 1973 this rate was equal to the central bank's discount rate, r_{cb}, plus a mark-up. In September 1973 a quota scheme for bank borrowing from the central bank was introduced. According to this system a bank has to pay a surcharge as soon as it exceeds its quota. Since

---

[30] A description of this instrument can be found in De Nederlandsche Bank, Kwartaalberichten, 1973 (2), pp. 43-54.

Table 4.9 Estimates of the banking sector's behaviour*

Results of the first stage

	RU_{-1}/FA^b_{-1}	$NDAS^b_{-1}/FA^b_{-1}$	$NDAL^b_{-1}/FA^b_{-1}$	NFA^b_{-1}/FA^b_{-1}	r_s	r_l	$r_f + \dot{e}^e$	$NDAS^p/FA^b_{-1}$	$NDALS/FA^b_{-1}$	$\Delta lq{\cdot}NDAS^p/FA^b_{-1}$	$\Delta SPL/FA^b_{-1}$
$\Delta RU / FA^b_{-1}$	-.7950 (2.00)	-.2340 (2.25)	-.2269 (2.79)	-.3402 (3.91)	0.1411 (0.39)	1.9591 (1.78)	0.3646 (1.44)	-.730 (1.58)	-.1358 (1.92)	-.0028 (1.58)	-.4125 (3.03)
$\Delta NDAS^b / FA^b_{-1}$	0.0	-.4858 (2.98)	-.4219 (4.29)	-.3539 (3.36)	0.1939 (0.26)	0.5437 (0.41)	-.3040 (1.04)	0.1339 (1.45)	0.2234 (2.69)	0.0044 (1.51)	0.4125 (2.50)
$\Delta NDAL^b / FA^b_{-1}$	-.2050 (2.00)	-.2802 (3.25)	-.1846 (1.51)	0.0	-.1647 (0.47)	2.2027 (1.16)	-.6668 (2.81)	-.0317 (0.71)	0.1221 (1.09)	0.0	0.0
$\Delta NFA^b / FA^b_{-1}$	0.0	0.0	-.1666 (5.26)	-.3059 (2.99)	-.1703 (.57)	-.7874 (0.88)	0.6062 (1.72)	-.0292 (0.86)	-.2097 (4.90)	-.0017 (1.89)	0.0
Σ	-1.0	-1.0	-1.0	-1.0	0.0	0.0	0.0	0.0	0.0	0.0	0.0

Results of the second stage***

	RU_{-1}/FA^b_{-1}	$NDAS^b_{-1}/FA^b_{-1}$	$NDAL^b_{-1}/FA^b_{-1}$	NFA^b_{-1}/FA^b_{-1}	r_s	r_l	$r_f + \dot{e}^e$	$NDAS^p/FA^b_{-1}$	$NDALS/FA^b_{-1}$	$\Delta lq{\cdot}NDAS^p/FA^b_{-1}$	$\Delta SPL/FA^b_{-1}$
$\Delta RU / FA^b_{-1}$	-.7950 (-)	-.2340 (-)	-.2269 (-)	-.3402 (-)	-.0069	-1.7099	0.3973	-.0691 (2.39)	-.1338 (7.02)	-.0029 (1.73)	-.4100 (3.21)
$\Delta NDAS^b / FA^b_{-1}$	0.0	-.4858 (-)	-.4219 (-)	-.3539 (-)	0.0466	0.5512	-.2778	0.1441 (2.55)	0.2283 (10.94)	0.0043 (1.60)	0.4100 (2.75)
$\Delta NDAL^b / FA^b_{-1}$	-.2050 (-)	-.2802 (-)	-.1846 (-)	0.0	0.0570	2.0388	-.7092	-.0431 (1.75)	0.1163 (3.72)	0.0	0.0
$\Delta NFA^b / FA^b_{-1}$	0.0	0.0	-.1666 (-)	-.3059 (-)	-.0967	-.8802	-.5897	-.0319 (1.34)	-.2109 (13.61)	-.0015 (1.13)	0.0
Σ	-1.0	-1.0	-1.0	-1.0	0.0	0.0	0.0	0.0	0.0	0.0	0.0

Table 4.9 (continued)

Results of the first stage

	$\Delta RES/FA^b_{-1}$	S1	S2	S3	FA^b/FA^b_{-1}	R^2(adj.)	s.e.e.	DW	Long-term coefficients** r_s	r_l	$r_l + \mathring{e}^e$
$\Delta RU / FA^b_{-1}$	0.4392	-.0073	-.0039	-.0065	0.3747	0.81	0.009	2.30	-.3474	0.0045	0.0569
	(6.27)	(1.31)	(0.72)	(1.22)	(5.22)						
$\Delta NDAS^b / FA^b_{-1}$	0.2499	0.0046	0.0147	-.0063	0.2118	0.55	0.011	2.11	3.6746	-9.2691	1.1814
	(3.02)	(0.74)	(2.37)	(1.45)	(2.51)						
$\Delta NDAL^b / FA^b_{-1}$	0.0	-.0173	-.0186	-.0051	0.1081	0.37	0.009	1.67	-6.0834	25.9961	-1.8824
		(4.11)	(4.83)	(1.44)	(4.07)						
$\Delta NFA^b / FA^b_{-1}$	-.6891	0.0053	0.0	0.0050	0.3051	0.85	0.008	1.93	2.7562	-16.7316	3.0069
	(8.41)	(1.85)		(1.83)	(7.07)						
Σ	0.0	0.0	0.0	0.0	1.0				0.0	0.0	0.0

Results of the second stage

	$\Delta RES/FA^b_{-1}$	S1	S2	S3	FA^b/FA^b_{-1}	R^2(adj.)	s.e.e.	DW	r_s	r_l	$r_l + \mathring{e}^e$
$\Delta RU / FA^b_{-1}$	0.4388	0.0071	0.0037	0.0062	0.3691	0.85	0.009	2.30	-.0002	0.0	0.0
	(7.15)	(1.69)	(1.01)	(1.80)	(21.88)				(0.04)		
$\Delta NDAS^b / FA^b_{-1}$	0.2521	0.0041	0.0146	-.0066	0.2074	0.76	0.010	2.11	-.0060	-0.0697	-.0058
	(3.55)	(0.87)	(3.43)	(1.65)	(11.54)				(0.29)	(0.65)	(0.27)
$\Delta NDAL^b / FA^b_{-1}$	0.0	-.0166	-.0183	-.0046	0.1159	0.61	0.009	1.68	-.0058	0.2162	-.0297
		(4.95)	(5.84)	(1.47)	(7.98)				(0.33)	(1.44)	(0.85)
$\Delta NFA^b / FA^b_{-1}$	-.6909	0.0055	0.0	0.0050	0.3076	0.90	0.007	1.92	0.0	-.1465	0.0354
	(9.83)	(2.01)		(2.02)	(20.96)					(2.61)	(2.17)
Σ	0.0	0.0	0.0	0.0	1.0				0.0	0.0	0.0

* The figures between brackets are the absolute values of the t-statistic. The variables: r_s, r_l and $r_f + \mathring{e}^e$ are multiplied by FA^b/FA^b_{-1}. During the second stage of the estimation procedure the interest rates' coefficients are derived by multiplyin2g the adjustment parameters and the long-term coefficients.

** Long-term coefficients are the parameters β_{jk} in equation (4.8). Coefficients that appeared to be wrongly signed are zero. Non-zero coefficients for which no absolute value of the t-statistic are published are obtained by inverting the coefficient matrix of adjustment parameters.

*** Note that the specification of the second stage is the same as that of the first stage. Thus in this case, the use of our two-stage procedure eliminates the specification bias.

October 1973 the banks have imposed an additional flexible mark-up on the loan rate, which depends on the tightness of the market for short-term investments. This mark-up is represented by $r_s - r_{cb}$. Other explanatory variables of r_{ls} are the private sector's demand for loans, measured by $[LS_{-1}/FA^b_{-1} - LS_{-2}/FA^b_{-2}]$, the tightness of credit ceilings represented by ncc, the discount rate and the lagged loan rate, which represents adjustments lags.

The estimation period of the equation of r_{ls} has been divided into two subperiods because of the above-described change of the regime in 1973. During the first period, which covers 1970:I to 1973:II the rate on bank loans is determined by the central bank's deposit rate only. For the period 1973:III - 1980:IV the other explanatory variables are also considered. The Durbin-Watson statistic of the relations estimated by OLS indicated first order autocorrelation in the disturbances. After correction for this autocorrelation, the results are

$$r_{ls} = \underset{(10.74)}{1.0009}\, r_{cb} + \underset{(4.43)}{0.589}$$

estimation period: 1970:I - 1973:II
R^2(adj.) = 0.91 DW = 1.53 $\rho = \underset{(0.99)}{0.044}$

$$r_{ls} = \underset{(13.32)}{0.951}\, r_{cb} + \underset{(1.92)}{0.137}\, r_{cb}(-1)$$
$$+ \underset{(1.83)}{1.553} \left\{ \frac{LS(-1)}{FA^b_{-1}} - \frac{LS(-2)}{FA^b_{-1}} \right\} + \underset{(1.65)}{0.078}\, ncc + \underset{(6.81)}{0.595}$$

estimation period:1973:III - 1980:IV
R^2(adj.) = 0.98 DW = 1.83 $\rho = \underset{(1.66)}{0.339}$

where the coefficient ρ is the estimated serial correlation coefficient and the absolute value of a parameter's t-statistic is shown between brackets below the relevant coefficient.[31]

---

[31] The estimated equations without correction for autocorrelation are

$$r_{ls} = \underset{(11.45)}{0.976}\, r_{cb} + \underset{(5.00)}{0.618}$$

estimation period: 1970: I - 1973: II
R^2(adj.) = 0.91 DW = 1.14

$$r_{ls} = \underset{(14.08)}{0.920}\, r_{cb} + \underset{(2.55)}{0.165}\, r_{cb}(-1)$$

The above-mentioned approximation of the mark up, $r_s - r_{cb}$, did not show up with a significant coefficient in any regression and thus is excluded from the ultimately selected relation. The coefficient of ncc is also slightly insignificant.

4.7 The foreigners' financial behaviour

The foreigners' investments in short-term and long-term domestic assets are endogenous. As in the preceding sections it is assumed that these flows can be represented by a partial adjustment specification. Contrary to the domestic sectors' behaviour only a very small part of the foreigners' portfolio is modelled. Consequently, the adding-up restrictions resulting from the balance sheet are neglected and the scaling variable need not be equal to the foreigners' total wealth. Another difference between the specification of the foreigners' and domestic sectors' behaviour is that the foreigners' demand function is not restricted to be linear homogenous in the scaling variable, W^f. The variable $1000/W^f$ has therefore been added to the relations. The multiplication of $1/W^f$ by 1000 has no other reason then to arrive at reasonable values of the corresponding coefficients.

The preferred equation of the foreigners' short-term investments is

$$\Delta NDAS^f/W^f = \underset{(4.05)}{0.500}\ NDAS^f(-1)/W^f + \underset{(3.06)}{0.091}\ (r_s - 0.5\cdot(\overset{\circ}{e}{}^e_{FR} + \overset{\circ}{e}{}^e_{UK}))$$

$$-\underset{(3.43)}{0.321}\ (r_{s,WG} + r_{s,US}) + \underset{(5.07)}{0.859}\ DUMS$$

$$+ \underset{(4.96)}{0.273}\ \ 1000.0/\ W^f + \underset{(2.55)}{0.932}$$

estimation period: 1970:I - 1980:IV
R^2(adj.) = 0.50 sse = 0.275 DW = 1.88

The dummy variable DUMS is 1 in 1970:III and 1970:IV and zero elsewhere. It represents extraordinary demand for Dutch assets. Most likely this demand resulted from an expected appreciation of the Dutch guilder (and the Deutsche

---

$$+ \underset{(1.93)}{1.644}\ \{ \frac{LS(-1)}{FA^b_{-1}} - \frac{LS(-2)}{FA^b_{-1}} \} + \underset{(2.67)}{0.091}\ ncc + \underset{(9.10)}{0.594}$$

estimation period:1973:III - 1980:IV
R^2(adj.) = 0.97 DW = 1.25

mark). In accordance with these facts, the expectations proxy indicates an expected appreciation of the guilder. However, the amount of the capital inflow is so large that a dummy variable had to be introduced in order to be able to describe it satisfactorily.

As might be expected, foreign investments rise when the expected yield on domestic assets - represented by ($r_s - 0.5\cdot(\mathring{e}^e_{FR} + \mathring{e}^e_{UK})$) - increases and declines when the yield on foreign short-term assets ($r_{s,WG} + r_{s,US}$) increases.

Since a significant part of the short-term capital flows is directly related to the imports of goods and services, some equations were estimated in which the scaling variable W^f was replaced by the Netherlands' imports. The resulting estimates were from a statistical point of view less satisfactory than those presented above.

The foreigners' investments in long-term domestic assets are comprised of portfolio investments, i.e. investments in shares and bonds. Direct investments are assumed to be exogenous. An increase in the (expected) domestic interest rate stimulates investments in bonds but discourages investments in shares. An additional variable representing the yield on domestic shares, r_{sh}, has been added to the list of explanatory variables. The time series of the foreigners' portfolio investments shows a structural change at the end of 1976. During the period 1970:I -1976:IV these investments exhibit a more or less gradual movement with dips at the end of 1973 and at the end of 1976. Starting with 1977:I the fluctuations and the average level of this time series increase. In order to investigate whether this shift corresponds with a structural change in the regression equation of the foreigners' long-term investments, the relation has been estimated for the period 1970:I-1976:IV and for the period 1977:I-1980:IV.

$$\Delta NDAL^f/W^f = \underset{(1.83)}{-0.065}\ NDAL^f(-1)/W^f - \underset{(3.67)}{0.135}\ (\mathring{e}^e_{fr} + \mathring{e}^e_{us})$$

$$+ \underset{(3.94)}{4.371}\ r_{sh} + \underset{(8.53)}{2.208}\ 1000/W^f - \underset{(1.96)}{0.456}\ S1 + \underset{(5.58)}{1.609}\ d7041 - \underset{(4.04)}{5.950}$$

estimation period: 1970:I - 1976:IV
R^2(adj.) = 0.83   sse = 0.454   DW = 2.30

$$\Delta NDAL^f/W^f = -0.094\ NDAL^f(-1)/W^f + 4.496\ (r_l - 0.5(r_{l,wg} + r_{l,uk}))$$
$$\quad\quad\quad\quad\quad (1.86) \quad\quad\quad\quad\quad\quad\quad\quad (1.80)$$

$$-0.382\ \mathring{e}^e_{fr} + 2.303\ S2 + 1.859\ S3 + 3.629\ d791 + 5.855$$
$$(1.75) \quad\quad (3.29) \quad\quad (2.62) \quad\quad (2.82) \quad\quad (2.44)$$

estimation period: 1977:I - 1980:IV
R^2(adj.) = 0.51 sse = 1.107 DW = 1.90

The estimated coefficients' value and the specification used are very different and thus affirm the observation of a structural shift in the time series at the end of 1986. The most obvious difference is that during the first subperiod the foreigners' investments are positively related to the yield on shares, whereas during the second subperiod they positively depend on the domestic long-term interest rate. Since the yield on shares and the domestic interest rate are negatively related, this implies that during the first subperiod the domestic long-term interest rate is negatively correlated with the foreigners' portfolio investments. When explaining the dummy variables we will elaborate this subject.

Chow's F-test of the equality of sets of coefficients in two linear regressions has been used as a formal test of the structural change at the end of 1976. For this aim the first relation has been re-estimated for the period 1970:I - 1977:IV and the second for the period 1976:I - 1980:IV. Chow's test, which, among others, is described in Johnston (1972, pp. 206, 207), tests whether the four observations added to the original sample can be considered to come from the same population. The relevant F-statistic is 22.46 for the case that the four quarters of 1977 are added to the sample 1970:I - 1976:IV and 6.84 when 1976 is added to the sample 1977:I - 1980:IV. The theoretical values of the F-statistic are respectively 3.63 (6.42) and 3.36 (5.67) for a significance level of 5 (1) percent. These calculations once again confirm our first impression of a structural shift at the end of 1976 in the time series of the foreigners' long-term portfolio investments in domestic assets.

Both equations contain a dummy variable representing extraordinary demand for Dutch long-term assets. The variable d7041 is 1 during 1970:IV, 1971:I and 1975:III. The huge amount of the capital inflow in 1970 and 1971 has already been mentioned when we described the foreigners' short-term investments. During this period foreigners bought large amounts of Dutch bonds so that during the second part of 1970 the Dutch long-term interest rate decreased more than abroad.[32] This illustrates the above-mentioned negative relation between the capital inflow and the long-term domestic interest rate. The capital inflow in

---

[32] See De Nederlandsche Bank, Kwartaalberichten, 1970 (4) and 1971 (1) for a brief description of these facts.

1975:III is caused by the weakness of the Deutsche mark which resulted from the lax German monetary policy. The Deutsche mark regained its strength when the German monetary authorities decided to loosen some capital controls.[33]

The dummy d791 equals 1 in 1979:I and also originates from commotion on the foreign exchange market. During the second part of 1978 the weak dollar created strains between the currencies participating in the snake arrangement. Moreover, the proposal for the creation of the European Monetary System lead investors to expect a realignment of the currencies concerned. Both events resulted in an increasing demand for Deutsche marks at the expense of, among other currencies, the Dutch guilder. After the realignment of the snake currencies on October 16, 1978 and especially in the first months of 1979, the value of the Dutch guilder gradually rose. These events on the foreign exchange market led to decreasing foreign demand for domestic assets during the second half of 1978 and a sharply increased interest from foreigners in Dutch bonds during the first quarter of 1979.[34] This shift in the foreigners' demand is extraordinarily large so that the dummy variable d791 had to be introduced to capture fully the foreign investors' renewed trust in the Dutch guilder.

In order to limit the inflationary effects on the domestic economy of foreign demand for Dutch assets during the early 1970s, the Dutch monetary authorities introduced the closed bond circuit for non-residents which was in effect from September 1971 until February 1974. As in Van Loo (1983), in some experiments the effect of this closed bond circuit has been represented by the premium on guilders available for non-residents from selling bonds to residents as a percentage of the free market exchange rate, bp. Contrary to our a priori expectation, it appeared that the coefficient of this variable was statistically insignificant (at the 5% level) when the relation was estimated for the period 1970:I-1976:IV, but significant when the relation was estimated for the entire period.

Under plausible assumptions the stock price is the present anticipated future profits, discounted at the real interest rate (see Gavin, 1989, p.184). Consequently, the stock price's percentage change is a function of the percentage change of the expected future profits and the percentage change in the real interest rate. We have assumed that the last two variables can be approximated by a weighted average of their observations during the last year so that

---

[33] See De Nederlandsche Bank, Kwartaalberichten 1975 (2), pp. 19 and 31.

[34] See De Nederlandsche Bank, Kwartaalberichten 1979 (1), p. 32.

$$r_{sh} = \underset{(2.03)}{0.536}\ \Sigma_{i=0}^{3}\ \alpha_i\ \mathring{\pi}_{-i} - \underset{(4.03)}{1.599}\ \Sigma_{i=0}^{3}\ \alpha_i(r_l(-i) - \mathring{p}_c(-i))$$

$$+ \underset{(4.25)}{0.192}\ S1 + \underset{(3.42)}{0.122}\ S2 + \underset{(2.57)}{0.095}\ S3 - \underset{(4.36)}{0.159}$$

estimation period: 1970:I-1976:IV
R^2(adj.) = 0.59 DW = 1.99

where $\alpha_i = (4-i)/10$, $i = 0,1,2,3$. The coefficients of the lag structures are estimated by means of the procedure developed in Almon (1965).[35]

4.8 The interest payments and receipts

In principle, the receipts and payments of interest are equal to the outstanding amount of debt times the relevant interest rate. For calculating these receipts and payments we need data on the amount and maturity structure of both foreigners' holdings of domestic assets and of inhabitants' holdings of foreign assets and of domestic government debt. For calculating the interest receipts of inhabitants on foreign assets we also need to know the currency in which these assets are denominated. Unfortunately however, reliable data of many of these variables are not available. Even if they were available or could be approximated in a more or less satisfactory way, then the calculation of the receipts on long-term investments would give rise to very long lag structures. In MORKMON for example, the maximum length of the lag structure in the government's payments of interest is 64 quarters. For the optimal control experiments such long lags

---

[35] This method assumes that a polynomial of fairly low degree can represent the lag coefficients. The degree of the polynomial and the number of lags have to be specified a priori. Given these values, the method defines new variables, whose coefficients correspond with the parameters of the polynomial. The number of these parameters is less than the number of lags. Thereafter these newly created variables are substituted in the original equation, which is estimated by OLS. The estimated parameters and t-values of the lagged variables' coefficients are derived from the estimated value and covariance of the polynomial's parameters. Two additional constraints can be imposed on the polynomial. The first one sets a hypothetical coefficient of the variable lead by one period at zero. The second constraint sets the hypothetical coefficient of the the variable lagged by one extra period than the number of lags at zero. These constraints are known as the near and far constraints respectively. Details with regard to the Almon scheme can be found in Almon (1965) and Johnston (1972), pp. 294-298. A description of the Almon procedure's implementation in the TSP-package is presented in Hall and Hall (1980), pp. 25, 26.

For estimating the coefficients in the equation of r_{sh}, the polynomial is assumed to be quadratic and far constraints are introduced.

should be approximated by shorter ones. Because of these two disadvantages of the method mentioned above, the interest receipts and payments are approximated by regression relations in which the proxies of the interest payments on outstanding debt serve as explanatory variables.

The inhabitants' receipts of interest from foreign investments is approximated by a regression equation in which the explanatory variable is the product of the foreign interest rate with the private sector's and the banks' holdings of foreign assets, $r_f \cdot (NFA^p + NFA^b)$. The resulting regression equation is

$$X_i = \underset{(17.35)}{2.89}\, r_f(-1) \cdot (NFA^p(-1) + NFA^b(-1)) - \underset{(3.05)}{526.290}$$

estimation period: 1970:I-1980:IV
R^2(adj.) = 0.88 DW = 1.53

In the relations of the interest payments to foreigners and those by the government, the payments on short-term and long-term debt are distinguished because these assets are endogenous. It is assumed that the interest payments on short-term debt depend on the stock of this debt lagged two quarters and that those on long-term debt depend on the outstanding debt of one year ago. Thus it is assumed that the average term of short-term debt is half a year and that the first payment of interest on long-term assets is one year after the issue of the bonds. Inspection of the graphs of the relevant variables affirms that this assumption gives rise to a better fit than when these payments are explained by the stock of the debt at the end of the present period. The average interest rate is selected in such a way that the resulting explanatory variables satisfactorily explain the payments.

The regression relation of the interest payments to foreigners is

$$M_i = \underset{(1.31)}{18.192}\, \Sigma_{j=2}^{3}\, 0.5\, r_s(-j)\, NDAS^f(-3) - \underset{(3.29)}{855.79}$$

$$+ \underset{(10.85)}{12.877}\, \Sigma_{j=1}^{3}\, 0.33\, r_l(-j)\, NDAL^f(-4)$$

estimation period: 1970:I-1980:IV
R^2(adj.) = 0.93 DW = 2.00 $\rho = \underset{(2.68)}{0.43}$

Inspection of the graphs of the government's interest payments reveals that this time series contains a trend and a clear seasonal pattern. The trend corresponds with the growth of the government's long-term debt, $NDAL^g$. During the greater part of the period considered, the seasonal pattern corresponds with the seasonal pattern in the government's short-term debt lagged two periods. The government's short-term debt consists of $NDAS^g$ and $FD^g{}_r$. The resulting relation is

$$ZRG = \underset{(14.53)}{1.153} \cdot 0.25\ \Sigma^{5}_{i=2}\ r_l(-i) \cdot NDAL^g(-4) + \underset{(3.52)}{1.107} \cdot r_s \cdot (NDAS^g(-2)$$

$$+ FD^g_r(-2)) - \underset{(2.34)}{252.41}$$

estimation period: 1970:I-1980:IV
R^2(adj.) = 0.90 DW = 2.12

The receipts and payments of interest are part of non-wage income and thus transmit developments of monetary variables to the real sector of the economy which is described in the next chapter.

Appendix A. A Critical Review of Some Specifications of the Multi-asset Partial Adjustment Model

In this Appendix we discuss some alternative specifications of the multi-asset partial adjustment model presented in the text. For convenience this model is reproduced here

$$\Delta A_{i,t} = \Sigma_{j=1}^{n} \delta_{ij} (A_{j,t}^{d} - A_{j,t-1}) \qquad i = 1,...,n \tag{A-1}$$

$$A_{j,t}^{d} = [\, \Sigma_{k=1}^{n} \beta_{jk}\, r_{kt} + \Sigma_{h=1}^{m} \gamma_{jh}\, X_{ht} + \alpha_j \,]\cdot W_t \qquad j = 1,...n \tag{A-2}$$

$$W_t = \Sigma_{i=1}^{n} A_{i,t} = \Sigma_{j=1}^{n} A_{j,t}^{d} \tag{A-3a}$$

$$\Sigma_{i=1}^{n} \delta_{ij} = 1 \quad \text{for all } j \tag{A-3b}$$

$$\Sigma_{j=1}^{n} \beta_{jk} = 0 \quad \text{for all } k \tag{A-3c}$$

$$\Sigma_{j=1}^{n} \gamma_{jh} = 0 \quad \text{for all } h \tag{A-3d}$$

$$\Sigma_{i=1}^{n} \alpha_i = 1 \tag{A-3e}$$

The fact that the (re)investment of assets is not costless is reflected by some of the coefficients δ_{ij}, being non-zero. In addition the constraint (A-3a) represents the assumption that the desired assets sum to the total wealth at the end of the period. Hence, the amounts of desired assets refer to both the investment of newly acquired wealth and the reinvestment of existing wealth, and thus these two types of investments are treated in the same manner. In particular it is implicitely assumed that the costs associated with the reinvestment of existing wealth are equal to the costs of investing newly acquired wealth.

Some authors, however, argue that these two types of investments should be distinguished from each other, because the costs of reinvesting an existing amount of wealth are about twice as high as the costs of investing new cash flows. The first transaction consists of both a purchase and a sale of assets whereas the investment of new cash flows gives rise to a purchase of assets only. In order to elucidate our choice, in this Appendix we review and assess some of these specifications used in other studies.

A method often used for separating these two effects in the portfolio adjustment model is to add the change in wealth ΔW_t, to the set of explanatory variables in (A-1)

$$\Delta A_{i,t} = \Sigma_{j=1}^{n} \delta_{ij} (A_{j,t}^{d} - A_{j,t-1}) + \mu_i \Delta W_t \qquad i=1,\ldots,n \tag{A-4}$$

This procedure has been applied in e.g. Ladenson (1971) and Clinton (1973).

Smith (1975) has argued that the model consisting of (A-1), (A-3a), and (A-4) overdescribes the portfolio disequilibria because according to (A-3a)

$$\Sigma_{j=1}^{n} (A_{j,t}^{d} - A_{j,t-1}) = \Delta W_t \tag{A-5}$$

As a consequence of the resulting multicollinearity, the coefficients in (A-4) cannot be meaningfully interpreted nor empirically identified. With a view to identifying the parameter values, Smith offers two alternative forms of (A-4).

The first alternative is to delete ΔW_t from (A-4). The resulting equation is (A-1) so that the previously mentioned disadvantage, namely that reinvestments and investments of new wealth are treated in the same way, still applies.

A second reformulation offered by Smith makes use of the following identity for the k-th discrepancy

$$A_{k,t}^{d} - A_{k,t-1} = \Delta W_t - \Sigma_{j\neq k}^{n} (A_{j,t}^{d} - A_{j,t-1}) \tag{A-6}$$

Then (A-4) is rewritten as

$$\begin{aligned}
\Delta A_{i,t} &= \Sigma_{j\neq k}^{n} \delta_{ij}(A_{j,t}^{d} - A_{j,t-1}) + \delta_{ik}(A_{k,t}^{d} - A_{k,t-1}) + \mu_i \Delta W_t \\
&= \Sigma_{j\neq k}^{n} \delta_{ij}(A_{j,t}^{d} - A_{j,t-1}) + \delta_{ik}[\Delta W_t - \Sigma_{j\neq k}^{n} (A_{j,t}^{d} - A_{j,t-1})] + \mu_i \Delta W_t \\
&= \Sigma_{j\neq k}^{n} (\delta_{ij} - \delta_{ik}) (A_{j,t}^{d} - A_{j,t-1}) + (\mu_i + \delta_{ik}) \Delta W_t \\
&= \Sigma_{j\neq k}^{n} d_{ij} (A_{j,t}^{d} - A_{j,t-1}) + h_i \Delta W_t
\end{aligned} \tag{A-7}$$

The adding up restrictions follow from

$$\Delta W_t = \Sigma_{i=1}^{n} \Delta A_{i,t} = \Sigma_{j\neq k}^{n} (\Sigma_{i=1}^{n} d_{ij}) (A_{j,t}^{d} - A_{j,t-1}) + \Sigma_{i=1}^{n} h_i \Delta W_t \tag{A-8}$$

According to Smith, (A-8) can always hold if and only if

$$\Sigma_{i=1}^{n} d_{ij} = 0 \qquad j \neq k \tag{A-9a}$$

$$\Sigma_{i=1}^{n} h_i = 1 \tag{A-9b}$$

In our view these conditions are not necessary for (A-8) to hold. Our opinion can easily be proved by an example in which the conditions (A-9a) and (A-9b) are violated whereas equation (A-8) is valid. Let us assume that the portfolio consists of three assets, n = 3, and that the values of the other variables and parameters are as shown in Table A-1. The parameter values $d_{i3} = 0$, i=1,2,3 illustrate the assumption that the third discrepancy is deleted from equation (A-4). One can easily verify that the selected values are in accordance with relation (A-8). The restrictions (A-9a) and (A-9b) are violated, however. They are

$$\Sigma_{i=1}^{3} d_{i1} = 0.5 \qquad \text{(A-10a)}$$

$$\Sigma_{i=1}^{3} d_{i2} = 0.75 \qquad \text{(A-10b)}$$

$$\Sigma_{i=1}^{3} h_{i} = 0.5 \qquad \text{(A-10c)}$$

This example clearly illustrates that the reformulated version (A-7) of (A-4) does not lead to an exact identification of the coefficients.

Table A-1 Assumed values of variables and parameters

i	d_{ij}			h_i	ΔW_t
	j=1	j=2	j=3		
1	0.25	0.25	0.0	0.3	
2	0.25	0.25	0.0	0.1	
3	0.00	0.25	0.0	0.1	
$A^d_{j,t} - A_{j,t-1}$	20	20	10		50

In our opinion this unsatisfactory result arises because (A-7) is merely a rewritten version of (A-4). No additional information has been used in the derivation of (A-7), whereas it is well-known that the solution of multicollinearity requires the use of some new information.[1] Very often this additional information consists of a priori restrictions on the parameters. As compared with (A-4), equation (A-1) incorporates the additional assumption that the increase in wealth, ΔW_t, is invested in the same way as the reinvestment of existing wealth. Consequently, the change of wealth is fully reflected in the differences between the desired stocks at the end of the period and the actual stocks at the end of the previous period, $A^d_{j,t} - A_{j,t-1}$.

[1] Compare the discussion of the multicollinearity problem in Section 2.5.4. In fact this is an example of perfect correlation between a set of variables and another variable.

Correctly specified models that distinguish the asset flows resulting from a redistribution of previous period wealth from those resulting from the increase of wealth, can be derived from (A-4) by introducing restrictive assumptions which clearly define the part of the flows caused by reinvestments and those resulting from new investments. An example of such a restrictive assumption, which also solves the multicollinearity problem, is the one that states that the $A^d_{j,t}$, j = 1,...,n only refer to the reinvestment of assets that were already available at the end of the previous period. Then (A-3a) is replaced by

$$W_{t-1} = \Sigma^n_{j=1} A^d_{j,t} \qquad \text{(A-3a')}$$

and the terms $A^d_{j,t} - A_{j,t-1}$, j = 1,...,n only refer to the reinvestment of previous period wealth. Consequently

$$\Sigma^n_{j=1} (A^d_{j,t} - A_{j,t-1}) = 0 \qquad \text{(A-11)}$$

From (A-4), and (A-11) it appears that the parameters δ_{ij} are constrained by

$$\Sigma^n_{i=1} \delta_{ij} = \delta' \qquad j = 1,...,n \qquad \text{(A-12)}$$

where δ' is a constant which is not restricted to 1, as was the case for (A-1) (see equation (4.4)).

These assumptions with regard to the $A^d_{j,t}$ reflect the reinvestment of available assets only. In order to fully describe the flows of assets, the model should be augmented with assumptions of the portfolio holders' attitude toward the current period's change of wealth. Basically, two assumptions have been used in the literature.

The first assumption is that a fixed proportion, μ_i, of the increase, in wealth is invested in asset i. Then the portfolio adjustment model consists of (A-4), (A-2), (A-3a'), (A-12) and the constrained

$$\Sigma^n_{i=1} \mu_i = 1 \qquad \text{(A-13)}$$

Note that the constraints (A-12) and (A-13) are induced by the additional information that $A^d_{j,t} - A_{j,t-1}$ only refers to the reallocation of existing wealth and that ΔW_t is the current period's increase of wealth. Under these assumptions, (A-12) - combined with (A-11) - states that a reallocation of wealth does not change the total value of it, whereas (A-13) reflects the fact that an increase in wealth should be held somewhere.

Friedman (1977) has criticized the assumption that the μ_i's are fixed. In his view "assuming that investors always allocate new cash flows in fixed proportions, regardless of market yields and other variables relevant to portfolio behavior, is in some sense more restrictive than assuming no distinction at all between allocation of new cash flow and reallocation of existing holdings". (Friedman, 1977, p. 669). He furthermore argues that only by chance will a growing portfolio ever reach an equilibrium if it is invested according to this model.

The second assumption with regard to the allocation of the increase in wealth meets Friedman's criticism. It assumes that the flow of newly investable funds are allocated according to whatever proportions the model indicates are the desired proportions, $a^d_{i,t}$. According to (4.5), which is reproduced as (A-2), $a^d_{i,t}$ equals

$$a^d_{i,t} = \Sigma^n_{k=1} \beta_{ik} r_{kt} + \Sigma^m_{h=1} \gamma_{ih} X_{ht} + \alpha_i \qquad j = 1,...n \qquad \text{(A-14)}$$

This "optimal marginal adjustment" model is developed in Friedman (1977) and replaces the fixed parameters μ_i in (A-4) by the desired proportions $a^d_{i,t}$, i.e.

$$\Delta A_{i,t} = \Sigma^n_{j=1} \delta_{ij} (A^d_{j,t} - A_{j,t-1}) + a^d_{i,t} \Delta W_t \qquad \text{(A-15)}$$

The model consists of the relations (A-2), (A-14), (A-15), (A-3a'), and the parameter constraints (A-12) and

$$\Sigma^n_{i=1} a^d_{it} = 1 \qquad \text{(A-16)}$$

Note that the constraints are once again induced by the additional information that $A^d_{j,t} - A_{j,t-1}$ only refers to a reallocation of wealth, whereas ΔW_t represents the change of wealth. An advantage of this model is that it explicitly takes into account that the costs of investing newly acquired wealth are less than those of reallocating the existing stocks of assets. In empirical studies the use of the optimal marginal adjustment model encounters two practical difficulties.[2] The first is that in models of complete balance sheets account has to be taken of various adding-up restrictions and many explanatory variables are included in the equations. The optimal marginal adjustment model nearly doubles the number of explanatory variables and thus reduces the degrees of freedom to an often unacceptably low figure. A second disadvantage of the model is that generally the data of $\Delta A_{i,t}$ i=1,...,n do not provide information on the reallocation and initial allocation of portfolios.

Hitherto the current period's change of wealth, ΔW_t, has been considered as one single item; it has not been divided into different categories. Some authors

---

[2] See Van Loo (1983), p 38.

drop this assumption. In Backus *et al.* (1980), for example, the change of wealth is divided into an expected and an unexpected part. At the beginning of the period, the portfolio holders incorporate the expected change of wealth in their desired stock of assets at the end of the period. A fixed proportion μ_i, of the unexpected change is allocated to assets i. The resulting model is

$$\Delta A_{it} = \Sigma_{j=1}^{n} \delta_{ij} (A_{j,t}^{d} - A_{j,t-1}) + \mu_i (W_t - {}_{t-1}W_t^e) \tag{A-17}$$

where

$$\Sigma_{j=1}^{n} A_{j,t}^{d} = {}_{t-1}W_t^e \tag{A-18a}$$

$$\Sigma_{i=1}^{n} \delta_{ij} = 1 \tag{A-18b}$$

$$\Sigma_{i=1}^{n} \mu_i = 1 \tag{A-18c}$$

and ${}_{t-1}W_t^e$ refers to the conditional expectation of W_t (conditioned on the information available at the end of period t-1). The constraints (A-18b) and (A-18c) reflect the statement that a change in (expected) wealth should be held somewhere. In fact, the disaggregation of the change in wealth in Backus *et al.* (1980) goes somewhat further than is assumed in (A-14). They disaggregate $W_t - {}_{t-1}W_t^e$ into p different sources of unanticipated changes in assets (such as unplanned saving or unexpected capital gains).

Another possible disaggregation of the change of wealth is presented in Brainard and Tobin (1968), where ΔW_t is divided into savings and capital gains/losses. It seems plausible to assume that capital gains and losses are held in the same asset from which they accrue and that during the present period new savings are held in a liquid form. The formula of this model could be

$$\Delta A_{it} = \Sigma_{j=1}^{n} \delta_{ij} (A_{j,t}^{d} - A_{j,t-1}) + \mu_{1i} \Delta W_{1t} + \mu_{2i} \Delta W_{2t} \tag{A-19}$$

where ΔW_{1t} (ΔW_{2t}) refers to capital gains/losses (new savings), the $A_{j,t}^{d}$ and δ_{ij} are constrained by (A-3a') and (A-12) respectively and the μ_{11} and μ_{2i} satisfy the constraints

$$\Sigma_{i=1}^{n} \mu_{ji} = 1 \qquad j = 1, 2 \tag{A-20}$$

The models presented above in which the current period's change in wealth is disaggregated are special forms of the specification with fixed coefficients consisting of equations (A-2), (A-4), (A-3a'), (A-12), and (A-13) and thus the same comments apply.

The discussion in this Appendix reveals that it is possible to incorporate into a multi-asset partial adjustment model the assumption that the reshuffling of existing wealth is more expensive than the investment of currently acquired cash flows. A correct specification, however, clearly indicates which part of the equations describes the reinvestment behaviour and which part refers to the investment of currently acquired wealth.

Appendix B Preliminary Estimates of the Private Sector's Financial Behaviour

In this Appendix we present the estimates of the unrestricted instrumental variables estimate. As is noted in Section 4.4.4 the cross-equation restrictions are automatically met. These estimates serve as starting values for the two stage procedure and inform the reader to a certain extent of the researcher's influence on the ultimately selected parameters.

Private Sector: unrestricted estimates*

	$\frac{M1_{-1}}{FA^p_{-1}}$	$\frac{NDAS^p_{-1}}{FA^p_{-1}}$	$\frac{NDAL^p_{-1}}{FA^p_{-1}}$	$\frac{NFA^p_{-1}}{FA^p_{-1}}$	$\frac{-LS_{-1}}{FA^p_{-1}}$	r_s	r_l	$r_f+\mathring{e}^e$	r_{ls}
$\Delta M1 / FA^p_{-1}$	-.7538 (5.63)	0.1369 (1.09)	0.2478 (1.73)	0.0566 (0.27)	0.1176 (0.67)	-.0230 (5.14)	-.0232 (2.36)	0.0002 (0.13)	0.0164 (2.36)
$\Delta NDAS^p / FA^p_{-1}$	0.0115 (0.05)	-.7254 (3.26)	-.6627 (2.61)	-.1485 (0.40)	-.2820 (0.91)	0.0543 (6.85)	0.0206 (1.18)	-.0065 (2.19)	-.0445 (3.62)
$\Delta NDAL^p / FA^p_{-1}$	-.0423 (0.26)	-.1213 (0.79)	-.3561 (2.03)	-.1930 (0.75)	-.3259 (1.52)	-.0152 (2.79)	-.0075 (0.63)	0.0041 (2.00)	0.0107 (1.25)
$\Delta FA^p / FA^p_{-1}$	0.0457 (0.60)	-.1329 (1.87)	-.1664 (2.05)	-.3724 (3.13)	-.2636 (2.66)	-.0026 (1.02)	0.0095 (1.71)	0.0010 (1.01)	0.0025 (0.64)
$-\Delta LS / FA^p_{-1}$	-.2611 (1.70)	-.1573 (1.09)	-.0626 (0.38)	-.3427 (1.42)	-.2460 (1.23)	-.0135 (2.62)	0.0639 (0.06)	0.0012 (0.63)	0.0149 (1.87)
Σ	-1.0	-1.0	-1.0	-1.0	-1.0	0.0	0.0	0.0	0.0

	Y / FA^p_{-1}	q	ncc	s1	s2	s3	FA^p / FA^p_{-1}	R^2(adj.)	s.e.e.	DW
$\Delta M1 / FA^p_{-1}$	0.5126 (3.45)	-.0445 (0.86)	-.0095 (1.79)	0.0107 (2.14)	0.0286 (5.81)	0.0034 (0.86)	0.0202 (0.17)	0.96	0.005	1.83
$\Delta NDAS^p / FA^p_{-1}$	-.3982 (1.51)	0.0262 (0.29)	-.0006 (0.07)	0.0 (0.0)	-.0174 (2.00)	0.0003 (0.05)	0.4870 (2.30)	0.76	0.009	1.57
$\Delta NDAL^p / FA^p_{-1}$	-.0191 (0.11)	-.0962 (1.53)	0.0136 (2.09)	-.0070 (1.15)	-.0023 (0.38)	-.0033 (0.68)	0.2830 (1.94)	0.75	0.006	1.71
$\Delta FA^p / FA^p_{-1}$	-.0035 (0.04)	0.0433 (1.49)	-.0019 (0.63)	-.0008 (0.28)	-.0007 (0.26)	-.0037 (1.67)	0.0795 (1.18)	0.28	0.003	2.54
$-\Delta LS / FA^p_{-1}$	-.0918 (0.54)	0.0712 (1.21)	-.0015 (0.25)	-.0029 (0.50)	-.0082 (1.45)	0.0033 (0.72)	0.1303 (0.95)	0.32	0.006	2.49
	0.0	0.0	0.0	0.0	0.0	0.0	1.0			

* The figures between brackets are the absolute values of the t-statistic. The variables: r_s, r_l, $r_f + \mathring{e}^e$ and r_{ls} are multiplied by FA^p/FA^p_{-1}.

Appendix C Preliminary Estimates of the Banks' Relations

In this Appendix we present the estimates of the unrestricted instrumental variables estimate of the banks' financial behaviour. As is noted in Section 4.4.4 the cross-equation restrictions are automatically met. These estimates serve as starting values for the two-stage procedure and inform the reader to a certain extent of the researcher's influence on the ultimately selected parameters.

The banking sector's financial behaviour: unrestricted estimates*

	$\frac{RU_{-1}}{FA^b_{-1}}$	$\frac{NDAS^b_{-1}}{FA^b_{-1}}$	$\frac{NDAL^b_{-1}}{FA^b_{-1}}$	$\frac{NFA^b_{-1}}{FA^b_{-1}}$	r_s	r_l	$r_f + \mathring{e}^e$	$\frac{NDAS^p}{FA^b_{-1}}$	$\frac{NDALS}{FA^b_{-1}}$
$\Delta RU / FA^b_{-1}$	-.8601 (6.26)	-.1787 (1.56)	-.1861 (2.08)	-.2963 (3.04)	0.1010 (0.28)	-1.8198 (1.66)	.3814 (1.42)	-.0884 (1.79)	-.1561 (2.05)
$\Delta NDAS^b / FA^b_{-1}$	0.4356 (2.81)	-.4665 (3.60)	-.3877 (3.83)	-.2759 (2.51)	0.2265 (.56)	1.1357 (.91)	-.7143 (2.35)	.2046 (3.66)	0.3160 (3.67)
$\Delta NDAL^b / FA^b_{-1}$	-.3095 (2.00)	-.2666 (2.07)	-.1859 (1.84)	-.0334 (.30)	-.1269 (0.32)	1.9013 (1.53)	-.5492 (1.81)	-.0536 (.96)	0.0793 (.92)
$\Delta NFA^b / FA^b_{-1}$	0.2666 (2.23)	-.0881 (.89)	-.2402 (3.09)	-.3944 (4.67)	-.2005 (.65)	-1.2172 (1.28)	.8821 (3.78)	-.0627 (1.46)	-.2393 (3.62)
Σ	-1.0	-1.0	-1.0	-1.0	0.0	0.0	0.0	0.0	0.0

	$\frac{\Delta lq \cdot NDAS^p}{FA^b_{-1}}$	$\frac{\Delta SPL}{FA^b_{-1}}$	$\frac{\Delta RES}{FA^b_{-1}}$	s1	s2	s3	FA^b/FA^b_{-1}	R^2(adj.)	s.e.e.	DW
$\Delta RU / FA^b_{-1}$	-.0028 (1.51)	-.3125 (1.90)	.4234 (5.14)	.0102 (1.76)	.0078 (1.35)	0.0076 (2.07)	0.3464 (4.21)	.86	.008	2.15
$\Delta NDAS^b / FA^b_{-1}$	0.0052 (2.46)	.4658 (2.51)	0.3789 (4.06)	.0128 (1.94)	.0193 (2.97)	-.0081 (1.93)	0.0806 (0.87)	.72	.009	2.10
$\Delta NDAL^b / FA^b_{-1}$	0.0001 (0.05)	-.0153 (.08)	-.0490 (.53)	-.0189 (2.88)	-.0195 (3.01)	-.0043 (1.04)	0.1508 (1.63)	.43	.009	1.75
$\Delta NFA^b / FA^b_{-1}$	-.0025 (1.53)	-.1380 (.97)	-.7533 (10.53)	-.0041 (0.81)	-.0076 (1.52)	0.0048 (1.49)	0.4222 (5.92)	.88	.007	2.04
	0.0	0.0	0.0	0.0	0.0	0.0	1.0			

* The figures between brackets are the absolute values of the t-statistic. The variables: r_s, r_l and $r_f + \mathring{e}^e$ are multiplied by FA^p/FA^p_{-1}.

5 THE NON-FINANCIAL SECTORS OF THE MODEL

5.1 Introduction

This chapter is devoted to the real part of the model. Since we are mainly concerned with monetary phenomena, the empirical modelling of these non-monetary sectors has been kept as simple as possible. The main structure of this part of the model can be illustrated by means of the well-known identity of gross domestic product.

$$Y \equiv CONS^{p} + I + G + (X - M) \tag{5.1}$$

where it is assumed that the government's expenditures for investment and consumption goods are incorporated in G, and net international transfer receipts form part of X and M. In order to illustrate the structure of the empirical model, we derive an alternative statement of (5.1) by subtracting net taxes (taxes, T, less domestic transfers, YT) from both sides and by disaggregating the balance on the current account

$$\begin{aligned} Y - (T - YT) \equiv {} & CONS^{p} + I + G - (T - YT) \\ & + X_g + X_{ng} + X_i - M_g - M_{ng} - M_i \end{aligned} \tag{5.2}$$

The exports and imports are divided into three sub-items, goods, services, and investment incomes. Of these the following are endogenous: the imports and exports of goods (M_g and X_g respectively), investment income, X_i, and payments on foreign investments in the Netherlands, M_i. The receipts and payments on international investments are assumed to be endogenous, because of their prominent role in the portfolio approach to exchange rate determination. Their relations are described in Section 4.8. The merchandise trade - represented by X_g and M_g - is determined by relative prices, income and the utilization rate of capital. The exogenous component of the current account - represented by X_{ng} and M_{ng} - consists of unilateral transfers and international trade in services, oil, natural gas, ships and aeroplanes. These parts of international trade are treated as exogenous variables, because the trade in these products is dominated by special events.

The domestic sector consists of firms, households and the government. The government sector is represented by G - (T - YT). The households determine the amount of private consumption, $CONS^{p}$, in identity (5.2) and play a role on the labour market and thus influence the wage rate. The investments in (5.2), I, are determined by the firms.

The behavioural equations of the real side of the model are estimated for non-seasonally adjusted quarterly data[1] during the period 1970:I-1980:IV. The definitional relations as well as the interaction between the real part and financial sectors of the model are presented in the next chapter, which contains the entire model.

The non-financial sector's behavioural equations are grouped into the following three broad categories: the labour market, the goods market (which also contains international trade), and wages and prices. With regard to the labour market, which is described in Section 5.2, it has been assumed that the supply of labour is exogenous, while the demand has been derived from a vintage-type production structure. The parameters of this production structure are used for deriving a time series of the utilization rate, q, which is an explanatory variable in many relations. The goods market is described in Section 5.3. As in the Dutch central bank's model MORKMON, De Nederlandsche Bank (1984), and Fair (1976), a behavioural equation of the supply of goods has been estimated (see Section 5.3.1). The remaining subsections of 5.3 specify the various demand functions for goods, *viz.* the consumption function, the investment function and the imports/exports relations. Then the investments in stocks can be derived by subtracting the demand from the supply of goods.

The variables in the identities (5.1) and (5.2) are in nominal terms, whereas the majority of the behavioural relations to be presented in the following sections refer to real variables, i.e. variables measured in constant prices. The prices transfer the quantity system into nominal terms. The regression relations of the prices are presented in Section 5.4. It has been assumed that the prices of the various goods are, among other things, determined by three cost components, *viz.* the price of imported goods, the user costs of capital and the wage rate. The equations of the last two cost components are also presented in Section 5.4. The price in domestic currency of imported goods results from a definitional relation which is presented in the next chapter.

5.2 The labour market

The demand for labour is assumed to be determined by capacity demand for labour and the degree of capacity utilization, i.e.

$$\mathring{a}^{d} = \mathring{a}^{*} + \beta(\mathring{y} - \mathring{y}^{*}) \tag{5.3}$$

---

[1] Our reasons for using non-seasonally adjusted data are listed in Section 4.3.3.

where
a^d = demand for labour
a^* = capacity demand for labour
y = actual output (in constant prices)
y^* = capacity output (in constant prices)
All variables in (5.3) are percentage changes indicated by a " $^\circ$ " above the variable. It is assumed that the adjustment of the actual employment to the demand for labour can be described by the partial adjustment model, i.e.

$$\mathring{a}_t - \mathring{a}_{t-1} = (1-\delta)(\mathring{a}^d_t - \mathring{a}_{t-1}) \tag{5.4}$$

where a_t refers to actual employment in period t.

Since the capacity demand for labour depends upon capacity output, equation (5.3) shows that the demand for labour by firms depends directly and indirectly upon y^*, which thus plays an important role in this part of the model. A main problem of estimating the capacity output is that no reliable data of the capital stock in use are available. In recent Central Planning Bureau models. see e.g. Van de Berg *et al.* (1983), a vintage approach has been applied to approximate this stock. For the present study an important disadvantage of this approach is that the capital stock is assumed to be a weighted sum of past investments, so that very long lags are introduced into the model. For example, vintage models of the Dutch economy indicate that during the 1970s the lifetime of the oldest equipment lies between 15 and 20 years, i.e. 60 and 80 quarters.[2] Such long lags can easily cause serious problems in the optimal control experiments to be presented in a subsequent chapter. More importantly, since we confine our attention to only slightly more than ten years, the chances are that this detailed approach would not change our results dramatically.[3]

Thus, we decided to estimate a model of capacity output which does not explicitly incorporate the capital stock. Examples of such models are presented in Barten *et al.* (1976), De Ridder (1977) and Driehuis, Heineken and De Savornin Lohman (1979). From these studies the last one has been selected, because its specification is rather flexible and the scrapping condition used in CPB models has been replaced by a more plausible replacement condition.

According to Driehuis *et al.* (1979) the percentage change in capacity output

---

[2] See e.g. Kuipers, Muysken and Van Sinderen (1979), Table 4.

[3] We do not want to dwell upon the other disadvantages of the CPB's vintage approach. A summary of the discussion of these models can be found in Driehuis and Van der Zwan (1978).

can be approximated by[4]

$$\mathring{y}^* = \frac{1}{\kappa} \cdot \frac{i}{y} (h^{\delta 1}) + \theta \Delta ly + \delta 1 \, \mathring{h} - \tau + \epsilon \tag{5.5}$$

where
i = total investment (in constant prices)
ly = economic lifetime
h = index of working hours
κ = capital-output ratio
τ = rate of technical and economic obsolescence
ϵ = rate of non-embodied capital-augmenting technical progress
This relation illustrates that a rise of total investments (as a share of total output and corrected for working time), an increase in working hours and a rise of the non-embodied capital-augmenting technical progress all increase the growth of capacity output. A shortening of the equipment's economic lifetime and a higher rate of technical and economic obsolescence reduce the growth of capacity output.

The growth in capacity demand for labour is represented by

$$\mathring{a}^* = \mathring{y}^* + \Phi \Delta ly - \delta 2 \, \mathring{h} - \mu - \sigma \tag{5.6}$$

where
μ = rate of embodied labour-augmenting technical progress
σ = rate of disembodied labour-augmenting technical progress
A growth of capacity output, thus, raises the capacity demand for labour. This demand declines if the equipment's economic lifetime decreases, if the number of working hours rises and if the rate of labour-augmented technical progress is positive.

The model's structural form is not estimated but its reduced form, which is obtained by substituting (5.5) and (5.6) into (5.3) and the resulting relation into (5.4). Then the equation to be estimated is the following relation of actual employment

[4] See Driehuis, *et al.* (1979), p. 159 and following for an extensive discussion of this approach.

$$\mathring{a} = \delta\mathring{a}_{t-1} + \text{ß}(1-\delta)\cdot\mathring{y} + [(1-\delta)\cdot(1-\text{ß})/\kappa]\cdot[i\cdot h^{\delta 1}/y_{t-1}]$$

$$+ (1-\delta)[(1-\text{ß})\theta + \Phi]\cdot\Delta ly + (1-\delta)[(1-\text{ß})\delta 1 - \delta 2]\cdot\mathring{h}$$

$$- (1-\delta)(1-\text{ß})(\tau-\epsilon) - (1-\delta)\cdot(\mu+\sigma) \tag{5.7}$$

One of the explanatory variables, namely the change in the economic lifetime cannot be observed and thus should be approximated.

Within the vintage type models, two methods can be distinguished for deriving the change in the economic lifetime. The first method, which is used in for example the CPB models, assumes that entrepreneurs scrap a vintage of equipment if the profits obtained from the use of this vintage are zero (the so-called scrapping condition). The alternative for this scrapping condition is the replacement condition. Then it is assumed that entrepreneurs replace equipment if the operating costs of old equipment are higher than the total costs of buying new equipment. Since, in general (see Driehuis *et al.* (1979), p.161) one considers the last condition to be more realistic than the scrapping condition, we use the replacement condition. Under this assumption entrepreneurs will replace equipment when the flexible costs of existing equipment per unit of product are equal to the total costs of new equipment per unit of product. The flexible costs of old equipment are comprised of labour costs and that of new equipment of labour costs and capital costs, so that the replacement condition is[5]

$$\Delta ly = [1 \ / \ (1 + C_t)]\cdot[(\mathring{p}_k - \mathring{w} - (\delta 1 - \delta 2)\mathring{h} + \sigma - \epsilon) \ / \ \mu + 1] \tag{5.8}$$

where
w = total wage per wage-earner
p_k = capital costs per unit of capital
C_t = the ratio in period t of labour costs and capital costs of the newest vintage, both per unit of product.

Assume that the influence of working time on the capacity output is the same as its effect on the growth in capacity demand for labour, $\delta 1$ is approximately equal to $\delta 2$, then C_t appears to be[6]

$$C_t = C_{t-1} \ [(1 + \mathring{w}) \ / \ (1 + \mathring{p}_k)]\cdot e^{-(\mu+\sigma-\epsilon)} \tag{5.9}$$

---

[5] For a derivation of this condition one is referred to Driehuis *et al.* (1979), pp. 162 and 163. They also show that under perfect competition, the scrapping condition used in the CPB-models equals this replacement criterium.

[6] See Driehuis *et al.* (1979), p. 163.

Relations (5.8) and (5.9) are used for deriving the time series of Δly and C_t. For deriving these series assumptions have to be made with regard to the value of μ, σ, ϵ and C_0 and with regard to the time series $\overset{\circ}{p}_k$. The formula used for approximating the latter is presented in the section on prices. Given these time series, the reduced form (5.7) can be estimated.

In the present study a slightly modified version of this relation has been estimated. This modification is introduced in order to meet to some extent the critique on the CPB model that applying the vintage approach to the whole sector of firms, implies the implicit assumption that the employment in *all* firms is mainly determined by capital formation. However, in the non-capital intensive sectors, such as building and construction and the non-capital intensive part of the services sector, employment is mainly determined by output. Driehuis *et al.* (1979) thus estimate (5.7) for the capital intensive sectors only. Since in the present model our main concern is not with the supply side of the economy, we have chosen another route, namely to add to the right-hand side of (5.7) the growth rate of the investment in dwellings as representative of the sales of the non-capital intensive sectors. Consequently $\overset{\circ}{y}$ and y_{t-1} in (5.7) now refer to the output of firms excluding investments in dwellings.

From some preliminary estimates of this modified and of the original (non-modified) version of (5.7) it appeared that the coefficient of $[i \cdot h^{\delta 1}/y_{t-1}]$ always had a negative sign. We therefore decided to assign an a priori value to this parameter. For the same reason Driehuis *et al.* fixed this parameter at 0.1. We have selected this coefficient from the range 0.05 to 0.25. The lowest value in this range appeared to yield the most satisfactory fit. Then, however the coefficient of $\overset{\circ}{h}$ appeared to be wrongly signed.[7] We therefore decided to assign an a priori value to this parameter too. From the range 0.05 to 0.2, the value 0.1 gives the best results. The ultimately preferred relation is

$$\begin{aligned}
\overset{\circ}{a} = \; & \underset{(3.87)}{0.560}\, \overset{\circ}{a}(-1) + \underset{(0.50)}{0.022}\, \Sigma^3_{j=0} (\overset{\circ}{y} - \overset{\circ}{i}_w)_{-j} + \underset{(-)}{0.05}\, [h^{0.75}/(y-i_w)]_{-1}\, \Sigma^3_{j=0}\, i_{-j} \\
& \underset{(-)}{-\,0.1}\, \Sigma^3_{j=0}\, 0.25\, \overset{\circ}{h}_{-j} + \underset{(1.70)}{0.002}\, \Delta ly + \underset{(2.21)}{0.018}\, \Sigma^3_{j=0}\, 0.25\, \overset{\circ}{i}_w(-j) + \underset{(2.43)}{0.003}\, S1 \\
& + \underset{(6.69)}{0.008}\, S2 + \underset{(4.19)}{0.004}\, S3 - \underset{(14.83)}{0.012}
\end{aligned}$$

estimation period : 1970:I - 1980:IV

R^2(adj.) = 0.66 DW = 1.33 h = 8.06

---

[7] This result may arise from the fact that the time series of $\overset{\circ}{h}$ does not show any fluctuation within the year and thus is an inadequate measure of the quarterly changes in working time.

Table 5.1 Estimates of the parameters of the vintage model's structural form

$ß = 0.05$	$\Phi = 0.023$
$\kappa = 8.36$	$\tau = 0.010$
$\delta 1 = 0.75$	$\mu = 0.0075$
$\delta 2 = 0.94$	$\sigma = 0.005$
$\theta = 0.004$	$\epsilon = 0.005$

Note: As in Driehuis *et al.* (1979) a priori values have been assigned to $\delta 1$, μ, $\sigma = \epsilon$. Given these a priori values the coefficients κ, ß, δ and τ can be derived from (5.7). However, the resulting estimated value of τ appeared to be negative and thus an a priori value has been assigned to it. For the estimation of Φ it is assumed that in the long run $\overset{\circ}{y}^* - \overset{\circ}{w}^* = \mu + \sigma$. Substitution of this condition and the estimates of $\delta 2$, μ and σ in equation (5.2) yields the following relation $\Phi \Delta ly = \delta 2 \overset{\circ}{h}$. Driehuis *et al.* (1979) estimate Φ by substituting the averages of Δly and $\overset{\circ}{h}$ into this relation. In the present study this mostly yields negative values for Φ, because during some quarters in the second half of the 1970s probably due to the increase in nominal interest rates Δly becomes positive. We therefore decided to use the negative values of Δly only for estimating Φ. In addition the coefficient of Δly has been multiplied by five. This factor has been introduced in order to obtain plausible values of θ. These implausible (negative) values may arise because contrary to Driehuis *et al.* (1979) we did not use long lags of the relative prices and interest rate for calculating Δly. They present estimates of the reduced form in which Δly is based upon unlagged relative prices and in which it is derived from a five-year moving average of relative prices. When the latter estimates are used, the coefficient of Δly is five times that obtained by using unlagged relative prices. See Driehuis *et al.* (1979) Table 5.

A priori values, derived from other studies of the Dutch supply side, have been assigned to some parameters e.g. δ_1 (see Table 5.1). Since the endogenous variable lagged one period is one of the explanatory variables, the DW-statistic is no longer useful. We therefore also present the value of Durbin's h-statistic. Under the null hypothesis of no serial correlation the h-test is approximately normally distributed with unit variance. These statistics indicate whether the error terms are serially correlated. Correction for this first order autocorrelation yields implausible results and thus the original estimates presented above are chosen.[8]

The estimates of the parameters of the model's structural form are presented in Table 5.1. They roughly correspond with those obtained in Driehuis *et al.* (1979). These estimated parameters are used for deriving the percentage change in the utilization rate. A series of utilization rates is calculated from these percentage changes by assuming that in 1977 the average utilization rate was equal to 100.

5.3 The goods market

5.3.1 *The supply of goods*

In many models of the Dutch economy, domestic production is the sum of the various expenditure functions. Thus no separate relation for production is estimated; behavioural equations of all components of domestic expenditure form its base. The disadvantages of this procedure arise from the resulting necessity to estimate a behavioural relation of the firms' investments in stocks. From a theoretical point of view these investments are difficult to explain. According to theory, firms produce in order to sell goods and stocks are regarded as remnants, which arise from stagnating demand or serve as a buffer for unexpected increases in sales. These theoretical difficulties are reflected in the bad results of empirical studies on investments in stocks. In addition in the National Accounts, from which the data used are derived, the investments in stocks are treated as a balancing item. Given these drawbacks of estimating the investments in stocks, we decided to follow the alternative route and estimated a function for production. Subsequently and in accordance with the treatment in the National Accounts, the investments in stocks are obtained as the difference between production and sales of firms.

Essentially, the relation describing the production consists of two parts, namely a target value of firms' production and an adjustment mechanism describing the adjustment of the actual production towards this target. The target results from the firms' objective to meet the demand and from the assumption that there are costs included in having the stocks of inventories deviate from β_1

---

[8] Note that the residuals in the relations presented in Driehuis *et al.* (1979) are also autocorrelated. The corresponding DW-statistic of their relations varies between 1.28 and 1.44 (See their Table 7, p. 178).

times sales,[9] where $\beta_1 > 0$. If firms were only interested in realizing these objectives, they would produce in period t according to the equation

$$y_t = E(v_t) + \beta_1 E(v_t) - n_{t-1} \tag{5.10}$$

where $E(v_t)$ are the expected sales and n_{t-1} is the stock of inventories at the beginning of the current period.

Since there are also adjustment costs, such as the costs of changing employment and of changing the capital stock, it is generally not optimal for firms to produce according to (5.10). Because of these adjustment costs firms will gradually change their production towards the level resulting from (5.10). This adjustment mechanism is obtained by minimizing the following one-period loss function[10]

$$q = \alpha_1[(1+\beta_1)E(v_t) - n_{t-1} - y_t]^2 + \alpha_2(y_t - y_{t-1})^2 \tag{5.11}$$

The first term represents the costs attached to discrepancies between the actual and the desired level of the production. The costs of changing the level of production are incorporated in the second term of (5.11). Notice that the form of (5.11) is the same as that of the objective function (4.1).

Minimizing (5.11) with respect to y_t thus yields the following partial adjustment mechanism

$$\Delta y_t = \theta\,[(1.0 + \beta_1)E(v_t) - n_{t-1} - y_{t-1}] \tag{5.12}$$

In Fair (1976) and in De Nederlandsche Bank (1984) the expectations are assumed to be formed rationally and thus $E(v_t)$ has been replaced by v_t. In view of our criticism of this strong form of rational expectations, described in Chapter 3, an alternative hypothesis has been introduced. Given the seasonal pattern in

---

[9] Of course, there are also costs associated with operating below full capacity level. These costs are incorporated in the price equations by means of the degree of capacity utilization. Then it is assumed that in the case of a low or decreasing degree of capacity utilization entrepreneurs will lower the price in order to increase the demand for their products and thus reduce the gap between the actual and the capacity level of output. The derivation presented in the text is based on Fair (1976).

[10] We have also estimated some relations that were derived from the error correction mechanism applied in Hendry and Von Ungern-Stenberg's (1981) study on consumers' expenditures. Then a term is added to the objective function that allows for more adjustment at a given cost when the target of y_t has changed than when it is constant. The relevant parameter appeared to be highly insignificant.

sales we assume that expected sales in a particular quarter equal those of the corresponding quarter in the previous year multiplied by one plus the last year's rate of growth, i.e.

$$E(v_t) = v^f_{t-4} \cdot [1.0 + 0.33\, \Sigma^3_{j=1}\, \mathring{v}^f_{t-j}] \qquad (5.13)$$

Dummy variables have been added to (5.12) in order to represent seasonal influences and the effects of the severe winter of 1979.

From a statistical point of view a satisfactory version of this model is

$$\underset{(3.55)}{\Delta y = 0.500}\, [(1.0 + \underset{(10.71)}{0.829})\, v^f_{t-4}\, \Sigma^3_{j=1}\, \mathring{v}^f_{-j} - n_{-1} - y_{-1}]$$

$$- \underset{(2.55)}{4574.47}\, d791 + \underset{(1.64)}{1754.17}\, S2 + \underset{(1.45)}{1334.27}\, S3 + \underset{(1.34)}{4862.16}$$

estimation period: 1970:I - 1980:IV
R^2(adj.) = 0.48 D.W. = 2.05

5.3.2 *Private consumption*

An important part of the demand for domestic goods, which is the subject of the present and next subsections, consists of the households' demand for consumption goods. Private consumption shows a strong seasonal pattern which in all likelihood represents the fact that different commodities are being purchased in different quarters of the year. The consumption in the present quarter differs from that in the corresponding quarter of the former year because of changes in income, (real) interest rates and prices. As in Davidson *et al.* (1978), p. 684, we have used the four-quarter or annual difference, Δ_4, of the consumption and income variables. In correspondence with other macro-econometric models of the Dutch economy two income variables are distinguished *viz.* disposable income of wage earners (inclusive of transfer payments), $YWTS^d$, and disposable non-wage income, Z^d. The ultimately chosen equation of the private consumption's value is[11]

---

[11] The relation does not contain $\Delta\Delta_4 Z^d$ because its coefficient appeared to be insignificant (t-value of about 0.5). It should be noticed that $CONS^p$ is in current prices so that the real interest rate most likely partly reflects a change of prices.

$$\Delta_4 CONS^p/CONS^p(-4) = \underset{(16.96)}{0.832}\ \Delta_4 YWTS^d/CONS^p(-4)$$

$$- \underset{(2.44)}{0.476}\ \Delta\Delta_4 YWTS^d/CONS^p(-4) + \underset{(5.12)}{0.229}\ \Delta_4\ Z^d/CONS^p(-4)$$

$$- \underset{(1.42)}{0.002}\ \{0.5\cdot(r_l+r_s) - \mathring{p}_c\} + \underset{(1.42)}{0.009}$$

estimation period: 1970: I - 1980: IV
R^2(adj.) = 0.83 DW = 1.99 $\rho = \underset{(1.76)}{-0.283}$

According to this relation consumers plan to spend in each quarter of the year the same as they spent in that quarter of the previous year modified by a proportion of their annual change in income [0.229 $\Delta_4 Z^d/CONS^p(-4)$ + 0.832 $\Delta_4 YWTS^d/CONS^p(-4)$], by whether this change in wage income is itself increasing or decreasing (-0.476 $\Delta\Delta_4 YWTS^d/CONS^p(-4)$) and by the level of the real interest rate -0.002 [$0.5(r_l+r_s)-\mathring{p}_c$]. Since the change of the four-quarter difference in wage income, $\Delta\Delta_4 YWTS^d/CONS^p(-4)$ is assumed to represent unexpected changes in income, the theoretically correct sign of its coefficient is negative. As expected, the proportion of a change in non-wage income used for consumption is smaller than the corresponding proportion of wage income. In some regressions the level of the real interest rate was replaced by its change. The corresponding coefficient appeared to be insignificant.

5.3.3 *Investment by firms*

The investments can be divided into three categories, namely: investments in dwellings, investments in ships and aeroplanes, and investments by firms in other fixed assets. Only the last type of investments is assumed to be endogenous, because they influence the capacity output, whereas other types of investments do not.[12] Henceforth, we use the term total investment by firms for investment in other permanent assets.

Total investments by firms can be divided into net investments and replacement investments. In a vintage model, replacement investments depend upon the stock of the oldest equipment in operation and the change in the economic lifetime, Δly. The first factor has not been included in the investment equation, because the model of capacity output presented in Section 5.2 does not contain any proxy of the stock of capital in use. Net investments dependent on the

---

[12] Investments in dwellings and those in ships and aeroplanes are exogenous too in most CPB-models (see, e.g. Van den Berg *et al.*, 1983, p. 35).

expected net yield of new investments and the expected demand for goods.[13]

The size of the effect of a certain increase of expected demand on net investment depends upon the present capacity utilization rate, q. If the latter is below its normal value then an expected increase in demand can be met without increasing capacity output and thus no net investments are required. An expected growth of demand will increase the capacity output desired and thus lead to net investments if q is above its normal level. We therefore decided to include the desired level of capacity output in the investment relation, where the desired capacity output is approximated as

$$y^{*d} = y^{*}_{-1} \cdot \{1.0 + 0.33 \cdot \Sigma^{3}_{j=1}\, \mathring{y}_{-j} + \alpha\, \Sigma^{3}_{j=0}\, 0.25(q-q_n)_{-j}\} \tag{5.14}$$

where
y^{*d} = the desired level of capacity output
q_n = the normal level of the utilization rate (= 0.95)
The capacity output in the previous period, y^{*}_{-1}, is derived from the supply side presented in Section 5.2. The expected increase in demand is assumed to be equal to the average of the percentage change of demand during the previous three quarters. The resulting desired level of capacity output does not show a seasonal pattern.

The expected yield on new investments is assumed to be negatively related to the percentage change in the user costs of capital and positively to the profit earned by firms.[14] Generally, the latter is approximated by disposable non-wage income. As argued by Keus (1980), an important disadvantage of this proxy is that it includes interest payments by firms. Consequently, the increase in interest payments by firms during the 1970s, which reduces the firms' net profits is measured as an increase in profits. For this reason only a part of non-wage income, $d_{pr} \cdot Z$, is considered to be firms' profits, π. The calculation of d_{pr} is based on information presented in Keus (1980). As in the MORKMON-model, writing-off is considered to be part of the firms' profits. The exact formula used for calculating firms' profits is set out in the Appendix which contains the list of symbols and also in the next chapter, which presents the entire model.

In addition to these explanatory variables of the investments by firms in equipment, i_{-sa}, seasonal dummies and a dummy representing the severe winter of 1979 have been included in the set of explanatory variables. The ultimately chosen relation is

---

[13] The same assumptions are made in Hasselman *et al.*, 1983, p. 35. Their way of modelling the influence of the expected demand on net investments forms the basis of the relation presented in the text.

[14] See, e.g. Branson (1979), pp. 230-233 for a derivation of this relation.

$$i_{-sa} = \underset{(5.21)}{0.464}\, i_{-sa}(-1) + \underset{(2.05)}{0.021}\, y^{*}(-1)\cdot\{1.0 + 0.33\cdot\Sigma_{j=1}^{3}\, \mathring{y}_{-j} + 0.1\, \Sigma_{j=0}^{3}\, (q-0.95)_{-j}\}$$

$$+ \Sigma_{j=0}^{3}\, \alpha_j\, (\mathring{\pi} - \mathring{p}_i)_{-j-4} + \Sigma_{j=0}^{7}\, \beta_j\, (\mathring{p}_k)_{-j-4} - \underset{(4.30)}{650.781}\, S1$$

$$- \underset{(3.29)}{361.850}\, S2 - \underset{(8.19)}{982.074}\, S3 - \underset{(4.76)}{861.989}\, dum7912 + \underset{(6.51)}{3646.050}$$

estimation period: 1970:I - 1980:IV
R^2(adj.) = 0.88 DW = 2.17 h = -0.70

The coefficients of the lag structure of $\mathring{\pi}$ and $\mathring{p}_k$ are estimated by means of the procedure developed in Almon (1965), see footnote 35 in Chapter 4, and are presented in Table 5.2. The coefficient 0.1 before the difference between the actual and normal level of the utilization rate has been selected from the range [0.1, 0.3].

Table 5.2 The lag structure in the investment relation*

j	$(\mathring{\pi} - \mathring{p}_i)_{-j-4}$ coefficient	t-statistic	$(\mathring{p}_k)_{-j-4}$ coefficient	t-statistic
0	1117.46	3.57	-4320.32	-3.17
1	838.092	3.57	-2616.43	-3.02
2	558.728	3.57	-1503.15	-1.83
3	279.364	3.57	-980.491	-1.07
4			-1048.44	-1.14
5			-1707.00	-1.99
6			-2956.17	-3.11
7			-4795.96	-3.27
Sum	2793.64	3.57	-19928.0	-3.41

* The lag structure of $\mathring{\pi} - \mathring{p}_i$ ($\mathring{p}_k$) is estimated under the assumption of a linear (quadratic) polynomial with end-point restriction for far (no end-point restrictions). See Chapter 4 footnote 35 for a description of the Almon procedure and a definition of the end-point constraints.

The several statistics indicate that the fit of this relation with the actual data is good. The explanatory variables represent, however, the net investments only, because the variables used for explaining the replacement investments appeared to have the wrong sign or to be highly insignificant. Most likely this result is partly due to the specification of the present model's supply side, which does not include a proxy for the capital stock in use nor for the lifetime of equipment in use.

In accordance with the arguments presented in Keus (1980), only a part of non-wage income is considered to be profits. Using the assumptions mentioned by Keus this part, d_{pr}, of non-wage income is approximated by annual data from the National Accounts. When simulating the model, it is assumed that the profits' part of non-wage income, is negatively related to the long-term interest rate. Since only annual data of d_{pr} are available, a relation has been estimated between d_{pr} and the yearly average of the long-term interest rate. The average interest rate of both the current and the preceding year have been used as explanatory variables in the regression. The best fit is obtained when the one-year lag was used. Then the estimated relation is

$$d_{pr} = \underset{(4.88)}{-0.332}\, r_l(-1) + \underset{(10.29)}{1.451}$$

estimation period: 1970-1980 (annual data)
R^2(adj.) = 0.70   DW = 1.98

The corresponding relation used in the quarterly model is

$$d_{pr} = -0.332 \cdot 0.25 \cdot \Sigma_{j=3}^{6}\, r_l(-j) + 1.451$$

In this manner an increase of the long-term domestic interest rate reduces the firms' profit and thus gives rise to a decrease of investments by firms.

5.3.4 *International trade in goods*

The transactions on the current account consist of merchandise trade, trade in services, investment income, investment payments and unilateral transfers. Part of merchandise trade, namely trade in aeroplanes and ships consists of a few very large transactions. Another part *viz.* trade in oil and natural gas is highly influenced by oil-price shocks. Because of their special characteristics, these two categories of international trade, imports and exports of ships and aeroplanes, and oil and natural gas are considered to be exogenous.

Trade in services consists of transportation income/expenditure, foreign tourists' expenditure in the Netherlands and Dutch tourists' expenditure abroad and other services income/expenditure. The imports and exports of services show a strong seasonal pattern caused by fluctuations within the year of tourists' expenditure. For the present study trade in services as well as unilateral transfers are assumed to be exogenous.

The import of goods - excluding ships, aeroplanes, oil and natural gas - depends on domestic demand, relative prices and the utilization rate of production capacity. The last variable represents the home pressure of demand effect, according to which a high level of the utilization rate will give rise to an increase in imports, because part of the home demand cannot be met by the domestic producers. In the Netherlands this phenomenon is also known as the Zijlstra effect.

The estimated equation for the volume of imported goods is

$$m_g = \underset{(14.46)}{0.256\, v} + \underset{(3.38)}{0.307\, i_n} + \underset{(2.83)}{80.00\, \Sigma_{j=1}^{4} \alpha_j\, q_{-j}} - \underset{(3.78)}{11913.8\, \Sigma_{j=1}^{7} \beta_j\, (p_m/p_v)_{-j}}$$

$$+ \underset{(3.37)}{544.36\, S1} - \underset{(7.01)}{2047.43\, S2} + \underset{(1.46)}{6640.83}$$

estimation period: 1970:I - 1980:IV
R^2(adj.) = 0.98 DW = 1.88

where $\alpha_1=\alpha_4=0.2, \alpha_2=\alpha_3=0.3; \beta_1=\beta_7=0.083, \beta_2=\beta_6=0.143, \beta_3=\beta_5=0.179$ and $\beta_4=0.19$. These weights are estimated by means of the Almon method under the assumption of a quadratic polynomial with zero constraints at both end-points. Domestic demand is represented by total expenditures, v, and investments in stocks, i_n. The influence of relative prices is captured by the ratio of the price of imported goods, p_m, to the price of domestic sales, p_v.

In some specifications we also introduced a measure of the uncertainty with regard to exchange rate movements in order to detect whether unexpected movements in exchange rates reduce imports. The coefficients of the proxies used appeared to have a wrong sign or to be statistically insignificant. The proxies used were the absolute value and the square of the difference between the expected and realized value of the exchange rate index.

The export of goods - excluding ships, aeroplanes, oil and natural gas - in essence depends upon the same factors as the import of goods. The demand for exports is approximated by an index of world imports. According to the home pressure of demand effect, a high utilization rate or an increase in this rate will depress the volume of exports, because domestic producers can easily sell their products at home. The price of competitors on foreign markets, p^f_{co}, and the price of exports, p^f_g, are expressed in foreign currency, because the foreign currency price of exports determines the demand by foreigners. The estimated relation is

$$x_g = \underset{(5.98)}{0.664\, x_g(-1)} + \underset{(14.38)}{223.23}\, [m_w - \underset{(5.98)}{0.664\, m_w(-1)}] - \underset{(1.78)}{36.187\, p^f_{ex}}$$

$$+ \underset{(1.59)}{23.453\, p^f_{exc}} + \underset{(1.85)}{1061.7742}$$

estimation period: 1970:I - 1980:IV
R^2(adj) = 0.98 DW = 2.18 h = -0.88

A Koyck lag has been used for describing the lagged influence of the relative prices (represented by p_g^f and p_{co}^f). on the volume of exports. The average adjustment lag is about three quarters. The volume of exports reacts immediately to a change in the volume of world trade. No significant impact of the home pressure of demand effect could be found.

5.4 Wages and prices

5.4.1 *Introduction*

The percentage changes in domestic prices are determined by the costs, the prices of foreign competitors and the utilization rate. A decreasing or a low level of the utilization rate as well as a gradual evolution of the foreign competitors prices will mitigate the price pushing influence of domestic costs on domestic prices.

Three types of costs are distinguished, *viz.* the costs of imported goods, the costs of labour, and the user costs of capital. The relative change of the costs of imported goods is the sum of the exchange rate's relative change and the relative change of the foreign price of these goods. Since these relations are merely definitions, we do not discuss them in this chapter but add them directly to the model, which is listed in the next chapter. The costs of labour consist of the wage bill corrected for the increase in labour productivity. The explanatory factors of the wage rate are described in Section 5.4.2, whereafter the approximation of the user costs of capital is presented in Section 5.4.3. After this explanation of the costs for domestic producers, the prices of their final goods are presented in Sections 5.4.4 to 5.4.6.

5.4.2 *The wage rate*

The percentage change of the wage bill per wage earner in firms depends upon changes in consumer prices, changes in the productivity of labour and changes in the share of taxes and premiums in the wage bill, as well as the level of unemployment (Phillips curve) and some dummy variables expressing special events.

During the estimation period, the effect of changes in consumer prices upon wages was determined by the automatic cost of living clauses in labour contracts. In the Netherlands these clauses imply that on January 1st and July 1st, respectively the average increase in prices during the period April-October and October-April respectively are included in the wage bill. As in Van den Berg *et al.* (1983) the average increase in prices during the period April-October has been approximated by 0.125 $\overset{\circ}{p}_{cI}$ + 0.375 $\overset{\circ}{p}_{cII}$ + 0.375 $\overset{\circ}{p}_{cIII}$ + 0.125 $\overset{\circ}{p}_{cIV}$ in order to take account of some overlap between quarters. Only in the first and third quarter of the year does this average increase in consumer prices give rise to an increase in the wage bill.

The general view is that it is not temporary fluctuations in labour productivity but the movement during a longer period of this productivity that will influence the wage bill. This effect can be incorporated in the model by a long distributed lag of the actual change in the productivity of labour, $\overset{\circ}{y} - \overset{\circ}{a}$, or by a much shorter lag of the change in labour productivity when the economy is at full capacity, $\overset{\circ}{y}^* - \overset{\circ}{a}^*$, which can be calculated from equation (5.6). In order to avoid very long lags, the second route has been selected. The lag structure is the same as the one used in Van den Berg *et al.* (1983) who apply the procedure for modelling the influence of labour productivity on the wage bill.

Part of the increase in the share of taxes and premiums in the total wage bill of firms will be compensated for in the wage rate. It has been assumed that this compensation effect can be approximated by a simple four-quarter moving average of this share's percentage change.

According to the traditional Phillips curve effect, the *level* of unemployment negatively relates to the increase in wages. Phillips notes that "a second factor influencing the rate of change of money wage rates might be the rate of change of the demand for labour, and so of unemployment" (Phillips, 1958, p.283). The KOMPAS model, Van den Berg *et al.* (1983), incorporates the influence of the *level* of the unemployment rate on the wage rate, whereas the MORKMON model relates the *changes* in the unemployment rate to wage changes.[15] In the present model we have tried to incorporate both effects in the wage rate equation. Although it can be argued that in all likelihood the resulting relation will be nonlinear, we have assumed that the two unemployment effects on the wage rate can be represented by a simple moving average of past unemployment rates and of the changes in these rates.

In addition to these more or less structural variables some dummy variables representing events specific for our estimation period have been included in the wage equation.[16] These events are the once-only payment of *f*400.- in 1970, represented by dum70 and the severe winter of 1979, represented by dumw2. The last dummy has to be included because the payments to compensate for delays due to frost are not included in the wage bill and thus the time series of

---

[15] See Siebrand and Swank (1986), p. 297 for the consequences of this different modelling of the relation between unemployment and the wage rate. It should be noted that in case of a vertical Phillips curve this trade-off does not exist.

[16] See also De Nederlandsche Bank (1984), p. 63.

the latter shows a dip which cannot be explained by the variables already included in the equation.

The ultimately selected equation of the percentage change in the wage bill per wage earner is

$$\mathring{w} = \underset{(2.17)}{0.816}\,(S1 + S3)\, \Sigma_{j=1}^{4} \alpha_j\, \mathring{p}_{c\,-j} + \underset{(1.60)}{0.805}\, \Sigma_{j=1}^{4} j/10\, (\mathring{y}^* - \mathring{a}^*)_{-j-2} +$$

$$+ \underset{(1.48)}{0.705}\, \Sigma_{j=0}^{7} \beta_j\, TS_{-j} - \underset{(1.65)}{0.267}\, \Sigma_{j=0}^{7} \beta_j\, [U/a_s]_{-j} - \underset{(4.24)}{0.032}\, dumw2$$

$$+ \underset{(2.52)}{0.028}\, dum70 + \underset{(2.11)}{0.017}\, S2 - \underset{(3.59)}{0.029}\, S4 + \underset{(1.53)}{0.017}$$

estimation period: 1970:I - 1980:IV
R^2(adj.) = 0.84 D.W. = 2.14

where $\alpha_1=\alpha_4=0.125$, $\alpha_2=\alpha_3=0.375$, $\beta_j = (j+1)/36$, j= 0,...,7 and the tax shifting variable TS is the percentage change in (TW + PW)/YW. The lag structure of TS, of $(\mathring{y}^* - \mathring{a}^*)$ and of the level of unemployment divided by the supply of labour, U/a_s, are obtained by means of the Almon procedure.[17]

The rather low value of the tax shifting variable's t-statistic is most likely due to the fact that this variable does not show much variation within a year. It should be noted, however, that the value of this statistic is sensitive for changes in the lag structures of $\mathring{y}^* - \mathring{a}^*$ and U/a_s. The t-statistic of TS's coefficient increases to 1.9, if slightly different specifications of these lag structures are used.[18]

As noted above the Phillips curve effect refers to the influence of both the level and the change of unemployment in the wage rate. The coefficients of the change of unemployment appeared to be statistically insignificant.

---

[17] All three lag schemes have been estimated under the assumption of a linear polynomial and end-point restrictions for near (see footnote 35 in Chapter 4 for details).

[18] The specification mentioned differed from the one presented in the text in that in the lag structure of U/a_s the zero constraint was near and that the lag structure of $\mathring{y}^* - \mathring{a}^*$ was 0.33 $(\mathring{y}^* - \mathring{a}^*)_{-1}$ + 0.34 $(\mathring{y}^* - \mathring{a}^*)_{-2}$ + 0.33 $(\mathring{y}^* - \mathring{a}^*)_{-3}$. The latter is the lag scheme used in Van den Berg *et al.* (1983). Then, however, the absolute values of the t- statistics of U/a_s, the price compensation term and of $\mathring{y}^* - \mathring{a}^*$ drop to 1.65, 1.76 and 0.39 respectively. This result also indicates that $(\mathring{y}^* - \mathring{a}^*)$'s coefficient is very sensitive for changes in its own lag structure.

5.4.3 *User costs of capital*

The user costs of capital consists of two parts, the depreciation costs and the interest payments on the initial investment, so that per unit these costs are:

$$p_k = p_i \cdot r + d \tag{5.15}$$

where p_k is the capital cost per unit, p_i is the purchase price of the capital goods, r is the interest rate and d is the depreciation costs per unit per period.

The level of depreciation costs per period depends upon the method used for calculating the annual depreciation of capital goods. As in Driehuis *et al.* (1979), these depreciation costs are approximated by the annuity formula, because according to Van Wallenburg (1977) it is most likely that the majority of Dutch firms uses this method.[19] When deriving the fixed amount of depreciation per period, d, it is assumed that the purchase value of the capital goods equals the sum of the discounted value of the constant amortization charges over the expected life of the investment, i.e.[20]

$$p_i = \Sigma_{j=0}^{lp-1} d\,(1+r)^j \tag{5.16}$$

where lp is the expected life of the investment. The value of d can be derived from (5.16) by subtracting (1+r) times (5.16) from (5.16), so that

$$d = p_i \cdot r \,/ [\,(1+r)^{lp} - 1] \tag{5.17}$$

The capital costs per unit are obtained by substituting this expression for d in equation (5.15), which yields

$$p_k = p_i \cdot r \,/\, [\,(1+r)^{lp} - 1\,] + p_i \cdot r = p_i \cdot r \cdot (1+r)^{lp} \,/\, [\,(1+r)^{lp} - 1\,] \tag{5.18}$$

which in continuous form equals[21]

$$p_k = p_i \cdot r \,/\, [\,1 - e^{-r \cdot lp}\,] \tag{5.19}$$

---

[19] See Van Wallenburg (1977), p. 57. It should be noted that this statement is not based on an analysis of the depreciation methods employed by Dutch firms but on a prior information.

[20] Contrary to e.g. Driehuis *et al.* (1979), no account has been taken of the influence of government's subsidies on the costs of a project.

[21] See e.g. Salter (1969), p. 20.

The relative change of the user costs is obtained by differentiating this formula

$$\mathring{p}_k = \mathring{p}_i + \{1 - r \cdot lp \;/\; [e^{r \cdot lp} - 1]\}\mathring{r} + \{r \;/\; [e^{r \cdot lp} - 1]\}\ \Delta lp \qquad (5.20)$$

According to Van Wallenburg (1977) most Dutch firms use a fixed life of equipment, when calculating the profitability of an investment project. Although the particular length of the expected lifetime differs per sector, in the majority of industries it is assumed, that this length is 10 years. In accordance with this usage, lp is assumed to be constant and equal to 40 (quarters). Then $\Delta lp=0.0$ and the third part of (5.20) disappears. In accordance with the assumption of an expected life of 10 years, r is represented by the long-term domestic interest rate.

5.4.4 *The price of consumption*

As explanatory variables of the price of consumption we have considered the price of all three costs categories, as well as the change in labour productivity when the economy is at full capacity and the utilization rate. In order to obtain plausible estimates, the coefficient of the price of imported consumption goods, p_{cm}, is set at the a priori value of 0.2. The same assumption is made in the MORKMON. The coefficient of the utilization rate's change appeared to be wrongly signed and insignificant so this variable is for that reason omitted. The preferred equation is

$$\mathring{p}_c = \underset{(-)}{0.20}\ \mathring{p}_{cm} + \underset{(1.91)}{0.132}\ \Sigma_{i=3}^{6}\ \alpha_i\ \mathring{p}_k(-i) + \underset{(4.93)}{0.472}\ \Sigma_{i=1}^{4}\ \beta_i\ \mathring{w}_g^f(-i)$$

$$-\ \underset{(2.46)}{0.408}\ (\mathring{y}^* - \mathring{a}^*)(-2) + \underset{(6.73)}{0.021}\ S2 + \underset{(1.95)}{0.006}\ S4 - \underset{(0.52)}{0.002}$$

estimation period: 1970:I-1980:IV
$R^2(adj) = 0.65$ DW = 2.23 $\rho = -0.22$
(1.75)

where $\alpha_1=0.1$, $\alpha_2=0.2$, $\alpha_3=0.3$, $\alpha_4=0.4$, $\beta_1=\beta_3=0.3$ and $\beta_2=0.4$. These coefficients are estimated by means of the Almon procedure, under the assumptions that for the lag structure of $\mathring{p}_k$ ($\mathring{w}_g^f$, wage rate corrected for absenteeism because of illness) the degree of the polynomial is one (two) and the appropriate end-point restrictions are near (both).

5.4.5 *The price of investments*

The percentage change of the price of investments in fixed assets is determined by the various costs and the utilization rate lagged one period. The latter has been included although its t-statistic is rather low. The change in the productivity of labour has been excluded, because its coefficient appeared to have the wrong sign. The ultimately selected equation is

$$\overset{o}{p}_i = \underset{(4.02)}{0.264\,\overset{o}{p}_{mi}} + \underset{(2.07)}{0.124\,\overset{o}{p}_{mi}(-1)} + \underset{(5.02)}{0.244\,\overset{o}{p}_k} + \underset{(1.73)}{0.0005\,q(-1)} + \underset{(1.85)}{0.136\,\overset{o}{w}{}^f_g(-4)}$$

$$- \underset{(1.81)}{0.305\,(\overset{o}{y}{}^* - \overset{o}{a}{}^*)(-2)} - \underset{(1.81)}{0.153\,(\overset{o}{y}{}^* - \overset{o}{a}{}^*)(-3)} - \underset{(1.41)}{0.039}$$

estimation period: 1970:I - 1980:IV
R^2(adj.) = 0.67 DW = 2.22

The coefficients of $(\overset{o}{y}{}^* - \overset{o}{a}{}^*)(-2)$ and $(\overset{o}{y}{}^* - \overset{o}{a}{}^*)(-3)$ are estimated by means of the Almon-method under the assumption of a linear polynomial and an end-point constraint for far (see footnote 35 in Chapter 4). Note that along with the current value of the percentage change of the price of imported investment goods, $\overset{o}{p}_{mi}$, the one period lagged value of this variable is also included in the equation. This lagged value has been added to the relation, because it appeared that whereas normally the correlation between the $\overset{o}{p}_i$ and $\overset{o}{p}_{mi}$ is greater than that between $\overset{o}{p}_i$ and $\overset{o}{p}_{mi}(-1)$ during certain periods notably in 1973, the relative magnitude of these correlations changed.

5.4.6 *The price of exports*

In addition to domestic costs, the price of exports, p_{ex}, will be influenced by the price of competitors on foreign markets, p_{exc}. Some preliminary regressions revealed that the single correlation between these two prices is high. However, this correlation reduces substantially if the price of imported raw materials is added to the equation. Furthermore, it appeared that during most periods the price of exports reacts on the *current* price of competitors but that for some quarters after the first oil-price shock it reacts on the price of competitors lagged two periods.[22] The option price theory offers a possible explanation for this

---

[22] This lag of two periods in the influence of the price of competitors on the price of exports does not exist if the former is approximated by the price of competitors used in MORKMON. The latter has not been used in the model, because its time series did not contain observations for the 1960s, so that it

difference in reaction to the competitors' price movements. According to this theory, economic agents adjust their decision variable - the price of exports - only if the change in the relevant uncertain variable - the price of foreign competitors - exceeds an upper or a lower bound. The price of exported goods is not changed if the change of the price of competitors remains between the upper and lower bound, which thus determine a range of inaction. As is shown in Dixit (1989), under very plausible assumptions an increase in uncertainty will dramatically widen this range of inaction. Thus, after the first-oil shock the resulting increase in uncertainty with regard to prices and exchange rates may have caused Dutch exporters to wait for a while before they followed their foreign competitors. We decided to assume that during the period 1973:IV-1974:III the price of exports is influenced by $\mathring{p}_{exc}(-2)$, whereas during the remaining periods it is influenced by the unlagged price of competitors. The ultimately selected relation is

$$\mathring{p}_{ex} = \underset{(3.21)}{0.776} \; \Sigma_{i=4}^{7} \alpha_i \; \mathring{w}_g^f(-i) + \underset{(4.15)}{0.3426} \; \mathring{p}_{mrm}$$

$$+ \underset{(3.36)}{0.270} \; [(1.0 - dum734) \cdot \mathring{p}_{exc} + dum734 \cdot \mathring{p}_{exc}(-2)] - \underset{(2.83)}{0.022}$$

estimation period: 1970:1 - 1980:IV
$\bar{R}$ (adj) = 0.49 DW = 2.11 $\rho = \underset{(1.78)}{-0.27}$

where dum734 is a dummy variable which is 1 during the period 1973:IV-1974:III, and p_{mrm} is the price index of imported raw material. As the relation illustrates, the price of exports depends upon the wage rate and the price of imported raw material. The coefficient of the user costs of capital appeared to be negative and/or highly insignificant.

This relation of the export price's percentage change concludes this chapter on the non-financial part of the model. The next chapter sets out the relations analysed in the previous and the present chapter, and also the definitional relations. Subsequently, the quality of the entire model is studied by means of a simulation during the sample period.

---

precluded the possibility of including distributed lags in the price terms of the equation of the exports of goods.

6 THE COMPLETE MODEL: INTEGRATION AND SIMULATION

6.1 Introduction

In this chapter the different pieces of the model described in the preceding two chapters are brought together and the interaction between the different parts (variables) is considered. These interactions come to the fore particularly in the results of a simulation of the model during the period 1970:I-1980:IV which concludes this chapter.

As in Jager (1981) and in accordance with our criticism of empirical tests of exchange rate determination presented in Chapter 2, especially Sections 2.5 and 2.6.1, the spot rate is derived from the balance of payments identity, which is a reflection of the foreign exchange market. The interest rates on short-term and long-term domestic assets are also derived from the market equilibrium in question. This practice of explaining the price of, or return on, a financial asset from its market equilibrium is known as the implicit explanation of the interest rate. It contrasts with the explicit explanation, which constitutes the estimation of a relation of the relevant interest rate (exchange rate). Den Butter (1986) examines the consequences of these two different types of modelling the interest rate on the simulation results of some small models. However, Den Butter does not estimate the parameters and thus does not address the question which of these two methods best describes the historical data.

An important characteristic of the implicit explanation is that the interest rate is the ultimate result of substituting the relevant estimated relations of the demand for financial assets in the market equilibrium. Consequently, the researcher cannot directly improve the explanatory power of the interest rate relation. If the resulting estimated values fit the historical data badly, then the researcher should re-examine all underlying demand relations. As far as we know, in the literature no attention has been paid to the conditions under which the implicit method gives reasonable results. This task is accomplished in the next section where we derive a relation between the explanatory power of the implicit method and the statistical characteristics of the relevant demand functions.

In Section 6.3 the main transmission mechanisms between the monetary and real part are described. Section 6.4 contains all equations of the model. The explanatory power of individual relations and of the entire model are described and illustrated in Section 6.5.

6.2 The implicit method for deriving interest rates and exchange rates

As noted in the introduction to this chapter, a main characteristic of the implicit method is that the explanatory quality of the rate concerned depends upon the estimated equations of the various sectors' demand for this particular financial asset. In this section we derive a relation between the characteristics of the demand functions and the explanatory power of the interest rate and exchange rate.

Suppose that there are n assets and that we want to derive the interest rate of the first asset, r_1. For convenience, let us in addition assume that this asset is demanded by just one sector, that the supply is exogenous, and that at the beginning of the period (the end of the previous period) desired and actual stocks are equal. Then the market is in equilibrium if

$$\Delta A_1^s = \Delta A_1^d \tag{6.1}$$

The implicit approach derives the interest rate from this market equilibrium. Essentially two methods can be distinguished. The first one is to use an iterative method which ensures that the market equilibrium always holds. For instance this procedure is used in the CPB models, see e.g. Van den Berg *et al.* (1983) and Hasselman *et al.* (1983). A disadvantage of this iterative procedure for the present study is that it cannot be applied in the optimal control programme which will be used in the next chapter. We therefore decided to use an alternative slightly less elegant method for deriving the interest rates from the market equilibrium. This method which has also been employed in Jager (1981 and 1982) and De Jong (1981) can be used in the optimal control experiments.

In order to explain this second method, let us consider the equilibrium condition (6.1). The change in asset demand ex post, ΔA_1^d, consists of the ex ante demand, $\Delta \bar{A}_1^d$, and an error term u. The ex ante demand is the fitted value resulting from a regression such as presented in Chapter 4. Let us assume that the demand for financial assets is estimated by multi-assets partial adjustment relations (see equation (4.8)). Then the demand ex post can be written as

$$\Delta A_1^d = \Delta \bar{A}_1^d + u$$

$$= [\ \Sigma_{j=1}^n \delta_{1j}\ (\ \Sigma_{k=1}^n \alpha_{jk} \cdot r_k \cdot W + \Sigma_{h=1}^n \beta_{jh} \cdot X_h\ -\ A_j(-1))/W(-1) + u\ ] \cdot W(-1)$$

$$= \ \Sigma_{j=1}^n \delta_{1j}\ \Sigma_{k=1}^n \alpha_{jk} \cdot W \cdot r_k + \Sigma_{j=1}^n \delta_{1j}\ (\Sigma_{h=1}^m \beta_{jh} \cdot X_h\ -\ A_j(-1)) + u \cdot W(-1) \tag{6.2}$$

The interest rate can be obtained by substituting equation (6.2) in the market equilibrium (6.1) and solving the resulting relation for the interest rate r_1, so that

$$r_1 = \{\Delta A_1^s - \Sigma_{j=1}^n \delta_{1j} \Sigma_{k=2}^n \alpha_{jk} \cdot W \cdot r_k + \Sigma_{j=1}^n \delta_{1j} (\Sigma_{h=1}^m \beta_{jh} \cdot X_h - A_j(-1))$$

$$- u \cdot W(-1)\} / \Sigma_{j=1}^n \delta_{1j} \cdot \alpha_{j1} \cdot W \qquad (6.3)$$

Relation (6.3) is an identity. The implicit method for deriving the interest rate consists of substituting the ex ante demand, $\Delta \bar{A}_1^d$, in the market equilibrium. The resulting equation is

$$r_1 = \{\Delta A_1^s - \Sigma_{j=1}^n \delta_{1j} \Sigma_{k=2}^n \alpha_{jk} \cdot W \cdot r_k$$

$$+ \Sigma_{j=1}^n \delta_{1j} (\Sigma_{h=1}^m \beta_{jh} \cdot X_h - A_j(-1))\} / \Sigma_{j=1}^n \delta_{1j} \cdot \alpha_{j1} \cdot W \qquad (6.4)$$

Comparing equation (6.4) with (6.3) we conclude that the interest rate obtained by the implicit method differs from its historical value by the term

$$- u \cdot W(-1) / \Sigma_{j=1}^n \delta_{1j} \cdot \alpha_{j1} \cdot W \qquad (6.5)$$

In this term the coefficients δ_{1j} and α_{j1} are constant. Mostly, the financial wealth of the sector concerned grows gradually so that the ratio W(-1)/W shows little fluctuation. This suggests that in many circumstances the disturbance term of the asset demand function is the main determining factor of the relevant rate's fit. If this disturbance term is small and more or less serially uncorrelated then we expect that the difference between the fitted and historical values of the interest rate will also be small and serially uncorrelated. If the asset demand function's error terms are not well-behaved, this feature will also characterize the difference between the fitted and historical value of the interest rate. Of course the magnitude of this effect depends upon the value of the denominator in (6.5), which is among other things determined by the size of the coefficients δ_{1j}, α_{j1}. The results of the application of the implicit method to be presented below confirm this relation between the asset demand function's error terms and the explanatory power of the interest (exchange) rate.

It can easily be shown that when the total demand of an asset is determined by various sectors, the difference between the fitted and actual values of the interest rate is the sum of terms like (6.5).

Let us now turn to the application of the implicit method for determining the exchange rate and the interest rate on short-term and long-term domestic assets. The interest rate on short-term domestic assets is derived from the following equilibrium condition

$$\Delta NDAS^{g} = \Delta NDAS^{p} + \Delta NDAS^{b} + \Delta NDAS^{f} \tag{6.6}$$

Substituting the behavioural equations of $\Delta NDAS^{p}$, $\Delta NDAS^{b}$ and $\Delta NDAS^{f}$ in (6.6) and solving the resulting relation for r_s yields

$$\begin{aligned} r_s = \{ & \Delta NDAS^{g} - (-.689\ NDAS^{p}_{-1} - 0.578\ NDAL^{p}_{-1} \\ & + 0.172\ LS_{-1} - 0.447\ Y + FA^{p}\cdot[0.013\ r_l - 0.005\ (r_f+\mathring{e}^{e}) \\ & - 0.036\ r_{ls} + 0.425] + FA^{p}_{-1}\cdot[0.0004\ S1 - 0.017\ S2 \\ & + 0.05\ q] -.4858\ NDAS^{b}_{-1} - 0.422\ NDAL^{b}_{-1} - 0.354\ NFA^{b}_{-1} \\ & + 0.144\ NDAS^{p} + 0.228\ NDALS + 0.004\ \Delta liq\cdot NDAS^{p} \\ & + 0.410\ \Delta SPL + 0.252\ \Delta RES + FA^{b}\cdot[0.551\ r_l \\ & - 0.278\ (r_f+\mathring{e}^{e}) + 0.207] + FA^{b}_{-1}\cdot[0.005\ S1 + 0.015\ S2 \\ & - 0.007\ S3] - 0.500\ NDAS^{f}_{-1} + 272.922 \\ & + W^{f}\cdot[-0.046(\mathring{e}^{e}_{fr} + \mathring{e}^{e}_{uk}) - 0.321\ (r_{s,wg} + r_{s,us}) + 0.859\ DUMS \\ & + 0.932] \} / \{ 0.047\ FA^{b} + 4.8559\ FA^{p} + 9.1380\ W^{f} \} \end{aligned} \tag{6.7}$$

The fitted values derived from (6.7), $\hat{r}_s$, and the historical values are shown in Figure 6.1. This figure makes clear that the fit of relation (6.7) is excellent.

The determination of the interest rate on long-term domestic assets appears to be an example of a less successful application of the implicit method. For the period 1977:I-1980:IV this interest rate is derived from the following equilibrium condition

$$\Delta NDAL^{g} = \Delta NDAL^{p} + \Delta NDAL^{b} + \Delta NDAL^{f} \tag{6.8-a}$$

During 1970:I-1976:IV the long-term interest rate is not an explanatory variable of $\Delta NDAL^{f}$, although r_l explains r_{sh} and thus indirectly influences $\Delta NDAL^{f}$. Therefore, for this period the modified equilibrium

Fig 6.1 The interest rate on short-term domestic assets

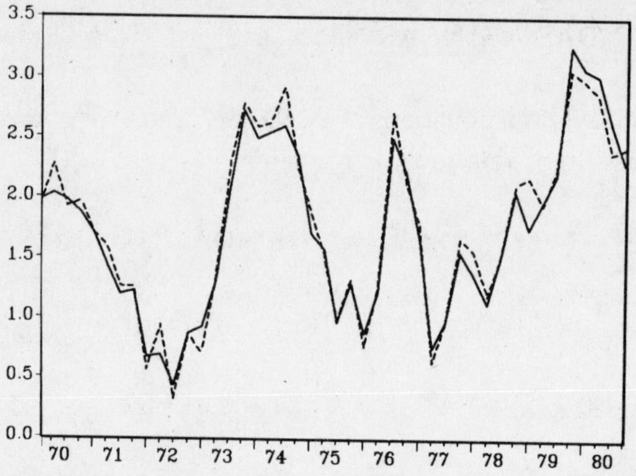

$$\Delta NDAL^g - \Delta NDAL^f = \Delta NDAL^p + \Delta NDAL^b \tag{6.8-b}$$

has been used. In order to obtain the relation of r_l for the period 1970:I-1980:IV, the behavioural equations of the variables at the right-hand side of (6.8-a) and (6.8-b) are substituted in these equilibrium conditions, whereafter the resulting relation is solved for r_l

$$\begin{aligned} r_l = \{&\Delta NDAL^g - d7076 \cdot \Delta NDAL^f - [-\ 0.144\ NDAL^p_{-1} + 0.111\ LS_{-1} \\ &- 0.099\ Y + FA^p \cdot [-.0085\ r_s + 0.003\ r_{ls} + 0.215] \\ &- FA^p_{-1} \cdot [0.0014\ q + 0.005\ S1] - .205\ RU_{-1} - 0.280\ NDAS^b_{-1} \\ &-.185\ NDAL^b - 0.043\ NDAS^p + 0.116\ NDALS + FA^b \cdot [0.057\ r_s \\ &- 0.007\ r_f + \mathring{e}^e + 0.116] - FA^b \cdot [0.017\ S1 + 0.018\ S2 \\ &+ 0.005\ S3] + (1.0 - d7067) \cdot (-.094\ NDAL^f_{-1} \\ &+ W^f \cdot [-2.248 \cdot (r_{l,wg} + r_{l,uk}) - 0.382\ \mathring{e}^e_{FR} + 2.303\ S2 \\ &+ 1.859\ S3 + 3.629\ d791 + 5.855]\ \} \\ &/ \{\ 0.3145\ FA^p + 2.0388\ FA^b + (1.0 - d7076 \cdot 449.576 \cdot W^f\ \} \end{aligned} \tag{6.9}$$

Fig 6.2 The interest rate on long-term domestic assets

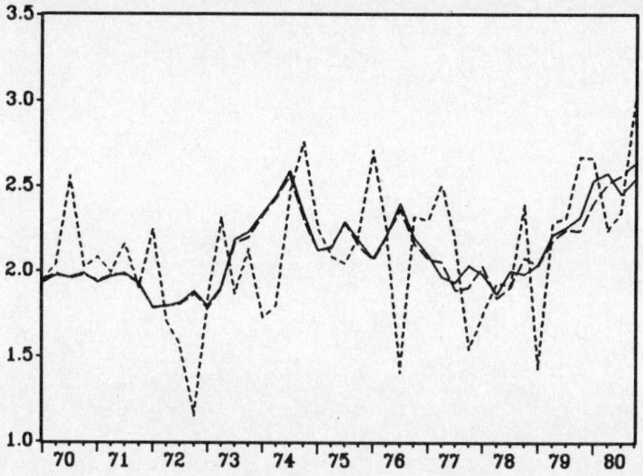

——— historical
. . . . . fitted (equation (6.9))
- - - fitted (equation (6.10))

The variable d7076 is a dummy variable which is 1.0 from 1970:I to 1976:IV and zero elsewhere. Figure 6.2 shows the fitted values calculated from (6.9), $\hat{r}_l$, and the historical values of the interest rate on long-term domestic assets. The fit of (6.9) appears to be rather bad. In order to detect the source of this result, features of the various behavioural relations' disturbance terms are presented in Table 6.1. When comparing the figures of the long-term domestic assets with those of the short-term domestic assets we note that the R^2(adj.) of the private and banking's sector demand relations are lower and that the denominator of r_l is about one third of the short-term interest rate's denominator. Given the fact that during the period 1970:I-1976:IV the foreign demand for long-term domestic assets does not directly influence the r_l, we conclude that the bad performance of (6.9) most likely originates from the behavioural relations of the domestic sectors. Therefore we have also calculated the fitted values of the interest rate on long-term domestic assets if equation (6.9) is corrected for the disturbance terms in the equations of $\Delta NDAL^p$ and $\Delta NDAL^b$, that is

$$\hat{r}'_l = (6.9) - [u_p.FA^p_{-1} + u_b.FA^b_{-1}] \,/\, [0.315 \cdot FA^p + 2.039 \cdot FA^b$$

$$+ (1.0 - d7067) \cdot 449.576 \cdot W^f] \qquad (6.10)$$

Table 6.1 Characteristics of disturbance terms of variables in equation (6.8)

asset	DW	R^2(adj.)	mean	standard deviation
$\Delta NDAS^p$	1.55	0.81	-213.99	1096.28
$\Delta NDAS^b$	2.11	0.76	3.62	532.53
$\Delta NDAS^f$	1.88	0.50	-7.57	123.75
denominator of r_s			664332.19	
$\Delta NDAL^p$	1.74	0.72	-33.26	909.51
$\Delta NDAL^b$	1.68	0.61	-14.94	570.14
$\Delta NDAL^{f**}$	1.90	0.51		
denominator of r_l			247785.55	

* The DW-statistic and the R^2(adj.) refer to the relations presented in Chapter 4 where the change in the asset is divided by FA^p_{-1}, FA^b_{-1} or W^f respectively. The mean and standard deviation refer to the disturbance terms of the variable listed in the row involved.
** The statistics shown in this row refer to the period 1977:I-1980:IV.

The variables u_p and u_b are the disturbance terms of $\Delta NDAL^p/FA^p_{-1}$ and $\Delta NDAL^b/FA^b_{-1}$, respectively. Since from 1970:I to 1976:IV r_l is derived from the condition (6.8-b), during this period the time series of $\hat{r}'_l$ corresponds with the historical values. A comparison of the time series of $\hat{r}'_l$, which is also presented in Figure 6.2, with the historical data reveals that this correction does indeed significantly improve the explanatory power of the relation during the second part of the sample period.

In order to improve the explanatory quality of the interest rate derived by means of the implicit method without the need of any correction, we should thus re-estimate the relations of $\Delta NDAL^p$ and $\Delta NDAL^b$. Since these equations form part of the private sector's and banks' portfolio this would imply that we should re-estimate all relations of these sectors' portfolio (see Chapter 4). Consequently, the other relations - particular those of the holdings of short-term domestic assets - will be affected so that the explanatory power of (6.7) might deteriorate to an unacceptable level. We have therefore decided in favour of an alternative route, namely to use the corrected version (6.10) in the simulation and optimal control experiments.

In accordance with our criticism in Section 2.6.1 on the assumption of perfect capital mobility, the endogenous exchange rate has been derived from the capital account of the balance of payments. This identity is

$$CA + \Delta NDAL^f + \Delta NDAS^f - \Delta NFA^p - \Delta NFA^b - \Delta RES + STATBB = 0.0 \quad (6.11)$$

The behavioural relations of $\Delta NDAL^f$, $\Delta NDAS^f$, ΔNFA^p and ΔNFA^b are substituted in (6.11). The resulting equation is rewritten so that the left-hand side consists of the terms containing the expected percentage change of the exchange rates and the right-hand side is comprised of the other variables, i.e.

$$- \{d7067 \cdot W^f \cdot 0.135 \cdot (\mathring{e}^e_{US} + \mathring{e}^e_{FR}) + (1-d7067) \cdot W^f \cdot 0.382 \cdot \mathring{e}^e_{FR}$$

$$+ (0.417\ FA^p + 0.590\ FA^b) \cdot (0.318 \mathring{e}^e_{US} + 0.51\ \mathring{e}^e_{WG} + 0.177\ \mathring{e}^e_{FR}$$

$$+ 0.055\ \mathring{e}^e_{UK}) = - CA + \Delta RES - STATBB - \Delta NDAL^f \backslash \{\mathring{e}^e\} + \Delta NFA^p \backslash \{\mathring{e}^e\}$$

$$+ \Delta NFA^b \backslash \{\mathring{e}^e\} \tag{6.12}$$

where $\Delta NDAL^f \backslash \{\mathring{e}^e\}$, $\Delta NFA^p \backslash \{\mathring{e}^e\}$ and $\Delta NFA^b \backslash \{\mathring{e}^e\}$ stand for the explanatory variables of the behavioural relations concerned excluding the exchange rate's expected percentage change. In order to endogenize the spot rate, the constituent parts of the expected percentage changes are made explicit, i.e. $\mathring{e}^e_{t+1}$ is rewritten as $\mathring{e}^e_{t+1} = (e^e_{t+1} - e_t)/e_t = e^e{}_{t+1}/e_t - 1$. This relation is used for deriving the expected levels from the expected percentage changes and the historical spot rates of the exchange rate.

The Dutch guilder - US dollar rate has been selected as the endogenous exchange rate. The other bilateral exchange rates are eliminated from (6.12) by using the following definitions

$$e_{WG} = e_{US} \cdot e_{US,WG} \tag{6.13-a}$$

$$e_{FR} = e_{US} \cdot e_{US,FR} \tag{6.13-b}$$

$$e_{UK} = e_{US} \cdot e_{US,UK} \tag{6.13-c}$$

During the simulations these identities and the definition of the effective exchange rate's percentage change presented in Section 4.3.4

$$\mathring{e} = 0.51\ \mathring{e}_{WG} + 0.318\ \mathring{e}_{US} + 0.117\ \mathring{e}_{FR} + 0.055\ \mathring{e}_{UK} \tag{6.14}$$

are used for obtaining these exchange rates.

Substituting identities (6.13-a), (6.13-b) and (6.13-c) and the identity $\mathring{e}^e_{US} = (e^e_{US,t+1} - e_{US,t})/e_{US,t}$ into (6.12) and solving the resulting relation for the Dutch guilder - US dollar rate yields

$$e_{US} = \{d7067 \cdot W^f \cdot 0.135 \cdot (e^e_{US} + e^e_{FR} \cdot e_{FR,US})$$

$$+ (1-d7067) \cdot W^f \cdot 0.382 \cdot e^e_{FR} \cdot e_{FR,US}$$

$$+ 0.457 \cdot W^f (e^e_{FR} \cdot e_{FR,US} + e^e_{UK}/e_{UK,US})$$

$$+ (0.417 \cdot FA^p + 0.590 \cdot FA^b) \cdot (0.318\ e^e_{US} + 0.51\ e^e_{WG} \cdot e_{EG,US}$$

$$+ 0.177\ e^e_{FR} \cdot e_{FR,US} + 0.055\ e^e_{UK} \cdot e_{UK,US})\} \ / \ \{CA - \Delta RES$$

$$+ STATBB + \Delta NDAL^f \backslash \{\mathring{e}^e\} + \Delta NDAS^f \backslash \{\mathring{e}^e\} - \Delta NFA^p \backslash \{\mathring{e}^e\}$$

$$- \Delta NFA^b \backslash \{\mathring{e}^e\}\} \tag{6.15}$$

The historical data of e_{US} and the fitted values resulting from (6.15) are plotted in Figure 6.3.A. As this figure illustrates the explanatory power of the relation is rather good. The same conclusion holds for the Dutch guilder / French franc

Fig 6.3.A The Dutch guilder / US dollar rate

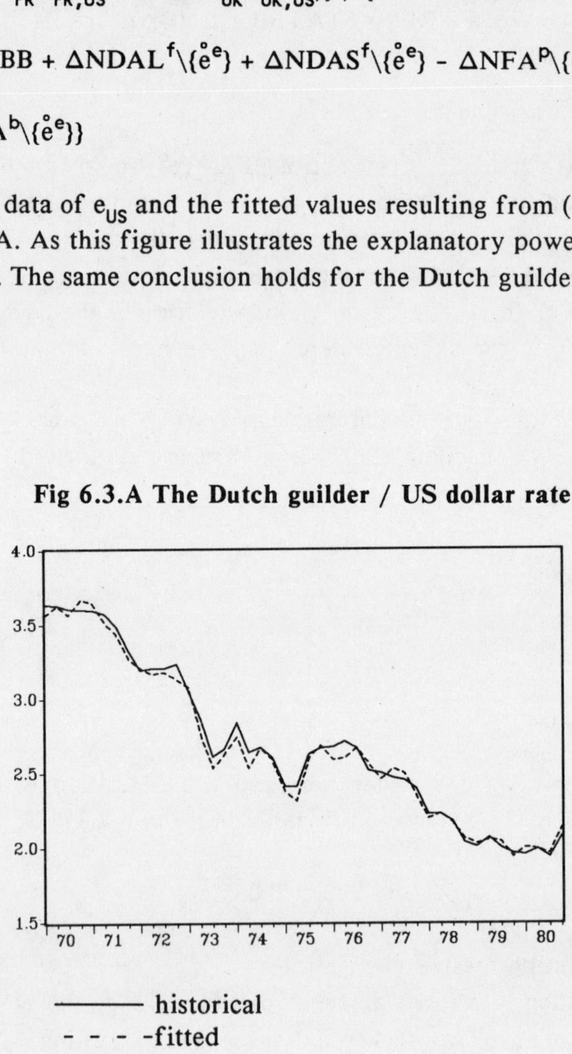

Fig 6.3.B The Dutch guilder / Deutsche mark rate

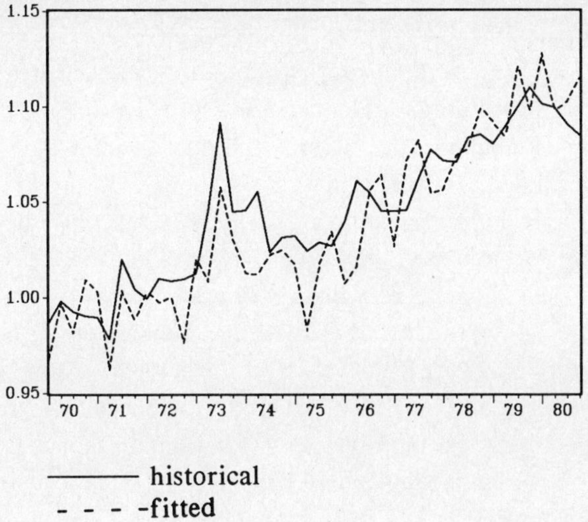

and the Dutch guilder / British pound sterling rate which are not shown. As Figure 6.3.B illustrates the time series of the Dutch guilder / Deutsche mark rate's fitted values satisfactorily track the historical series.

Fig. 6.4 Accumulation and exchange rate dynamics

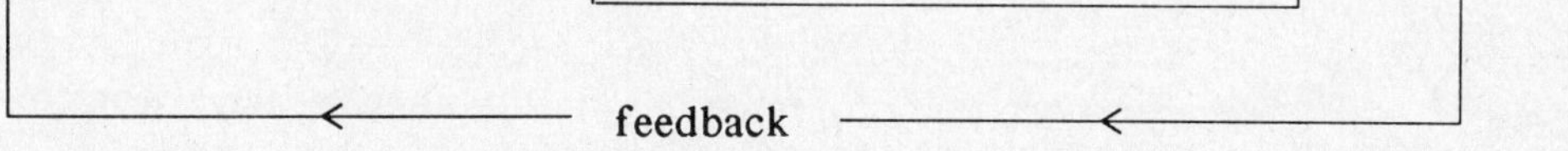

6.3 The interaction between the monetary and real part

The main links between the monetary and real sectors of the model are illustrated in Figures 6.4 and 6.5. Figure 6.4, which is the empirical counterpart of Figure 2.1, shows the current account's influence on asset accumulation and exchange rate determination. The balance on current account determines the change in the non-bank sector's financial assets and thus influences indirectly, through the sector's portfolio behaviour, the interest rates and exchange rate. It also has a direct influence on the expected percentage change of the exchange rate, see Section 4.3.5, and the exchange rate itself (equation (6.15)).

The model's main interrelations between the monetary and the real part are summarized in Figure 6.5. This figure clearly shows that the long-term domestic interest rate forms one of the main forces of the monetary transmission. It influences the profit of firms, the user costs of capital and the interest payments to foreigners and those by the government.

The long-term interest rate's effect on the user costs of capital is very important, because the latter influences many variables in the real part of the model. It is one of the explanatory variables of the price of investments and that of consumption goods and thus p_k influences the private sector's investment and consumption decisions. Another important channel is that the user costs of capital along with the wage rate determines the change of the time of equipment in use and thus the change of production capacity, which in turn affects the utilization rate. The latter influences the volume of exports and imports and thus through the current account the stocks of financial assets. The utilization rate also has a direct influence on the privates sector's portfolio selection. The change of the lifetime of equipment in use also affects the demand for labour and hence unemployment, which in its turn is a determining factor of the wage rate. The wage rate is among the explanatory variables of domestic prices, p_i and p_c, and thus influences domestic expenditures.

The long-term interest rate directly and indirectly affects consumption expenditures. Its direct influence results from the real interest rate term in the consumption function. (The short-term interest rate causes $CONS^p$ by the same manner.) The indirect effect of r_l results from its influence on the amount of interest payments by the government and to foreigners which both form part of non-wage income that in turn affects private consumption.

An increase on the long-term interest rate decreases firms' profits and thus has a contractionary effect on domestic investments. The reduction in profits leads to a lower return on shares.

By definition, the percentage change of the exchange rate determines the percentage change of the domestic currency price of imported goods, such as $\mathring{p}_{mc}$,

Fig. 6.5 Relations between the monetary and real sector

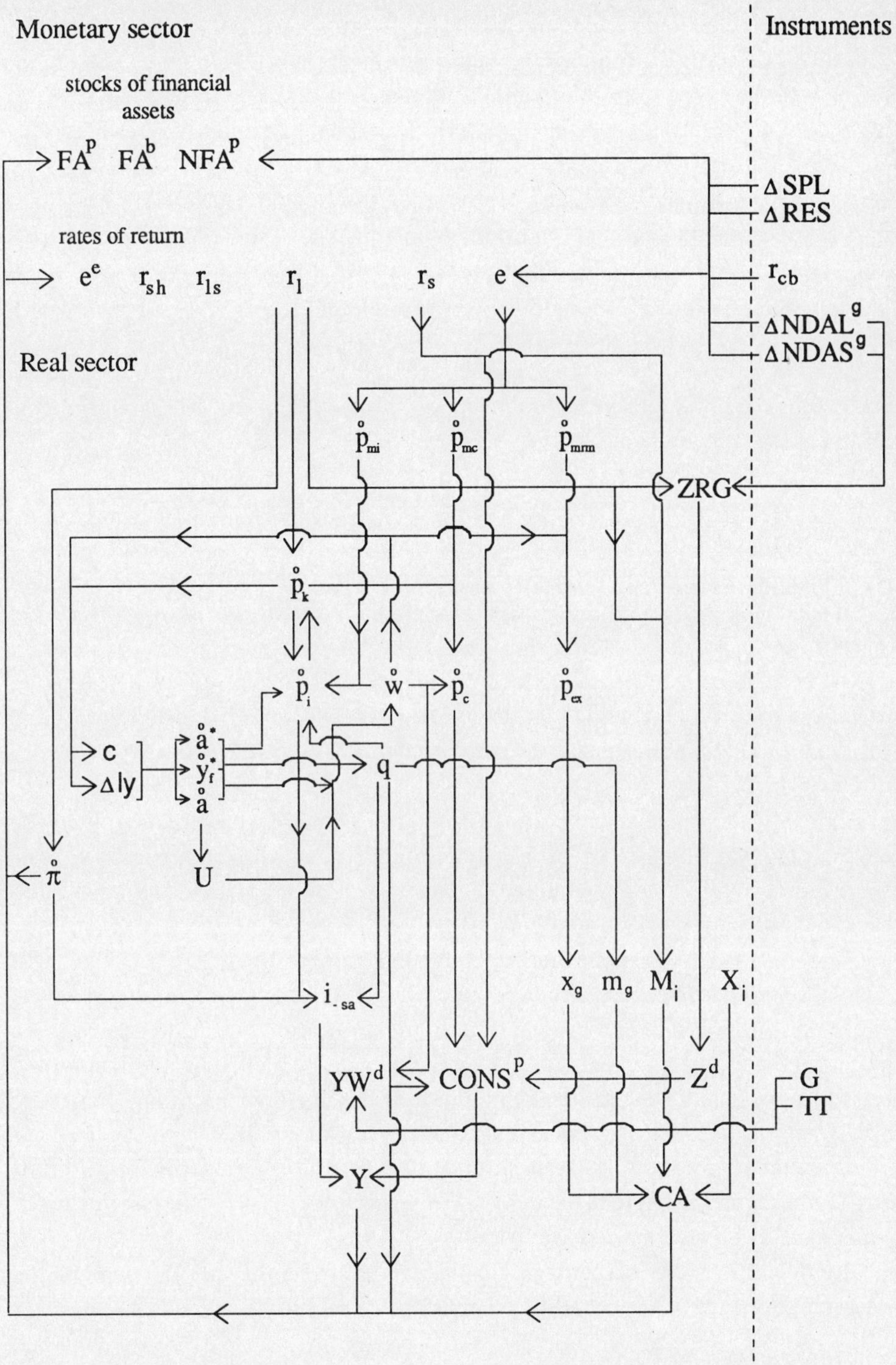

$\overset{\circ}{p}_{mi}$, and $\overset{\circ}{p}_{mrm}$. Since these prices form part of the price of various expenditures, the exchange rate through imported inflation indirectly influences the expenditure decisions of the private sector.

On the extreme right-hand side of Figure 6.5 we have listed the instruments of economic policy. Most instruments affect monetary variables. The government's financing of the budget deficit influences the holdings by the private sector and by the banking sector of domestic long-term and short-term assets. In this manner the amount of the budget deficit and the way of financing it influence the determination of domestic interest rates. Since the interest receipts on the government debt form part of the private sector's non-wage income, the budget deficit indirectly affects domestic expenditure. Of course the government expenditure which caused the deficit directly increases the domestic expenditure. Taxes, on the other hand, reduce disposable income. These instruments of economic policy play an important role in the next chapter where we apply optimal control techniques in order to determine the optimal exchange rate regime of a small industrial country.

6.4 The equations of the quarterly model

Money (M1: currency and demand deposits)

The private sector's demand for money

$$M1 = FA^{p}\cdot[-0.0138\ r_s - 0.0219\ r_l - 0.0005\ (r_f+\overset{\circ}{e}^{e}) + 0.2164]$$
$$+ 0.7719\ Y + FA^{p}_{-1}\cdot[-.0013\ q + 0.0046\ S1 + 0.0220\ S2$$
$$+ 0.0066\ S3]$$

Unborrowed reserves

The banks' demand for unborrowed reserves

$$RU = 0.205\ RU_{-1} - 0.234\ NDAS^{b}_{-1} - 0.227\ NDAL^{b}_{-1} - 0.340\ NFA^{b}_{-1}$$
$$+ FA^{b}\cdot[-\ 0.0069\ r_s - 0.017\ r_l + 0.004\ (r_f+\overset{\circ}{e}^{e}) + 0.369]$$
$$- 0.069\ NDAS^{p} - 0.1338\ NDALS - 0.0029\ \text{dliq}\ NDAS^{p}$$
$$- 0.410\ \Delta SPL + 0.439\ \Delta RES + FA^{b}_{-1}\cdot[0.007\ S1 + 0.004\ S2$$
$$+ 0.006\ S3]$$

Short-term domestic assets

The private sector's demand

$$NDAS^p = 0.311\ NDAS^p_{-1} - 0.578\ NDAL^p_{-1} + 0.172\ LS_{-1} - 0.447\ Y + FA^p \cdot [0.0486\ r_s + 0.013\ r_l - 0.005\ (r_f + \mathring{e}^e) - 0.036\ r_{ls} + 0.425] + FA^p_{-1} \cdot [0.0004\ S1 - 0.017\ S2 + 0.05\ q]$$

The banks' demand

$$NDAS^b = 0.514\ NDAS^b_{-1} - 0.422\ NDAL^b_{-1} - 0.354\ NFA^b_{-1} + 0.144\ NDAS^p + 0.228\ NDALS + 0.004\ dliq\ NDAS^p + 0.410\ \Delta SPL + 0.252\ \Delta RES + FA^b \cdot [0.047\ r_s + 0.551\ r_l - 0.278\ r_f + \mathring{e}^e + 0.207] + FA^b_{-1} \cdot [0.004\ S1 + 0.015\ S2 - 0.007\ S3]$$

Foreigners' demand

$$NDAS^f = 0.500\ NDAS^f_{-1} + 272.922 + W^f \cdot [0.091\ (r_s - 0.5 \cdot (\mathring{e}^e_{FR} + \mathring{e}^e_{UK})) - 0.321\ (r_{s,WG} + r_{s,US}) + 0.859\ DUMS + 0.932]$$

The interest rate on short-term domestic assets derived from the market equilibrium

$$r_s = \{\Delta NDAS^g - (-.689\ NDAS^p_{-1} - 0.578\ NDAL^p_{-1} + 0.172\ LS_{-1} - 0.447\ Y + FA^p \cdot [0.013\ r_l - 0.005\ (r_f + \mathring{e}^e) - 0.036\ r_{ls} + 0.425] + FA^p_{-1} \cdot [0.0004\ S1 - 0.017\ S2 + 0.050\ q] -.4858\ NDAS^b_{-1} - 0.422\ NDAL^b_{-1} - 0.354\ NFA^b_{-1} + 0.144\ NDAS^p + 0.228\ NDALS + 0.004\ dliq\ NDAS^p + 0.410\ \Delta SPL + 0.252\ \Delta RES + FA^b \cdot [0.551\ r_l - 0.278\ (r_f + \mathring{e}^e) + 0.207] + FA^b_{-1} \cdot \{0.005\ S1 + 0.015\ S2 - 0.007\ S3\} - 0.500\ NDAS^f_{-1} + 272.922 + W^f \cdot [-0.046\ (\mathring{e}^e_{FR} + \mathring{e}^e_{UK})) - 0.321\ (r_{s,WG} + r_{s,US}) + 0.859\ DUMS + 0.932]\ \} / \{\ 0.047\ FA^b + 4.8559\ FA^p + 9.1380\ W^f\ \}$$

Short-term bank loans

The private sector's demand

$$LS = -1.0\cdot\{-\ 0.045\ NDAS^{p}_{-1} - 0.363\ NFA^{p}_{-1} + 0.770\ LS_{-1}$$
$$-\ 0.195\ Y + FA^{p}\cdot[-0.013\ r_s + 0.003\ (r_f+\mathring{e}^{e}) + 0.018\ r_{ls} + 0.025]$$
$$+\ FA^{p}_{-1}\cdot[0.09\ q - 0.005\ S2]\}$$

Interest-rate setting by banks

1970:I - 1973:II

$$r_{ls} = 1.0009\ r_{cb} + 0.589$$

1973:III - 1980:IV

$$r_{ls} = 0.951\ r_{cb} + 0.137\ r_{cb}(-1)$$
$$+\ 1.553\ [LS_{-1}/FA^{b}_{-1} - LS_{-2}/FA^{b}_{-2}] + 0.077\ ncc + 0.594$$

Long-term domestic assets

The private sector's net demand

$$NDAL^{p} = 0.856\ NDAL^{p}_{-1} + 0.112\ LS_{-1} - 0.099\ Y + FA^{p}\cdot[-.0085\ r_s$$
$$+\ 0.0031\ r_l + 0.003\ r_{ls} + 0.215] - FA^{p}_{-1}\cdot[0.14\ q + 0.005\ S1]$$

The banks' net demand

$$NDAL^{b} = -0.205\ RU_{-1} - 0.280\ NDAS^{b}_{-1} + 0.815\ NDAL^{b} - 0.043\ NDAS^{p}$$
$$+\ 0.116\ NDALS + FA^{b}\cdot[0.057\ r_s + 2.039\ r_l - 0.007\ (r_f+\mathring{e}^{e})$$
$$+\ 0.116] - FA^{b}\cdot[0.017\ S1 + 0.018\ S2 + 0.005\ S3]$$

Foreigners' demand

1970:I - 1976:IV

$$NDAL^{f} = 0.936\ NDAL^{f}_{-1} + 2207.673 + W^{f}\cdot\{4.371\ r_{sh}$$
$$-\ 0.135\ (\mathring{e}^{e}_{FR} + \mathring{e}^{e}_{US}) - 0.456\ S1 + 1.609\ d7041 - 5.950\}$$

1977:I - 1980:IV

$$NDAL^{f} = 0.906\ NDAL^{f}_{-1} + W^{f}\cdot\{4.496\ (r_{l} - 0.5(r_{l,WG} + r_{l,UK}))$$
$$- 0.382\ \mathring{e}^{e}_{FR} + 2.303\ S2 + 1.859\ S3 + 3.629\ d791 + 5.855\}$$

Long-term domestic interest rate derived from the market equilibrium

$$r_{l} = \{\ \Delta NDAL^{g} - d7076\cdot\Delta NDAL^{f} - [-\ 0.144\ NDAL^{p}_{-1} + 0.112\ LS_{-1}$$
$$- 0.099\ Y + FA^{p}\cdot[-.0085\ r_{s} + 0.003\ r_{ls} + 0.215]$$
$$- FA^{p}_{-1}\cdot[0.14\ q + 0.005\ S1] -.205\ RU_{-1} - 0.280\ NDAS^{b}_{-1}$$
$$-.185\ NDAL^{b} - 0.043\ NDAS^{p} + 0.116\ NDALS + FA^{b}\cdot[0.057\ r_{s}$$
$$- 0.007\ (r_{f}+\mathring{e}^{e}) + 0.116] - FA^{b}\cdot[0.017\ S1 + 0.018\ S2$$
$$+ 0.005\ S3] + (1.0 - d7067)\cdot(-.094\ NDAL^{f}_{-1}$$
$$+ W^{f}\cdot[-2.248\cdot(r_{l,WG} + r_{l,UK}) - 0.382\ \mathring{e}^{e}_{FR} + 2.303\ S2$$
$$+ 1.859\ S3 + 3.629\ d791 + 5.855]\ \}$$
$$/\ \{\ 0.3145\ FA^{p} + 2.0388\ FA^{b} + (1.0 - d7076\cdot 449.576 W^{f}\ \}$$

The yield on shares

$$r_{sh} = 0.536\ \Sigma^{3}_{i=0}\ \alpha_{i}\ \mathring{\pi}_{-i} - 1.599\ \Sigma^{3}_{i=0}\ \alpha_{i}(r_{l}(-i) - \mathring{p}_{c}(-i))$$
$$+ 0.192\ S1 + 0.122\ S2 + 0.095\ S3 - 0.159$$

Demand for foreign assets

The private sector's net demand

$$NFA^{p} = -\ 0.267\ NDAS^{p}_{-1} - 0.278\ NDAL^{p}_{-1} + 0.360\ NFA^{p}_{-1}$$
$$+ 0.486\ LS_{-1} - 0.030\ Y + FA^{p}\cdot[-.013\ r_{s} + 0.006\ r_{l}$$
$$+ 0.003\ (r_{f}+\mathring{e}^{e}) + 0.014\ r_{ls} + 0.115] + FA^{p}_{-1}\cdot[0.129\ q - 0.007\ S3]$$

The banks' net demand

$$NFA^{b} = -\ 0.167\ NDAL^{b}_{-1} + 0.694\ NFA^{b}_{-1} + FA^{b}\cdot[0.308 - 0.097\ r_{s}$$
$$- 0.880\ r_{l} + 0.590\ r_{f}+\mathring{e}^{e}] - 0.032\ NDAS^{p} - 0.211\ NDALS$$
$$- 0.002\ dliq\ NDAS^{p} - 0.691\ \Delta RES + FA^{b}_{-1}\cdot[0.006\ S1 - 0.005\ S3]$$

Definitions of sectors' net financial assets

$$FA^p = W^p + NDAS^f + NDAL^f + DI^f$$

$$W^p = W^p_{-1} + CA + FT^g + \Delta W^p{}_{ex}$$

$$FA^b = W^b - LS + NDAS^p + NDALS + FA^b{}_{ex}$$

Exchange rate determination

$$e_{us} = [d7067 \cdot W^f \cdot 0.135 \cdot (e^e_{US} + e^e_{FR})$$
$$+ (1 - d7067) \cdot W^f \cdot 0.382 \cdot e^e_{FR} + 0.457 \cdot W^f \cdot (e^e_{FR} + e^e_{UK})$$
$$+ (0.3171\ FA^p + 0.5897\ FA^b) \cdot (0.318 e^e_{US} + 0.51\ e^e_{WG} + 0.177\ e^e_{FR}$$
$$+ 0.055\ e^e_{UK})] / [CA - \Delta RES + STATBB + \Delta NDAL^f \backslash \{\mathring{e}^e\}$$
$$+ \Delta NDAL^f \backslash \{\mathring{e}^e\} - \Delta NFA^p \backslash \{\mathring{e}^e\} - \Delta NFA^b \backslash \{\mathring{e}^e\}]$$

$$CA = X_g + X_i + X_r - M_g - M_i - M_r + D_s + \Delta TCS + SD_{cu}$$

$$e_{FR} = e_{US} \cdot e_{FR,US}$$

$$e_{UK} = e_{US} \cdot e_{UK,US}$$

$$e_{WG} = e_{US} \cdot e_{WG,US}$$

$$\mathring{e} = 0.318\ \mathring{e}_{US} + 0.510\ \mathring{e}_{WG} + 0.055\ \mathring{e}_{UK} + 0.117\ \mathring{e}_{FR}$$

Formation of exchange rate expectations

$$\mathring{e}^e_{i,t+1} = \alpha_{o,t}\ [\mathring{p}_{n,t+1} - \mathring{p}_{i,t+1}]^e + \alpha_{1,t}[e_{i,t+1} CA_{i,t+1} - CA_{n,t+1}]^e \qquad i = US, UK$$

$$\mathring{e}^e{}_{FR,t+1} = \alpha_{0t} + [\mathring{p}_{n,t+1} - \mathring{p}_{FR,t+1}]^e + \alpha_{1t}[e_{FR,t+1} CA_{FR,t+1} - CA_{n,t+1}]^e$$
$$+ \alpha_{2t}\{\tilde{e}_{FR} - e_{FR}) / e_{FR}$$

$$\mathring{e}^e{}_{WG} = (\tilde{e}_{WG} - e_{WG}) / e_{WG}$$

$$\mathring{e}^e = 0.318\ \mathring{e}^e_{US} + 0.510\ \mathring{e}^e_{WG} + 0.055\ \mathring{e}^e_{UK} + 0.117\ \mathring{e}^e_{FR}$$

The non-monetary sectors

Labour market

$$\mathring{y}^*_f = \frac{0.25}{8.36} \cdot \{ \Sigma^3_{j=0} (i_{-sa})_{-j} / (y_f(-1) - i_w(-1))\} \cdot h^{0.75} + 0.004\ \Delta ly$$

$$+ 0.5\ \Sigma^3_{j=0} \mathring{h}_{-j} - 0.005$$

$$y^*_f = y^*_f(-1) \cdot (1.0 + \mathring{y}^*_f)$$

$$\mathring{a}^* = \mathring{y}^*_f + 0.022\ \Delta ly - 0.1875\ \Sigma^3_{j=0} \mathring{h}_{-j} - 0.0125$$

$$\Delta ly = -.25\ [(\mathring{w}^f_g - \mathring{p}_k)/0.0075 + 1\ ] / [\ 1 + C\ ]$$

$$C = C_{-1}\ [\ (1 + \mathring{w}) / (1 + \mathring{p}_k)\ ]\ e^{-0.0075}$$

where $C_{1970:I} = 2.15$

$$\mathring{a} = 0.560\ \mathring{a}(-1) + 0.005\ \Sigma^3_{j=0} (\mathring{y}_f - \mathring{i}_w)_{-j} + 0.018\ \Sigma^3_{j=0} 0.25\ i_w(-j)$$

$$+ 0.0125\ \Sigma^3_{j=0} i_{-sa}(-j) / [y_f(-1) - i_w(-1)]\ h^{0.75} + 0.002\ \Delta ly$$

$$- 0.025\ \Sigma^3_{j=0} \mathring{h}_{-j} + 0.003\ S1 + 0.008\ S2 + 0.004\ S3 - 0.012$$

$$a = a_{-1} \cdot (1.0 + \mathring{a})$$

$$a_{se} = qase \cdot a$$

Supply of goods

$$y = y_{-1} + 0.500\ [1.0 + 0.829\ v_{f,-4}\ 0.33\ \Sigma^3_{j=1} \mathring{v}_{f,-j} - y_{-1} - n_{-1}]$$

$$- 4574.47\ d7912 + 1754.17\ S2 + 1334.27\ S3 + 4862.16$$

Demand for goods

Private consumption

$$CONS^p = CONS^p_{-4} + 0.832\ \Delta_4 YWTS^d - 0.476\ \Delta\Delta_4 YWTS^d + 0.229\ \Delta_4 Z^d$$

$$- 0.002\ \{\ 0.5(r_l + r_s) - \mathring{p}_c\} \cdot CONS^p_{-4} + 0.009 \cdot CONS^p_{-4}$$

Investments by firms

$$i_{-sa} = 0.464\ i_{-sa}(-1) + 2793.64\ \Sigma^7_{j=4} \alpha_j\ (\mathring{\pi} - \mathring{p}_i)_{-j} + \Sigma^{11}_{j=4} \beta_j\ (\mathring{p}_k)_{-j}$$

$$+ 0.021\ y^*_{f-1}\ \{1.0 + \Sigma^3_{j=1} \mathring{y}_{f-j} + 0.1\ \Sigma^3_{j=0} (q-0.95)_{-j}\} - 650.781\ S1$$

$$- 361.850\ S2 - 982.074\ S3 - 861.989\ dum7912 + 3646.050$$

where $\alpha_4 = 0.4$, $\alpha_5 = 0.3$, $\alpha_6 = 0.2$, and $\alpha_7 = 0.1$
$\beta_4 = -4320.32$, $\beta_5 = -2616.43$, $\beta_6 = -1503.15$, $\beta_7 = -980.49$, $\beta_8 = -1048.44$, $\beta_9 = -1707.00$, $\beta_{10} = -2956.17$, $\beta_{11} = -4795.96$

Imports of goods

$$m_g = 0.256\, v + 0.307\, i_n + 80.00\, \Sigma_{j=1}^{4} \alpha_j\, q_{-j} - 11913.8\, \Sigma_{j=1}^{7} ß_j\, (p_m/p_v)_{-j}$$
$$+ 544.36\, S1 - 2047.43\, S2 + 6640.83$$

where $\alpha_1 = \alpha_4 = 0.2$, $\alpha_2 = \alpha_3 = 0.3$; $ß_1 = ß_7 = 0.083$, $ß_2 = ß_6 = 0.143$, $ß_3 = ß_5 = 0.179$ and $ß_4 = 0.19$

Exports of goods

$$x_g = 0.664 x^{g}_{-1} + 223.33[m_w - 0.664\, m_w(-1)] - 36.187\, p^f_{ex}$$
$$+ 23.453\, p^f_{exc} + 1061.774$$

Costs and prices

The wage rate

$$\mathring{w} = 0.816\, (S1 + S3)\, \Sigma_{j=1}^{4} \alpha_j\, \mathring{p}_{c\ -j} + 0.805\, \Sigma_{j=1}^{4} j/10\, (\mathring{y}^*_f - \mathring{a}^*)_{-j-2}$$
$$+ 0.705\, \Sigma_{j=0}^{7} [(j+1)/36]\, TS - 0.267\, \Sigma_{j=0}^{7} [(j+1)/36].[U/a_s]_{-j}$$
$$- 0.032\, dumw2 + 0.028\, dum70 + 0.017\, S2 - 0.029\, S4 + 0.017$$

where $\alpha_1 = \alpha_4 = 0.125$, $\alpha_2 = \alpha_3 = 0.375$

$$w = w_{-1} \cdot (1.0 + \mathring{w})$$

$$w^f_g = w^f / \tau$$

$$\mathring{w}^f_g = \mathring{w} - \mathring{\tau}$$

User costs of capital

$$\mathring{p}_k = \mathring{p}_i + \{1 - r_l \cdot 40 / [e^{r \cdot 40} - 1]\} \mathring{r}_l \quad \text{where } r = r_l$$

The price of consumption

$$\mathring{p}_c = 0.20\, \mathring{p}_{mc} + 0.132\, \Sigma_{i=3}^{6} \alpha_i\, \mathring{p}_k(-i) + 0.472\, \Sigma_{i=3}^{n} ß_i\, \mathring{w}^f_g(-i) +$$
$$- 0.408\, (\mathring{y}^* - \mathring{a}^*)(-2) + 0.021\, S2 + 0.006\, S4 - 0.002$$

where $\alpha_1 = 0.1$, $\alpha_2 = 0.2$, $\alpha_3 = 0.3$, $\alpha_4 = 0.4$, $ß_1 = ß_3 = 0.3$ and $ß_2 = 0.4$.

$$p_c = p_c(-1)\cdot(1.0 + \mathring{p}_c)$$

The price of investments

$$\mathring{p}_i = 0.264\ \mathring{p}_{mi} + 0.124\ \mathring{p}_{mi}(-1) + 0.244\ \mathring{p}_k + 0.0005\ q(-1)$$
$$+ 0.136\ \mathring{w}^f_g(-4) - 0.305\ (\mathring{y}^* - \mathring{a}^*)(-2) - 0.153\ (\mathring{y}^* - \mathring{a}^*)(-3)$$
$$- 0.039$$

$$p_i = p_i(-1)\cdot(1.0 + \mathring{p}_i)$$

The price of exports

$$\mathring{p}_{ex} = 0.078\ \mathring{w}^f_g(-4) + 0.155\ \mathring{w}^f_g(-5) + 0.233\ \mathring{w}^f_g(-6) + 0.311\ \mathring{w}^f_g(-7)$$
$$+ 0.342\ \mathring{p}_{mrm} + 0.270\ [(1.0 - dum734)\cdot\mathring{p}_{exc} + dum734\cdot\mathring{p}_{exc}(-2)]$$
$$- 0.022$$

$$p_{ex} = p_{ex}(-1)\cdot(1.0 + \mathring{p}_{ex})$$

$$\mathring{p}_m = \mathring{p}^f_m + \mathring{e}$$

$$p_m = p_m(-1)\cdot(1.0 + \mathring{p}_m)$$

$$\mathring{p}_{mc} = \mathring{p}^f_{mc} + \mathring{e}$$

$$\mathring{p}_{mi} = \mathring{p}^f_{mi} + \mathring{e}$$

$$\mathring{p}_{mrm} = \mathring{p}^f_{mrm} + \mathring{e}$$

$$\mathring{p}_{exc} = \mathring{p}^f_{exc} + \mathring{e}$$

$$p^f_{ex} = p^f_{ex}(-1)\cdot(1.0 + \mathring{p}_{ex} - \mathring{e})$$

Definitions

$$X_g = x_g\cdot p_{ex}(-1)\cdot(1.0 + \mathring{p}_{ex})\cdot 0.01$$

$$M_g = m_g\cdot p_m(-1)\cdot(1.0 + \mathring{p}_m)\cdot 0.01$$

$$X = X_g + X_i + X_r$$

$$q = q_{-1}\cdot(1.0 + \mathring{y}_f - \mathring{y}^*_f)$$

$$\mathring{q} = (q - q_{-1})/q_{-1}$$

$$n = n_{-1} + i_n$$

$$cons^p = 100\cdot CONS^p/p_c$$

$$v = cons^p + i_{-sa} + i_{wo} + x_g + v_{ex}$$

$$v_f = v - v_{f,ex}$$

$$y_f = y - m_g - m_r$$

$$y_{ni} = y_f + g_w + x_p - m_p + R_{tt}$$

$$R_{tt} = (X/p_m - X/p_{ex})\cdot 100 + R^r_{tt}$$

$$I_{-sa} = p_i \cdot i_{-sa} \cdot 0.01$$

$$U = a_s - a_w - a_g - a_{se}$$

$$TS = [(TW + PW)/YW - (TW_{-1} + PW_{-1})/YW_{-1}] \;/\; (TW_{-1} + PW_{-1})/YW_{-1}$$

$$Y = CONS_p + I_{-sa} + YW^g + X_g - M_g + Y_{ex}$$

The income distribution

$$Z = Y + ZRG - YW^f - YW^g + X_{g\,-\,M} - T_{is} + Z_{ex}$$

$$YW^f = (1.0 - qase)\cdot a \cdot w$$

$$YW = YW^f + YW^g$$

$$YS = a_{se} \cdot w$$

$$YS^d = YS - (TW/YW)\cdot YS - PZ$$

$$YW^d = YW - TW - PW$$

$$Z^d = Z + ZRG + X_i - M_i - TZ - (1.0 - TW/YW)\cdot YS$$

$$YWTS^d = YW^d + YT^d + YS^d$$

$$w^f = YW^f / a_w$$

$$\pi = Z\cdot\{1.451 - 0.332\cdot 0.25\cdot[r_l(-3) + r_l(-4) + r_l(-5) + r_l(-6)]\}$$
$$+ DEP^f - TZ - (1.0 - TW/YW).YS$$

$$\mathring{\pi} = (\pi - \pi_{-1})/\pi_{-1}$$

$$X_i = 2.89\, r_f(-1)\cdot(NFA^b_{-1} + NFA^p_{-1}) - 526.290$$

$$M_i = 18.192\, \Sigma^3_{j=2}\, 0.5\, r_s(-j)\, NDAS^f_{-3} - 855.79$$
$$+ 12.877\, \Sigma^3_{j=1}\, 0.33\, r_l(-j)\, NDAL^f_{-4}$$

The government

$$\Delta NDAL^g = FD^g - \Delta NDAS^g - FD^g_r$$

$$ZRG = 1.153 \cdot 0.25\ \Sigma^5_{j=2}\ r_l(-j) \cdot NDAL^g_{-4} + 1.107 \cdot r_s \cdot [NDAS^g_{-2} + FD^g_r(-2)] - 252.41$$

$$FD^g = T - G + SD^g$$

$$T = TW + TZ + T_{is} + O_g$$

$$G = G_w + G_x + ZRG + G_r$$

6.5 Simulation results

In order to investigate the quality of the entire model some dynamic simulations have been performed for the period 1970:I-1980:IV. In these simulations the historical values of the exogenous variables are used, whereas the lagged endogenous variables are replaced by the simulated values of the endogenous variables for the previous periods.

As a consequence of the long-term domestic interest rate's bad fit, the following additional assumptions are introduced in order to reduce accumulation of disturbing influences on other variables:

- the domestic long-term interest rate is represented by (6.10) instead of (6.9);
- in the relation of r_l the (lagged) amounts of the various assets are fixed at their historical values and a dummy variable is added to capture the peak of r_l in 1974:III;
- C(t-1) in the equation of C(t) is fixed at its historical value;
- all variables in the $\mathring{p}_k$ relation are lagged one period and an exogenous correction factor $\Delta\mathring{p}_k$ is added to this equation;
- in the definitions of the private and banking sector's financial assets the terms $NDAS^f$, $NDAL^f$, $NDAS^p$, and LS are replaced by $NDAS^f_{-1} + \Delta NDAS^f$, $NDAL^f_{-1} + \Delta NDAL^f$, $NDAS^p_{-1} + \Delta NDAS^p$, and $LS_{-1} + \Delta LS$, where $\Delta NDAS^f$, $\Delta NDAL^f$, ΔLS and $\Delta NDAS^p$ are fixed at their historical level;
- the term $\mathring{e}$ in the definition of the percentage change of the price of imported goods is replaced by $\mathring{e}(-1) + \Delta\mathring{e}$, where $\Delta\mathring{e}$ is assumed to be exogenous.

The assumptions with regard to the prices of imports and with regard to the definition of the private and banking sector's financial assets are made in order to guarantee the convergence of the algorithm.

Table 6.2 Mean and inequality coefficients*

variable	mean historical	mean simulated	RMSE	Theil	Theil**
M1	45444.11	46287.66	1686.662	0.018	0.014
RU	-362.506	-65.3678	799.4487	0.280	0.171
$NDAS^p$	23223.71	23450.07	1145.543	0.023	0.035
$NDAS^b$	13042.95	12900.55	1094.268	0.039	0.061
$NDAS^f$	1003.909	919.9500	145.8131	0.075	0.047
LS	38777.00	37598.55	4083.618	0.048	0.036
$NDAL^p$	58756.84	60965.59	4345.683	0.034	0.017
$NDAL^b$	52628.02	53148.93	1850.768	0.016	0.029
$NDAL^f$	11311.09	9336.243	2281.929	0.102	0.016
$NDAS^f$	1003.909	919.9500	145.8131	0.075	0.047
NFA^p	46924.18	48507.00	3040.133	0.029	0.030
NFA^b	4491.841	4952.864	2649.335	0.209	0.214
FA^p	135571.9	141612.3	9866.975	0.034	0.011
FA^b	69800.34	70937.05	3109.043	0.021	0.026
$\Delta M1/FA^p$	0.007603	0.007451	0.012337	0.260	0.258
$\Delta RU/FA^b$	-0.00090	-0.00041	0.008708	0.228	0.226
$\Delta NDAS^p/FA^p$	0.004596	0.004606	0.004160	0.117	0.119
$\Delta NDAS^b/FA^b$	0.005697	0.005516	0.008137	0.254	0.256
$\Delta NDAL^p/FA^p$	0.010011	0.010918	0.008661	0.302	0.311
$\Delta NDAL^b/FA^b$	0.025568	0.025180	0.007813	0.143	0.163
$\Delta NFA^p/FA^p$	0.011026	0.010604	0.011075	0.413	0.405
$\Delta NFA^b/FA^b$	-0.00309	-0.00119	0.010481	0.288	0.248
$\Delta LS/FA^p$	0.010182	0.008552	0.009117	0.381	0.333
$\Delta NDAL^f$	406.6137	330.2357	224.1894	0.160	0.139
$\Delta NDAS^f$	2.500000	1.059278	121.8500	0.619	0.589
r_{ls}	2.409573	2.407489	0.088200	0.018	0.018
r_s	1.746100	1.627300	0.341700	0.093	0.080
r_l	2.120500	2.083200	0.153200	0.036	0.037
e_{US}	2.690000	2.653464	0.067643	0.012	0.012
e_{FR}	0.561590	0.553844	0.014093	0.013	0.012
e_{WG}	1.044072	1.030193	0.025343	0.012	0.011
e_{UK}	6.006670	5.926621	0.151074	0.012	0.011
r_{sh}	-0.00369	-0.03672	0.082114	0.543	0.556
$\mathring{e}$	-0.00420	-0.00344	0.023892	0.581	0.600

e	1.049309	1.041445	0.023718	0.011	0.011
$\mathring{y}^*$	0.006360	0.006126	0.001486	0.106	0.113
y^*	43211.41	43003.23	315.3793	0.004	0.004
Δlv	0.011968	-0.00737	0.243370	0.402	0.406
C_t	2.331400	2.336632	0.056243	0.012	0.012
$\mathring{a}$	-0.00029	-0.00068	0.003271	0.429	0.439
$\mathring{y}^* - \mathring{a}^*$	0.010195	0.010636	0.005549	0.222	0.228
y	82694.55	82537.41	2604.849	0.016	0.016
$CONS^p$	31195.29	31758.84	778.2669	0.012	0.010
i_{-sa}	7077.825	6995.386	381.4643	0.027	0.030
m_g	21693.40	21620.11	1773.965	0.041	0.041
x_g	20261.23	19945.43	718.7374	0.018	0.017
X_g	18491.06	18226.40	704.5931	0.018	0.018
M_g	19557.82	19439.29	1709.932	0.042	0.042
$\mathring{w}$	0.026616	0.029350	0.009908	0.134	0.135
$\mathring{p}_k$	0.020317	0.021059	0.023614	0.320	0.314
$\mathring{p}_c$	0.018783	0.020138	0.008492	0.200	0.211
$\mathring{p}_i$	0.017085	0.017966	0.009442	0.212	0.221
$\mathring{p}_{ex}$	0.011701	0.014252	0.018785	0.360	0.369
$\mathring{\pi}$	5544.052	5343.602	564.2255	0.049	0.058
$\mathring{p}_{mi}$	0.014766	0.015889	0.023794	0.401	0.431
$\mathring{p}_{mrm}$	0.017162	0.018166	0.023959	0.289	0.305
$\mathring{p}_{mc}$	0.011837	0.012592	0.023892	0.349	0.360
p^f_g	86.22261	89.31723	4.010867	0.022	0.021
$\mathring{p}_{exc}$	0.019021	0.019777	0.023892	0.296	0.310
p_m	88.09309	87.82634	1.841577	0.010	0.011
X_i	2240.068	2350.512	386.5340	0.074	0.075
M_i	2166.137	1583.502	844.0402	0.195	0.077
Y	53767.57	54145.30	1687.248	0.015	0.014

* The figures refer to a simulation of the entire model. During the simulation run the coefficients of the exchange rate expectations generating functions are re-estimated at the beginning of each year. From these equations the expected levels of the exchange rates are derived so that the expected percentage changes are endogenous.

** Theil's inequality coefficient of the simulation in which the expected percentage changes of the exchanges rates are exogenous and equal to those used for estimating the model.

Table 6.2 reports for the most important endogenous variables the mean of the historical and the simulated time series, the root-mean-squared error, RMSE, and the inequality coefficient of Theil. The last two coefficients are defined as, respectively, $\sqrt{\Sigma (X_t^s - X_t)^2/n}$ and $\sqrt{\Sigma (X_t^s - X_t)^2}/[\sqrt{\Sigma X_t^{s2}} + \sqrt{\Sigma X_t^2}]$, where X_t^s is the simulated and X_t the historical time series and n the number of periods. The Theil-coefficient is a standardization of the RMSE.

The second, third and fourth column in Table 6.2 contain the summary statistics of a simulation in which at the end of every year the relations of the exchange rate's percentage change are re-estimated for the period from 1967:II to the fourth quarter of the year concerned. These regressions are used for deriving the exchange rates' expected percentage change for the four quarters of the next year. Then the expected levels of the exchange rates are calculated as

$$e_{t+1}^e = e_t \cdot (1.0 + \mathring{e}^e) \tag{6.16}$$

Conditional on these expected levels the expected percentage changes are made endogenous by adding the following definitions to the model

$$\mathring{e}^e = (e_{t+1}^e - e_t) \, / \, e_t \tag{6.17}$$

The last column of Table 6.2 shows Theil's inequality coefficients of a simulation in which the exchange rates' expected percentage changes are exogenous and equal to the ones used for estimating the relations. A comparison of the Theil coefficients for the two simulations reveals that the results are more or less the same. The levels and changes of various stocks of financial assets perform better when the exchange rates' expected percentage changes are endogenous, whereas the exchange rates fit the historical data best when these percentage changes are exogenous. The differences are, however, small so that no firm conclusion can be drawn. In order to facilitate the discussion of the quality of the simulations, Figures 6.6 and following show the time series of the historical and simulated values of the model's most important variables.

As both the inequality coefficients and Figures 6.6.A and 6.6.B indicate the simulated time series of the domestic interest rates track their historical values rather well during the entire period. The simulated series of these interest rates are smaller than their historical values at the beginning and at the end of the 1970s. During the greater part of 1974, 1975 and 1976 the simulated values are larger than the historical ones. As is shown by Figure 6.6.B, these deviations of the simulated from the historical time series can most likely be ascribed to the remaining forecasting errors in the domestic long-term interest rate. The inequality coefficient and RMSE of the return on shares is rather high. Two explanations for this disappointing performance of r_{sh} can be mentioned. Firstly, the R^2(adj.) of the equation was 0.59, and thus the fit of the estimated relation was rather low. The second possible explanation is that the simulated time series of one of the explanatory variables, $\overset{\circ}{p}_c$, does not track the historical values very well. However, the inequality coefficient of $\overset{\circ}{p}_c$ is not very high.

The Figures 6.7.A to 6.7.D and the corresponding inequality coefficients in Table 6.2 indicate that the simulation describes the historical time series of the level of the four endogenous exchange rates in satifactory way. Figure 6.7.B seems to suggest that the Dutch guilder/Deutsche mark rate is an exception. We should keep in mind, however, that the difference between the highest and lowest value of this exchange rate is much smaller than for the other exchange rates. Thus a particular deviation is much more accentuated in the graph of the Dutch guilder/Deutsche mark rate than in the figures of the other exchange rates. Of course, it remains interesting for future research to study the effects of alternative expectation schemes on the performance of these rates.

In both simulations, the simulated time series of the various financial stocks closely track the historical data. The simulated values are so good that we do not present graphs of the simulated and historical levels of these assets. In many cases the two curves cannot be distinguished from each other. As an inspection of the inequality coefficients reveals, the first differences of the simulated stocks (as a part of the particular sector's stock of financial assets) differ more than the corresponding levels from their historical value. The graphs of these series are presented in Figures 6.6.A-6.6.K. For the changes in the foreigners' investments in short-term domestic assets the inequality coefficient is higher than 0.6. This is about twice as high as those of the other changes in financial assets. From Figure 6.8.J we conclude that this lack of correspondence between the two time series results from the irregular behaviour of the historical data, probably reflecting speculative movements. For the $\Delta NFA^p/FA^p$ which has an inequality coefficient that is about 1.5 times that of the other assets, the opposite holds; the simulated series shows more irregular movements than the historical one. At times the simulated series of the change in short-term loans by the private sector also differs remarkably from its historical path. The corresponding inequality coefficient is also higher than those of the other changes in holdings of financial assets. The model satisfactorily simulates the remaining financial flow variables. For the private holdings of domestic short-term assets the simulation is very good indeed. The simulated series perfectly track even the sharp fluctuations in the historical series in 1976 and 1977.

The historical and simulated paths of various variables of the real part of the model are presented in Figures 6.9.A - 6.9.H. As these figures and the corresponding inequality coefficients and RMSEs show, the model simulates reasonably well the historical times series of the majority of variables from the model's non-financial sector. For some variables, such as private consumption, the value of imported and that of exported goods, as well as the percentage change of the wage rate, the fit is very good. Even the simulated time series of investment by firms (in constant prices), which is generally regarded to be difficult to explain, follows the historical data quite well. The fluctuations in the simulated series roughly correspond with those in the historical data. The fact that in the years 1972 and 1974 the simulated series is higher and from 1974:III to 1977:III it is lower than the historical level can be ascribed to the lagged influence of the long-term domestic interest rate. As Figure 6.6.B shows, the latter differs from its historical rate during 1970:I-1972:III and the greater part of the period 1974-1976. The level of the simulated time series of the imports of goods (in constant prices) roughly corresponds with the historical level. This series' fluctuations, however, very often do not correspond with the actual ones. A similar remark can be made with regard to the percentage change of the user costs of capital. According to the values of the inequality coefficients, the quality of the simulated times series of the percentage changes of the various prices is roughly the same as that of the changes in the stocks of financial assets and thus rather good. As mentioned before, when comparing the quality of the various simulated time series, we should keep in mind that, in general, it is easier to explain (forecast) the level than the percentage change or first difference of a variable.

To conclude, except for some variables such as the private holdings of foreign assets, the model describes the historical data in a satisfactory manner. Especially the simulated series of the four exchange rates follow their historical rates reasonably well. These exchange rates will play a dominant role in the next chapter.

6.6 Concluding remarks

This chapter presents the results of the model's dynamic simulation. Attention is paid especially to the implicit method used for deriving the interest and exchange rates. The time series obtained by the use of this method well describe the interest rate on short-term domestic assets and the four exchange rates. The method is less successful for explaining the historical times series of the long-term domestic interest rate.

As argued in Section 6.2 in all probability the performance of the interest rate on long-term domestic assets can be improved by re-estimating the relevant asset demand equations. We should be aware, however, that these relations form part of a portfolio, so that the improvement of the fit of one relation easily goes at the expense of the fit of the relations of the other assets/liabilities in the particular portfolio. Maybe the disappointing result with regard to the long-term interest rate reflects the inappropriateness of the partial adjustment model for explaining investments in long-term assets. A reason for this might be that the partial adjustment model is a one-period horizon model that inadequately takes account of the multi-period character of investments in long-term assets.

Although we have introduced some assumptions in order to restrict the detrimental effects of the bad fit of the long-term interest rate, during some subperiods the differences between the simulated and historical time series of this variable are fairly large. These differences may have caused divergences between the simulated and historical time series of other variables, most notably the short-term interest rate, changes in the holdings of some financial assets, the percentage change of the user costs of capital, and the investments by firms. Notwithstanding these deficiencies, the simulations indicate that the explanatory power of the model is good. In particular, the fit of the exchange rate equations is satisfactory. The good performance of the exchange rate relations is an important finding because (1) the explanation of exchange rate movements forms a main theme of this study, (2) the exchange rate equations play a major role in the next chapter, where the model is used for investigating various exchange rate regimes, and (3) exchange rate movements are difficult to explain as appears from other attempts at modelling exchange rates.

Fig 6.6.A The interest rate on short-term domestic assets

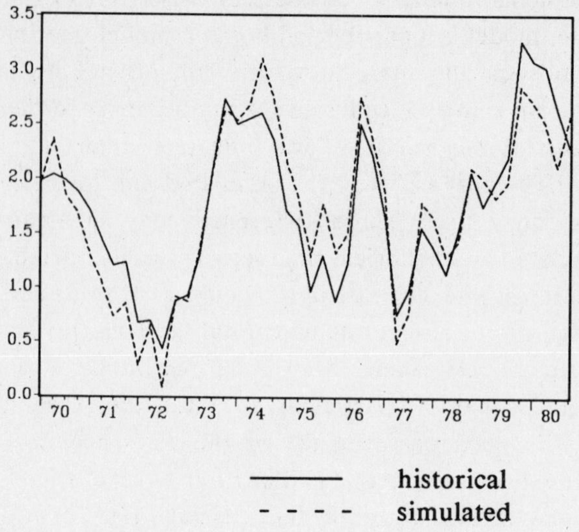

Fig 6.6.B The interest rate on long-term domestic assets

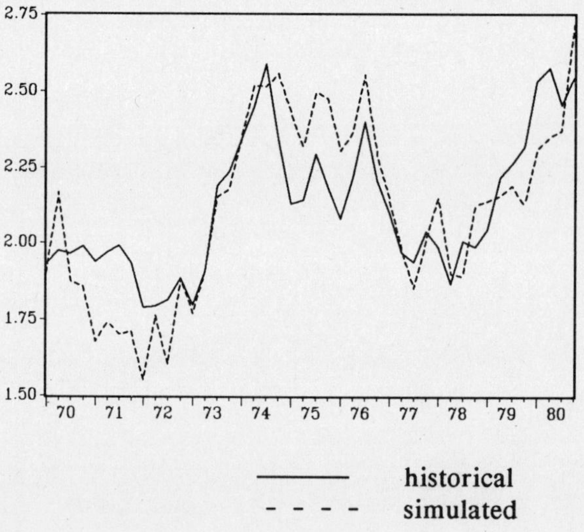

Fig 6.7.A The Dutch guilder / US dollar rate

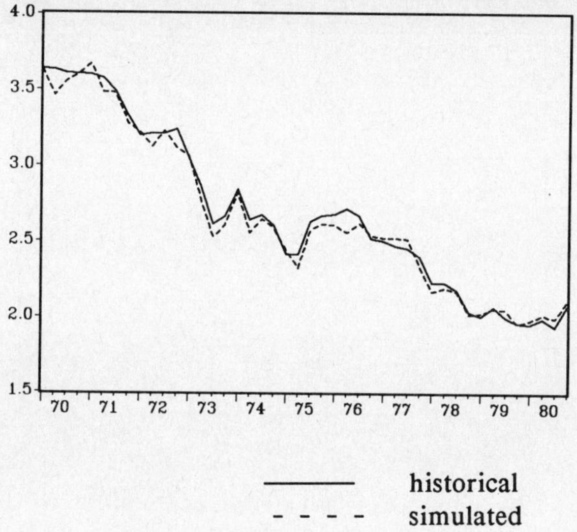

Fig 6.7.B The Dutch guilder / Deutsche mark rate

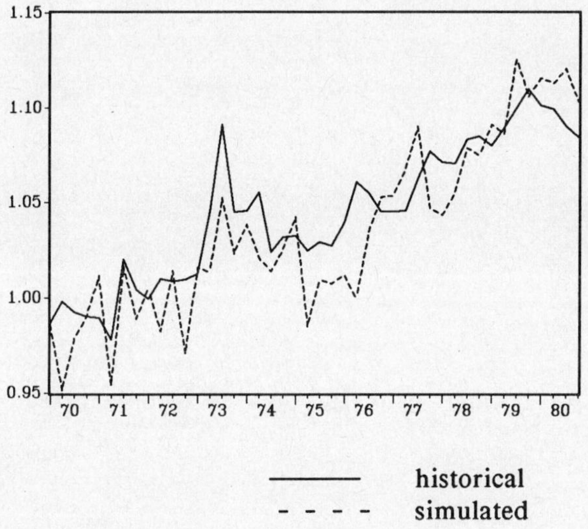

Fig 6.7.C The Dutch guilder / French franc rate

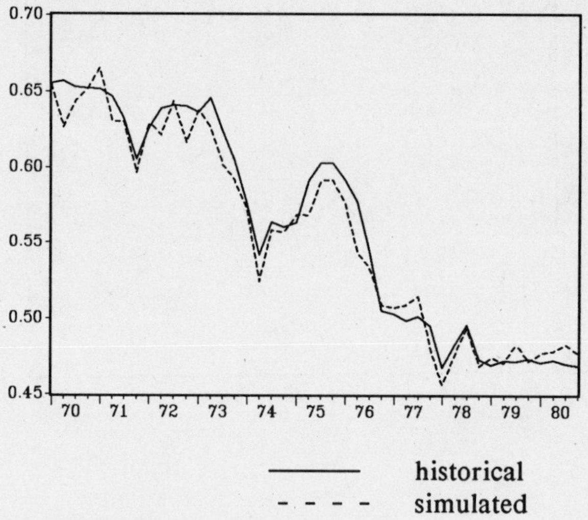

Fig 6.7.D The Dutch guilder / Britsh pound sterling

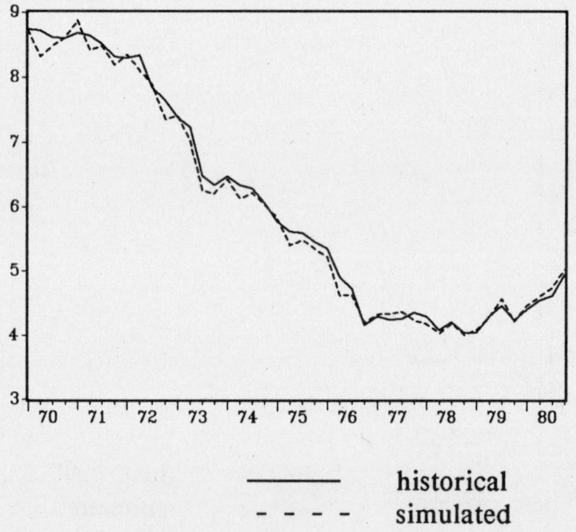

Fig 6.8.A ΔM1 / FA^p

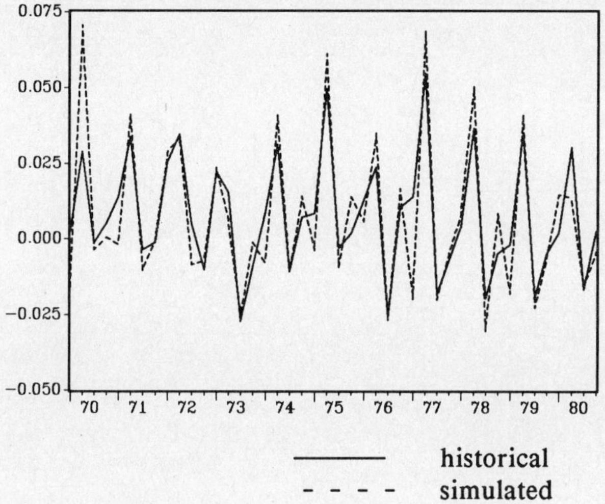

Fig 6.8.B ΔRU / FA^b

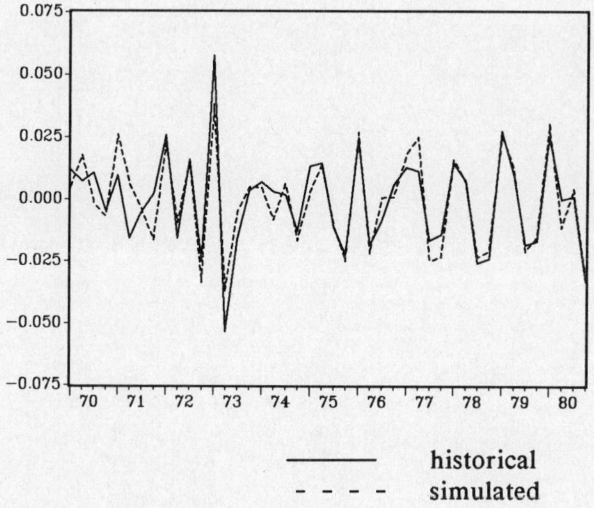

Fig 6.8.C $\Delta NDAS^p / FA^p$

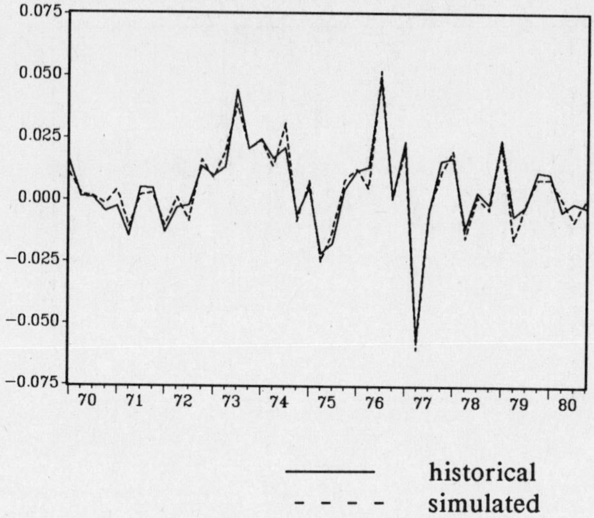

Fig 6.8.D $\Delta NDAS^b / FA^b$

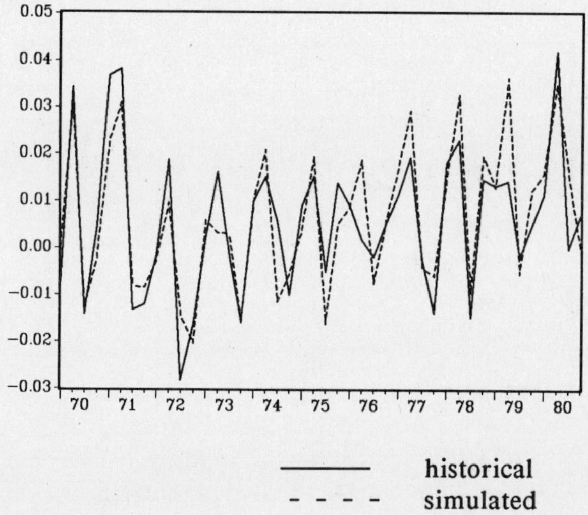

Fig 6.8.E $\Delta NDAL^p / FA^p$

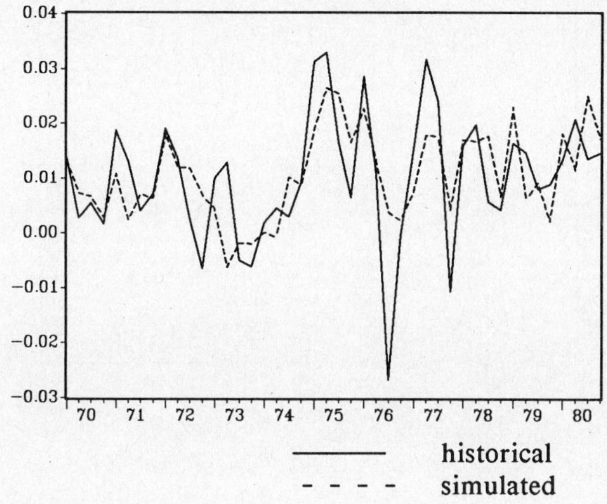

Fig 6.8.F $\Delta NDAL^b / FA^b$

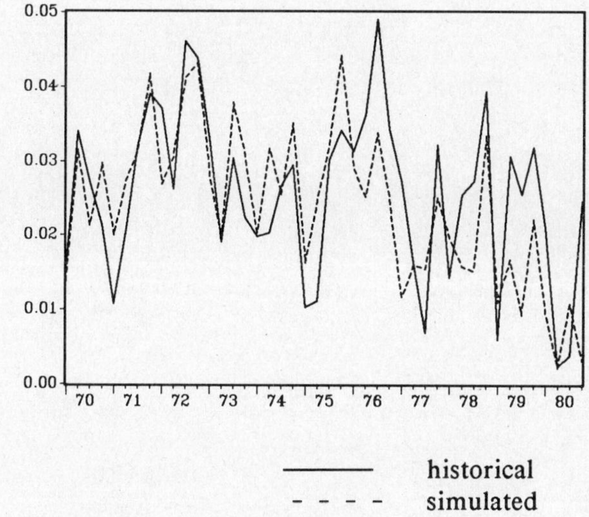

Fig 6.8.G $\Delta NFA^p / FA^p$

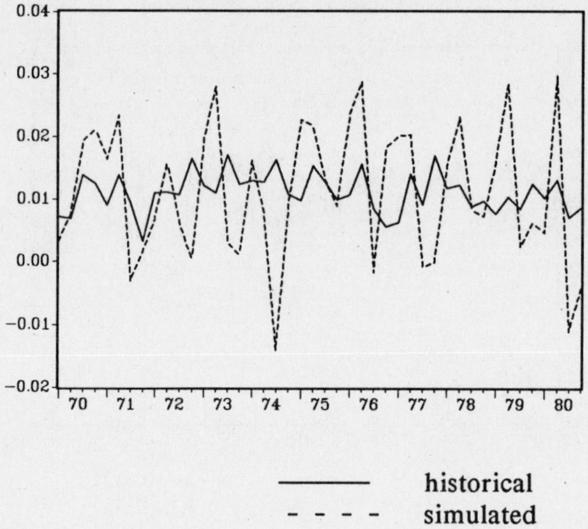

Fig 6.8.H $\Delta NFA^b / FA^b$

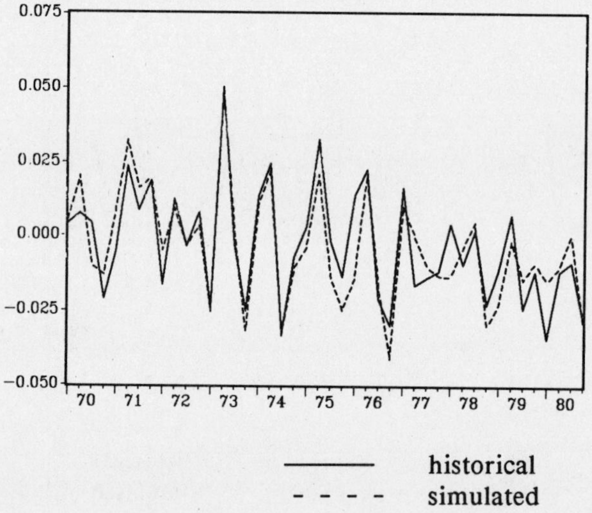

Fig 6.8.I $\Delta LS^p / FA^p$

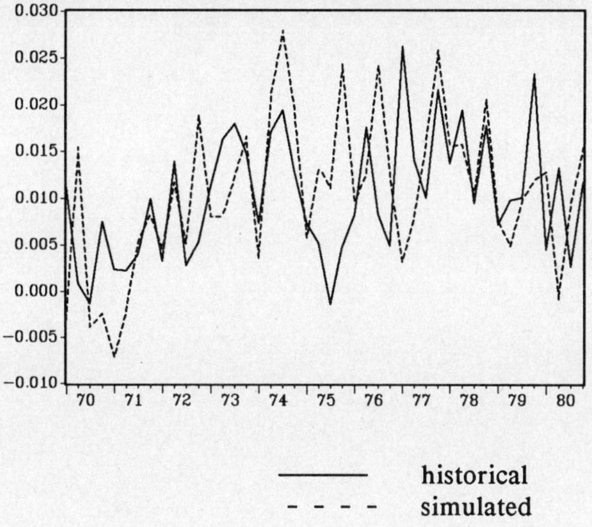

Fig 6.8.J $\Delta NDAS^f$

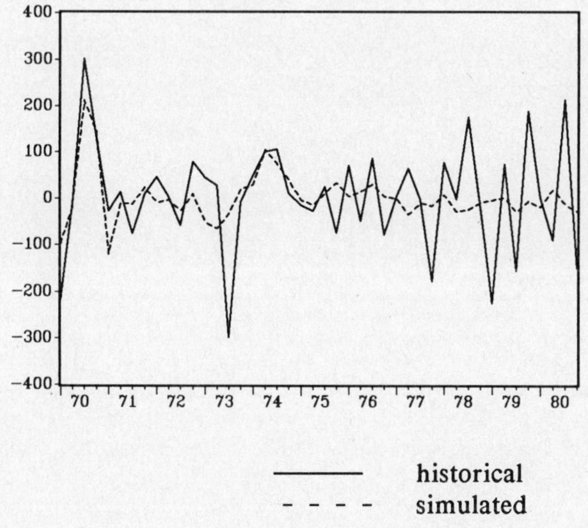

Fig 6.8.K $\Delta NDAL^{f}$

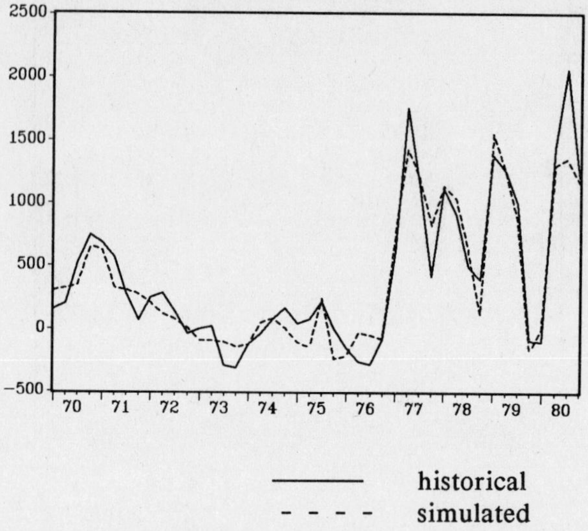

Fig 6.9.A Imports of goods (current prices)

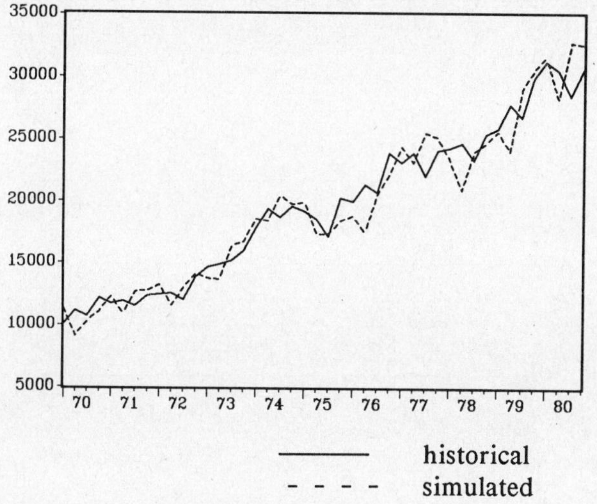

Fig 6.9.B Imports of goods (constant prices)

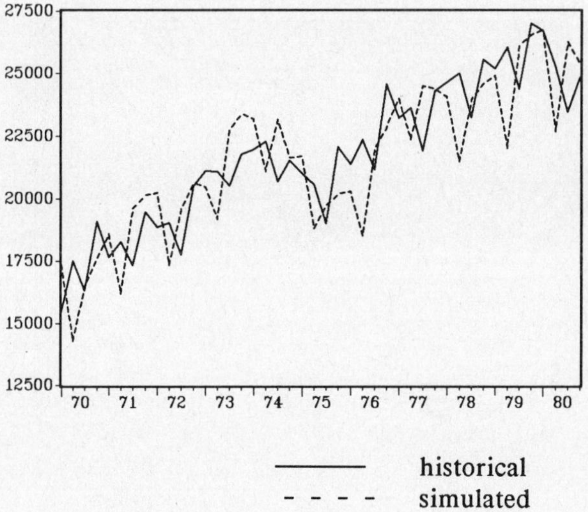

Fig 6.9.C Exports of goods (current prices)

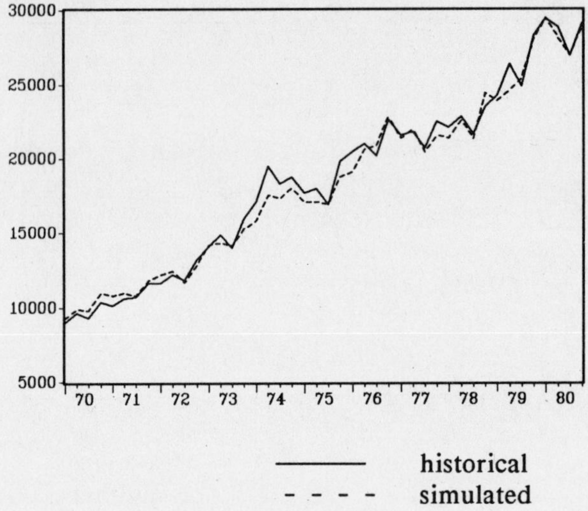

Fig 6.9.D Exports of goods (constant prices)

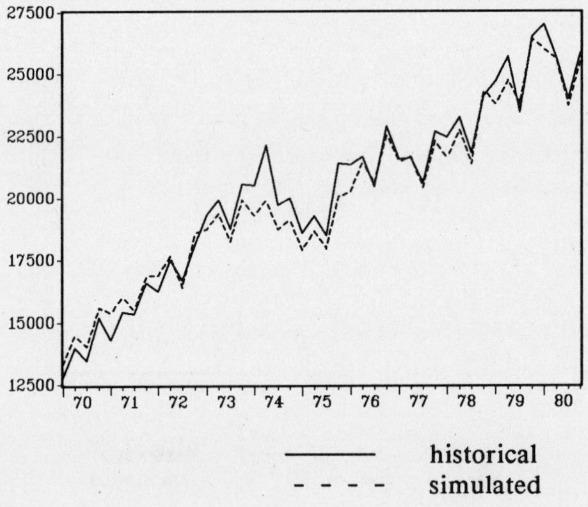

Fig 6.9.E User costs of capital (percentage change)

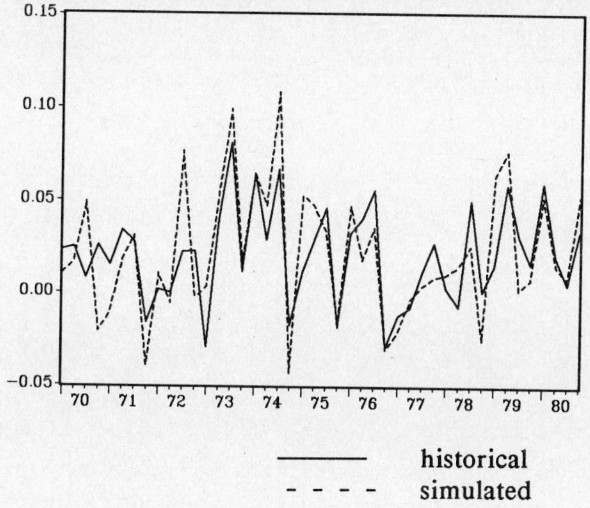

Fig 6.9.F Wage rate (percentage change)

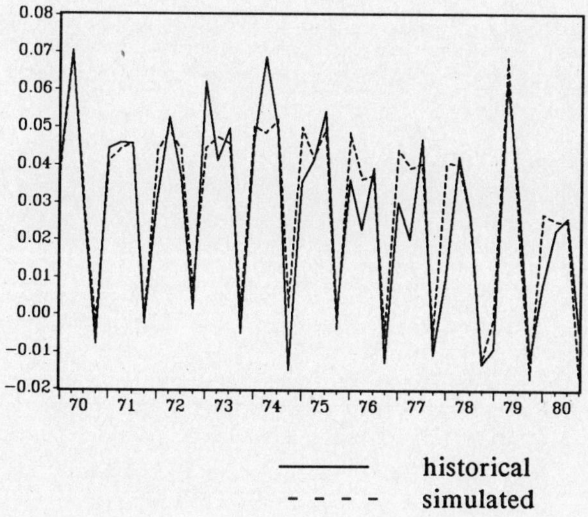

Fig 6.9.G Private consumption (current prices)

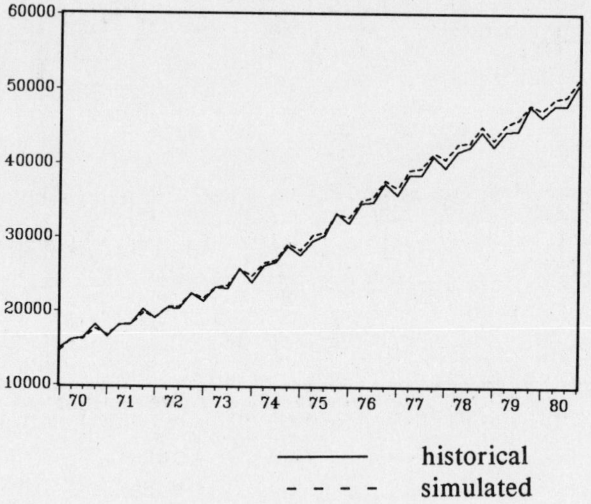

Fig 6.9.H Investments by firms (constant prices)

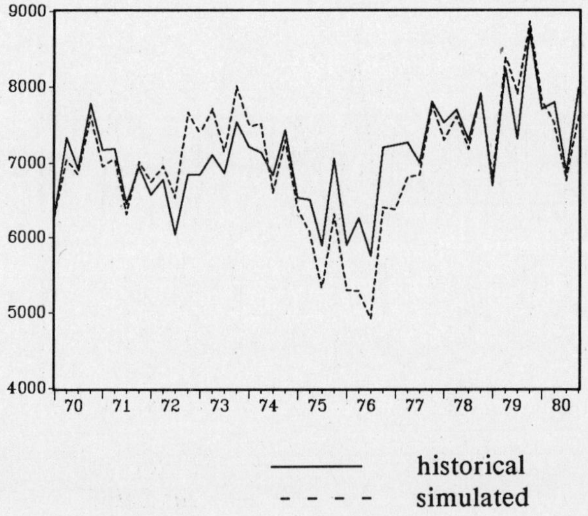

7 OPTIMAL ECONOMIC POLICY UNDER VARIOUS EXCHANGE RATE REGIMES

7.1 Introduction

This chapter is devoted to the second main theme of the present study, namely the analysis of different exchange rate regimes. Regimes considered for a small industrialized country are, a system of floating rates, one of fixed rates, and three crawling peg schemes. Under a crawling peg regime, the authorities accept the obligation to defend a particular value of the exchange rate, the peg rate, by maintaining the market rate within some band around the peg. The peg rate can be changed, but only gradually and in small steps.

The majority of studies on the crawling peg system are restricted to developing countries. A crawling peg regime can, however, also be of relevance for industrialized countries, in particular for the members of the European Monetary System. As has been set out in Chapter 1, the Delors committee's proposals aim at an European Monetary Union. This union would be characterized by fixed exchange rates and free movement of capital. Some are sceptical with regard to the possibility and/or desirability of a fixed peg for the EMS currencies. They argue that the success of the EMS can partly be ascribed to some members' use of capital controls. In this way these particular monetary authorities, most notably those of Italy and France, have limited capital outflow in order to defend their currency's exchange rate. According to the Delors commission's proposals, however, all barriers to the free movement of capital have to be removed. Consequently, in the future the fixed intra-EMS exchange rates cannot be defended by means of limiting capital flows. Persistent differences in economic performance, especially in rates of inflation, will still require a realignment of the exchange rates. If capital controls are completely removed while inflation differentials persist, the chances are that at times investors expect a devaluation of a weak currency. They will speculate on this and may force the particular central bank to devalue its currency. Thus the monetary authorities would be incapable of deciding the timing of EMS realignments, and the system would be exposed to repeated speculative attacks and devaluations.

Recent studies present two arguments for the proposition that there is a great chance that the EMS will develop into this undesirable situation. Firstly, according to Grilli (1989) the optimal level of the inflation rate is higher for the South European countries than for other members of the EMS, so that it is desirable for South European countries to opt for inflation rates that are higher than those in other European countries. Consequently, inflation differentials remain and exchange rate realignments are still necessary. Secondly, Giavazzi and Pagano (1989) argue that the mismanagement of public debt might give rise to a speculative attack on the 'soft' currency's exchange rate. If speculators expect a devaluation, the central bank has to increase the domestic interest rate in order to defend the currency. For the treasury, however, an interest rate rise may create large problems if it coincides with the expiry of a large amount of public debt that needs to be reissued. To avoid reissuing at high rates, the treasury may decide to turn to the central bank for a loan until interest rates fall. The resulting increase of liquidity will fuel the speculation against the domestic currency and will make devaluation more likely than it would otherwise be. This conflict between the central bank and the treasury is more serious in countries where public debt is both high and concentrated at short maturities, where large quantities of debt expire at the same time and where the treasury is allowed substantial recourse to central bank loans.

In order to avoid these undesirable events of a fixed peg, one could opt for a more flexible exchange rate system. A natural candidate is the crawling peg. In fact, in a recent article Dornbusch (1988) appears to be an adherent of a crawling peg scheme for the EMS currencies.

In the literature on the crawling peg system attention is focused almost exclusively on rules for the peg based on the purchasing power parity. Exceptions to this rule are the articles of Amman and Jager, who study the properties of various guidelines. A disadvantage of their analysis is that it is based upon a small Keynesian econometric model. It lacks a supply side so that the influence of net investments on capital stock and a labour market are missing. In addition, the financial sector of the model is rather rudimentary. In this chapter we investigate whether the results obtained in Jager and Amman's analyses still hold if use is made of a model that incorporates these sectors. In this manner some light is shed on the robustness of the peg rules. In the event of a supporting outcome, they are serious candidates for guidelines in an EMS with free movement of capital.

Before we can deal with the main objective of this chapter in Section 7.5, first in Section 7.2 we describe the framework used for analysing the alternative exchange rate regimes. It appears that the optimal control technique is highly recommended. This procedure, however, requires that the model is linear and that the decision-makers' desired paths of the objective variables and of instruments as well as the weights in the objective function are made explicit. Since the present model is non-linear, a linear approximation of it is derived in Section 7.3. The derivation of the desired paths and of the weights in the loss function is presented in Section 7.4. As mentioned, Section 7.5 contains the analysis of the various exchange rate regimes. The chapter closes with some concluding remarks in Section 7.6.

7.2 The framework for analysing different exchange rate systems[1]

In order to assess alternative exchange rate regimes, the criteria used for comparing the different regimes should be made clear. The most appropriate method for the appraisal depends on the nature of these criteria.

In the literature several criteria have been suggested. First, it has been argued that the speed of the exchange rate adjustment should reflect the change in the underlying equilibrium rate. It seems that in this respect, the crawling peg stands midway between the great variability of the floating rate regime and the irregular adjustment in a fixed but adjustable peg. Secondly, a regime should diminish the chance of speculative disturbances. The advantages of a crawling peg in this respect have been pointed out in the previous section. Thirdly, an exchange rate regime should allow for changes in the real rate in order to generate the necessary adjustments in the economy, most notably in the balance of payments. Often the inability of the crawling peg for allowing changes in the real exchange rate has been considered as its major disadvantage. This reasoning is based on the implicit assumptions that the rule should be based on the purchasing power parity. However, alternative formulas are possible and analyzed in this chapter. Fourthly, the exchange rate system should smooth the adjustment of the economy to various types of exogenous shocks. Finally, the implications for other instruments of economic policy, especially monetary policy, should be considered.

From this brief review of the criteria for appraising exchange rate arrangements, we conclude that the method used for assessing different exchange rate regimes should consider the functioning of the entire economy. Moreover, it is desirable that the method allows for studying the exchange rate regimes under various exogenous shocks. Finally, it should take into account that a particular exchange rate regime affects the use of other instruments of economic policy. For example, at times the domestic interest rate has to be raised in order to defend a speculative attack on the domestic currency. Consequently, a simulation method is not useful because this procedure assumes that instruments are exogenous or are related to other variables in a fixed manner (by means of reaction equations, see e.g. De Jong (1981)).

The optimal control technique is, as far as we know, the only method which incorporates all these desirable elements. It allows us to study the consequences

[1] The first part of this section is based on Sections 2 and 3 in Jager and Amman (1986). Some of the issues on the optimal control approach presented in the second part of this section can also be found in Westaway and Wren-Lewis (1990).

of a particular exchange rate regime for the whole economy and it also derives the wanted (desired) changes in the other instruments. This does not mean that this method does not show any disadvantages. The critique on the application of optimal control for macro-economic policy analysis can be classified into three groups, namely criticism referring to: the numerical values of the parameters, the rules versus discretion debate, and expectations and optimal control.

Optimal control experiments can only be derived for a quantitative model. Hence, the conclusions drawn only apply to the particular model. This disadvantage also pertains to simulation methods. In this study we use the empirical model developed in the preceding three chapters. Consequently, strictly speaking the results only refer to the Netherlands during the 1970s. Of course, the conclusions can be generalized to models (economies) that show similar characteristics. Nevertheless, the results remain rather specific. This is re-iterated by the fact that the results also depend upon the particular authorities' objective function and desired paths of targets and instruments. Moreover, hardly any exact data on the decision makers' desires are available. However, it can be argued that this disadvantage does not refer to the optimal control procedure but to the fact the decision makers' preferences are too vague.

Up to now it is implicitly assumed that the model is the right representation of the economy, which of course is not true. The fact that the parameter values of the economy's true model are unknown, has been a reason for some to argue that 'fine tune' policies may make matters worse. They prefer the use of simple fixed rules (rules without feedback) to flexible rules or discretionary policy. With fixed rules the actual and future values of the policy instruments are determined at the beginning of the planning period. Flexible rules or contingent policies specify the values of policy instruments as functions of the information that will be available when these instrument values will actually have to be assigned. Although many are of the opinion that preferably policy is determined by rules rather than unpredictable actions, they do not claim that fixed rules dominate flexible ones. Buiter (1981), for example, has shown that even if expectations are rationally formed, a contingent policy will dominate a fixed rule. Of course this does not imply that a bad discretionary policy will always dominate a fixed rule but rather that the optimal policy will always, given the information available, take the form of a contingent response. In addition the adherents of fixed rules concentrate on one particular instrument and neglect that in order to defend this rule, from time to time the government has to change the values of other policy instruments. For example, if a government has committed itself to a fixed value of the exchange rate, at times the discount rate has to be changed in order to fulfill this commitment. Constraining an instrument to be equal to a fixed value changes the character of the particular variable from instrument to a target of economic policy.

The third group of objections to the use of optimal control for policy evaluation refers to the treatment of expectations. As has been pointed out by Lucas (1976) the private sector's expectations (and decisions rules) depend on the type of policy implemented. In an optimal control experiment the optimal policy differs from the historical one so that expectations and expectations generating functions differ from their historical values. In many (simulation) models no account is taken of these changes of expectations. In our model expectations depend by means of the expectations generating function on changes in policy instruments. However, contrary to the simulation run reported in the preceding chapter, technical restrictions prevented us from re-estimating the parameters in this function. So in the simulation runs the Lucas critique is met. It should be noted that the same criticism applies to simulations in which some exogenous variables differ from their historical values. In order to completely meet Lucas' critique, forward looking expectations should be incorporated in the model. Then, however, the problem of time-inconsistency comes to the fore. This problem is first noted by Kydland and Prescott (1977) and arises as follows. By announcing future policy measures the government will influence the private sector's expectations for the future state of the economy. That will in turn lead to a certain response by the private sector in the current period. Having induced this first-period response, the government will discover that it can improve its position in the second period by re-optimizing and carrying out a different policy from the one it originally announced, even when the information has not changed. As has been argued by Hughes Hallett (1986) this argument implausibly supposes that agents can have rational expectations about economic activity but not about the government's policy. Since the expectations in the present model are not forward looking, we will not deal with possible solutions of the time-inconsistency problem.[2]

When applying the optimal control method in Section 7.5, we do not add various exogenous disturbances to the equations in order to study the economy's functioning under different shocks. Instead the optimal control experiments are calculated for a period during which several large shocks took place, namely the first part of the 1970s. This period is characterized by several great exogenous shocks, in particular the inflow of US dollars into Western Europe at the

[2] Solutions for the time-inconsistency problem consist of ways to enforce the government's commitment to the ex ante optimal policy. Rules rather than discretion can be used, although these rules should be credible. Reputation can serve as a mechanism to enforce commitment (see, Rogoff, 1987, for a survey). Another solution suggested in Kotlikoff, Persson and Svensson (1988) involves formulating a "social" contract that specifies the ex ante optimal policy and that can be "sold" by successive old generations to successive young generations. A detailed treatise of rational expectations and optimal control can be found in the Chapters 7 to 10 of Holly and Hughes Hallett (1989).

beginning of the 1970s, which represents an important monetary shock, and the first oil shock of 1973/74, that stands for a great real shock.

7.3 Deriving the linearization of the model

7.3.1 *The technique*

As in Friedman (1975) the method used for deriving the linearizations of the model is the truncation, after the first-order terms, of a set of Taylor series expansions. Let $y = f(\mathbf{z})$ be a single-valued function, for scalar y and vector **z** and assume that f is at least twice differentiable. Then Taylor's theorem states that

$$y(\mathbf{z}^0 + \delta\mathbf{z}) = f(\mathbf{z}^0) + \nabla f(\mathbf{z}^0)'\delta\mathbf{z} + \tfrac{1}{2}\,\delta\mathbf{z}'\nabla^2 f(\mathbf{z}^0)\delta\mathbf{z} + \ldots. \tag{7.1}$$

where $\mathbf{z}^0$ is a particular value of **z**, $\delta\mathbf{z}$ is a vector of small displacements in **z** about $\mathbf{z}^0$, $\nabla f(\mathbf{z}^0)$is the vector of first partial derivatives of $f(\mathbf{z})$ evaluated at $\mathbf{z}^0$ and $\nabla^2 f(\mathbf{z}^0)$ is the matrix of second partial and cross partial derivatives of $f(\mathbf{z})$ evaluated at $\mathbf{z}^0$. Equation (7.1) is incomplete in that it omits a series of higher-order terms in higher-order derivatives.

The linearization technique used in this chapter assumes that the second- and higher-order terms of the expansions are small within limited ranges of the state of the economy so that the nonlinear equation can be approximated by the linear

$$y^0(\mathbf{z}^0 + \delta\mathbf{z}) = f(\mathbf{z}^0) + \nabla f(\mathbf{z}^0)'\delta\mathbf{z} \tag{7.2}$$

and y^0 is treated as an approximation of y.

A linearization of a nonlinear equation means that the several variables in the nonlinear terms are separated into individual terms consisting of one variable and a parameter. Assuming that **z** is a vector of n elements the resulting linearized relation is

$$y = \alpha_0 + \alpha_1 z_1 + \alpha_2 z_2 + \ldots + \alpha_n z_n \tag{7.3}$$

where the α_i, i=1,...,n are the elements of the gradient vector ∇f in equation (7.2), i.e.

$$\alpha_i = \delta y/\delta z_i \quad i=1,\ldots,n \tag{7.4}$$

The terms (7.4) are evaluated at $\mathbf{z}^0$. The coefficient α_0 represents the sum of three components: the nonlinear function's constant term, the evaluation at $\mathbf{z}_0$ of the nonlinear terms in the function (the $f(\mathbf{z}^0)$ term in (7.2)), and the product of the variables in the nonlinear terms multiplied by their partial derivatives (the $-\nabla f(\mathbf{z}^0)'\mathbf{z}^0$ components of $\nabla f(\mathbf{z}^0)'\delta\mathbf{z}$ in (7.2)).

This procedure transforms the nonlinear relation y = f(z) into the linear equation (7.3) with time-varying coefficients. The standard version of the optimal control programme used in Section 7.5 assumes that the model is linear and that its coefficients are constant. We, therefore, decided that in general the coefficient's time series in the linearized relations is replaced by its mean, so that the parameters in the linear model are constant. This procedure is not applied in those cases that the assumption of constant parameters significantly deteriorates the particular equation's fit. The worsening of the fit can occur because one or more of the coefficients' time series is not more or less constant or because the original, nonlinear, equation contains a structural shift. The model contains two structural changes. The first one arises at the end of 1973:II, when the form of the relation of the interest rate on short-term domestic assets changes (see Section 4.6). The second structural change occurs at the end of 1976:IV in the relation of the foreigners' investments in long-term domestic assets (see Section 4.7). Since the substitution method is used for deriving the exchange rate and the interest rate on short-term and long-term domestic assets, the structural shift at the end of 1976:IV also influences the equation of the Dutch guilder/US dollar exchange rate and that of the long-term domestic interest rate (see Section 6.2).

The structural shift at the end of 1976:IV is not a part of the linearized model, because the optimal control experiments are derived for the period 1970:I -1976:IV only. The reason for restricting the optimal control experiments to a subperiod of the estimation period is that the central memory of the computer used for calculating the optimal control solutions appeared to be too small for calculating these solutions for the entire period. This problem could be solved by reducing the number of periods. We selected the subperiod 1970:I-1976:IV instead of 1977:I-1980:IV in order to incorporate the effects of various exogenous shocks into the analysis (see the end of Section 7.2) and in order to enhance a comparison with the results in the studies by Jager and Amman, who derived their results for the same period. The optimal control programme has been amended in order to incorporate the possibility of parameter changes at the end of 1973:II and at some other points in time (see Section 7.3.2).

7.3.2 *Forms of nonlinearities in the model*

The monetary part of the model contains the majority of the nonlinear functions. The two main sources of these nonlinearities are the specification of the assets demand functions and the use of the substitution approach for deriving the short-term domestic interest rate, the long-term domestic interest rate and the endogenous exchange rate.

The general specification of the assets' demand functions is represented by equation (4.8) which for convenience is reproduced here as equation (7.5)

$$\frac{\Delta A_{it}}{W_{t-1}} = \Sigma_{j=1}^{n} \delta_{ij} \cdot \alpha_j \frac{W_t}{W_{t-1}} + \Sigma_{j=1}^{n} \delta_{ij} \Sigma_{k=1}^{n} \beta_{jk} r_{kt} \frac{W_t}{W_{t-1}}$$

$$+ \Sigma_{j=1}^{n} \delta_{ij} \Sigma_{h=1}^{m} \gamma_{jh} \frac{X_{ht} \cdot W_t}{W_{t-1}} - \Sigma_{j=1}^{n} \delta_{ij} \frac{A_{j,t-1}}{W_{t-1}}$$

$$+ \mu_i \frac{Z_t}{W_{t-1}} + \frac{v_{it}}{W_{t-1}} \qquad i = 1,...,n \qquad (7.5)$$

In order to linearise these relations, they are first multiplied by W_{t-1}. Then (7.5) changes in

$$\Delta A_{it} = \theta_1 W_t + \Sigma_{k=1}^{n} \theta_{ik} r_{kt} W_t + \Sigma_{h=1}^{m} \theta_{ih} X_{ht} W_t + \Sigma_{j=1}^{n} \theta_{ij} A_{j,t-1} + \mu_i Z_t + v_{it}$$

$$i=1,...,n \qquad (7.6)$$

$$\theta_1 = \Sigma_{i=1}^{n} \delta_{ij} \alpha_j$$

$$\theta_{ik} = \Sigma_{j=1}^{n} \delta_{ij} \beta_{jk}$$

$$\theta_{ih} = \Sigma_{j=1}^{n} \delta_{ij} \gamma_{jh}$$

The procedure described in the former subsection is used for linearizing relation (7.6). Terms like $\theta_{ih} X_{ht} W_t$ are replaced by $\lambda_1 X_{ht} + \lambda_2 W_t + \lambda_3$ where $\lambda_1 = \theta_{ih} W_t$, $\lambda_2 = \theta_{ih} X_{ht}$ and $\lambda_3 = -\theta_{ih} X_{ht} W_t$.

For example, the nonlinear relation of the private sector's holdings of short-term domestic assets is

$$NDAS^p = 0.308\ NDAS^p_{-1} - 0.578\ NDAL^p_{-1} + 0.172\ LS_{-1}$$

$$- 0.447\ Y + FA^p \cdot [0.0486\ r_s + 0.013\ r_l - 0.005\ (r_f + \mathring{e}^e)$$

$$- 0.036\ r_{ls} + 0.425] + FA^p_{-1} \cdot [0.051\ q + 0.0004\ S1 - 0.018\ S2] \qquad (7.7)$$

The corresponding linear relation is

$$NDAS^p = 0.308\ NDAS^p_{-1} - 0.582\ NDAL^p_{-1} + 0.172\ LS_{-1}$$

$$- 0.447\ Y + \alpha_0 + \alpha_1\ FA^p + \alpha_2\ r_s + \alpha_3\ r_l + \alpha_4\ (r_f + \mathring{e}^e)$$

$$+ \alpha_5\ r_{ls} + \alpha_6\ FA^p_{-1} + \alpha_7\ q + \alpha_8\ S1 + \alpha_9\ S2 \qquad (7.8)$$

where $\alpha_0 = -\ FA^p \cdot [0.0486\ r_s + 0.013\ r_l - 0.005\ (r_f + \mathring{e}^e)$

$- 0.036\ r_{ls}] - FA^p_{-1} \cdot [0.051\ q + 0.0004\ S1 - 0.018\ S2]$

$\alpha_1 = 0.0486\ r_s + 0.013\ r_l - 0.005\ (r_f + \mathring{e}^e) - 0.036\ r_{ls} + 0.425$

$\alpha_2 = 0.0486\ FA^p$

$\alpha_3 = 0.013\ FA_p$

$\alpha_4 = -0.005\ FA^p$

$\alpha_5 = -0.036\ FA^p$

$\alpha_6 = 0.0004\ S1 - 0.018\ S2 + 0.05\ q$

$\alpha_7 = 0.05\ FA^p_{-1}$

$\alpha_8 = 0.0004\ FA^p_{-1}$

$\alpha_9 = -\ 0.018\ FA^p_{-1}$

In principle, the coefficients $\alpha_0,\ldots,\alpha_9$ vary per period. The linearization procedure replaces a nonlinear relation with constant parameters by a linear one with time-varying parameters. This method is used for deriving linear versions of all assets' demand functions.

The second group of nonlinear functions consists of the short-term interest rate, the long-term interest rate and the exchange rate. As has been set forth in Section 6.2, these rates are derived from the particular market's equilibrium condition. The resulting relations contain rather complicated nonlinear terms. This is illustrated by equation (6.7), the relation of the short-term interest rate, which is reproduced as equation (7.9)

$$r_s = \{\Delta NDAS^g + \Delta NDAS^s_r - (-.6887\ NDAS^p_{-1} - 0.578\ NDAL^p_{-1}$$
$$+ 0.172\ LS_{-1} - 0.447\ Y + FA^p \cdot [0.013\ r_l - 0.005\ (r_f + \mathring{e}^e)$$
$$- 0.036\ r_{ls} + 0.425] + FA^p_{-1} \cdot [0.0004\ S1 - 0.018\ S2$$
$$+ 0.05\ q] - 0.4858\ NDAS^b_{-1} - 0.422\ NDAL^b_{-1} - 0.354\ NFA^b_{-1}$$
$$+ 0.144\ NDAS^p + 0.228\ NDALS + 0.004\ dliq\ NDAS^p$$
$$+ 0.410\ \Delta SPL + 0.252\ \Delta RES + FA^b \cdot [0.551\ r_l$$
$$- 0.278\ r_f + \mathring{e}^e + 0.207 + FA^b_{-1} \cdot \{0.004\ S1 + 0.015\ S2$$
$$- 0.007\ S3\} - 0.500\ NDAS^f_{-1} + 272.922 + W^f \cdot [-0.091 \cdot 0.5$$
$$(\mathring{e}^e_{fr} + \mathring{e}^e_{uk})) - 0.321\ (r_{s,wg} + r_{s,us}) + 0.859\ DUMS$$
$$+ 0.932] \} / \{ 0.047\ FA^b + 4.8559\ FA^p + 9.1380\ W^f \} \qquad (7.9)$$

The complex nonlinear terms arise because the expression $\{\Delta NDAS^g .... + 0.932\}$, which contains some products, is divided by $\{0.047\ FA^b + 4.8559\ FA^p + 9.1380\ W^f\}$. In order to simplify the linearization procedure we have defined an extra variable, say r'_s, which consists of the numerator of the equation of r_s. This relation has been linearized in the same manner as the asset demands function. The nonlinear formula of the short-term interest rate can be written as

$$r_s = r'_s / \{ 0.047\ FA^b + 4.8559\ FA^p + 9.1380\ W^f \} \qquad (7.10)$$

The linear form of this relation is

$$r_s = \lambda_0 + \lambda_1 r'_s + \lambda_2 FA^b + \lambda_3 FA^p + \lambda_4 W^f \qquad (7.11)$$

where

$$\lambda_0 = 0.047\ FA^b + 4.8559\ FA^p + 9.1380\ W^f$$

$$\lambda_1 = 1.0 / \{ 0.047\ FA^b + 4.8559\ FA^p + 9.1380\ W^f \}$$

$$\lambda_2 = - 0.047 \cdot r'_s / \{ 0.047\ FA^b + 4.8559\ FA^p + 9.1380\ W^f \}^2$$

$$\lambda_3 = - 4.8559 \cdot r'_s / \{ 0.047\ FA^b + 4.8559\ FA^p + 9.1380\ W^f \}^2$$

$$\lambda_4 = -9.1380 \cdot r'_s / \{ 0.047\ FA^b + 4.8559\ FA^p + 9.1380\ W^f \}^2$$

As in the linear relations mentioned before, the time-varying coefficients λ_0, λ_2, λ_3 and λ_4 are replaced by their means. The time series of λ_1, however, shows a trend so that replacing λ_1 by its mean significantly deteriorates the equations fit. Its value, therefore, is allowed to change stepwise in the following periods 1971:I, 1972:I, 1973:III, 1974:I and 1975:I. During the period 1970:I-1970:IV, λ_1 is represented by its mean for this subperiod. The same holds for the other subperiods.

As has been extensively discussed in Chapter 6, the fit of the long-term interest rate is rather disappointing. During the simulation experiments, presented in that chapter, many endogenous explanatory variables have been fixed at their historical values. The contribution to the explanation of r_l is represented by rlex. Then the nonlinear relation for the period 1970:I-1976.IV is

$$r_l = \{\Delta NDAL^g - [(0.057\ FA^b - 0.0085\ FA^p) \cdot r_s + 0.003\ FA^p\ r_{ls}$$
$$- 0.007\ FA^b (r_f + \mathring{e}^e) - 0.382\ W^f\ \mathring{e}^e_{FR} \}$$
$$/ \{ 0.3145\ FA^p + 2.0388\ FA^b \} + rlex \tag{7.12}$$

where FA^p and FA^b are assumed to be exogenous. The linearized form is

$$r_l = \lambda_1\ \Delta NDAL^g + \lambda_2\ r_s + \lambda_3\ r_{ls} + \lambda_4\ r_f + \mathring{e}^e + \lambda_5\ \mathring{e}^e_{FR} + rlex \tag{7.13}$$

where

$$\lambda_1 = 1.0 / \{ 0.3145\ FA^p + 2.0388\ FA^b \}$$

$$\lambda_2 = (0.057\ FA^b - 0.0085\ FA^p) / \{ 0.3145\ FA^p + 2.0388\ FA^b \}$$

$$\lambda_3 = 0.003\ FA^p / \{ 0.3145\ FA^p + 2.0388\ FA^b \}$$

$$\lambda_4 = -0.007\ FA^b / \{ 0.3145\ FA^p + 2.0388\ FAb \}$$

$$\lambda_5 = -0.382\ W^f / \{ 0.3145\ FA^p + 2.0388\ FA^b \}$$

The time series of λ_1 has a strong trend term and therefore is allowed to change in the following quarters 1971:I, 1972:I, 1973:III, 1975:I and 1976:I. Although the times series of λ_2, λ_3, λ_4 and λ_5 are rather stable, the coefficients derived from these series are also allowed to change at these moments because the approximation of the original nonlinear equations is rather rough.

Equation (6.15), which is reproduced as (7.14), is the nonlinear relation of the Dutch guilder / US dollar exchange rate

$$\begin{aligned} e_{US} = &\{d7067 \cdot W^f \cdot 0.135 \cdot (e^e_{US} + e^e_{FR} \cdot e_{FR,US}) \\ &+ (1-d7067) \cdot W^f \cdot 0.382 \cdot e^e_{FR} \cdot e_{FR,US} \\ &+ 0.457 \cdot W^f (e^e_{FR} \cdot e_{FR,US} + e^e_{UK} / e_{UK,US}) \\ &+ (0.417 \cdot FA^p + 0.590 \cdot FA^b) \cdot (0.318\, e^e_{us} + 0.51\, e^e_{WG} \cdot e_{WG,US} \\ &+ 0.177\, e^e_{FR} \cdot e_{FR,USf} + 0.055\, e^e_{UK} \cdot e_{UK,US})\} \,/\, \{CA - \Delta RES \\ &+ STATBB + \Delta NDAL^f \backslash \{\mathring{e}^e\} + \Delta NDAS^f \backslash \{\mathring{e}^e\} - \Delta NFA^p \backslash \{\mathring{e}^e\} \\ &- \Delta NFA^b \backslash \{\mathring{e}^e\}\} \end{aligned} \tag{7.14}$$

where $\Delta NDAL^f \backslash \{\mathring{e}^e\}$, $\Delta NDAS^f \backslash \{\mathring{e}^e\}$, $\Delta NFA^p \backslash \{\mathring{e}^e\}$ and $\Delta NFA^b \backslash \{\mathring{e}^e\}$ represent the particular asset demand functions' explanatory variables except for the exchange rate expectations (see Section 6.2).

For the period 1970:I-1976:IV, the linearized version is

$$e_{US} = \lambda_0 + \lambda_1\, e^e_{US} + \lambda_2\, e^e_{UK} + \lambda_3\, e^e_{FR} + \lambda_4\, e^e_{WG} + \lambda_5\, DEN_{US} \tag{7.15}$$

where

$$\begin{aligned} \lambda_0 = &-\{d7067 \cdot W^f \cdot 0.135 \cdot (e^e_{US} + e^e_{FR} \cdot e_{FR,US}) \\ &+ (1-d7067) \cdot W^f \cdot 0.382 \cdot e^e_{FR} \cdot e_{FR,US} \\ &+ 0.457 \cdot W^f (e^e_{FR} \cdot e_{FR,US} + e^e_{UK} / e_{UK,US}) \\ &+ (0.417 \cdot FA^p + 0.590 \cdot FA^b) \cdot (0.318\, e^e_{us} + 0.51\, e^e_{WG} \cdot e_{WG,US} \\ &+ 0.177\, e^e_{FR} \cdot e_{FR,USf} + 0.055\, e^e_{UK} \cdot e_{UK,US})\} \,/\, DEN_{US} \end{aligned}$$

$$\lambda_1 = (0.135 \cdot W^f + 0.133 \cdot FA^p + 0.188 \cdot FA^b) \,/\, DEN_{US}$$

$$\lambda_2 = (0.457 \cdot W^f + 0.023 \cdot FA^p + 0.032 \cdot FA^b) \,/\, e_{UK,US} \cdot DEN_{US}$$

$$\lambda_3 = (0.974 \cdot W^f + 0.074 \cdot FA^p + 0.104 \cdot FA^b) \cdot e_{FR,US} \,/\, DEN_{US}$$

$$\lambda_4 = (0.213 \cdot FA^p + 0.301 \cdot FA^b) \cdot e_{WG,US} \,/\, DEN_{US}$$

$$\lambda_5 = -\{d7067 \cdot W^f \cdot 0.135 \cdot (e^e_{US} + e^e_{FR} \cdot e_{FR,US})$$

$$+ (1 - d7067) \cdot W^f \cdot 0.382 \cdot e^e_{FR} \cdot e_{FR,US}$$

$$+ 0.457 \cdot W^f (e^e_{FR} \cdot e_{FR,US} + e^e_{UK} / e_{UK,US}$$

$$+ (0.417 \cdot FA^p + 0.590 \cdot FA^b) \cdot (0.318\ e^e_{us} + 0.51\ e^e_{WG} \cdot e_{WG,US}$$

$$+ 0.177\ e^e_{FR} \cdot e_{FR,USf} + 0.055\ e^e_{UK} \cdot e_{UK,US}))\} \,/\, DEN^2_{US}$$

$$DEN_{US} = CA - \Delta RES + STATBB + \Delta NDAL^f \backslash \{\mathring{e}^e\} + \Delta NDAS^f \backslash \{\mathring{e}^e\}$$

$$- \Delta NFA^p \backslash \{\mathring{e}^e\} - \Delta NFA^b \backslash \{\mathring{e}^e\}$$

It appeared that the time series of λ_i, i = 0,...,5 are badly represented by their mean. The coefficients λ_i, i = 1,...,5 are reasonably constant only for some subperiods. As in the two interest equations the parameters' values are allowed to change at 1971:I, 1972:I, 1973:III, 1975:I and 1976:I. The time series of λ_0 is added to the relation as an exogenous explanatory variable.

A simulation with the linearized model reveals that in general this model gives a good representation of the nonlinear model. Only the simulated time series of the exchange rates and the domestic interest rates show relative large differences from their historical values in the neighbourhood of periods where the parameters' values change. In order to prevent these differences significantly affecting the optimal control experiments, we have added an exogenous correction term to the relations of r_s, r_l and e_{US}.

Hitherto some parameters in the linear model are assumed to be time-varying although the corresponding coefficients in the nonlinear model are constant. The nonlinear model itself also contains some time-varying coefficients, namely those in the relation of the exchange rates' expected percentage change (see Section 4.3.5). The expected levels of the exchange rates are calculated as

$$e^e_{t+1} = e_t \cdot (1.0 + \mathring{e}^e) \tag{7.16}$$

In this relation $\mathring{e}^e$ is replaced by the equation used for approximating the particular expected percentage change (equations (4.12), (4.13) and (4.14)). The parameters in the resulting nonlinear equation are time-varying, because they are estimated by means of the rolling regressions procedure. The procedure described in Section 7.2.1 is used for linearizing this equation. As is described in Section 6.5 in the non-linear model these parameters are re-estimated at the end of every year. In order to approximate this practice as much as possible, the relevant parameters are assumed to change in 1971:I, 1972:I, 1973:III, 1975:I, and 1976:I.

The definitional relation of the expected percentage changes are

$$\mathring{e}^e = (e^e_{t+1} - e_t) / e_t = e^e_{t+1} / e_t - 1.0 \tag{7.17}$$

The corresponding linear equation is

$$\mathring{e}^e = \lambda_0 + \lambda_1 e^e_{t+1} + \lambda_2 e_t \tag{7.18}$$

where

$$\lambda_0 = -e^e_{t+1} / e_t - 1.0$$

$$\lambda_1 = 1.0 / e_t$$

$$\lambda_2 = -e^e_{t+1} / e_t^2$$

The coefficients of e^e_{t+1} and e_t are reasonably constant in the subperiods 1970:I-1973:II and 1973:III-1976:IV. The difference between this linear relation and the historical values are added to the equation as an exogenous correction term.

The nonlinear terms in the other relations of the model are less complicated than those of the interest rate and exchange rate equations. They all consist of the product or quotient of two variables. In many cases the time series of the linearized parameters are represented in a satisfactory manner by their means. The few exceptions to this rule are listed in Table 7.1. For each of the subperiods indicated the coefficients of the explanatory variables in the equation of these five endogenous variables are set equal to their mean for the subperiod concerned. In this way a reasonable approximation of the non-linear relation is obtained.

7.3.3 *Other modifications*

It is possible that under one or more of the exchange regimes to be studied in the next section, the optimal path of some variable largely diverges from its historical track. In that case the equilibrium on the markets for domestic short term assets, condition (6.6), for domestic long-term assets, condition (6.8-b), and the equilibrium on the balance of payments, condition (6.11) might be violated

Table 7.1 Other linearized relations with time-varying parameters

Endogenous variable	Number of subperiods distinguished*
X_g, M_g	2
X_i, M_i	2
U	6

* If this column contains a 2 then the subperiods during which the parameters are constant are 1970:I-1973:II and 1973:III-1976:IV. If a 6 is mentioned, the subperiods are 1970:I-1970:IV, 1971:I-1971:IV, 1972:I-1973:II, 1973:III-1974.IV, 1975:I-1975:IV and 1976:I-1976:IV.

to a great extent. In order to avoid such unrealistic results, we have defined additional variables which are set equal to the difference between the supply and demand on the these markets. These excess demand or supply variables are added to the state vector, which is the vector in the optimal control algorithm containing the current and lagged endogenous variables. The desired values of the excess demand or supply variables are zero and the weights in the loss function are set equal to 10.

The state vector has also been extended because, as is shown in Amman and Jager (1987), the calculations of optimal currency pegs requires that the definitions of the pegs, formulas (7.21) and (7.22) in Section 7.5, are added to the system. Consequently, the state vector is extended by the number of additional equations. However, it appeared that when these relations where added to the original linearized version of the model, the central memory of the computer was again too small. In order to solve this problem, we decided to delete the last period of some long lags from the model. The value of the coefficient in question has been spread over the other parameters in the lag structure concerned. The variables that are deleted are $\mathring{\pi}_{-6}$, $\mathring{p}_{i,-6}$ and $\mathring{p}_{k,-6}$ from the relation of investments, $p_{g,-6}$ and $p_{v,-6}$ from the equation of real imports of goods, TS_{-6} and $[U/a_s]_{-6}$ from the wage rate relation, and $\mathring{w}$ from the percentage change in the export price of goods.

It appeared that for some periods the linearized form of the definitional relation of the amount of labour used by firms gives rise to negative values of the unemployment rate. This result arose from the linearization of the definition of labour used by firms. The coefficient of a_{-1} in this linearized equation is high (0.9997). This parameter has therefore been reduced from 0.9997 to 0.85 and the constant term has been increased.

7.4 The desired paths and the weights in the loss function

7.4.1 *The desired paths of economic targets*

As far as possible we have used official publications for deriving the time series of the target variables' desired values. It should be mentioned that, generally, official publications are very vague about the exact preferred path of an objective variable or of an instrument. Consequently, the time series of target values are subjective approximations of the decision-makers' preferences. When no clear estimate could be derived from the publications, we have chosen target values that are more favourable than the historical values. For instance, the selected values of the desired level of real national income are higher than the historical values. The reason for this choice is that the objective function is quadratic. Consequently, a realization that is better than the target value gets the same penalty as a realized value that differs from the target value by the same amount but that is less favourable than the target value. In order to avoid policy makers being penalized for doing better than they first thought possible, we have corrected the particular desired values.

The targets of economic policy can be divided into two groups, *viz.* ultimate and intermediate targets. As ultimate targets we consider the level of economic growth, the stability of this growth, the rate of inflation, measured by $\overset{\circ}{p}_c$, the balance on the current account, and the unemployment rate. They provide the guideline for the performance of policy instruments. Intermediate targets, that are included in our analysis, are the exchange rate parity of the Dutch guilder *vis-à-vis* the Deutsche mark and the French franc, and the liquidity ratio. Intermediate targets are a mixture of targets and instruments. This mixed character of an intermediate target can nicely be illustrated by comparing our treatment of the liquidity ratio with that in Jager (1981). Jager lists the liquidity ratio in the set of instruments. The reason is that, except for the discount rate, his model does not contain the instruments of monetary policy that are directly controlled by the monetary authorities. The numerator of the liquidity ratio, the value of primary and secondary liquidity, represents the effects of these instruments (see Jager, 1981, p. 162).

Since we use non-seasonally adjusted data, the time series of the economic growth, the rate of inflation, the balance on the current account, and the unemployment rate contain a seasonal pattern. Generally, however, the authorities' target values refer to the particular variable's annual value. Therefore, we do not include the current value of these variables but their average during the last four quarters in the objective function. An additional advantage of this choice proceeds from the fact that the calculated optimal paths of optimal control experiments exhibit irregular behaviour at the beginning and at the end of the period concerned. By using the four-quarter moving average in the objective function, we reduce the influence of the last three quarters and thus diminish the impact of end-effects on the solutions.

The time series of the desired level of real national income[3] is derived as follows. Until 1971:IV the level is obtained by assuming an annual growth rate of 8 per cent. From 1972:I to 1974:VI this annual rate is reduced to 4 per cent, and for 1975 and 1976 this rate is 3 per cent[4]. For every quarter the resulting time series exceeds the time series of actual values for the average during the last four quarters of real national income.

In addition to a high level of economic activity, the authorities prefer a stable time pattern of this growth to an irregular evolution. This objective is reflected by the growth rate of real national income. Since this is an independent objective, representing a characteristic quite different from the level of economic growth, the desired values are not derived from the preferred path of real national income. In order to represent the desired uniform pattern, the target values should reflect the directly obtainable growth rate. The target values are derived from the growth rates used for calculating the structural budget deficit. From 1970:I to 1971:IV this rate is 4.8 per cent per year. For the period 1972-1975 the desired value is an annual rate of 4.2 per cent, whereas in 1976 it is decreased to 3.75 per cent per year. According to Sterks (1982), for the first years these growth rates reflect merely an expectation. From the budget plan for 1973 onwards the growth rates represent an objective of economic policy (see Sterks, 1982, p. 172).

---

[3] Note that in Jager (1981) and in subsequent studies by Jager and Amman, the economic growth target is approximated by the real national product, whereas we use the real national income. Like us, Jager is of the opinion that national income is the appropriate measure for representing the desired level of economic growth. Nevertheless, he uses national product because his model lacks an (un)employment variable. His reasoning is that by using national product instead of national income, the employment target is also indirectly incorporated in the optimization procedure. Since our model contains a labour market, we need not make this restrictive assumption, but can explicitly incorporate both the growth and unemployment target in the optimal control experiments.

[4] From 1972:I onwards, this time series of the desired level of real national income is less ambitious than the one used in the studies by Amman and Jager. For these periods the gap between desired path and the actual path of the four-quarter-average of real national income appeared to be very large. As a result the optimal control algorithm forced the interest rates to be negative in order to reach this path. In order to avoid such unrealistic results we have chosen the target values mentioned in the text. These values meet the same criterion as those used by Jager and Amman, i.e. they exceed the actual values. The reason why the gap between the actual and the desired time series is less in the studies by Jager and Amman is that they use the current value instead of the four-quarter-average in the objective function.

During the greater part of the 1960s and the early 1970s, the level of the Dutch national product was at or slightly below the full-employment level. Hence it is reasonable that no explicit target of the unemployment rate was published. When from 1972 onwards the unemployment rate rose considerably, the authorities still did not decide upon a particular level for the desired unemployment rate. They only stated that they aimed to reduce current unemployment. As far as we were able to trace, it was not until the second half of the 1970s that a concrete desired level of the number of unemployed employees was published. In accordance with these findings the preferred level of the unemployment rate is calculated as follows. From 1976 to 1980 the desired level is 3.25 per cent. This is roughly one per cent below the yearly average of the actual unemployment rate. During the period 1972:I-1975:IV the desired level is set at the four-period moving average minus one percent. For the years 1970 and 1971 it is assumed that the desired level equals the actual level of the average of last year's unemployment rate.

As in Jager(1981), the desired inflation rate is set at an annual rate of 2.5 per cent. This percentage is mentioned as the desired rate in Bestek '81, p. 20. It is less than the preferred value specified in the EEC's Members' Resolution of December 5, 1972. According to that resolution, these countries aimed at reducing the increase in consumer prices to an annual rate of 4 per cent in 1973 (see Miljoenennota 1974, pp.12 and 13). The chosen rate thus corresponds with the lowest desired value.

The time series of the desired values of the current account's surplus is set at 1 percent of the net national product, $0.01 \cdot (Y - DEP^f)$. De Nederlandsche Bank mentions this target several times (see, for instance, De Nederlandsche Bank, Verslag over het boekjaar 1969, p. 59 and De Nederlandsche Bank, Verslag over het boekjaar 1973, pp. 62 and 63). This norm is an approximation of the value of the Dutch development aid. The reasoning behind this norm is that the developing countries should be enabled to spend their receipts in the Dutch economy without creating an excess demand on the Dutch goods market. As a consequence expenditure by Dutch inhabitants has to be reduced to the amount of the development aid. An additional reason to strive for a surplus on the current account of the balance of payments is that such a surplus enhances the investors' confidence in the value of the Dutch guilder.

The liquidity ratio has been the main target for the domestic monetary policy throughout the period analysed. In the model this ratio is defined as $lq = (M1 + NDAS^p + NDAS^f)/(4.0 \cdot (Y - DEP^f))$. Almost every year, the central bank's annual report contains a discussion of the actual and desired movement of this ratio[5]. These statements of the monetary authorities' desires are used for deriving the time series of target values. Accordingly, for the years 1974 and 1975 desired values equal actual values, although these are rather high (about 36 per cent). The reason is that the authorities accepted the high values of the liquidity ratio, because the Dutch economy showed clear signs of weakening. For 1976 the desired value is 1 per cent lower than for 1975, whereas for the years 1970 to 1973, the desired values are about 33 per cent.

7.4.2 *The desired paths of instruments*

The authorities' instruments of economic policy included in our model can be divided into two groups, namely those belonging to monetary policy and those belonging to fiscal policy. Instruments of monetary policy are: the change in international monetary reserves, the change of the discount rate, the parity of the Dutch guilder *vis-à-vis* the Deutsche mark and *vis-à-vis* the French franc, special loans granted by the central bank, and liquidity requirements on short-term deposits. Instruments belonging to fiscal policy are government expenditures, various taxes and the financing of a budget deficit. The latter can be financed by issuing bonds, $\Delta NDAL^{g}$, or by increasing the government's short-term debt held by banks, $\Delta NDAS^{g} = \Delta NDAS^{b}$ and changes in other short-term assets and liabilities, such as cash positions, FD^{gr}. When comparing this list of instruments with those mentioned in previous chapters, especially in Sections 4.6, 6.3 and 6.4, it appears that the measure of the tightness of credit ceilings, ncc, is not used in the optimal control experiments. The reason is that this instrument has been used in the period 1977:I-1980:IV only. As mentioned in Section 7.3.1, we were forced to restrict the optimal control experiments to the period 1970:I-1976:IV so that these instruments could be deleted from the linearized model.

For several instruments of economic policy no time series of desired values can be found in official publications. Nor does the economic theory present any suggestion. The only information we have is that in many circumstances there are costs associated with changing the instrument's value. These costs can be costs associated with implementing the change of the policy or costs resulting from the private sector's increased uncertainty of the government's behaviour. Hence we have assumed that the desired value of the change of the instrument concerned is equal to zero. This assumption of a desired value equal to zero is made for the change in international monetary reserves, the change of the discount rate, the change of parity rates, special loans granted to by the central bank, and the

---

[5] A list of quotations from the central bank's annual reports dealing with the liquidity ratio can be found in Fase (1985), pp. 100-105.

monetary financing of the government's budget deficit.

The target values of the change of the various taxes are obtained by a applying a similar reasoning. These values are calculated according to the formula $1.16 \cdot \overset{\circ}{y} \cdot TTY_{-1}$, where $\overset{\circ}{y}$ represents the particular tax base and TTY_{-1} is the value of the tax in the previous period. The factor 1.16 is the macro-economic progression factor. The amount of taxes resulting from the use of this formula represents the amount obtained when the government does not alter the tax rates.

The time series of the desired amount of bonds to be issued for financing the government's budget deficit is derived from the figures published under the structural budget policy. For the years 1970, 1971, 1972, and 1973 these figures are obtained from various issues of De Miljoenennota. For 1974 and later years we have used the figures published in Sterks (1982), p.214.

In order to avoid the algorithm calculating unreasonable results at the end of the period used in the optimal control experiments, a transversality condition has been introduced for the level of international monetary reserves. In accordance with the target values for the change in international reserves its level in 1976:IV is assumed to be the same as in 1970:I. It should be noted that the literature is not very clear with regard to the appropriate level of international monetary reserves.[6]

7.4.3 *The weights in the loss function*

The results of the optimal control experiments depend to a great extent upon the weights in the loss function. These weights should reflect the authorities' preference scheme. Various methods for deriving these weights have been suggested and used in the literature[7]. Since, we are only interested in investigating the robustness of the results obtained in Jager and Amman (1986), we have decided to derive the weights in the loss function from those used in that study. These weights have been derived by means of the revealed preference method presented in Friedlaender (1973). During the period 1967-1970 the main economic variables behaved in a smooth and relatively predictable manner. When deriving the weights of the target variables it has been assumed that during this period actual policy is a good reflection of desired policy. Details of the assumptions underlying this derivation can be found in Jager (1981), pp. 197-

---

[6] See Jager (1981), pp. 162, 163.

[7] See the introduction of Brandsma *et al*. (1988) for a review of the various methods. They also mention several studies in which the preferences of Dutch policy makers are estimated.

Table 7.2 The weights in the loss function

Variable	Weight	
j	p_j	p_{JA}
y	0.0000106	19
$\mathring{y}$	0.0016612	15
$\mathring{p}_c$	0.2133895	8
CA	0.0000102	7
U	23661.687*	
e_{WG}	0.0002001	2
e_{FR}	0.0002516	2
lq	2963916.8	30
ΔRES	0.00048	30
Δr_{cb}	0.0003105	30
$\Delta NDAS^g$	0.0002731	50
$\Delta NDAL^g$	0.0000146	50

* This weight has been derived by assuming that the sum of squares equals that of $\mathring{y}$.

206. In Jager and Amman (1986) the weights of the instruments and of the exchange rate obtained by means of the revealed preference method serve as a first estimate only. The ultimately selected weights of these variables are also determined by the "necessity to keep their optimal time paths within politically acceptable limits and within the fluctuation margin around the parity" (Jager and Amman, 1986, p. 14).

In order to keep the results of the present experiment as comparable as possible with those obtained by Jager and Amman, the following formula is used for deriving the weights in the objective function

$$\Sigma^n_{t=1} p_{JA,y} (y_{JA,t} - \tilde{y}_{JA,t})^2 = \Sigma^n_{t=1} p_y (y_t - \tilde{y}_t)^2 \tag{7.19}$$

where $y_{JA,t}$, $\tilde{y}_{JA,t}$, $p_{JA,y}$ are respectively, the observation in period t of a variable, its target value and its weight in the loss function, used in Jager and Amman's paper. The symbols y_t, $\tilde{y}_t$, p_y represent the corresponding variables in our model. Equation (7.19) represents the assumption that the variable's contribution in the quadratic loss is the same in both models. From (7.19) the weight p_y can be calculated as

$$p_y = \Sigma^n_{t=1} p_{JA,y} (y_{JA,t} - \tilde{y}_{JA,t})^2 / \Sigma^n_{t=1} (y_t - \tilde{y}_t)^2 \tag{7.20}$$

The weights obtained by this procedure are presented in Table 7.2. The table also contains the corresponding weights used in the studies by Jager and Amman. The differences between the two sets of weights can be ascribed to the different dimensions of the variables concerned.

7.5 Optimal economic policy under various exchange rate regimes

7.5.1 *The various exchange rate regimes*

As was mentioned in the introduction to this chapter, the aim of the analysis is to study the robustness of the results obtained in Jager (1985) and in Jager and Amman (1986). The first regime to be considered is a floating rate regime. This is followed by five other systems, namely the arrangement that actually existed for the Dutch guilder, a system of fixed exchange rates, and three crawling peg rules.

There are no peg rates under a system of *freely floating exchange rates*. We therefore decided to replace the peg rates of the French franc and the Deutsche mark in the formulas of the exchange rate expectations by the actual rate lagged one period. Another characteristic of this regime is that the monetary authorities do not intervene in the foreign exchange market. This is implemented in the optimal control experiments by transferring the level and change in international monetary reserves to the vector of exogenous variables. The change of these reserves is set equal to zero and its level is made constant during the entire period.

The Dutch guilder/French franc rate also floats in the five other systems to be studied, which differ with regard to the exchange rate regime of the Dutch guilder against the Deutsche mark. These arrangements have in common that the authorities use the instruments of economic policy in order to keep the market rate within a range around a parity rate. The maximum deviation of the market rate from the peg is chosen to be 2.5 per cent, which implies a band width of 5 per cent. The fluctuation margin is more or less the same as the one used in the various exchange rate arrangements which were in force during the post-World War II period.

The first of these systems to be considered is the one that was actually in operation during the period considered. During this period the Dutch authorities strived to peg the guilder to a strong currency, *viz*. the Deutsche mark. As in Jager (1985), we, therefore, call this the *strong currency option*. The aim of this policy is to reduce domestic inflation. In the optimal control experiments the desired time path of the parity rate is assumed to be exogenous and is set equal to the actual parity of the Dutch guilder against the Deutsche mark in the period concerned. Note that since the present model contains the nominal Dutch guilder/Deutsche mark rate, it gives a better representation of this regime than Jager's model could, because that model only contains the guilder's effective exchange rate.

The third arrangement to be considered is the system of a *fixed* Dutch guilder/Deutsche mark rate. The value of the parity is set equal to the parity rate in 1970:I. Since, during the 1970s, the Dutch guilder has slightly depreciated against the Deutsche mark, this regime can be considered as the super-strong currency option. By comparing the model's behaviour under the fixed regime with that under the strong currency option, we are able to investigate whether the Dutch authorities would have done a better job if they had fixed the guilder against the Deutsche mark from the beginning of the 1970s.

Crawling peg rules can be divided into two groups, namely systems that allow for discretionary peg adjustments and systems where the peg adjusts according to a formula[8]. The *restricted peg* is included as a representative of the discretionary peg systems. Under this system the maximum change of the peg equals the percentage that the upper and lower intervention points differ from the peg. As has been mentioned above, this percentage is 2.5.

We study two alternatives of a crawling peg system characterized by a peg that adjusts according to a formula. In the first arrangement the parity change is determined by recent changes in the actual exchange rate. The reasoning underlying this rule is that the central banks cannot resist prolonged market forces. The particular formula is

$$\tilde{e}_{t,WG} = \tilde{e}_{t-1,WG} + \alpha\,(e_{t-1,WG} - e_{t-2,WG}) \tag{7.21}$$

where e_{WG} and $\tilde{e}_{WG}$ represent the market rate and the parity rate of the guilder against the Deutsche mark, respectively. In Jager and Amman (1986) and Amman and Jager (1988) an iterative procedure is used for determining the optimal value of the adjustment coefficient α. The optimal value appeared to be 1.06. This value has been used in the guidelines studied in this chapter.

The second rule is the well-known and frequently studied guideline according to which regular changes of the parity rate reduce the gap between the current rate and the rate that corresponds with purchasing power parity. In applying this rule, the choice of the appropriate price index is ambiguous. The adjustment of the balance of trade involves both the ratio of domestic to foreign prices of traded goods and the ratio of the domestic price of non-traded to that

---

[8] A description of the pros and cons of the various arrangements can be found in Jager and Amman (1986), pp. 14-18.

of traded goods. Jager and Amman attempt to approximate these two relative prices by introducing two parity rules: one determined by the terms of trade on the export side and the other by the terms of trade on the import side. A disadvantage of these two price indices is that both refer to traded goods only, whereas the prices of both traded and non-traded goods are involved in the adjustment process. Moreover, as has been mentioned in Section 2.6.4, the purchasing power parity refers to aggregate price indices containing both traded and non-traded goods. We, therefore, do not use these two price indices, but base the purchasing power parity rule on the consumer price indices. These indices contain both tradeable and non-tradeable goods. The resulting parity rule is

$$\tilde{e}_{t,WG} = \tilde{e}_{t-1,WG} + \beta\,(\overset{\circ}{p}_{c,t-1} - \overset{\circ}{p}_{WG,t-1}) \tag{7.22}$$

The optimal values of the adjustment parameters in the two purchasing power parity rules used in Jager and Amman (1986) are 1.18 and 0.04, and thus differ substantially from each other. Because of this great difference we do not use these values but select the value that reflects the assumption that on average the percentage change in the parity rate equals the percentage change in relative prices. The corresponding value of β is 1.0229. This variant is chosen in order to highlight the consequences of adhering to a purchasing power parity rule.

7.5.2 *The results*

Optimal policies are calculated for the six exchange rate regimes described in the preceding subsection. The main characteristics of the model's behaviour under each of these six regimes are presented in this subsection.

In order to increase the comparability of the model's characteristics under the various exchange rate systems, all optimal control runs have been subjected to the following conditions. Firstly, except for the penalty for the divergence of the market exchange rate from the parity rate and for the change of the parity, the penalties of the instruments and targets of economic policy are the same for all arrangements. If necessary, the penalties for the difference between the target rate and the market rate are changed in order to guarantee that the rate remains within the band. The penalty for the exchange rate parity's change has been used for restricting the change of the parity rate per period. Secondly, the level of the monetary reserves in 1976:IV has been required to be equal to the level at the beginning of the period. In this way, it is impossible that the optimal policy consists of exhausting the stock of monetary reserves. Such a policy would lead to too great a burden for the policies from 1977 onwards, the period after the period investigated. The level at the end of the period is set equal to the level in 1970:I rather than to any other figure, in order to increase the comparability of the results under the floating rate regime with those of the other arrangements.

In Table 7.3 we present each exchange rate arrangement's total costs and the costs of deviating from the desired paths of the various ultimate targets. The discretionary crawling peg appears to be the system with the lowest total costs and thus it can be regarded as the optimal exchange rate arrangement. This finding is in accordance with that in Jager (1985), but contrasts with the results in Amman and Jager (1987) and Jager and Amman (1986). In the last two studies the optimal system appears to be a crawling peg rule based on recent changes in the exchange rate, such as the peg represented by equation (7.21). According to Table 7.3, in our study this system is the second-best exchange rate arrangement. Combining our result with those obtained by Amman and Jager, we conclude that under various circumstances a crawling peg based on recent changes in the exchange rate or a discretionary crawling peg proves to be the optimal or near-optimal exchange rate system.

The costs of the objective variables indicate that except for the costs of the percentage change in real national income, a crawling peg system is the optimal exchange rate arrangement. Apparently, the crawling peg systems represent a good balance between the rigidity of fixed exchange rates and the instability of floating rates. These results affirm our suggestion in the introduction that for an industrialized country variants of a crawling peg system deserve more attention than currently is done in the majority of the literature.

Note that the total costs of the fixed exchange rate system are higher than those of the strong currency option. So, conditional on the preference function used, the Dutch monetary authorities correctly decided not to fix the guilder against the Deutsche mark at the value of the parity rate of 1970. However, as is shown in Figure 7.1.B, the optimal time path of the exchange rate under the discretionary crawling peg, the optimal exchange rate arrangement, suggests that they would have done an even better job if they had appreciated the guilder against the Deutsche mark in 1970, whereafter they should have depreciated it in 1973 and 1974.

Table 7.3 shows that, except for the percentage change of real national income, under the purchasing power parity rule (PPP-rule) the costs of deviations from the desired time path differ greatly from the corresponding costs under the other exchange rate regimes. The total costs, the costs of deviations from the desired path of the current account, and the costs of deviations from the desired inflation target are the highest of all arrangements. The costs are the lowest for deviations from the preferred level of the unemployment rate and deviations from the target of the level of real national income (the latter measured by its uncorrected costs). This suggests an extreme

Table 7.3 Costs of the various systems[a]

Exchange rate system	Total costs[b,c]	Real national income level[b]	Real national income % change	inflation rate	current account	unemployment rate
-floating	1844.45 (1844.46)	3738.11 (13404.77)*	76.86	233.16	165.60	86.40
-strong currency	1782.32 (1782.34)	4147.44 (18839.91)	70.98	259.16	164.38	85.07
-fixed	1846.81 (1846.82)	4707.21 (19278.50)	70.00*	258.90	140.97	88.63
crawling peg variants						
-discretionary	1678.89* (1678.91)*	3982.47 (15994.71)	73.03	213.18*	141.84	91.22
-formula (7.21)	1757.71 (1757.72)	5424.37 (19110.00)	70.23	220.91	109.30*	95.16
-PPP-rule	2465.29 (2465.31)	3426.54* (17847.38)	73.55	301.32	341.31	71.70*

a. An asterisk indicates the best record in the column.
b. As is shown in Figure 7.2.A, during some periods under floating exchange rates the optimal time path of the level of real national income exceeds the time path of the desired values. Since the loss function is quadratic, costs are assigned to the values higher than the desired values. In order to prevent policy makers being penalized for doing better than they first thought possible, we have recalculated the costs by increasing the target values with a constant term. This constant term is equal to the largest difference between the optimal path under floating and the original target values of the level of real income. These costs are the figures between brackets.
c. The actual total costs are the amounts in this column multiplied by 100,000.

Fig 7.1.A The Dutch guilder / Deutsche mark rate under various exchange rate regimes

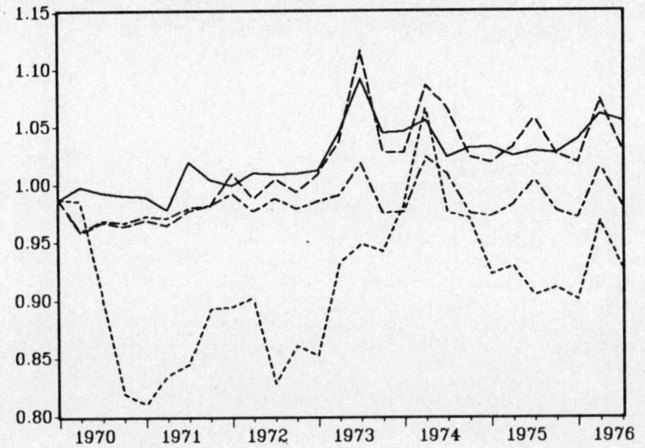

——— historical ------- strong currency
---------- floating -------- fixed

Fig 7.1.B The Dutch guilder / Deutsche mark rate under crawling peg variants

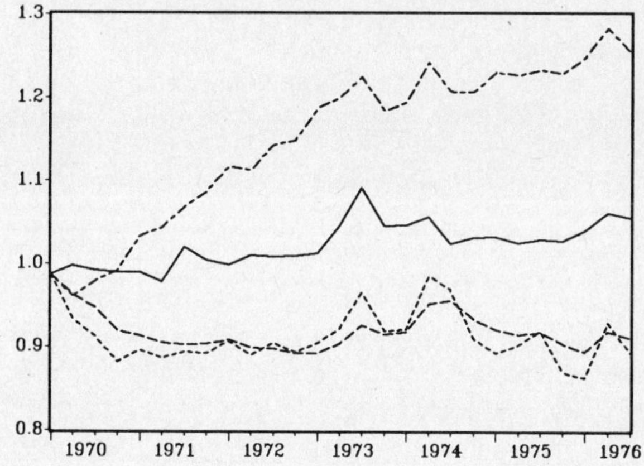

——— historical ------- formula (7.21)
---------- discretionary -------- PPP-rule

Table 7.4 Mean and standard deviation of the optimal paths[a]

Exchange rate system	Real national[b] income mean	st. dev.	Inflation[c] rate mean	st. dev.
-floating	60838.97*	5037.55	1.71	0.44
-strong currency	59341.16	4569.31	1.78	0.45
-fixed	59373.92	4397.89*	1.76	0.48
crawling peg variants				
-discretionary	60139.8	4591.57	1.69*	0.43*
-formula (7.21)	59634.7	4505.46	1.71	0.44
-formula (7.22)	59427.8	5203.18	1.81	0.55

Exchange rate system	current[b] account mean	st. dev.	unemployment[c] rate mean	st. dev.
-floating	1273.16	714.38	2.64	1.20
-strong currency	1310.9	667.05	2.62	1.20
-fixed	1232.2	628.69	2.65	1.25
crawling peg variants				
-discretionary	1214.46	657.12	2.67	1.26
-formula (7.21)	1123.36	562.02*	2.70	1.30
-PPP-rule	1686.12	1003.45	2.52*	1.05

a. All variables are four-period moving averages.
An asterisk indicates the best record.
b. In million of guilders.
c. In percent points.

behaviour of the economy under the purchasing power parity rule. This impression is reaffirmed by the optimal time paths of the exchange rate shown in Figures 7.1.A and 7.1.B. Except for the PPP-formula, the guilder appreciates against the Deutsche mark. The guilder depreciates under the PPP-rule. As expected, the figures in Tables 7.3 and 7.4 indicate that the depreciation generates inflation and that the resulting improvement of competitiveness stimulates economic activity. In Table 7.4 the unemployment rate ranks the lowest and the domestic inflation rate the highest of all alternatives. The high inflation rate is due to the increase of import prices. The low unemployment rate results from the improved competitiveness of the domestically produced Dutch products, which substitutes domestic for foreign production.

Note that for the various exchange rate regimes the levels of real national income differ more from each other than the levels of national product in the studies by Amman and Jager. Although it is difficult to interpret optimal control results, it might be that the greater differences in the present study result from the supply effects. These effects are incorporated in our model but not in the one used by the two authors mentioned above. Another possible cause of the greater dispersion in our results is the possible importance of the difference between these two variables, *viz.* the influence of changes in the terms of trade on real income.

In order to shed light on the possible size of the terms of trade effect, we present in Figure 7.2 the size of the terms of trade effect and the level of both real national income and real national product. The figures of these three variables are drawn for the case of floating exchange rates and for that of the PPP-regime. These two arrangements have been selected because as is shown in Figure 7.1 the exchange rate exhibits the most extreme behaviour under these two regimes. As Figure 7.2 shows, the terms of trade effect is large for the floating rate regime and relatively small under the PPP-rule. The Dutch guilder appreciates under floating rates (see Figure 7.1). This appreciation generates a positive terms of trade effect and worsens the competitiveness of Dutch products. Figure 7.2.B shows that during several years the domestic production is more or less the same as under the PPP-rule. Thus, during these years the worsening in competitiveness is compensated by the positive terms of trade effect. Consequently, real national income is higher than under the PPP-regime (Figure 7.2.A). However, after some time the consequences of the worsening of competitiveness come to the fore in the form of a sudden and large decline in domestic production in 1974. Thereafter real production remains at a level significantly lower than the corresponding level under the PPP-regime. The time patterns in Figure 7.2 illustrate that the terms of trade effect occurs almost immediately after a change in the exchange rate, whereas changes in relative rices influence the real side of the economy with lags of many periods. The fact

Fig 7.2.A The optimal time path of real income[a,b]

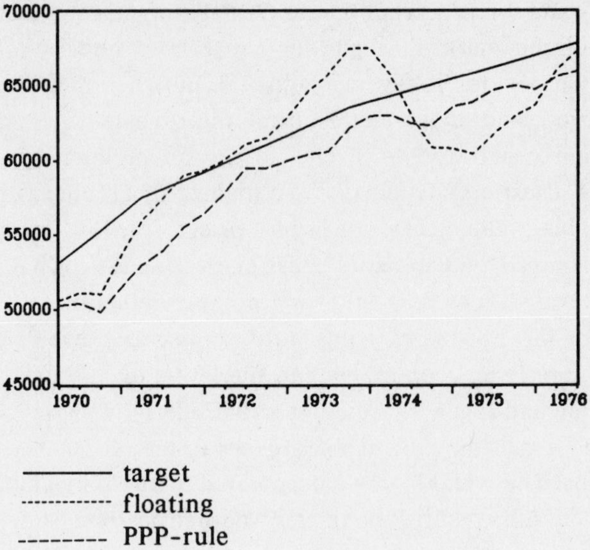

Fig 7.2.B The optimal time path of real product[a,b]

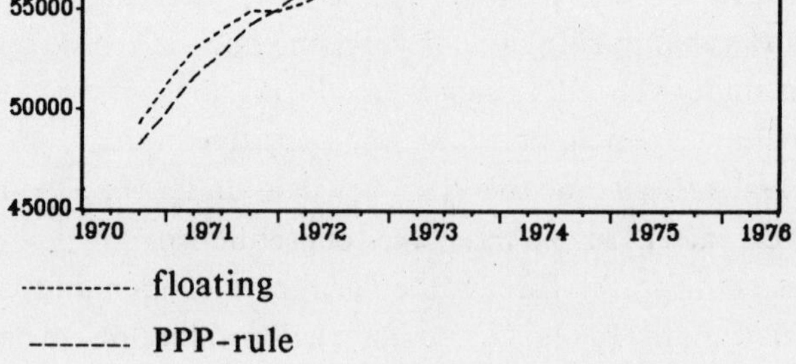

Fig 7.2.C The optimal time path of the terms of trade effect[a]

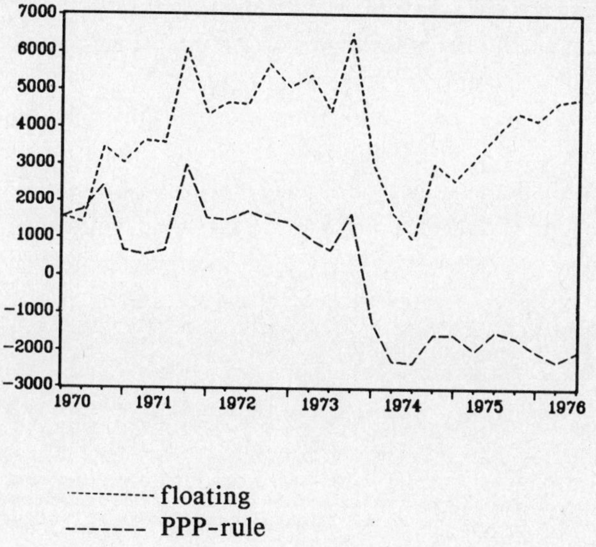

Fig 7.3 The optimal and historical time paths of the current account[a,b]

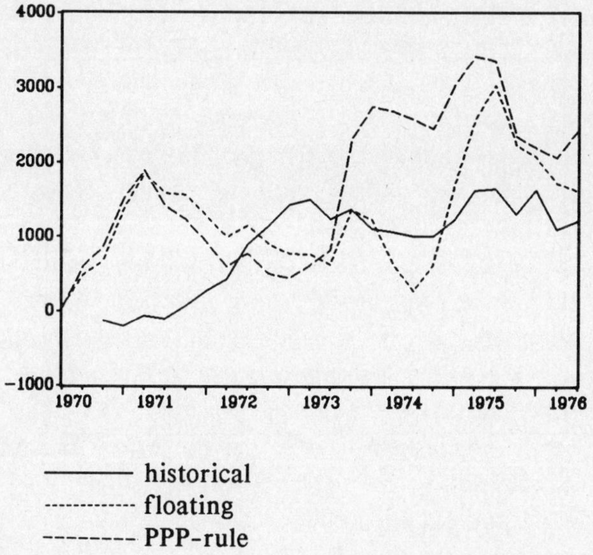

a. In million of guilders.
b. Four-period moving average.

that the terms of trade effect is felt immediately, might be the reason why in Figures 7.1.A and 7.1.B all optimal time paths show an appreciation of the exchange rate in the first period(s); this advantage is easily obtained.

The time patterns of the variables under a system of floating and under the PPP-rule in Figures 7.1.A and 7.1.B and in Figures 7.2.A - 7.2.C offer an opportunity for presenting some interesting conclusions on the potential effectiveness of a devaluation of the guilder. As is well-known, according to the opinion of the Dutch monetary authorities a devaluation is useless. The wages will increase as a result of indexation for price rises and will soon nullify the initial improvement in competitiveness. The present model incorporates this feature of full price indexation in the wage equation (see Section 5.4.2). In Figure 7.2.B its supposed effect seems to be displayed by the fact that from 1970 to 1974 the level of real production is almost the same for both exchange rate regimes. Most likely, the reason is that under floating rates, relative to the PPP variant, the positive terms of trade effect on production, which runs via national income, and the resulting higher domestic demand compensates the worsening of competitiveness. Under the PPP-rule it is just the other way round: the positive effect of increased competitiveness is reduced by means of the negative terms of trade effect on income and thus on production. However, the decline in production under floating exchange rates in mid-1974 suggests that after a lag of about three years the negative effects of a worsening of competitiveness dominate. This happens even though compared with the level at the end of 1970, in the meantime the exchange rate has depreciated. The continuing increase of production under the PPP-rule seems to reaffirm the long-lasting influence of changes in competitiveness. From these results we conclude that in the short run a depreciation and an appreciation of the currency exhibit a similar effect on domestic production; the terms of trade effect and the change in competitiveness compensate each other. However in the medium term (about three to four years) the change in competitiveness seems to dominate so that a depreciation has a stimulating effect and an appreciation leads to a reduction in production. In an optimal control run the instruments change along with the endogenous variables so that an explanation of the results is difficult. It should, therefore, be mentioned that this is a possible interpretation of the results of the optimal control runs.

Figure 7.3 illustrates the consequences of the worsening in competitiveness resulting from the exchange rate appreciation on the current account. From mid-1973 until 1975, under the floating rate regime the balance on the current account is much lower than under the PPP-rule.

Finally, we want to draw attention to the consequence of including the level of the real national income rather than that of the real national product in the objective function for the optimal use of international reserves under the various exchange rate regimes. As has been mentioned in footnote 2 of Section 7.4.1 Jager and Amman assume that the economic growth target can be represented by the level of real national product. In the studies by Jager and Amman, optimal policies tended to exhaust the reserves during the first quarters of the period. Consequently, they had to assign a rather high penalty to the use of international monetary reserves in order to prevent the stock becoming negative. In the experiments presented in the present study we were not forced to increase the penalty for using these reserves drastically. The reason is obvious. In our model the appreciation resulting from the decline of reserves has two opposite effects. It reduces real income and real production by means of a worsening of competitiveness but it increases these variables via the beneficial effect on the terms of trade. These two opposite effects prevent extreme behaviour, such as a sale of the total stock of international monetary reserves.

7.6 Concluding remarks

In the present chapter we have used the optimal control technique in order to study the characteristics of a small industrialized economy under different exchange rate regimes. The optimal control technique has been applied in order to take account of the fact that the authorities can and, in general, will behave differently under the various exchange rate systems.

From the optimal control experiments presented in the preceding section we conclude that the total costs of the objective function are lowest for the discretionary crawling peg, which consequently is regarded as the optimal exchange rate arrangement. Except for the stability of real national income, the costs of each individual objective variable is minimal for one of the crawling peg variants. These favourable outcomes for the crawling peg variants correspond with the results obtained by Jager and Amman, who use a model that differs in many respects from ours. Consequently, this result is rather robust. From this we conclude that for a small industrialized country a crawling peg system could be a good alternative to a system of floating or fixed exchange rates. In the introduction of this chapter we considered various possible problems associated with the implementation of a system of fixed exchange rates in Europe. On the basis of the present analysis we recommend the following solution to these problems: a variant of the crawling peg as the exchange rate regime for the members of the European Monetary System.

Some other interesting conclusions can be drawn from the results of the optimal control experiments. Firstly, it appears that except for the PPP-rule, the optimal exchange rate appreciates relative to its historical value. Secondly, the results illustrate the opposite influences of an exchange rate change on the terms of trade and on the competitiveness. These influences are, moreover, of such a size that in the next three to four years national production is not affected. However, after this period a depreciation does turn out to be effective after all, and stimulates production. Finally, the inclusion of the level of real income instead of the level of real production in the loss function prevents the optimal policy being that the monetary authorities should sell the total stock of international monetary reserves.

8 SUMMARY AND CONCLUDING REMARKS

8.1 Introduction

As was mentioned in Chapter 1, this study had two main objectives. The first was to investigate the sources of the various models' bad performance in explaining the exchange rate and if possible to improve these methods. The second aim was to analyse alternative exchange rate systems, in particular different specifications of the crawling peg. In this chapter we summarize our findings and indicate possible areas for future research.

The sections of this chapter correspond with the objectives of the book. In Section 8.2 aspects of modelling and estimating models of exchange rate determination are discussed. Given the prominent role of expectations formation for exchange rate determination, a separate chapter, Chapter 3, was devoted to it. The conclusions of that chapter are presented in Section 8.3. In Section 8.4 the results with regard to the different exchange rate regimes and the pros and cons of the optimal control technique for studying economic problems are discussed. Finally in Section 8.5, we map out lines for future research.

8.2 Exchange rate determination

8.2.1 *Theory*

The general framework of the asset market approach to exchange rate determination has been sketched in Chapter 2. In accordance with the dominant role of financial flows on the foreign exchange markets, this theory assumes that in the short run the exchange rate is determined by financial market conditions. Along with the interest rates and the expected exchange rate, the exchange rate fluctuates in order to equilibrate the desired and actual stocks of financial assets. The dynamics towards the long-run equilibrium are determined by the financing of the deficit on the government's budget, disequilibria on the goods market, and the balance on the current account. The current account influences the accumulation of financial stocks and may also affect the expectations of exchange rates and interest rates.

In our view, in principle this structure of the asset market approach to exchange rate determination can be regarded as a good reflection of the actual behaviour of foreign exchange markets. Hence, our criticism of the theoretical model is directed to the way this framework has been given concrete form in the majority of studies on exchange rate determination. A shortcoming of nearly all theoretical models is that the set of assets is assumed to be restricted to non-interest-bearing money and bonds.

8.2.2 *Quasi-reduced form versus structural form*

Our main criticism with regard to the studies on exchange rate determination concerns the empirical tests of the models (see Section 2.5.2). In nearly all studies the theoretical model is tested by means of a quasi- or semi-reduced form equation of the model. These relations can be regarded as a mixture of the structural form and reduced form relations. Whereas reduced form equations are obtained by fully solving the model for the endogenous variables, the quasi-reduced form relations can be obtained by partly solving the underlying model for the endogenous variables. Quasi-reduced form equations share with the structural form relations the property that endogenous variables are included in the set of explanatory variables. Consequently, unbiased estimation of the parameters requires a simultaneous estimation technique.

Two important shortcomings of the quasi-reduced form relations should be mentioned. The first drawback also holds for reduced form relations. It is that since the coefficients are obtained by partly solving the model, they are combinations of the parameters of the original structural model. In many cases the estimated values of the semi-reduced form parameters do not provide enough information for deriving the structural form coefficients, so that it is hard or impossible to judge whether the estimated equation validates the particular exchange rate model. Secondly, the chances are that the use of the semi-reduced form equations introduces multicollinearity and sign reversals (see Section 2.5.4). These problems arise because the quasi-reduced form relation is obtained by substituting several structural form equations into each other. If a structural form equation contains a variable that is highly correlated with an explanatory variable in another structural form relation, then both explanatory variables will appear as explanatory variables in the quasi-reduced form equation. Thus the latter contains multicollinearity, whereas this was not the case with the structural form relations. Assigning a priori values to certain variables does not solve the multicollinearity problem; sign reversals may still be present. From these problems associated with the use of semi-reduced form relations, we conclude that it is preferable to test exchange rate models by means of estimating the structural form of the model. This is done in Chapters 4 to 6.

In accordance with our criticism concerning the use of semi-reduced form relations, in the present study a structural form approach is applied; as a result the exchange rate and the short-term and long-term interest rates have been derived from the equilibrium conditions of the relevant markets. It appears that the resulting exchange rates and the short-term interest rate on domestic assets closely resemble their historical rates. However, the thus obtained time series of the interest rate on long-term domestic assets did not track the historical rate in a satisfactory way.

8.2.3 *Specification and estimation of asset demand functions*

When estimating and specifying the model we have also paid attention to some other weaknesses of tests on exchange rate determination. Firstly, in many studies it is assumed that desired stocks are always equal to actual stocks. As mentioned in Section 2.6.1, we questioned the reality of this assumption. Hence, the asset demand functions used in our model allow for a gradual adjustment of desired stocks to actual stocks. We have used the multi-asset partial adjustment model in order to give concrete form to the non-instantaneous adjustment of desired to actual stocks. As has been correctly argued in Smith (1975), many specifications of this model overdescribe the portfolio disequilibria. In these wrong specifications the accumulation of financial wealth is contained twice in the relation. Smith, therefore, suggests two reformulations of these incorrect specifications. In Appendix A to Chapter 4 we prove by means of a simple example, that one of these reformulations, the one used in for instance Van Loo (1983), does not solve the relevant problem. The reason is that the model does not make explicit whether the reinvestment of available assets and the investment of newly acquired financial wealth are treated equally or that these two types of investments are assumed to be influenced by different motives. If the latter assumption holds, then the identification of the parameters requires that it be clear which part of the relation stands for the reinvestment of existing wealth and which part reflects the investment of new wealth. When specifying the asset demand functions, we have used the other respecification of the two suggested by Smith. Underlying this specification is the assumption that the two types of investments can be regarded as one item. Motives for this assumption are: available data on the changes in assets do not enable us to distinguish between the two types of investments, and a reasonable specification which distinguishes between the new investments and the reinvestments becomes too complicated to be used for estimating all assets of a portfolio.

When estimating the multi-asset partial adjustment model for the assets of a particular sector's balance sheet, account has to be taken of various cross-equation restrictions. In addition the model is nonlinear in its parameters; many estimated parameters are the sum of products of adjustment coefficients and other parameters. Thus it is difficult to estimate each coefficient of the structural form and simultaneously consider the relevant cross-equation restrictions. This problem has been solved by applying an amended version of the two-stage procedure used in De Nederlandsche Bank (1984). This method is described in Section 4.3.2. During the first stage of this method, the adjustment parameters are estimated. Conditional on these estimated values of the adjustment coefficients, estimates of the other parameters in the product terms mentioned above are derived in the second stage. A disadvantage of this procedure is that, in all likelihood, the estimated values of the adjustment parameters differ from those which would have been obtained if these coefficients were re-estimated conditional on the estimated values of the other parameters obtained at the end of the second stage. In order to reduce this difference, the first stage of our procedure differs from that of the method applied in De Nederlandsche Bank (1984). During the first stage of the latter method except for the adjustment parameters, no insignificant coefficients are set equal to zero. During this stage of our procedure we delete those highly insignificant and wrongly signed coefficients that are not (the sum of) a product of an adjustment parameter and another coefficient. When estimating the relations of the banking sector by means of this amended procedure, it appeared that the estimated values of the first estimation of the second stage were at once satisfactory.

Another problem concerning the estimation of exchange rate models is that the estimation by means of OLS would yield inconsistent estimates. There are two reasons for this. Firstly, many of the explanatory variables and the independent variable - the flows of funds in our model and the exchange rate in the quasi-reduced form equations - are simultaneously determined. Secondly, the expected (change of the) exchange rate is one of the independent variables. Since expectations cannot be observed, they have to be approximated. The differences between the proxy and the true expectations are incorporated in the disturbance term and so the expectations proxy and the disturbance term are correlated and the resulting estimates are inconsistent.

An instrumental variables technique can be used for solving this inconsistency problem. An essential but often neglected aspect of this method is the proper selection of instrumental variables. These variables should be highly correlated with the variable they replace and uncorrelated with the disturbance term of the equation concerned. Small-sample theory indicates that the estimates are biased if use is made of the two-stage least squares procedure, which assumes that the set of instrumental variables consists of the entire set of predetermined variables. In order to prevent this bias, the set of instrumental variables should be reduced. We have selected from the set of preliminary variables of the financial part of the model, those variables for which the correlation coefficient with the interest rates and (expected) exchange rate changes is greater than 0.5. This selection procedure can be considered as a workable mixture of the causal ordering procedure suggested by Fisher (1965) and the use of canonical regressions proposed by Bowden and Turkington (1984).

8.2.4 *Stability of relations and time series*

In order to avoid problems associated with the instability of time series, nearly all equations are estimated for first differences or percentage changes of the endogenous variable. As is well-known, the time series of these forms are more stable than those of the corresponding level. The Dickey-Fuller test has been used for investigating stationarity of the level and relative first difference of the time-series of exchange rates. In accordance with findings in other studies, the time series of the levels appeared to be non-stationary and those of the relative first differences appeared to be stationary. We therefore decided to calculate a proxy of the expected percentage change instead of the level of the exchange rates.

The relevance of considering the possible instability of time series also came to the fore with respect to foreigners' investments in long-term domestic assets. This time series shows a structural shift at the end of 1976. These investments are comprised of investments in bonds and in shares. The estimated equations reveal that from 1970:I to 1976:IV this capital inflow is caused by the yield on domestic shares, whereas during the years 1977 to 1980 the interest rate on domestic bonds appeared to be the relevant domestic return variable. In addition some experiments with alternative specifications indicate the importance of considering the possibility of structural shifts for the significance of coefficients and in particular for the influence of the closed bond circuit, which was in operation from September 1971 until February 1974. As in Van Loo (1983) this restriction is represented by the premium on guilders available for non-residents from selling bonds to residents as a percentage of the free market exchange rate. Contrary to our a priori expectation, the coefficient of this variable appeared to be statistically insignificant when the relation was estimated for the subperiod 1970:I-1976:IV, but it was significant when the equation was estimated for the entire period. This result highlights the importance of tests on structural changes of the time series of endogenous variables.

8.2.5 *The goods market*

In many studies of exchange rate behaviour, the goods market is not considered, or is treated in a very rudimentary way. Our model contains a goods market and as a result allows for the interaction between exchange rates and real phenomena such as investment by firms and its effect on capacity output. Since our main concern is with the financial sectors, the real side of the model is kept as simple as possible. To some extent this part of the model shows much similarity with the real part of MORKMON, the model used by the Dutch central bank.

Notable distinctions between the non-financial sectors in our model and those of other models of the Dutch economy (including MORKMON) are the specification of the consumption function and the approximation of firms' profits. Private consumption shows a strong seasonal pattern which in all likelihood reflects the fact that different commodities are being purchased in different seasons. In other models this seasonal influence is captured by seasonal dummies. However, since it is likely that this seasonal pattern is caused by quarterly differences in the consumption pattern, it is preferable to capture this in a more systematic way. We decided to use the specification presented in Davidson *et al.* (1978), which relates the consumption in a particular quarter to the consumption in the same quarter of the year before. Consequently, the dependent variable is the four-quarter difference of the consumption. The estimated relation appeared to explain the movements in the historical data reasonably well.

Another distinction has to do with the fact that in other models of the Dutch economy the firms' profits are represented by disposable non-wage income. As argued in Keus (1980), an important disadvantage of this proxy is that it includes interest payment by firms, so that the increase of these payments during the 1970s, which reduces the actual profits, is measured as an increase in profits. Based on the assumptions made in Keus (1980), we have constructed a proxy of firms' profits by subtracting from non-wage income those items that refer to the firms' payments of interest. The resulting variable appeared to be highly significant in the investment function.

8.2.6 *Other aspects of exchange rate determination*

Some aspects of exchange rate models, which are mentioned in Chapter 2 as items that are capable of improvement, are not discussed in this book and are therefore left as subjects for future research. These items are: the treatment of capital gains/losses and the effects of extending the portfolio to include gold and shares.

Since exchange rates show large fluctuations, the effect of the resulting capital gains is likely to be reasonably large. The potential importance of capital gains and losses is reinforced by the fact that in several countries, including the Netherlands and Japan, the income from capital gains is not taxed, whereas the receipts of dividend and interest are. This gives the portfolioholders an incentive to invest in assets with a high capital gain and a low dividend. Most likely this tax-system gives rise to higher fluctuations in exchange rates than would be the case if the tax on income from capital gains/losses were the same as that on income from dividend and interest receipts.[1]

We did not consider the effects of capital gains/losses because of the lack of data on the currency denomination of the inhabitants' stocks of foreign assets. Hence, any result in this respect would be rather artificial, because it fully depends upon the assumptions made with regard to the currency of denomination of the foreign assets.

8.3 Expectations formation

Expectations, and especially exchange rate expectations, form an important aspect of both theoretical and empirical studies of exchange rate behaviour. Although many expectations hypotheses have been proposed in the literature, not a single hypothesis has been generally accepted. This gives us a reason to investigate the essential elements of expectations formation in Chapter 3. In our opinion three features are relevant. First, by their very nature expectations can be based only on available data and thus the same should hold for their proxy. Secondly, expectations formation means acquiring knowledge about the future so the model should incorporate a learning process. Thirdly, the analysis of the results of a particular model or test are highly facilitated if the influence of the expectations can be separated from the effect a particular variable has on the expectations proxy itself.

These three criteria concerning expectations formation are not of equal importance and one or two of them need not apply. It is self-evident that expectations can be derived only from available data, and thus that the data-availability condition should always be imposed. In some studies it suffices to require that the expectations proxy meets this criterion only. If, for example, we are only interested in estimating the influence of expectations, then it suffices to impose the data-availability criterion upon the proxy. In addition, the identification criterion might then be useful too. A correct evaluation of different policy rules, however, requires that the identification criterion is met and that a learning process is included in the model. The reason is that the results of such an analysis very much depend on the way economic agents revise their

---

[1] Note the similarity with the stock exchange. According to Viner the fact that in Japan income from capital gains is not taxable, causes a greater volatility on the Tokyo Stock Exchange than is usual for the New York Stock Exchange. See Viner (1987), p. 85.

expectations.

The three criteria were used for assessing the various expectations hypotheses and methods for estimating models with expectations. This assessment revealed that of the hypotheses considered, the weak forms of the rational expectations hypothesis meet the three criteria best. Our final judgement of these hypotheses depends on the particular method used for approximating the expectations. From the assessment of the various estimation methods we concluded that, provided the prior values are appropriately chosen, both the multi-state Kalman filter and the "rolling regressions" approach meet all three criteria. As a result, one of these two methods should be used for approximating weak forms of the rational expectations hypothesis. The exact form of the expectations generating function and the variables to be included in the information set depend on the particular problem at hand. In our model we used the "rolling regressions" procedure for deriving expectations of the relative change of exchange rates.

8.4 Exchange rate regimes and optimal control experiments

8.4.1 *Alternative exchange rate regimes*

The second theme of the present study was the determination of the characteristics of a small industrialized economy under different exchange rate regimes. As was mentioned in Chapter 1, we were particularly interested in comparing the performance of the economy under crawling peg rules with its performance under alternative exchange rate regimes. The optimal control technique has been applied in order to take account of the fact that in all likelihood the authorities will behave differently under the various exchange rate systems.

The total welfare costs appeared to be lowest for the discretionary crawling peg, which consequently was the optimal exchange rate arrangement. Except for the percentage change in real national income, the welfare costs of pursuing the ideal time path for each individual objective variable is minimal when one of the crawling peg variants is used. These favourable outcomes for the crawling peg variants correspond with the results obtained by Jager and Amman. Consequently, the results are rather robust. From this we conclude that for a small industrialized country a crawling peg system could be an attractive alternative to a system of floating or fixed exchange rates. In particular, a variant of the crawling peg could be a solution for the potential problems associated with implementing the Delors commission's proposal for introducing fixed exchange rates in the European Monetary System. These problems attach to striving simultaneously for complete capital liberalisation and completely fixed exchange rates.

Some other interesting conclusions can be drawn from the results of the optimal control experiments. The results illustrate the opposite influences of an exchange rate change on the terms of trade and on the competitiveness. These influences are, moreover, of such a size that in the next period of three to four years national production is not affected. After three to four years a depreciation does turn out to be effective after all, and stimulates production. Furthermore, the inclusion of the level of real income instead of the level of real production in the loss function prevents the optimal policy being that the monetary authorities should sell the total stock of international monetary reserves.

8.4.2 *Possible applications of optimal control experiments in economics*

At first sight optimal control experiments might be useful in the following three areas of economic research: the determination of optimal economic policies, the investigation of the characteristics of econometric models, and the evaluation of alternative proposals. In order to evaluate the pros and cons of using this technique for problems, we first discuss problems we have met when using this method.

Compared with a simulation study, the computation of optimal control experiments requires more data: the desired time paths of targets and instruments and the weights (penalties) in the loss function. As was pointed out in Section 7.4, in general no exact figures of these variables and parameters are available. As a result, the researcher is forced to make estimations and approximations.

Another problem concerns the elimination of unrealistic solutions. As was mentioned in Section 7.4, optimal control solutions exhibit irregular and unrealistic behaviour at the end and at the beginning of the period concerned. In addition, in many instances the method will give rise to economically unrealistic solutions. For example, given the first estimates of the penalties in the loss function, the optimal time paths of the discount rate and consequently of other interest rates became zero. The reason is simply that in this way economic activity was stimulated. Large fluctuations in public expenditures form another example of unrealistic or unacceptable solutions. By means of increasing the penalties of instruments in the loss function, these unrealistic results can be eliminated. However, this once again introduces a subjective element into the analysis; what is considered to be economically or politically unacceptable?

These two types of problems are typical for optimal control experiments and necessitate the researcher having to make some more or less subjective decisions.

Hence, the value of the results of optimal control experiments will increase when the importance of these subjective choices can be reduced or eliminated.

This brings us to the fields in which the application of optimal control techniques can deliver potentially fruitful results. Given the prominent place in the optimal control method of targets, instruments, and the trade-off between the various objectives, it seems to be the ideal method for selecting the best economic policies. However, the subjective decisions mentioned above preclude a straightforward application of the method for these types of problems. When possible, these choices should be taken by the decision-makers themselves. This suggests that optimal control experiments are particularly useful for small problems with a limited number of decision-makers, so that the objective represents the preferences of just a limited number of people. Then the penalties of deviations from the desired paths of targets and instruments can be determined by means of an iterative procedure between the researcher and the decision-makers. In such a procedure the researcher presents the optimal control solutions and the decision-makers use these solutions for indicating the value of the parameters in the loss function. Consequently, optimal control is less appropriate for determining the optimal macro-economic policy. However, this does not imply that optimal control is totally useless for deriving the most favourable (optimal) macro-economic policy. The technique can be fruitfully used to improve existing scenarios. For example, suppose that the government wants to reduce the level of unemployment and that the central planning bureau has presented a list of measures to be taken in order to reduce unemployment. Then an optimal control run in which a high penalty is assigned to deviations from the desired level of unemployment will deliver a set of optimal time paths of instruments which is most effective in reducing unemployment. In addition optimal control experiments can be used in order to obtain a first idea of the appropriate form of contingent rules.

Essentially, the same procedure can be used for investigating the characteristics of macro-economic models, especially of large models. Often in these models the number of interactions between the variables is high, so that it is difficult to judge whether the feed back mechanisms between the various blocks are plausible. Although, simulation studies can shed light on the characteristics of the model, these studies are limited to studying the effects of an exogenous shock on the endogenous variables. In simulation studies the endogenous variables are the result and not the original cause of changes. The optimal control technique can deliver additional information because it emphasises the influence of endogenous variables (objectives) on the instruments, which are exogenous in simulation runs. In this type of applications, the coefficients in the loss function do not represent the preferences of a particular group of economic agents, but the researcher's interest in knowing the dynamics of a particular part of the model, or the optimal time paths of instruments resulting from emphasizing a certain objective. The only limitation might be the size of the central memory of the computer used and the efforts needed for linearizing a nonlinear model.

When comparing different economic situations (environments), such as alternative exchange rate systems, the subjective decisions are also made by the researcher. However, in contrast to analysing the dynamics of the model, the objective function does not reflect the researcher's preferences. The fact that he takes the decisions need not be a disadvantage. The aim of the analysis is not to determine the best policy, but to compare the evolution of variables under different circumstances. As long as the ranking of the alternatives is unaffected by the subjective decisions, the analysis is fruitful. In Chapter 7, therefore, we used the same set of parameters in the objective function for studying the alternative exchange rate regimes. This was done except, of course, for the decisions that shape the specific features of the exchange rate arrangements: the penalties of the difference between the peg rate and the actual rate and of changes of the peg rate. The optimal control experiments indicate whether, assuming that the authorities behave optimally, the alternative regimes will give rise to a very different or an almost similar performance of the economy. Since the technique explicitly considers the fact that the policy makers' reactions are affected by a change in the regime, optimal control experiments have to be preferred to simulation studies. As was argued in Section 7.3, this is the reason why we used optimal control for studying different exchange rate regimes.

In the preceding paragraphs we stressed the subjectivity involved in applying optimal control. The reader might have received the impression that the results of this method are more sensitive to subjective decisions made when carrying out the analysis, than are alternative methods. We are of the opinion that this technique forces the researcher to state explicitly the assumptions which are implicitly made when other methods are used. For instance, when determining the effect of a change in an exogenous variable on the economy by means of a simulation run, one implicitly assumes that the authorities do not react at all. When applying optimal control the decision-makers are allowed to react, and the researcher has to assign costs to the use of particular instruments.

8.5 Suggestions for future research

8.5.1 *Extensions and modifications of the model*

As was mentioned in Section 4.7 the possibility of investments in shares is only considered when estimating the foreign investments in long-term domestic assets.

The model lacks a full description of the market for shares. A possible route for future research is to extend the model with the market for shares in order to investigate the effect on the results obtained.

In this study we did not extend the investment opportunities to include gold because in our opinion gold is not relevant for explaining the movements of the exchange rate of a small country. However, in periods of turbulence the price of gold could be an important determining factor of fluctuations in the exchange rate between two important currencies, such as the Japanese yen, the Deutsche mark and the US dollar. Future research of the bilateral exchange rate between two of these countries should therefore allow for the possibility of investing in gold.

We did not consider the influence of capital gains/losses arising from exchange rate changes on the portfolio selection because of the lack of data on the currency denomination of inhabitants' stock of foreign assets. Maybe for other countries corresponding data are more readily available so that a model including the influences of capital gains/losses could be estimated for these countries. If no data on the currency denomination of inhabitant's holdings of foreign assets become available in future research one could try to derive a proxy of these stocks. In this respect a detailed study of the investment policy of a number of large Dutch funds, pension funds and mutual funds with respect to the currency of denomination of their foreign investments could be fruitful. Note that in such a study attention should also be paid to the hedging policy of these funds. Provided that the amount of the investments considered are large enough, the results obtained might be assumed to be representative of the currency of denomination of all inhabitants' foreign assets, so that a financial model with capital gains/losses on foreign assets can be estimated for the entire economy.

As was mentioned in Section 4.2, the partial adjustment model is a one-period horizon model, whereas it is reasonable that a multi-period model more adequately reflects the long-term character of investments in bonds and shares. As a result, it would be worthwhile for future research to develop and estimate a multi-period model for investments in long-term assets.

In Section 6.2 the exchange rate relation derived from the implicit method appeared to fit the historical data well. So within the sample used for estimating the relation, this method appeares to be quite successful. It would be interesting to study in future research the out-of-sample (forecasting) quality of this relation.

A related interesting area for future research is the investigation of the sensitivity of time series of capital flows for structural changes. In particular it would be worthwhile to study the capital inflows for the Netherlands and West-Germany. Such a study would enable us to determine whether structural shifts in the time series of foreigners' investments in the Netherlands are caused by factors that are typical for the Dutch economy or whether they can be explained by more general phenomena. In addition such a study could elucidate phenomena, such as the effects of the German announcement of the introduction of a withholding tax and the possible change of the substitutability between the Dutch and German assets as a consequence of the introduction of the European Monetary System.

8.5.2 *Econometric issues*

When estimating the parameters of the financial model, account had to be taken of various cross-equation restrictions. As was described in Section 4.3.2, we have applied an amended version of the two-stage procedure used by De Nederlandsche Bank in order to include these restrictions in the estimation procedure. Future research might be dedicated to the robustness of this technique and to the development of other methods for estimating this type of models.

In Section 4.3.3 we presented a new method for selecting instrumental variables. This method can be regarded as a practical mixture of the causal ordering procedure suggested by Fisher (1965) and the use of canonical correlations proposed by Bowden and Turkington (1984). It might be worthwhile for future research to study the effects of different selection procedures of instrumental variables. These methods should also pay attention to the correlation of the instrumental variables with the relevant disturbance term. When selecting the instrumental variables, we did not consider this correlation because we estimated all relations of a particular sector's demand system simultaneously. Consequently, it is very likely that a particular instrumental variable is correlated with the disturbance term of one relation but uncorrelated with that of another. We, therefore, recommend research to start on the most appropriate method for selecting the instrumental variables for different single equation models. The results thus obtained might throw some light on the procedures to be used for selecting the instrumental variables when estimating a whole system of equations simultaneously.

8.5.3 *Expectations formation*

As was argued in Section 3.2, the way economic agents form expectations is important for evaluating different policy regimes. Currently, however, data on the expectations formation are not available. Future research, should, therefore be directed towards obtaining information on the explanatory variables of expectations. This could be done by means of periodic interviews. These interviews should not be restricted to asking the persons' expectations but should, in particular, be directed towards detecting the persons' motives for forming this particular expectation.

It would be interesting for future research to study the effects on the estimated parameters of assuming different expectations schemes. Of course, it is recommended that these expectations hypotheses meet the three criteria developed in Section 3.2. In addition, research could be directed towards studying the effects of neglecting these criteria in order to arrive at information on the bias resulting from this neglect.

8.5.4 Exchange rate regimes and optimal control

In order to investigate the robustness of the results presented in Section 7.5.2, it is recommended that optimal control experiments be conducted under different assumptions and for different models. For example, it is well-known that the instruments of monetary policy can be changed much more easily than those of fiscal policy. In the present study account has been taken of this phenomenon by assigning appropriate values to the penalties in the loss function. In future research some or all of these instruments could be assumed to be exogenous, or it could be assumed that only some of these instruments can be used. Another route for studying the robustness of the results is to apply the optimal control experiments a. on models which contain the extensions recommended in Section 8.5.1, or b. on multi-country models.

During the optimal control experiments, the parameters in the formulas of expectations formation were set equal to the values obtained during the simulation runs. It would be desirable to update these parameters during the optimal control runs, so that the influence of different policies on the expectations formation is considered (adaptive learning). We were unable to implement these procedures, because when writing these conclusions (January 1990) the software on stochastic control could only handle very small models (up to 20 equations). It is interesting for future research to take account of this interaction between expectations formation and optimal economic policy. Given the present computational limitations, it is recommended that future research should start with small models and then be extended to larger (more realistic) models as soon as new software becomes available.

Appendix: List of Symbols and Description of the Data of the Quarterly Model

The meaning of the symbols of both the theoretical and empirical part of this study as well as the sources of the data used for estimating the empirical model are listed in this Appendix. The greater part of the data used for estimating the non-financial sectors of the model are provided by De Nederlandsche Bank N.V.. A description of the sources and methods used for deriving these data can be found in Boeschoten *et al.* (1984). Some of these series are also published in De Nederlandsche Bank (1982[a], 1982[b] and 1983). As the source of the latter we mention, DNB, Kwartaalconfrontatie van middelen en bestedingen.

For many quarterly time series published in these publications, originally only annual data were available, so that an approximation method had to be used for deriving the quarterly figures. Essentially two methods have been applied *viz.* the one presented in Boot *et al.* (1967) and the method published in Ginsburgh (1973). The latter uses the quarterly time series of a related phenomenon for approximating the quarterly figures from annual data, whereas the former method only smoothly distributes the annual data over the quarters. A brief description of both methods and the method used for deriving the series listed in "Kwartaalconfrontatie van middelen en bestedingen" can be found in De Nederlandsche Bank (1982[a]).

The main source of the time series of foreign variables is the International Financial Statistics published by the International Monetary Fund. Some series are also published in special supplements of this publication. As an abbreviation of this source we mention IFS and if relevant we also refer to the particular supplement.

The time series of domestic monetary variables are obtained from various issues of De Nederlandsche Bank, Kwartaalberichten. The tables, columns and/or items mentioned refer to the 1979(1) (June 1979) issue. Annual interest rates are devided by four in order to obtain quarterly figures which have the same dimension as the expected percentage change in the exchange rate. The interest rates and exchange rates are quarterly averages. Quarterly averages are preferred to end-of-period figures, because the financial flows in the model refer to the entire quarter and not just the end of the quarter.

In the empirical model upper case symbols refer to values in current prices, whereas lower case symbols refer to variables expressed in constant prices (of 1977). Prices, interest rates and exchange rates are also represented by lower case symbols. In Section 2.5 some lower case symbols refer to the logarithm of the particular variable. Generally Arabic characters refer to variables and Greek symbols stand for parameters. Symbols which refer to variables (parameters) in general - for example the vectors x_t, y_t and z_t in Chapter 3 and the parameteres α, β etc. in various formules - are not included in this list. The following notation has been used for operators

- $^{\circ}$ above a variable indicates its relative change
- Δ before a variable denotes its first difference
- Δ_4 before a variable denotes its four periods difference
- a lag of a variable is indicated by a subscript or by a number between brackets; e.g. x_{-1} or x(-1)
- the expected value of avariable is indicated by a superscript ^{e} or by the operator E(..); e.g. x^e or E(x)
- the asterisk * refers to a foreign variable, see Chapter 2
- $\tilde{}$ above a variable indicates its target value, see Chapter 7. If this variable is an exchange rate then this value corresponds with its parity rate
- a bar above a variable denotes its long-term value, see Chapter 2
- a $\hat{}$ above a parameter refers to its estimated value
- the superscript ^{d} stands for demand or desired amount
- the superscript ^{s} refers to supply
- the subscript $_{n}$ refers to the variable's normal value
- the subscript $_{JA}$ refers the particular variable's value in the studies by Jager and Amman, see Chapter 7
- a(.) is demand for foreign money and foreign bonds, see Chapter 2
- b(.) is demand for domestic bonds, see Chapter 2
- B backshift operator, $B^n x_t = x_{t-n}$
- bf(.) demand for domestic and foreign bonds, see Chapter 2
- f(.) demand for foreign bonds, see Chapter 2
- m(.) demand for domestic money, see Chapter 2
- m_r(.) demand for real money balances, see Chapter 2
- $\backslash \{\overset{\circ}{e}^{e}\}$ after a variable indicates the explanatory variables of the particular variable except for the exchange rate expectations, see Chapter 7

Abbreviations

Estimation methods

IV	Instrumental variables estimator
OLS	Ordinary least squares
SURE	Seemingly unrelated regressions estimators
TSLS	Two-stage least squares

Statistical terms

R^2	Coefficient of determination
R^2(adj.)	Coefficient of determination adjusted for degrees of freedom
DW	Durbin-Watson statistic

h	Durbin's h-statistic on serial correlation. This statistic is approximately normally distributed with unit variance.
ρ	Serial correlation coefficient when during the estimation a correction is made for the first order autocorrelation in the disturbance terms
s.e.e.	Standard error of the regression
F(n,d)	F-statistic for n degrees of freedom in the numerator and d degrees of freedom in the denumerator
ARIMA	Autoregressive Integrated Moving Average
VAR	Vector Autoregressive

List of variables

A	The stock of foreign money and foreign bonds: see Chapter 2.
A_i	The amount of asset i: see Chapter 4.
a	Labour used by firms $a = a_{se} + a_w$
a^*	Capacity demand for labour: see Section 5.2.
a_g	Wage earners in the government sector, in men years Source: Boeschoten *et al.*
a_s	Supply of labour $a_s = a_w + a_g + a_{se} + U$
a_{se}	Self-employed working population Source: Boeschoten *et al.*
a_w	Wage earners in firms, in men years Source: Boeschoten *et al.*
B	The stock of domestic bonds: see Chapter 2.
BF	The stock of domestic and foreign bonds: see Chapter 2
BB_{ex}	Exogenous parts of the balance of payments (on cash basis) This variable consists of not yet categorized payments. Source: DNB, table 6.1, item 3
bp	Premium on guilders available from non-residents from selling bonds to residents as a percentage of the commercial exchange rate. Proxy to capture the effect of the closed bond guilder circuit for non-residents, calculated from the averages of the highest and lowest premium during a week Source: DNB, table 9.7

C — The ratio of labour costs and capital costs of the newest vintage, both per unit of product: see Chapter 5.

C — Currency
Source: DNB, table 3.1, column 2

C^g — Currency held by local authorities.
Defined as 0.13 times the volume of narrowly defined money held by local authorities
Source: DNB, table 3.1, column 18. The coefficient of 0.13 has been calculated from Cramer and Reekers (1972), pp. 10-11.

C^p — Currency held by the private sector
$C^p = C - C^g$.

CA — Current account of the Netherlands (cash basis)
In Chapter 2, CA refers to the current account of the domestic country.

CA_{FR} — Current account of France (in billions of French francs)
The imports and exports of France (in billions of US dollars) are published in the IFS, Supplement on Trade Statistics. These figures are transferred into French francs by means of the $e_{FR,US}$ rate.

CA_{UK} — Current account of the United Kingdom (in billions of pound sterling).
The imports and exports of the United Kingdom (in billions of US dollars) are published in the IFS, Supplement on Trade Statistics. These figures are transferred into pound sterling by means of the $e_{UK,US}$ rate.

CA_{US} — Current account of the United States (in billions of US dollars)
The imports and exports of the United States (in billions of US dollars) are published in the IFS, Supplement on Trade Statistics.

$CONS^p$ — Value of private consumption
Source: DNB, Kwartaalconfrontatie van middelen en bestedingen

$cons^p$ — Private consumption in prices of 1977
Source: DNB, Kwartaalconfrontatie van middelen en bestedingen

CSM — The accumulation of special mutations: see further SM and RESA.

d — Depreciation costs per unit per period: see Section 5.4.2.

D — Demand deposits
Source: DNB table 3.1, columns 3 and 4

D^p — Demand deposits held by the private sector
$D^p = D - D^g$.

D_s — Balance of unilateral income transfers
Source of the unilateral income transfers paid and received: DNB, Kwartaalconfrontatie van middelen en bestedingen

DEN_{US} — Denominator in the relation of the Dutch guilder U.S. dollar exchange rate, equation (7.15)
$DEN_{US} = CA - \Delta RES + STATBB + \Delta NDAL^f \backslash \{\mathring{e}^e\} + \Delta NDAS^f \backslash \{\mathring{e}^e\} - \Delta NFA^p \backslash \{\mathring{e}^e\} - \Delta NFA^b \backslash \{\mathring{e}^e\}$

DEP^f — Depreciation by firms
Source: DNB, Kwartaalconfrontatie van middelen en bestedingen

D^g — Deposits of the central government
$D^g = DG^b + DG^{cb}$

DG^b — Deposits of the central goverment with giro institutions
These institutions belong to the banks.
Source: DNB, table 2.1, column 31

DG^{cb} — Deposits of the central goverment with the central bank
Source: DNB, table 2.1, column 31

DGL — Demand deposits held by local authorities
Defined as 0.87 times the volume of narrowly defined money held by local authorities. See further C^g.

DI^f — Direct foreign investments
Source: DNB, table 6.1, item b(2)

d_{pr} — Factor used for approximating the part of non-wage income that can be considered to be profits
This factor is supposed to be constant within the year.
Source: CBS, N.A., table 1, items in the numerator 1.2.06, 1.2.08, 1.2.11 and 1.2.13. The denominator is non-wage income.

DUMS — Dummy variable in the foreigner's flow of short-term domestic assets representing extraordinary demand:
DUMS is 1 in 1970.III, 1970:IV and 1975:III and zero elsewhere.

d791 — Dummy variable representing extraordinary foreign demand for domestic long-term assets:
d791 is 1.0 in 1979:I and zero elsewhere.

d7912 — Dummy variable representing the severe winter of 1979:
d791 is 1.0 in 1979:I, -1.0 in 1979:II and zero elsewhere.

dum70 — Dummy variable in the equation of the percentage change in the wage rate representing the once only payment of *f*400. in 1970:
dum70 is 1.0 in 1970:II and 1970:III and zero elsewhere.

dum7041 — Dummy variable representing foreigners' extraordinary demand for domestic long-term assets:
dum7041 is 1.0 in 1970:IV, 1971:I and 1975:III and zero elsewhere.

dum734 — Dummy variable in the relation of price of exports
This dummy expresses the influence of the first oil crisis:
dum734 is 1.0 during the period 1973:IV - 1974:III and zero elsewhere.

dumw2 — Dummy variable representing the severe winter of 1979:
dumw2 equals 1.0 in 1979:I and is zero elsewhere.

e — Exchange rate, domestic price of foreign currency

e_{WG} — The spot rate of the Dutch guilder against the Deutsche mark (quarterly average) $e_{WG} = e_{US}/e_{US,WG}$

$\tilde{e}_{WG}$ — The parity rate of the Dutch guilder/Deutsche mark exchange rate (quarterly average)
Source: DNB, table 9.4

e_{FR} — The spot rate of the Dutch guilder against the French franc (quarterly average) $e_{FR} = e_{US}/e_{US,FR}$

$\tilde{e}_{FR}$ — The parity rate of the Dutch guilder/French franc exchange rate
During periods where no parity rate existed, this time series equals the spot rate.
Source: DNB, table 9.4

$e_{FR,US}$ — The spot rate of the French franc against the US dollar (quarterly average)
Source: IFS

e_{UK} — The spot rate of the Dutch guilder against the British pound sterling (quarterly average)
$e_{UK} = e_{US} \cdot e_{UK,US}$

$e_{UK,US}$ — The spot rate of the British pound sterling against the US dollar (quarterly average)
Source: IFS

e_{US} — The spot rate of the Dutch guilder against the US dollar (quarterly average)
Source: IFS

$e_{US,WG}$ — The spot rate of the Deutsche mark against the US dollar (quarterly average)
Source: IFS

F — Stock of bonds denominated in foreign currency: see Chapter 2.

FA^b — Financial assets of the banking sector
$FA^b = RU + NDAS^b + NDAL^b + NFA^b$

FA^p	Financial assets of the private sector $FA^p = M1 + NDAS^p + NDAL^p + NFA^p - LS$
FD^g	Financial deficit of the government Source: DNB, table 5.1, row 7 and table 5.2, row 7
FD^g_r	Part of the government's financial deficit that is not financed by means of $\Delta NDAL^g$ or $\Delta NDAS^g$
G	Government expenditures: see Section 5.1 and Chapter 6.
G_w	Total sum of wages paid by the government Source: Boeschoten *et al.*
g_w	Idem, in prices of 1977 Source: Boeschoten *et al.*
G_x	Value of autonomous expenditures by the government These expenditures include the public expenditure on goods and services (exclusive of the wages, G_w) and gross investments by the government. Source: Boeschoten *et al.*
G_r	Other government expenditures, such as transfer payments Source: Boeschoten *et al.*
h	Index of working hours in firms Source: Boeschoten *et al.*
I	Total investments, excluding those in inventories by the private sector Source: DNB, Kwartaalconfrontatie van middelen en bestedingen
i	Idem, in prices of 1977
INT	Foreign exchange market interventions by the central bank, approximated by the change in the international monetary reserves of De Nederlandsche Bank corrected for special mutations and swap arrangements Source: DNB, table 4.2
I_n	Investments in stocks of inventories ($I_n = \Delta N$) Source, DNB, Kwartaalconfrontatie van middelen en bestedingen
i_n	Idem, in prices of 1977
I_{sa}	Gross investments in ships and aeroplanes Source: Boeschoten *et al.*
i_{sa}	Idem, in prices of 1977

I_{-sa} Gross investments by firms excluding those in ships and aeroplanes, in current prices
$I_{-sa} = I - I_{sa} - I_w$

i_{-sa} Idem, in prices of 1977
$i_{-sa} = i - i_{sa} - i_w$

I_t The set of information on time t, see Chapter 3.

I_w Total investments in dwellings in current prices
Source: DNB, Kwartaalconfrontatie van middelen en bestedingen

i_w Idem, in prices of 1977
Source: DNB, Kwartaalconfrontatie van middelen en bestedingen

ly Economic lifetime used in the vintage model: see Section 5.2.

lp Expected life of an investment used for determining the user costs of capital: see Section 5.4.2.

LBL^b Bonds issued by banks valued at par
Calculated by accumulating flows, to start from zero at the end of 1956
Source: DNB, table 7.1

liq The percentage of the banks' short-term liabilities that should be held as domestic short-term assets
This percentage refers to an average per period.
Source, DNB, table 8.1, column 2

LM^f Mortgage loans supplied by foreigners to domestic borrowers
Calculated by accumulating flows to start from zero at the end of 1956
Source: DNB, table 7.1

LP^f Private placements of domestic borrowers with foreigners
Calculated by accumulating flows to start from zero at the end of 1956
Source: DNB, table 7.1

lq Liquidity ratio
$lq = (M1 + NDAS^p + NDAS^f)/(4.0 \cdot (Y - DEP^f))$

LS Short-term bank loans (granted to the private sector)
Source: DNB, table 2.1, column 8, including the central bank

M Total imports of goods and services in current prices
Source: DNB, Kwartaalconfrontatie van middelen en bestedingen
In Chapter 2 the symbol of M is the stock of domestic money.

m Idem, in prices of 1977
Source: DNB, Kwartaalconfrontatie van middelen en bestedingen
In Chapter 2 m also refers to the logarithm of domestic money.

M_{FR}	Imports of France (in billions of US dollars) Source: IFS, Supplement on Trade Statistics
M_{UK}	Imports of the United Kingdom (in billions of US dollars) Source: IFS, Supplement on Trade Statistics
M_{US}	Imports of the US (in billions of dollars) Source: IFS
M_g	Imports of goods, excluding ships, aeroplanes, oil and natural gas $M_g = M - M_{og} - M_{sa} - M_s - M_p$
m_g	Idem, in prices of 1977 $m_g = m - m_{og} - m_{sa} - m_s - m_p$
M_i	Investment income paid to foreigners Source: DNB, table 6.2, item 8a
M_{ng}	Imports not included in M_g and M_i $M_{ng} = M - M_g - M_i$
M_{og}	Imports of oil and natural gas Source: Boeschoten *et al.*
m_{og}	Idem, in prices of 1977 Source: Boeschoten *et al.*
M_p	Income paid to foreigners Source: DNB, Kwartaalconfrontatie van middelen en bestedingen
m_p	Idem, in prices of 1977 Source: DNB, Kwartaalconfrontatie van middelen en bestedingen
M_r	Imports excluding the imports of goods and investment income received from foreigners $M_r = M - M_g - M_i$
M_s	Imports of services in current prices Source: DNB, Kwartaalconfrontatie van middelen en bestedingen
m_s	Idem, in prices of 1977 Source: DNB, Kwartaalconfrontatie van middelen en bestedingen
M_{sa}	Imports of ships and aeroplanes Source: Boeschoten *et al.*
m_{sa}	Idem, in prices of 1977 Source: Boeschoten *et al.*
m_w	Index of world imports Source: Boeschoten *et al.*

M1 Money: currency and demand deposits
$M1 = D + C - (C^g + DGL)$
Source: DNB, table 3.1

N Stock of foreign money: see Chapter 2.

n Stock of inventories
$n = \Sigma i_n = n(-1) + i_n$

ncc Net credit ceiling: variable to capture the tightness of this ceiling. Equals unity since 1977: III and zero elsewhere
Source: Van Loo (1983), p. 322

NCI Net capital inflow: see Chapter 2.

$NDAL^b$ Long-term net domestic assets of banks
Source: stocks DNB, table 2.1, column 22 minus column 40 and shares emitted by banks. The stock of shares has been calculated by accumulating flows, starting from zero at the end of 1956
Source of the flows: DNB, table 7.1 (net supply minus net demand)

$NDAL^f$ Long-term net domestic assets held by foreigners
Calculated by accumulating flows, starting from zero at the end of 1953 Source of the flows: DNB, table 7.1 (Net supply of foreigners, minus net demand of private placements and mortgage loans)

$NDAL^g$ Long-term net domestic assets held by the government
This item wholy consists of liabilities. The stock at the end of 1978 is the sum of LB^g and LP^g in Van Loo (1983)
Source of the flows: DNB, table 7.1

$NDAL^p$ Long-term net domestic assets held by the private sector.
This stock is made up of the private sector's cumulative net supply on the domestic stock market and the stock of long-term deposits with banks.
$NDAL^p = NDALS + NDALC^p$

NDAL1 Long-term deposits with banks
Source: DNB, table 2.1, column 41

NDAL2 Savings certificates to bearer issued by banks
Source: DNB, table 2.1, column 42

NDAL3 Genuine savings deposits with banks
Source: DNB, table 2.1, column 43

$NDALC^p$ The private sector's cumulative net supply on the domestic capital market
$NDALC^p = NDAL^g - NDAL^b - NDAL^f$

NDALS The private sector's long-term time and saving deposits with banks
NDALS = NDAL1 + NDAL2 +NDAL3

$NDAS^f$ Short-term net domestic assets held by foreigners
Calculated by accumulating flows, starting form zero at the end of 1953 Source of the flows: DNB, table 6.3, column 15

$NDAS^b$ Short-term time and savings deposits by banks
Source: DNB, table 3.1, columns 8 and 10

$NDAS^f$ Short-term time and savings deposits held by the foreign sector
It should be noted that $NDAS^f$ also contains demand deposits other money market titles and short-term credit.
Calculated by accumulating flows, starting from zero at the end of 1953
Source of the flows: DNB, table 6.3, row 15

$NDAS^g$ Short-term time and savings deposits by banks held by the local authorities.
Defined as 0.73 times the volume of near money held by local authorities
Source: DNB, table 3.1, columns 14 and 18. The coefficient 0.73 has been taken from Van Loo (1973), who bases it on information provided by DNB

$NDAS^p$ Short-term time and savings deposits by banks held by the private sector
$NDAS^p = NDAS^b - NDAS^g - NDAS^f$

$NDLS^g$ Short-term domestic liablities of the government
$NDLS^g = NDAS^b$

$NFA^b =$ $NFAS^b + NFAL^b$

$NFA^p =$ $NFAS^p + NFAL^p$

$NFAL^b$ Long-term foreign assets held by banks
Calculated by accumulating and decumulating flows to start from 8.8 billion guilders at the end of 1977 (see Den Butter, Fase en Huyser, 1979, table 2)
Source of the flows: DNB, table 6.1, item 5a

$NFAL^p$ Long-term net foreign assets held by the private sector
Calculated by accumulating flows, to start from zero at the end of 1953
Source of the flows: DNB, table 6.3, item 11

NFAS = $NFAS^p + NFAS^b$

$NFAS^b$ Short-term net foreign assets held by banks
Calculated by accumulating flows, to start from -4.6 billion guilders at the end of 1977 (see Den Butter, Fase and Huyser, 1979, table 2)
Source of the flows: DNB, table 6.1, items 5b and 5c

$NFAS^p$ Short-term net foreign assets of the private sector
Stocks are calculated by accumulating flows, starting from zero at the end of 1953
Source of the flows: DNB, table 6.3, row 18

O_g Other receipts of the government

P Index of domestic price level: see Chapter 2

p Logarithm of domestic price level: see Chapter 2

PT Social insurance premiums paid on transfer income
Source: Boeschoten *et al.*

PW Social security premiums paid on wage income
Source: Boeschoten *et al.*

PZ Social insurance premiums paid by the self-employed

p_c Index of consumer prices (1977 = 100)
$P_c = 100.\ CONS^p/cons^p$

p_{exc} Price of competitors at foreign markets (1977 = 100)
Source: The annual data of the price of competitors at foreign markets (double weighted) are from CPB, Centraal Economisch Plan 1982. Quarterly data are derived by means of Ginburgh's method. As the related quarterly series we used the export unit value index of industrial countries published in the IFS

p^f_{exc} Price of competitors at foreign markets expressed in foreign currency (1977 = 100)

p^f_{ex} The price of exported goods expressed in foreign currency
$p^f_{ex} = p_{ex}/e = p^f_{ex}(-1)\cdot(1.0 + \mathring{p}_{ex} - \mathring{e})$

p_{FR} Index of consumer prices in France
Source: IFS, Supplement on Price Statistics

p_i Index of the price of investment goods (1977 = 100)
$p_i = 100\ I_{-sa}/i_{-sa}$

p_j Penalty of variable j in the loss function: see Chapter 7.

$p_{JA,y}$ Penalty of variable y in the loss function used by Jager and Amman: see Chapter 7.

p_k Index of user costs of capital (1977 = 100)
Construction: see Chapter 5.

p_m — Index of prices of imported goods (1977 = 100)
$p_m = 100 \cdot M_g / m_g$

p_{mc} — Index of the price of imported consumer goods (1977 = 100)
Source: Boeschoten *et al.*

p_{mi} — Index of price of imported investment goods (1977 = 100)
Source: Boeschoten *et al.*

p_{UK} — Index of consumer prices in the United Kingdom
Source: IFS, Supplement on Price Statistics

p_{US} — Index of consumer prices in the United States
Source: IFS, Supplement on Price Statistics

q — Utilization rate
$q = 100 \cdot y / y^*$
In Chapter 2 the symbol q refers to the real exchange rate.

qase — The share of the self employed working population in the total working force of firms
$qase = a_{se} / a$

R — Bank reserves
Source: DNB, table 2.1, columns 3 and 5

R_{tt} — Gains and losses as a result of changes in the terms of trade
Source: Boeschoten *et al.*

R^r_{tt} — The exogenous part of R_{tt}
Source: Boeschoten *et al.*

r — Interest rate: see Chapters 2 and 5.

r_{CB} — Discount rate
Source: DNB, table 9.1

REG — Regulation variable to capture the prohibition for banks to pay interest on short-term guilder deposits
Equals:
1. 1972: II - 1973: II
0.5 1973: III - 1974: I
0.25 1974: II - 1975: IV
0 elsewhere
Source: Den Butter, Fase and Huyser (1979) p. 186

RES — International monetary reserves of De Nederlandsche Bank N.V.
Source: DNB table 2.4, item 1 (net total), corrected for special changes item B of that table

RESA — The central bank's international reserves adjusted for special mutations and swap arrangements
RESA = RES - CSM - SWAP

r_f — Interest rate on foreign assets measured as
$r_f = \{0.318\,(r_{s,US} + r_{l,US}) + 0.51\,(r_{s,WG} + r_{l,WG}) + 0.055\,(r_{s,UK} + r_{l,UK}) + 0.117\,(r_{s,FR} + r_{l,FR})\} / 2$
The weights are explained in Section 4.3.4.

RL — Bank demand for discounts and advances (including special loans) from the central bank
Source: DNB, table 2.1, column 30

r_l — Long-term interest rate measured as the average yield on the latest three long-term central goverment bonds
Source: DNB, table 9.2

rlex — The contribution to the explanation of the long-term domestic interest rate of variables that during the simulation are assumed to be exogenous in the r_l-relation

r_{lf} — Long-term foreign interest rate
$r_{lf} = 0.318\, r_{l,US} + 0.51\, r_{l,WG} + 0.055\, r_{l,UK} + 0.117\, r_{l,FR}$
The weights are explained in Section 4.3.4.

r_{ls} — Interest rate on short-term bank loans measured as the average of the minimum and maximum of the overdraft rate (other than stocks)
Source: DNB: table 9.2

$r_{l,FR}$ — Interest rate on long-term government bonds in France
Source: IFS

$r_{l,UK}$ — Interest rate on long-term government bonds in the United Kingdom
Source: IFS

$r_{l,US}$ — Yield of government bonds in the United States
Source: IFS

$r_{l,WG}$ — Interest rate on long-term government bonds in West Germany
Source: IFS

RR — Required reserves of banks
Source: DNB, table : Main figures of the money market

r_s — Interest rate on short-term government debt, measured as the rate on three month loans to local authorities
Source: DNB, table 9.2

r_{sf} — Short term foreign interest rate
$r_{sf} = 0.318\, r_{s,US} + 0.51\, r_{s,WG} + 0.055\, r_{s,UK} + 0.117\, r_{s,FR}$
The weights are explained in Section 4.3.4.

$r_{s,FR}$ Call money rate in France
Source: IFS

r_{sh} The yield on domestic shares approximated by the percentage change of the index of share prices of internationals at the Amsterdam Stock Exchange
Source: DNB, table 9.3

$r_{s,UK}$ Treasury bill rate in the United Kingdom
Source: IFS

$r_{s,US}$ Treasury bill rate in the United States
Source: IFS

$r_{s,WG}$ Call money rate in West Germany
Source: IFS

r_{st} Interest rate on short term time and savings deposits measured as the rate on three month time deposits
Source: DNB, table 9.2

RU Non-borrowed reserves of banks
RU = R - RL

S1,S2
S3,S4 Seasonal dummies: S1 is 1 in the first quarter and zero in the remaing quarters etc.

SD_{ca} Statistical discrepancy in the capital account
This correction factor arises because of registration differences between the flows in table 7.1 and those in table 6.1 of DNB

SD_{cu} Statistical discrepancy in the current account
Source: Boeschoten *et al.*

SD_g Statistical differences between the government's budget deficit on a transaction base and that on a cash base
Source: Boeschoten *et al.*

SL Special loans granted by the central bank
Source: DNB, table 8.1

SM Special mutations of the central bank's international reserves
Source: DNB, table 2.4, item B

SS Short-term government debt
Flows are determined by (parts of) the liquidity-surplus (DNB, table 5.1, items 10a (1) and 10b, and table 5.2, item 10). The stock of SS has been calculated by accumulating flows. As a reference the stock at the end of 1978 has been taken. This stock 19380 consists of holdings of the central bank and banks (DNB, table 2.1, columns 6 and 7) and the holdings of the private sector.
Source: DNB, table 3.1, columns 6 and 7 minus 0.27 times the volume of near money held by local authorities
Source: DNB, table 3.1, column 14. The coefficient of 0.27 has

been taken from Van Loo (1983) p. 332, who bases this on information provided by DNB.

SS^b Short-term goverment debt held by banks
Source: stock at the end of 1978: DNB, table 2.1, columns 6 and 7, flows: DNB table 5.1, item 10, b (1) and 10, b (2) and table 5.2, item 10, a (2)

SS^p Short-term goverment debt held by the private sector
Source: DNB, table 3.1, columns 6 and 7 minus 0.27 times the volume of near money held by local authorities
Source: DNB, table 3.1, column 14. The coefficient of 0.27 has been taken from Van Loo (1983), p. 332, who bases this on information provide by DNB.

STATBB Several exogenous items of the balance of payments on cash basis:
- unilateral capital transfers (DNB:, table 6.1 item 2.a)
- direct investments (idem, item 2b)
- long-term credits (idem, item 3)
- other long-term capital flows (idem, item 2b(4))
- capital flows of the government (idem, item 2 d)
- payments which are not yet classified (idem, item 3)
- allocation of Special Drawing Rights (idem, item 6)
- statistical differences resulting from different registration manners in table 7.1 and 6.1 (6.3) of portfolio investments by foreigners

SWAP Dollar swaps, temporary sales of dollars by the central bank to the banking system for a specified period
Source: DNB, table 8.2

T Total amount of taxes: see Section 5.1 and Chapter 6.

T_{is} Indirect taxes minus subsidies
Source: Boeschoten *et al.*

TB Trade balance: see Chapter 2.

TCS Short term trade credit.
Source: Boeschoten *et al.*

TS Tax shifting variable in the wage rate equation
TS is the percentage change in (TW + PW)/YW.

TT Taxes on transfer payments
Source: Boeschoten *et al.*

TW Taxes on wage income
Source: Boeschoten *et al.*

TZ Taxes on non-wage income
Source: Boeschote *et al.*

U	Unemployment Source: Boeschoten *et al.*
V	Total sales $V = Y - I_n$
v	Idem, in prices of 1977 $v = y - i_n$
v_{ex}	Exogenous part of v
v_f	Sales by firms $v_f = v - v_{f,ex}$ Source: Boeschoten *et al.*
$v_{f,ex}$	Exogeneous part of v_f Source: Boeschoten *et al.*
W	Stock of financial wealth: see Chapter 2.
W^b	Balancing item of the banking sector's balance sheet $W^b = FA^b - LS$
W^b_{ex}	Exogenous part of W^b
W^p	Balancing item of the private sector's balance sheet $W^p = FA^p + NDAS^f + NDAL^f$
w^f	Total wage per wage-earner in firms $w^f = YW^f / a_w$
w^f_g	Total wage per wage-earner in firms corrected for absenteeism because of illness $w^f_g = w^f/\gamma$ Source: Boeschoten *et al.*
W^f	Proxy of foreign wealth; scaling variable in the equations of foreign investments in the Netherlands W^f is approximated by a weighted sum of the GNPs
X	Total exports of goods and services in current prices Source: DNB, Kwartaalconfrontatie van middelen en bestedingen
x	Idem, in prices of 1977 Source: DNB, Kwartaalconfrontatie van middelen en bestedingen
Xfr	Exports of France (in billions of US dollars) Source: IFS, Supplement on Trade Statistics
X_{uk}	Exports of the United Kindom (in billions of US dollars) Source: IFS, Supplement on Trade Statistics
X_{us}	Exports of the US (in billions of dollars)

	Source: IFS
Xg	Exports of goods, excluding ships, aeroplanes, oil and natural gas $X_g = X - X_{og} - X_{sa} - X_s - X_p$
x_g	Idem, in prices of 1977 $x_g = x - x_{og} - x_{sa} - x_s - x_p$
X_i	Investment income received from foreigners Source: DNB, table 6.2, item 3a
X_{ng}	Exports not included in Xg and X_i $X_{ng} = X - X_g - X_i$
X_{og}	Exports of oil and natural gas Source: Boeschoten *et al.*
x_{og}	Idem, in prices of 1977 Source: Boeschoten *et al.*
X^p	Variables that permanently influence the current account: see Chapter 2.
X_p	Income received from foreigners Source: DNB, Kwartaalconfrontatie van middelen en bestedingen
x_i	Idem, in prices of 1977 Source: DNB, Kwartaalconfrontatie van middelen en bestedingen
X_r	Exports excluding the exports of goods and investment income received from foreigners $X_r = X - X_g - X_i$
X_s	Exports of services in current prices Source: DNB, Kwartaalconfrontatie van middelen en bestedingen
x_s	Idem, in prices of 1977 Source: DNB, Kwartaalconfrontatie van middelen en bestedingen
X_{sa}	Exports of ships and aeroplanes Source: Boeschoten *et al.*
x_{sa}	Idem, in prices of 1977 Source: Boeschoten *et al.*
X^t	Variables that transitorily influence the current account: see Chapter 2
Y	National income (value of gross national product, market price) Source: Boeschoten *et al.*
y	Idem, in prices of 1977 In Chapter 2, y refers to the logarithm of Y

y^* Capacity output (in constant prices)

Y_{ex} Exogenous part of national income
Source: Boeschoten *et al.*

Y_f Production by firms (gross value added by firms, market price)
Source: Boeschoten *et al.*

y_f Idem, in prices of 1977

y_{ni} National income in constant prices
Source: Boeschoten *et al.*

YS^d Calculated disposable wage income of the self-employed
$YS^d = YS - (TW/YW) \cdot YS - PZ$

YS Calculated wage income of the self-employed working population
$Y_s = a_{se} \cdot w$

YT Transfer payments from the government to the household sector
Source: CBS, NA, table 4, items 4.2.63 + 4.2.65 + 4.2.66 + 4.5.52 - 4.2.05 for annual figures. The quarterly figures are constructed by means of the method presented in Boot *et al.*
(See Boeschoten *et al.*)

YT^d Disposable income from transfer payments by the government

YW Total wages
$YW = YW^f + YW^g$

YW^d Disposable wage income, excluding the income of the self-employed
$YW^d = YW - TW - PW$

YW^g Total wages paid by the government
Source: DNB, Kwartaal-confrontatie van middelen en bestedingen

YW^f Total wages paid by firms
Source: DNB, Kwartaal-confrontatie van middelen en bestedingen

$YWTS^d$ Disposable wage and transfer income, including calculated wage income of the self-employed
$YWTS^d = YW^d + YT^d + YS^d$

Z Non-wage income
Source: DNB, Kwartaal-confrontatie van middelen en bestedingen

ZRG Interest payments to the private sector by the government
Source: Boeschoten *et al.*

Z^d Disposable non-wage income
$Z^d = Z + ZRG + X_i - M_i - TZ - (1.0 - TW/YW) \cdot YS$

Z_{ex}	Exogenous component of non-wage income $Z_{ex} = Z - (Y + ZRG - YW^{f} - YW^{g} + X_{g-M} - T_{is})$
γ	Correction factor with regard to absenteism because of illness
δ_1	Elasticity of capacity output with regard to working hours
δ_2	Elasticity of capacity demand for labour with regard to working hours
ϵ	Rate of non-embodied capital-augmenting technical progress
θ	Elasticity of capacity output with regard to a change in the economic life-span of equipment
Φ	Elasticity of capacity demand for labour with regard to a change in the economic life-span of equipment
κ	Capital-output ratio
μ	Rate of embodied labour-augmenting technical progress
π	Profits of firms $\pi = Z \cdot d_{pr} + DEP^{f} - TZ - (1.0 - TW/YW) \cdot YS$ The term $Z \cdot d_{pr}$ contains calculated wage income of the self-employed working population. Since is not apart of the firms' profit this calculated income is subtracted from $Z \cdot d_{pr} + DEP^{f}$ - In Chapter 2 the symbol π refers to the rate of inflation. - In Chapter 3 the symbol π refers to reduced form coefficients.
σ	Rate of disembodied labour-augmenting technical progress
τ	Rate of technical and economic obsolence

References

Abraham, F, 1985, Efficiency, predictability and news on the foreign exchange markets; Floating exchange rates versus adjustable E.M.S. rates, Weltwirtschaftliches Archiv 121 (1), 18-32.

Adam, M.-C. and G. Melard, 1987, Why are European interest rates poor predictors of inflation?, Working Paper 8703, DULBEA, Free University of Brussels.

Almon, S, 1965, The distributed lag between capital appropriations and expenditures, Econometrica 33 (1), 178-196.

Amano, A., 1983, A structural approach to capital flows and exchange rates, in Klein, L.R. and W.E. Krelle, eds., Capital Flows and Exchange Rate Determination, Springer Verlag, Vienna, 3-28.

Amano, A, 1986, Exchange rate simulations: A comparative study, European Economic Review 30 (1), 137-148.

Amman, H.M. and H. Jager, 1987, Optimal economic policies under a crawling-peg exchange-rate system, in Carraro, C. and D. Sartore, eds., Developments of Control Theory for Economic Analysis, Martinus Nijhoff Publishers, Dordrecht, 105-126.

Amman, H.M. and H. Jager, 1988, Constrained control algorithm for non-linear control problems, International Journal of System Science, 19 (9),1781-1793.

Anema, W.J. and C.J. Jepma, 1978, De effectieve wisselkoers als maatstaf voor de opwaardering van de gulden, Economisch Statistische Berichten 3166, 792-796.

Arrow, K.J., 1978, The future and the present in economic life, Economic Inquiry 16 (2), 157-169.

Artus, J. R., 1976, Exchange rate stability and managed floating: the experience of the Federal Republic of Germany, IMF Staff Papers 23 (2), 312-333.

Artus, J.R. and A.K. McGuirk, 1981, A revised version of the multilateral exchange rate model, IMF Staff Papers 28 (2), 275-309.

Athans, M., 1974, The importance of Kalman filtering methods for economic systems, Annals of Economic and Social Measurement 3 (1), 49-64.

Attfield, C.L.F., 1980, Expected income in the demand for money: An unobservable variable analysis, Journal of Monetary Economics 6 (4), 573-586.

Backus, D., W.C. Brainard, G. Smith and J. Tobin, 1980, A model of U.S. financial and nonfinancial economic behavior, Journal of Money, Credit and Banking 12 (2), 259-293.

Backus, D. and D. Purvis, 1980, An integrated model of household flow-of-funds allocations, Journal of Money, Credit and Banking 12 (2), 400-421.

Baillie, R.T. and D.D. Selover, 1987, Cointegration and models of exchange rate determination, International Journal of Forecasting 3 (1), 43-51.

Barro, R.J., 1977, Unanticipated money growth and unemployment in the United States, American Economic Review 67 (2), 101-115.

Barten, A.P., G. d' Alcantara and C.J. Carrin, 1976, COMET: A medium term macroeconomic model for the European Economic Community, European Economic Review 7 (1), 63-115.

Begg, D.K.H., 1982, The Rational Expectations Revolution in Macroeconomics: Theories and evidence, Philip Allen Publishers, Oxford.

Berg, P.J.C.M. van den, F.J.H. Don, and J. Sandee, 1983, KOMPAS: Kwartaalmodel voor prognose, analyse en simulatie, Central Planning Bureau, CPB-monografie 26, The Hague.

Bhandari, J.S. and B.H. Putnam, eds., 1983, Economic Interdependence and Flexible Exchange Rates, The MIT Press, Cambridge Mass..

Bigman, D., 1984, Semi-rational expectations and exchange-rate dynamics, Journal of International Money and Finance 3 (1), 51-66.

Bisignano, J. and K. Hoover, 1982, Some suggested improvements to a simple portfolio balance model of exchange rate determination with special reference to the US dollar/Canadian dollar rate, Weltwirtschaftliches Archiv 118 (1), 19-38.

Blume, L.E. and D. Easley, 1982, Learning to be rational, Journal of Economic Theory 26 (2), 340-351.

Blume, L.E., M.M. Bray and D. Easley, 1982, Introduction to the stability of rational expectations equilibrium, Journal of Economic Theory 26 (2), 313-317.

Blundell-Wignall, A. 1984, Exchange rate modelling and the role of asset supplies. The case of the Deutschemark effective rate 1973 to 1981, The Manchester School of Economic and Social Studies, 52 (1), 14-27.

Boeschoten, W.C., R. Cossee, N.J.A. van der Hoeven, P. Kramer and P.D. van Loo, 1984, Basisgegevens MORKMON gebruikt voor schattingen, De Nederlandsche Bank, paper 8416, Amsterdam.

Bomhoff, E.J. and P. Korteweg, 1983, Exchange-rate variability and monetary policy under rational expectations: Some Euro-American experience, 1973-1979, Journal of Monetary Economics 11 (1), 169-206.

Boot, J.C.G., W. Feibes and J.H.C. Lisman, 1967, Further methods of derivation of quarterly figures from annual data, Applied Statistics 16 (1), 65-75.

Boughton, J.M., 1984, Exchange rate movements and adjustment in financial markets: Quarterly estimates for major currencies, IMF Staff Papers 31 (3), 445-468.

Bowden, R.J. and D.A. Turkington, 1984, Instrumental Variables, Cambridge University Press, Cambridge.

Box, G.E.P. and Jenkins G., 1976, Time Series Analysis: Forecasting and control, Holden Day, San Francisco, revised edition.

Brainard, W. C. and J. Tobin, 1968, Pitfalls in financial model building, American Economic Review 58 (2), Papers and Proceedings, 99-122.

Brandsma, A.S., G.M.M. Gelauff, B. Hanzon, and A.M.A. Schrijver, 1988, Retracing the preference behind macroeconomic policy: The Dutch experience, De Economist 136 (4), 468-490.

Branson, W.H., 1968, Financial Capital Flows in the U.S. Balance of Payments, North Holland, Amsterdam.

Branson, W.H., 1977, Asset markets and relative prices in exchange rate determination, Sozialwissenschaftlichen Annalen 1 (1), 69-89.

Branson, W.H., 1979, Macroeconomic Theory and Policy, Harper and Row Publishers, New York, second edition.

Branson, W.H., 1984, Exchange rate policy after a decade of "floating", in Bilson, J.F.O. and R.C. Marston, eds., Exchange Rate Theory and Practice, The University of Chicago Press, Chicago, 79-108.

Branson, W.H., Halttunen H. and Masson P., 1977, Exchange rates in the short-run: The dollar-deutsche mark rate, European Economic Review 10 (3), 303-324.

Branson, W.H. and J.P. Love, 1988, U.S. manufacturing and the real exchange rate, in Marston, R.C., ed., Misalignment of Exchange Rates: Effects on Trade and Industry, University of Chicago Press, Chicago, 241-270.

Bray, M., 1982, Learning, estimation and the stability of rational expectations, Journal of Economic Theory 26 (2), 318-339.

Brodsky, D.A. 1982, Arithmetic versus geometric effective exchange rates, Weltwirtschaftliches Archiv 118 (3), 546-562.

Brundy, G.M. and Jorgenson D.W., 1971, Efficient estimation of simultaneous equations by instrumental variables, The Review of Economics and Statistics, 53 (3), 207-224.

Buiter, W.H., 1980, The macroeconomics of dr. Pangloss, A critical survey of the new classical macroeconomics, The Economic Journal 90 (1), 34-50.

Buiter, W.H., 1981, The superiority of contingent rules over fixed rules in models with rational expectations, The Economic Journal 91 (3), 647-670.

Burmeister, E. and S.J. Turnovsky, 1977, Perfect foresight, expectational consistency and macroeconomic equilibrium, Journal of Political Economy 85 (2), 379-393.

Butter, F.A.G. den, 1986, Macro-economische Modelbouw en Monetaire Transmissie, Ph.D. dissertation, Erasmus University, Rotterdam.

Butter, F.A.G. den, M.M.G. Fase and A.P. Huyser, 1979, Het netto buitenlands actief van de handelsbanken: Een econometrische analyse voor Nederland 1960: II - 1975: IV, Maandschrift Economie 43 (4), 161-190.

Cagan, P., 1956, The monetary dynamics of hyperinflation, in Friedman, M., ed., Studies in the Quantity Theory of Money, The University of Chicago Press, Chicago.

Capel, J.J. and E. de Jong, 1988[a], The variance and covariance of risk premia and expected spot rates: Does a rational expectation bias exist?, Research Memorandum 8808, Department of Economics, University of Amsterdam.

Capel, J.J. and E. de Jong, 1988[b], Has the rational expectation proxy biased the evidence on a risk premium in the forward exchange market?, Research Memorandum 8809, Department of Economics, University of Amsterdam.

Chouraqui, J.-C., M. Driscoll and M.-O. Strauss-Khan, 1988, The effects of monetary policy on the real sector: An overview of empirical evidence for selected OECD economies, Working Papers no. 51, OECD, Paris.

Christofides, L.N., 1976, Quadratic costs and multi-asset partial adjustment equations, Applied Economics 8 (3), 301-305

Clements, K.W. and J.A. Frenkel, 1980, Exchange rate money and relative prices: The dollar-pound in the 1920s, Journal of International Economics 10 (2), 249-262.

Clinton, K. 1973, Pitfalls in financial model building: Comment, American Economic Review 63 (6), 1003, 1004.

Cramer, J.S. and G.M. Reekers, 1972, Het Houderschap van Liquiditeiten in Nederland, Amsterdam.

Cuddington, J.T., 1983, Currency substitution, capital mobility, and money demand, Journal of International Money and Finance 2 (1), 111-133.

Cuddington, J.T. and Gluck J.A., 1983, Exchange rate forecasting and the international diversification of liquid asset holdings, Seminar Papers no. 245, IIES, Stockholm.

Cumby, R.E., J. Huizinga and M. Obstfeld, 1983, Two-step two-stage least squares estimation in models with rational expectations, Journal of Econometrics 21 (2), 333-355.

Currie, D., 1985, Macroeconomic policy design and control theory - A failed partnership?, The Economic Journal 95 (2), 285-306.

Cyert, R.M. and M.H. de Groot, 1974, Rational expectations and Bayesian analysis, Journal of Political Economy 28 (3), 521-536.

Darby, M.R., 1976, Rational expectations under conditions of costly information, The Journal of Finance 31 (3), 889-895.

Davidson, J.E.H., D.F. Hendry, F. Srba and S. Yeo, 1978, Econometric modelling of the aggregate timeseries relationship between consumers' expenditure and income in the United Kingdom, The Economic Journal 88 (4) 661-692.

De Macedo, J.B., J.A. Goldstein and D.M. Meerschwam, 1984, International portfolio diversification: Short-term financial assets and gold, in Bilson, J.F.O. and R.C. Marston, eds., Exchange-rate Theory and Practice, The University of Chicago Press, Chicago, 199-232.

De Nederlandsche Bank, 1982[a], Kwartaalconfrontatie van Middelen en Bestedingen 1957-1980, Kluwer, Deventer.

De Nederlandsche Bank, 1982[b], Kwartaalberichten, 1982 (3), 78-85.

De Nederlandsche Bank, 1983, Kwartaalberichten, 1983 (3), 78-85.

De Nederlandsche Bank, 1984, MORKMON: Een kwartaal model voor macro-economische beleidsanalyse, Monetaire Monografieën no. 2, Kluwer, Deventer.

Denton, F.T. , 1978, Single-equation estimators and aggregation restrictions when equations have the same set of regressors, Journal of Econometrics 8, 173-179.

Dixit, A., 1989, Entry and exit decisions under uncertainty, Journal of Political Economy 97 (3), 620-638.

Dongelmans, A.M. and M.M.G. Fase, 1975, Hoofdcomponenten van de rente in Nederland: 1971-1974, Bank- en Effectenbedrijf 24 (10), 363-369.

Dooley, M. and P. Isard, 1980, Capital controls, political risk, and deviations from interest rate parity, Journal of Political Economy, 88 (2), 370-384.

Dooley, M. and P. Isard, 1982, A portfoliobalance rational expectations model of the dollar-mark exchange rate, Journal of International Economics 12 (3/4), 257-276.

Dominguez, K.M., 1986, Are foreign exchange rates rational? New evidence from survey data, International Finance Discussion Papers no 281, Federal Reserve Board, Washington D.C.

Dornbusch, R., 1976, Expectations and exchange rate dynamics, Journal of Political Economy 84 (6), 1161-1176.

Dornbusch, R., 1983, Exchange rate risk and the macroeconomics of exchange rate determination, in Hawkins, R., R.M. Levich and C.G. Wihlborg, eds., The Internationalization of Financial Markets and National Economic Policy, JAI Press, Greenwich Conn., 3-27.

Dornbusch, R., 1988, The European Monetary System, the dollar and the yen, in Giavazzi, F., S. Micossi and M. Miller, eds., The European Monetary System, Cambridge University Press, Cambridge, 23-41.

Dornbusch, R. and P. Krugman, 1976, Flexible exchange rates in the short run, Brookings Papers on Economic Activity 3, 537-575.

Dornbusch, R. and J.A. Frankel, 1987, The flexible exchange rate system: Experience and alternatives, NBER Working Paper no. 2464, Cambridge.

Driehuis, W., 1972, Fluctuations and Growth in a Near Full Employment Economy: A quarterly econometric analysis of the Netherlands, Rotterdam University Press, Rotterdam.

Driehuis, W., K.A. Heineken and A.F. de Savornin Lohman, 1979, De werkgelegenheid in kapitaalgebruikende bedrijfstakken, in Klant J.J., W. Driehuis, H.J. Bierens and A.J. Butter, eds., Samenleving en Onderzoek, Stenfert Kroese, Leiden, 147-182.

Driehuis, W. and A. van der Zwan (eds.), 1978, De Voorbereiding van het Economisch Beleid Kritisch Bezien, Stenfert Kroese, Leiden.

Driskill, R.A., 1981[a], Exchange rate overshooting, the trade balance and rational expectations, Journal of International Economics 11 (3), 361-377.

Driskill, R.A, 1981[b], Exchange rate dynamics: An empirical investigation, Journal of Political Economy 89 (2), 357-371.

Driskill, R.A. and S.M. Sheffrin, 1981, On the mark: Comment, American Economic Review 71 (5), 1068-1074.

Dunnen, E. den, 1985, Instrumenten van het geld- en valutamarktbeleid in Nederland, Serie Bank- en Effectenbedrijf no. 21, NIBE, Amsterdam.

Edison, H.J., 1985, The rise and fall of sterling: Testing alternative models of exchange rate determination, Applied Economics 17 (6), 1003-1021.

Fair, R.C., 1976, A Model of Macroeconomic Activity: Volume II: The empirical model, Ballinger Publishing Company, Cambridge.

Fair, R.C., 1984, Specification, Estimation and Analysis of Macroeconomic Models, Harvard University Press, Cambridge.

Fase, M.M.G., 1985, Monetary control; The Dutch experience, in Ewijk, C. van and J.J. Klant, eds., Monetary Conditions for Economic Recovery, Martinus Nijhoff Publishers, Dordrecht, 95-125.

Fase, M.M.G. and M. van Nieuwkerk, 1975, Anticipated inflation and interest rates in an open economy, in Masera S., A. Fazio and T. Padoa-Schioppa, eds., Econometric Research in European Central Banks, Banca d'Italia, Rome, 297-321.

Feige, E.H. and D.K. Pearce, 1976, Economically rational expectations: Are innovations in the rate of inflation independent of innovations in measures of monetary and fiscal policy?, Journal of Political Economy 84 (3), 499-522.

Fisher, F.M., 1965, The choice of instrumental variables in the estimation of economy-wide econometric models, International Economic Review 6 (3), 245-274.

Fischer, S., 1980, On activist monetary policy with rational expectations, in Fischer, S., ed., Rational Expectations and Economic Policy, The University of Chicago Press, Chicago, 211-247.

Fischer, S., 1981, Relative shocks, relative price variability, and inflation, Brookings Papers on Economic Activity 2, 381-431.

Fourgeaud, C., C. Gourieroux and J. Pradel, 1984, Rational expectations models and bounded memory, Econometrica 53 (4), 977-985.

Frankel, J.A., 1979[a], The diversifiability of exchange risk, Journal of International Economics 9 (3), 379-393.

Frankel, J.A., 1979[b], On the mark: A theory of floating exchange rates based on real interest differentials, American Economic Review 69 (4), 610-622.

Frankel, J.A., 1981, On the mark: Reply, American Economic Review 71 (5), 1075-1082.

Frankel, J.A., 1982[a], In search of the exchange risk premium: A six-currency test assuming mean-variance optimization, Journal of International Money and Finance 1 (2), 255-274.

Frankel, J.A., 1982[b], A technique for extracting a measure of expected inflation from the interest rate term structure, The Review of Economics and Statistics 64 (1), 135-141.

Frankel, J.A., 1983[a], Estimation of portfolio-balance functions that are mean-variance optimizing: The mark and the dollar, European Economic Review 23 (2), 315-327.

Frankel, J.A., 1983[b], Monetary and portfolio-balance models of exchange rate determination, in Bhandari J.S. and B.H. Putnam, eds., Economic Interdependence and Flexible Exchange Rates, Cambridge, Mass., 84-115.

Frankel, J.A., 1984, Tests of monetary and portfolio balance models of exchange rate determination, in Bilson, J.F.O. and R.C. Marston, eds., Exchange Rate Theory and Practice, The University of Chicago Press, Chicago, 239-260.

Frankel, J.A. and K. Froot, 1985, Using survey data to test some standard propositions regarding exchange rate expectations, Working Paper no. 1672, National Bureau of Economic Research, Cambridge, Mass..

Frankel, J.A. and K. Froot, 1986, Short-term and long-term expectations of the yen/dollar rate: Evidence from survey data, International Finance Discussion Papers no.292, Federal Reserve Board, Washington D.C.

Frenkel, J.A., 1975, Inflation and the formation of expectations, Journal of Monetary Economics 1 (4), 403-421.

Frenkel, J.A., 1981, The collapse of purchasing power parities during the 1970's, European Economic Review 16 (1), 145-165.

Frenkel, J.A. and C.A. Rodriguez, 1982, Exchange rate dynamics and the overshooting hypothesis, IMF Staff Papers 29 (1), 1-30.

Friedlaender, A.F., 1973, Macro policy goals in the postwar period: A study in revealed preference, Quarterly Journal of Economics 87, 25-43.

Friedman, B.M., 1977, Financial flow variables and the short-run determination of long-term interest rates, Journal of Political Economy 85 (4), 661-669.

Friedman, B.M., 1979, Optimal expectations and the extreme information assumptions of 'rational expectations' macromodels, Journal of Monetary Economics 5 (1), 23-41.

Friedman, B.M., 1980, Survey evidence on the 'rationality' of interest rate expectations, Journal of Monetary Economics 6 (2), 453-465.

Friedman, B. M. and V. V. Roley, 1979, Investors' portfolio behavior under alternative models of long-term interest rate expectations: Unitary, rational or autoregressive, Econometrica 47 (6), 1475-1497.

Friedman, B.M. and V. V. Roley, 1980, Models of long-term interest rate determination, The Journal of Portfolio-Management 6 (3), 35-45.

Fukao, M., 1983, The risk premium in the foreign exchange market, in Klein L.R. and W.E. Krelle, eds., Capital Flows and Exchange Rate Determination, Springer-Verlag, Vienna, 99-125.

Fuller, W.A., 1976, Introduction to Statistical Time Series, John Wiley and Sons, New York,

Furstenberg, G.M. von, 1981, Incentives for international currency diversification by U.S. financial investors, IMF Staff Papers 28 (3), 477-494.

Gavin, M., 1989, The stock market and exchange rate dynamics, Journal of International Money and Finance 8 (2), 181-200.

Gelauff, G.M.M., 1988, Crude expectations in a general equilibrium model, Research Memorandum no. 44, Central Planning Bureau, The Hague.

Genberg, H., 1981, Effects of central bank intervention in the foreign exchange market, IMF Staff Papers 28 (3), 451-476.

Giavazzi, F. and M. Pagano, 1989, Confidence crises and public debt management, Discussion Paper no. 318, Centre for Economic Policy Research, London.

Ginsburgh, V.A., 1973, A further note on the derivation of quarterly figures consistent with annual data, Applied Statistics 22 (3), 368-374.

Glynn, L., 1988, The forex game, Institutional Investor, June, 35-41.

Goldstein, M., 1984, The exchange rate system: Lessons of the past and options for the future, IMF Occasional Papers no. 30, Washington.

Goldstein, M. and M.S. Kahn, 1985, Income and price effects in foreign trade, in Jones R.W. and P.B. Kenen, eds., Handbook of International Economics, North Holland, Amsterdam, 1041-1105.

Gottfries, N., 1985, Multiple perfect foresight equilibriums and convergence of learning processes, Journal of Money, Credit and Banking 17 (1), 111-117.

Gottfries, N. and T. Persson, 1986, Empirical examinations of the information sets of economic agents, IIES, Seminar Paper no. 349, Stockholm.

Grauwe, P. de, 1988, On the nature of risk in the foreign exchange markets: Evidence from the dollar- and the EMS-markets, International Research Paper no. 56, Katholieke Universiteit Leuven, Leuven.

Grauwe, P. de, M. Fratianni and M.K. Nabli, 1985, Exchange Rates Money and Output: The European experience, MacMillan, London.

Grilli, V., 1989, Exchange rates and seigniorage, European Economic Review 33 (2/3), 580-587.

Gylfason, T. and J.F. Helliwell, 1983, A synthesis of Keynesian, monetary, and portfolio approaches to flexible exchange rates, The Economic Journal 93 (4), 820-831.

Haan, H. de, S. Korteweg, S.K. Kuipers and J.K.T. Postma, 1979, Het Moderne Geldwezen, part III, North Holland, Amsterdam.

Haas, R.D. and W.E. Alexander, 1979, A model of exchange rates and capital flows: The Canadian floating rate experience, Journal of Money, Credit and Banking 9 (4), 467-482.

Hacche, G. and J.C. Townend, 1983, Some problems in exchange rate modelling: The case of sterling, in Klein L.R and W.E. Krelle, eds., Capital Flows and Exchange Rate Determination, Springer-Verlag, Vienna, 127-162.

Hakkio, C.S., 1984, A re-examination of purchasing power parity: A multi-country and multi-period study, Journal of International Economics 17 (3/4), 265-277.

Hall, B.H. and R.E. Hall, 1980, Time Series Processor, version 3.5, user's manual, London, Ontario.

Hansen, L.P. and Sargent T.J., 1980, Formulating and estimating dynamic linear rational expectations models, Journal of Economic Dynamics and Control 2 (1), 7-46.

Hansen, L.P. and Sargent T.J., 1982, Instrumental variables procedures for estimating linear rational expectations models, Journal of Monetary Economics 9 (2), 263-296.

Harris, R.G. and D.D. Purvis, 1981, Diverse information and market efficiency in a monetary model of the exchange rate, The Economic Journal 91 (4), 829-847.

Hasselman, B.H., Okker V.R. and Haan R.J.A. den, 1983, FREIA: Een macro-economisch model voor de middellange termijn, Central Planning Bureau, Monografie 25, The Hague.

Haynes, S.E. and J.A. Stone, 1981, On the mark: Comment, American Economic Review 71 (5), 1060-1067.

Haynes, S.E. and J.A. Stone, 1982, Spurious tests and sign reversals in international economics, Southern Economic Journal 48 (4), 868-876.

Helliwell, J., 1969, A structural model of the foreign exchange market, The Canadian Journal of Economics 2 (1), 90-105.

Hendry, D.F. and T. von Ungern-Stenberg, 1981, Liquidity and inflation effects on consumers' expenditures, in Deaton A., ed., Essays in the Theory and Measurement of Consumer Behaviour, Cambridge University Press, Cambridge, 237-260.

Hodrick, R.J., 1987, The Empirical Evidence on the Efficiency of Forward and Futures Foreign Exchange Markets, Harwood Academic Publishers, London.

Holly, S. and A.J. Hughes Hallett, 1989, Optimal Control, Expectations and Uncertainty, Cambridge University Press, Cambridge.

Holtham, G., 1986, Exchange rates in the OECD INTERLINK model: Specification and simulation properties, European Economic Review 30 (1), 199-235.

Hooper, P, 1983, Movements of the dollar's real exchange rate over ten years of floating: A structural analysis, paper presented at the Third International Symposium on Forecasting, Philadelphia, Penn., June 7-8.

Hooper, P., 1986, Exchange rate simulation properties of the MCM, European Economic Review 30 (1), 171-198.

Hooper, P., R.D. Haas, S.A. Symansky and L. Stekler, 1983, Alternative approaches to general equilibrium modeling of exchange rates and capital flows: The MCM experience, in Klein, L.R. and W.E. Krelle, eds., Capital Flows and Exchange Rate Determination, Springer-Verlag, Vienna, 29-60.

Hooper, P. and J. Morton, 1982, Fluctuations in the dollar: A model of nominal and real exchange rate determination, Journal of International Money and Finance 1 (1), 39-56.

Hughes Hallett, A.J., 1986, Is time inconsistent behaviour really possible?, CEPR Discussion Paper no. 138, Centre for Economic Policy Research, London.

Intrilligator, M.D, 1978, Econometric Models, Techniques and Applications, North-Holland Publishing Company, Amsterdam.

Isard, P., 1977, How far can we push the 'law of one price'?, American Economic Review 67 (5), 942-948.

Isard, P., 1983, What's wrong with empirical exchange rate models: Some critical issues and new directions, International Finance Discussion Papers no. 226, Federal Reserve Board, Washington D.C..

Isard, P., 1987, Lessons from empirical models of exchange rates, IMF Staff Papers 34 (1), 1-28.

Jacobs, R.L., 1982, The effects of errors in variable tests for a risk premium in forward exchange rates, The Journal of Finance 37 (3), 667-677.

Jager, H., 1981, De Behoefte aan Internationale Monetaire Reserves als Uitvloeisel van Optimale Economische Politiek, Ph.D. dissertation, Groningen.

Jager, H., 1982, Optimal exchange-rate policy in an open economy, De Economist 130 (2), 228-263.

Jager, H., 1985, The optimal exchange-rate system and its significance for economic recovery, in Ewijk, C. van and J.J. Klant, eds., Monetary Conditions for Economic Recovery, Martinus Nijhoff Publishers, Dordrecht, 187-220.

Jager, H. and H.M. Amman, 1986, Optimal sliding exchange-rate rules for a small industrial country: An empirical application of nonlinear control theory, Research Memorandum no 8610, Department of Economics, University of Amsterdam.

Johnston, J., 1972, Econometric Methods, McGraw-Hill, New York, second edition.

Jong, E. de, 1981, De invloed van reactievergelijkingen op de eigenschappen van een econometrisch model, Institute for Economic Research, University of Groningen, Research Memorandum no. 82.

Jong, E. de, 1983, Wisselkoersfluctuaties op korte termijn en recente wisselkoerstheorieën; Een beknopt overzicht, Maandschrift Economie 47 (5), 224-241.

Jong, E. de, 1985, A limited information method for approximating exchange rate expectations, mimeo.

Jong, E. de, 1986, Consistent estimation of simultaneous models with partly rational expectations, Research Memorandum no. 8604, Department of Economics, University of Amsterdam.

Jong, E. de, 1988, Expectation formation: Criteria and an assessment, De Economist 136 (4), 435-467.

Jong, E. de, 1990, On the dynamics and structure of multi-asset financial models, Research Memorandum no. 9030, Department of Economics, University of Amsterdam.

Judge, G.G., W.E. Griffiths, R. Carter Hill and T.-C. Lee, 1980, The Theory and Practice of Econometrics, John Wiley and Sons, New York.

Keller, A.A., 1984, Semi-reduced forms of econometric models, in Ancot, J.P., ed., Analysing the Structure of Economic Models, Martinus Nijhoff Publishers, Dordrecht, 89-113.

Keus, J., 1980, Rendementen die geen winsten zijn, Economisch Statistische Berichten 3247, 335-340.

Keynes, J.M., 1936, The General Theory of Employment, Interest and Money, MacMillan, London.

Kiviet, J.F., 1985, The importance and performance of tests for the selection of instrumental variables, University of Amsterdam, mimeo.

Koedijk, K.G. and M. Ott, 1987, Risk aversion, efficient markets and the forward exchange rate, Review of the Federal Reserve Bank of St. Louis 69 (6), 5-13.

Kohlhagen, S.W., 1977, 'Rational' and 'endogenous' exchange rate expectations and speculative capital flows in Germany, Weltwirtschaftliches Archiv 113 (4), 624-643.

Kool, C.J.M., 1989, Recursive Baysian Forecasting in Economics: The muti state Kalman filter, Ph.D. dissertation, Erasmus University, Rotterdam.

Kotlikoff, L.J., T. Persson and L.E.O. Svensson, 1988, Social contracts as assets: A possible solution to the time-inconsistency problem, American Economic Review 78 (4), 662-677.

Kouri, P.J.K., 1976, The exchange rate and the balance of payments in the short run and the long run: A monetary approach, The Scandinavian Journal of Economics 78 (2), 280-304.

Kouri, P.J.K. and M.G. Porter, 1974, International capital flows and portfolio equilibrium, Journal of Political Economy 82 (3), 443-467.

Kuipers, S.K., B.W.A. Jongbloed, G.H. Kuper and E. Sterken, 1990, CESAM: The CCSO annual model of the Dutch economy, Economic Modelling, 220-250.

Kuipers, S.K., J. Muysken and J. van Sinderen, 1979, The vintage approach to output and employment growth in The Netherlands, 1921 to 1976, Weltwirtschaftliches Archiv 115 (3), 485-507.

Kydland, F.E. and E.C. Prescott, 1977, Rules rather than discretion: The inconsistency of optimal plans, Journal of Political Economy 85 (3), 473-491.

Ladenson, M.L., 1971, Pitfalls in financial model building: Some extensions, American Economic Review 61 (1), 179-186.

Lafrance, R. and D. Racette, 1985, The Canadian-US dollar exchange rate: A test of alternative models for the seventies, Journal of International Money and Finance 4 (2), 237-252.

Loo, P.D. van, 1983, A Sectoral Analysis of the Dutch Financial System, Stenfert Kroese, Leiden.

Lucas, R.E., 1976, Econometric policy evaluation: A critique, in Brunner, K. and A.H. Meltzer, eds., The Phillips Curve and Labour Markets, Carnegie - Rochester Conference Series on Public Policy 1, 19-46.

Lucas, R.E. and T.J. Sargent, 1981, Introduction, in Lucas, R.E. and T.J. Sargent, eds., Rational Expectations and Econometric Practice, George Allen and Unwin, London, xi-xl.

MacDonald, R., 1983, Some tests of the rational expectations hypothesis in the foreign exchange market, Scottisch Journal of Political Economy 30 (3), 235-250.

MacDonald, R., 1988, Floating Exchange Rates: Theories and evidence, Unwin Hyman, London.

Marwah, K. and L.R. Klein, 1983, A model of foreign exchange markets: Endogenising capital flows and exchange rates, in Klein, L.R. and W.E. Krelle, eds., Capital Flows and Exchange Rate Determination, Springer-Verlag, Vienna, 61-95.

Marwah, K., L.R. Klein and R.G. Bodkin, 1985, Bilateral capital flows and the exchange rate: The case of the U.S.A. vis-a-vis Canada, France, West Germany and the U.K., European Economic Review 29 (1), 89-110.

Mathieson, D.J., 1977, The impact of monetary and fisal policy under flexible exchange rates and alternative expectation structures, IMF Staff Papers 24 (3), 535-568.

Mayer, C. and M. Mors, 1985, Company expectations and new information: An application of Kalman filters, Discussion Paper no. 62., Centre for Economic Policy Research, London.

McCallum, B.T., 1976, The role of speculation in the Canadian forward exchange market: Some estimates assuming rational expectations, The Review of Economics and Statistics 59 (2), 145-151.

McCallum, B.T., 1976, Rational expectations and the natural rate hypothesis: Some consistent estimates, Econometrica 44 (1), 43-52.

Meese, R.A., 1986, Testing for bubbles in exchange markets, A case of sparkling rates?, Journal of Political Economy 94 (2), 345-373.

Meese, R.A., and K. Rogoff, 1983a, Empirical exchange rate models of the seventies: Do they fit out of sample?, Journal of International Economics 14 (1/2), 3-24.

Meese, R.A. and K. Rogoff, 1983b, The out-of-sample failure of empirical exchange rate models: Error or misspecification?, in Frenkel, J., ed., Exchange Rates and International Macroeconomics, The University of Chicago Press, Chicago, 67-112.

Meese, R.A. and Rogoff, K., 1985, Was it real? The exchange rate - interest differential relation, 1973-1984, International Finance Discussion Papers no. 268, Board of Governors of the Federal Reserve, Washington.

Meese, R.A. and K.J. Singleton, 1982, On unit roots and the empirical modeling of exchange rates, Journal of Finance 37 (4), 1029-1035.

Miles, M.A. and M.B. Stewart, 1980, The effects of risk and return on the currency composition of money demand, Weltwirtschaftliches Archiv 116 (4), 613-626.

Mitchell, B.M. and Fisher, F.M., 1970, The choice of instrumental variables in the estimation of economy-wide econometric models: Some further thoughts, International Economic Review 11 (2), 226-234.

Murphy, R.G. and C. van Duyne, 1980, Asset market approaches to exchange rate determination: A comparative analysis, Welwirtschaftliches Archiv 116 (4), 627-655.

Mussa, M., 1978, The exchange rate, the balance of payments, and monetary and fiscal policy under a regime of controlled floating, in Frenkel, J.A. and H.G. Johnson, eds., The Economics of Exchange Rates: Selected studies, Addison-Wesley, Reading Mass., 47-65.

Muth, J.F., 1961, Rational expectations and the theory of price movements, Econometrica 129 (3), 315-335.

Nieuwkerk, M. van, 1979, The covering of exchange risks in the Netherlands' foreign trade: A note, Journal of International Economics 9 (1), 89-93.

Nieuwkerk, M. van, 1981, De financiering van het betalingsbalanstekort, in Dunnen, E. den, M.M.G. Fase and A. Szasz, eds., Zoeklicht op Beleid, Stenfert Kroese, Leiden, 241-267.

Obstfeld, M., 1983, Exchange rates, inflation, and the sterilization problem: Germany, 1975-1980, European Economic Review 21 (1), 161-189.

Obstfeld, M. and A.C. Stockman, 1985, Exchange-rate dynamics, in Jones R.W. and P.B. Kenen, eds., Handbook of International Economics, North-Holland, Amsterdam, 917-977.

Officer, L.R., 1976, The purchasing-power-parity theory of exchange rates: A review article, IMF Staff Papers 23 (1), 1-60.

Owen, D., 1986, Money, Wealth and Expenditure: Integrated modelling of consumption and portfolio behaviour, Cambridge University Press, Cambridge.

Pauly, P., 1983, Inequality constraints in a multi-country exchange rate model, mimeo.

Pauly, P. and C.E. Petersen, 1986, Exchange rate responses in the LINK system, European Economic Review 30 (1), 149-170.

Pesaran, M.H., 1985, Formation of inflation expectations in British manufacturing industries, The Economic Journal 95 (4), 948-975.

Pesaran, M.H., 1988, The Limits to Rational Expectations, Basil Blackwell, Oxford.

Phillips, A.W., 1954, Stabilization policy in a closed economy, The Economic Journal 64 (2), 290-323.

Phillips, A.W., 1958, The relation between unemployment and the rate of change of money wage rates in the United Kingdom, 1861-1957, Economica 25 (4), 283-299.

Protopapadakis, A.A. and H.R. Stoll, 1986, The law of one price in international commodity markets: A reformulation and some formal tests, Journal of International Money and Finance 5 (3), 335-360.

Rasulo, J. and D. Sykes Wilford, 1980, Estimating monetary models of the balance of payments and exchange rates: A bias, Southern Economic Journal 47 (1), 136-146.

Rhomberg, R.R., 1976, Indices of effective exchange rates, IMF Staff Papers 23 (1), 88-112.

Ridder, P.B. de, 1977, Een jaargangenmodel met vaste technische coefficiënten en in kapitaal geïncorporeerde arbeidsbesparende technische vooruitgang, Central Planning Bureau, Occasional Paper no. 14, The Hague.

Rogoff, K., 1987, Reputational constraints on monetary policy, in Brunner, K. and A.H. Meltzer, eds., Bubles and Other Essays, Carnegie-Rochester Conference Series on Public Policy no. 26, 141-183.

Roley, V. V., 1983, Symmetry restrictions in a system of financial asset demands: Theoretical and empirical results, The Review of Econonomics and Statistics 65 (1), 124-130.

Salter, W.E.G., 1969, Productivity and Technical Change, Cambridge University Press, Cambridge, second edition.

Saracoglu, R., 1984, Expectations of inflation and interest determination, IMF Staff Papers 31 (1), 141-178.

Sargent, T.J., 1971, A note on the "accelerationist" controversy, Journal of Money, Credit and Banking 83 (3), 721-725.

Sargent, T. J., 1973, Rational expectations, the real rate of interest, and the natural rate of employment, Brookings Paper on Economic Activity 2, 429-472.

Sheffrin, S.M., 1983, Rational Expectations, Cambridge University Press, Cambridge.

Shiller, R.J., 1978, Rational expectations and the dynamic structure of macroeconomic models: A critical review, Journal of Monetary Economics 4 (1), 1-44.

Siebrand, J.C., 1988, Macroeconomic modelling for economic policy, in Driehuis, W., M.M.G. Fase and H. den Hartog, eds., Challenges for Macroeconomic Modelling, North Holland, Amsterdam, 99-135.

Siebrand J.C. and J. Swank, 1986, An evaluation of the Morkmon model, De Economist 134 (3), 289-300.

Simon, H.A., 1959, Theories of decision-making in economics and behavioral science, American Economic Review 49 (3), 253-283.

Sims, C.A., 1980, Macroeconomics and reality, Econometrica 48 (1), 1-48.

Sims, C.A., 1982, Policy analysis with econometric models, Brookings Papers on Economic Activity 1, 107-152.

Smith G., and W. Brainard, 1976, The value of a priori information in estimating a financial model, The Journal of Finance 31 (5), 1299-1322.

Smith, P.N. and M.R. Wickens, 1986, An empirical investigation into the causes of failure of the monetary model of the exchange rate, Journal of Applied Econometrics 1 (2), 143-162.

Snippe, J., 1983, Economic rationality and the formation of expectations: A critical analysis, Memorandum from the Institute of Economic Research, Faculty of Economics, University of Groningen.

Snippe, J., 1985, Macroeconomic Adjustment Processes: A sequential analytical approach, Ph.D. dissertation, Groningen.

Snippe, J., 1986, Varieties of rational expectations: Their differences and relations, Journal of Post Keynesian Economics 8 (3), 427-437.

Stein, J.L., 1980, The dynamics of spot and forward prices in an efficient foreign exchange market with rational expectations, American Economic Review 70 (4), 565-583.

Sterken, E., 1986, Een monetair model voor Nederland, CCSO-Reeks no.1, Groningen.

Sterks, C.G.M., 1982, Begrotingsnormen, Ph.D. dissertation, University of Groningen.

Stoll, H.R., 1968, An empirical study of the forward exchange market under fixed and flexible exchange rate systems, Canadian Journal of Economics 1 (1), 55-78.

Swany, P.A.V.B. and G.J. Schinasi, 1986, Should fixed coefficients be reestimated every period for extrapolation?, International Finance Discussion Paper no. 287, Board of Governors of the Federal Reserve, Washington D.C.

Theil, H., 1971, Principles of Econometrics, John Wiley and Sons, New York.

Thomas, J.J. and K.F. Wallis, 1971, Seasonal variation in regression analysis, Journal of the Royal Statistical Society, series A 134, part 1, 57-72.

Viaene, J.M. and C. de Vries, 1985, Welfare implications of foreign exchange intervention: Theory and measurement, in Peeters, T., P. Praet and P. Reding, eds., International Trade and Exchange Rates in the Late Eighties, North-Holland, Amsterdam, 299-322.

Viner, A., 1987, Inside Japan's Financial Markets, The Economist Publications, London.

Visser, H., 1989, Exchange rate theories, De Economist 137 (1), 16-46.

Wallenburg, M. van, 1977, Theorie en Praktijk van de Winstbepaling, Samson Uitgeverij, Alphen aan de Rijn.

Wallis, K.F., 1974, Seasonal adjustment and relations between variables, Journal of American Statistical Association 69 (1), 18-31.

Wallis, K.F., 1980, Econometric implications of the rational expectations hypothesis, Econometrica 48 (1), 49-73.

Wartna, J.A., 1974, Bouw en Gebruik van Econometrische Modellen, Universitaire Pers Rotterdam, Rotterdam.

Westaway P. and S. Wren-Lewis, 1990, Is there a case for the MTFS?, CEPR Discussion Paper no. 411, Centre of Economic Policy Research, London.

Wilde, S. de, 1975, Dollarswaps als geldmarktinstrument, Bank- en Effectenbedrijf 24 (7/8), 295-297.

Williamson, J., 1983, The exchange rate system, Policy Analysis for International Economics no. 5, Institute for International Economics, Washington.

Woo, W.T., 1985, The monetary approach to exchange rate determination under rational expectations: The dollar-deutschmark rate, Journal of International Economics 18 (1/2), 1-16.

Wyplosz, C.A., 1983, The exchange and interest rate term structure under risk aversion and rational expectations, Journal of International Economics 14 (1/2), 123-139.

Zellner, A., 1986, Biased predictors, rationality and the evolution of forecasts, Economics Letters 21 (1), 45-48.

AUTHOR INDEX

Vol. 261: Th.R. Gulledge, Jr., N.K. Womer, The Economics of Made-to-Order Production. VI, 134 pages. 1986.

Vol. 262: H.U. Buhl, A Neo-Classical Theory of Distribution and Wealth. V, 146 pages. 1986.

Vol. 263: M. Schäfer, Resource Extraction and Market Structure. XI, 154 pages. 1986.

Vol. 264: Models of Economic Dynamics. Proceedings, 1983. Edited by H.F. Sonnenschein. VII, 212 pages. 1986.

Vol. 265: Dynamic Games and Applications in Economics. Edited by T. Başar. IX, 288 pages. 1986.

Vol. 266: Multi-Stage Production Planning and Inventory Control. Edited by S. Axsäter, Ch. Schneeweiss and E. Silver. V, 264 pages. 1986.

Vol. 267: R. Bemelmans, The Capacity Aspect of Inventories. IX, 165 pages. 1986.

Vol. 268: V. Firchau, Information Evaluation in Capital Markets. VII, 103 pages. 1986.

Vol. 269: A. Borglin, H. Keiding, Optimality in Infinite Horizon Economies. VI, 180 pages. 1986.

Vol. 270: Technological Change, Employment and Spatial Dynamics. Proceedings 1985. Edited by P. Nijkamp. VII, 466 pages. 1986.

Vol. 271: C. Hildreth, The Cowles Commission in Chicago, 1939–1955. V, 176 pages. 1986.

Vol. 272: G. Clemenz, Credit Markets with Asymmetric Information. VIII, 212 pages. 1986.

Vol. 273: Large-Scale Modelling and Interactive Decision Analysis. Proceedings, 1985. Edited by G. Fandel, M. Grauer, A. Kurzhanski and A.P. Wierzbicki. VII, 363 pages. 1986.

Vol. 274: W.K. Klein Haneveld, Duality in Stochastic Linear and Dynamic Programming. VII, 295 pages. 1986.

Vol. 275: Competition, Instability, and Nonlinear Cycles. Proceedings, 1985. Edited by W. Semmler. XII, 340 pages. 1986.

Vol. 276: M.R. Baye, D.A. Black, Consumer Behavior, Cost of Living Measures, and the Income Tax. VII, 119 pages. 1986.

Vol. 277: Studies in Austrian Capital Theory, Investment and Time. Edited by M. Faber. VI, 317 pages. 1986.

Vol. 278: W.E. Diewert, The Measurement of the Economic Benefits of Infrastructure Services. V, 202 pages. 1986.

Vol. 279: H.-J. Büttler, G. Frei and B. Schips, Estimation of Disequilibrium Models. VI, 114 pages. 1986.

Vol. 280: H.T. Lau, Combinatorial Heuristic Algorithms with FORTRAN. VII, 126 pages. 1986.

Vol. 281: Ch.-L. Hwang, M.-J. Lin, Group Decision Making under Multiple Criteria. XI, 400 pages. 1987.

Vol. 282: K. Schittkowski, More Test Examples for Nonlinear Programming Codes. V, 261 pages. 1987.

Vol. 283: G. Gabisch, H.-W. Lorenz, Business Cycle Theory. VII, 229 pages. 1987.

Vol. 284: H. Lütkepohl, Forecasting Aggregated Vector ARMA Processes. X, 323 pages. 1987.

Vol. 285: Toward Interactive and Intelligent Decision Support Systems. Volume 1. Proceedings, 1986. Edited by Y. Sawaragi, K. Inoue and H. Nakayama. XII, 445 pages. 1987.

Vol. 286: Toward Interactive and Intelligent Decision Support Systems. Volume 2. Proceedings, 1986. Edited by Y. Sawaragi, K. Inoue and H. Nakayama. XII, 450 pages. 1987.

Vol. 287: Dynamical Systems. Proceedings, 1985. Edited by A.B. Kurzhanski and K. Sigmund. VI, 215 pages. 1987.

Vol. 288: G.D. Rudebusch, The Estimation of Macroeconomic Disequilibrium Models with Regime Classification Information. VII, 128 pages. 1987.

Vol. 289: B.R. Meijboom, Planning in Decentralized Firms. X, 168 pages. 1987.

Vol. 290: D.A. Carlson, A. Haurie, Infinite Horizon Optimal Control. XI, 254 pages. 1987.

Vol. 291: N. Takahashi, Design of Adaptive Organizations. VI, 140 pages. 1987.

Vol. 292: I. Tchijov, L. Tomaszewicz (Eds.), Input-Output Modeling. Proceedings, 1985. VI, 195 pages. 1987.

Vol. 293: D. Batten, J. Casti, B. Johansson (Eds.), Economic Evolution and Structural Adjustment. Proceedings, 1985. VI, 382 pages. 1987.

Vol. 294: J. Jahn, W. Krabs (Eds.), Recent Advances and Historical Development of Vector Optimization. VII, 405 pages. 1987.

Vol. 295: H. Meister, The Purification Problem for Constrained Games with Incomplete Information. X, 127 pages. 1987.

Vol. 296: A. Börsch-Supan, Econometric Analysis of Discrete Choice. VIII, 211 pages. 1987.

Vol. 297: V. Fedorov, H. Läuter (Eds.), Model-Oriented Data Analysis. Proceedings, 1987. VI, 239 pages. 1988.

Vol. 298: S.H. Chew, Q. Zheng, Integral Global Optimization. VII, 179 pages. 1988.

Vol. 299: K. Marti, Descent Directions and Efficient Solutions in Discretely Distributed Stochastic Programs. XIV, 178 pages. 1988.

Vol. 300: U. Derigs, Programming in Networks and Graphs. XI, 315 pages. 1988.

Vol. 301: J. Kacprzyk, M. Roubens (Eds.), Non-Conventional Preference Relations in Decision Making. VII, 155 pages. 1988.

Vol. 302: H.A. Eiselt, G. Pederzoli (Eds.), Advances in Optimization and Control. Proceedings, 1986. VIII, 372 pages. 1988.

Vol. 303: F.X. Diebold, Empirical Modeling of Exchange Rate Dynamics. VII, 143 pages. 1988.

Vol. 304: A. Kurzhanski, K. Neumann, D. Pallaschke (Eds.), Optimization, Parallel Processing and Applications. Proceedings, 1987. VI, 292 pages. 1988.

Vol. 305: G.-J.C.Th. van Schijndel, Dynamic Firm and Investor Behaviour under Progressive Personal Taxation. X, 215 pages. 1988.

Vol. 306: Ch. Klein, A Static Microeconomic Model of Pure Competition. VIII, 139 pages. 1988.

Vol. 307: T.K. Dijkstra (Ed.), On Model Uncertainty and its Statistical Implications. VII, 138 pages. 1988.

Vol. 308: J.R. Daduna, A. Wren (Eds.), Computer-Aided Transit Scheduling. VIII, 339 pages. 1988.

Vol. 309: G. Ricci, K. Velupillai (Eds.), Growth Cycles and Multisectoral Economics: the Goodwin Tradition. III, 126 pages. 1988.

Vol. 310: J. Kacprzyk, M. Fedrizzi (Eds.), Combining Fuzzy Imprecision with Probabilistic Uncertainty in Decision Making. IX, 399 pages. 1988.

Vol. 311: R. Färe, Fundamentals of Production Theory. IX, 163 pages. 1988.

Vol. 312: J. Krishnakumar, Estimation of Simultaneous Equation Models with Error Components Structure. X, 357 pages. 1988.

Vol. 313: W. Jammernegg, Sequential Binary Investment Decisions. VI, 156 pages. 1988.

Vol. 314: R. Tietz, W. Albers, R. Selten (Eds.), Bounded Rational Behavior in Experimental Games and Markets. VI, 368 pages. 1988.

Vol. 315: I. Orishimo, G.J.D. Hewings, P. Nijkamp (Eds.), Information Technology: Social and Spatial Perspectives. Proceedings, 1986. VI, 268 pages. 1988.

Vol. 316: R.L. Basmann, D.J. Slottje, K. Hayes, J.D. Johnson, D.J. Molina, The Generalized Fechner-Thurstone Direct Utility Function and Some of its Uses. VIII, 159 pages. 1988.

Vol. 317: L. Bianco, A. La Bella (Eds.), Freight Transport Planning and Logistics. Proceedings, 1987. X, 568 pages. 1988.

Vol. 318: T. Doup, Simplicial Algorithms on the Simplotope. VIII, 262 pages. 1988.

Vol. 319: D.T. Luc, Theory of Vector Optimization. VIII, 173 pages. 1989.

Vol. 320: D. van der Wijst, Financial Structure in Small Business. VII, 181 pages. 1989.

Vol. 321: M. Di Matteo, R.M. Goodwin, A. Vercelli (Eds.), Technological and Social Factors in Long Term Fluctuations. Proceedings. IX, 442 pages. 1989.

Vol. 322: T. Kollintzas (Ed.), The Rational Expectations Equilibrium Inventory Model. XI, 269 pages. 1989.

Vol. 323: M.B.M. de Koster, Capacity Oriented Analysis and Design of Production Systems. XII, 245 pages. 1989.

Vol. 324: I.M. Bomze, B.M. Pötscher, Game Theoretical Foundations of Evolutionary Stability. VI, 145 pages. 1989.

Vol. 325: P. Ferri, E. Greenberg, The Labor Market and Business Cycle Theories. X, 183 pages. 1989.

Vol. 326: Ch. Sauer, Alternative Theories of Output, Unemployment, and Inflation in Germany: 1960–1985. XIII, 206 pages. 1989.

Vol. 327: M. Tawada, Production Structure and International Trade. V, 132 pages. 1989.

Vol. 328: W. Güth, B. Kalkofen, Unique Solutions for Strategic Games. VII, 200 pages. 1989.

Vol. 329: G. Tillmann, Equity, Incentives, and Taxation. VI, 132 pages. 1989.

Vol. 330: P.M. Kort, Optimal Dynamic Investment Policies of a Value Maximizing Firm. VII, 185 pages. 1989.

Vol. 331: A. Lewandowski, A.P. Wierzbicki (Eds.), Aspiration Based Decision Support Systems. X, 400 pages. 1989.

Vol. 332: T.R. Gulledge, Jr., L.A. Litteral (Eds.), Cost Analysis Applications of Economics and Operations Research. Proceedings. VII, 422 pages. 1989.

Vol. 333: N. Dellaert, Production to Order. VII, 158 pages. 1989.

Vol. 334: H.-W. Lorenz, Nonlinear Dynamical Economics and Chaotic Motion. XI, 248 pages. 1989.

Vol. 335: A. G. Lockett, G. Islei (Eds.), Improving Decision Making in Organisations. Proceedings. IX, 606 pages. 1989.

Vol. 336: T. Puu, Nonlinear Economic Dynamics. VII, 119 pages. 1989.

Vol. 337: A. Lewandowski, I. Stanchev (Eds.), Methodology and Software for Interactive Decision Support. VIII, 309 pages. 1989.

Vol. 338: J.K. Ho, R.P. Sundarraj, DECOMP: an Implementation of Dantzig-Wolfe Decomposition for Linear Programming. VI, 206 pages. 1989.

Vol. 339: J. Terceiro Lomba, Estimation of Dynamic Econometric Models with Errors in Variables. VIII, 116 pages. 1990.

Vol. 340: T. Vasko, R. Ayres, L. Fontvieille (Eds.), Life Cycles and Long Waves. XIV, 293 pages. 1990.

Vol. 341: G.R. Uhlich, Descriptive Theories of Bargaining. IX, 165 pages. 1990.

Vol. 342: K. Okuguchi, F. Szidarovszky, The Theory of Oligopoly with Multi-Product Firms. V, 167 pages. 1990.

Vol. 343: C. Chiarella, The Elements of a Nonlinear Theory of Economic Dynamics. IX, 149 pages. 1990.

Vol. 344: K. Neumann, Stochastic Project Networks. XI, 237 pages. 1990.

Vol. 345: A. Cambini, E. Castagnoli, L. Martein, P. Mazzoleni, S. Schaible (Eds.), Generalized Convexity and Fractional Programming with Economic Applications. Proceedings, 1988. VII, 361 pages. 1990.

Vol. 346: R. von Randow (Ed.), Integer Programming and Related Areas. A Classified Bibliography 1984–1987. XIII, 514 pages. 1990.

Vol. 347: D. Ríos Insua, Sensitivity Analysis in Multi-objective Decision Making. XI, 193 pages. 1990.

Vol. 348: H. Störmer, Binary Functions and their Applications. VIII, 151 pages. 1990.

Vol. 349: G. A. Pfann, Dynamic Modelling of Stochastic Demand for Manufacturing Employment. VI, 158 pages. 1990.

Vol. 350: W.-B. Zhang, Economic Dynamics. X, 232 pages. 1990.

Vol. 351: A. Lewandowski, V. Volkovich (Eds.), Multiobjective Problems of Mathematical Programming. Proceedings, 1988. VII, 315 pages. 1991.

Vol. 352: O. van Hilten, Optimal Firm Behaviour in the Context of Technological Progress and a Business Cycle. XII, 229 pages. 1991.

Vol. 353: G. Ricci (Ed.), Decision Processes in Economics. Proceedings, 1989. III, 209 pages. 1991.

Vol. 354: M. Ivaldi, A Structural Analysis of Expectation Formation. XII, 230 pages. 1991.

Vol. 355: M. Salomon, Deterministic Lotsizing Models for Production Planning. VII, 158 pages. 1991.

Vol. 356: P. Korhonen, A. Lewandowski, J. Wallenius (Eds.), Multiple Criteria Decision Support. Proceedings, 1989. XII, 393 pages. 1991.

Vol. 358: P. Knottnerus, Linear Models with Correlated Disturbances. VIII, 196 pages. 1991.

Vol. 359: E. de Jong, Exchange Rate Determination and Optimal Economic Policy Under Various Exchange Rate Regimes. VII, 270 pages. 1991.